# JONAS MEKAS

# " SCRAPBOOK " OF THE SIXTIES

WRITINGS
1954–2010

SPECTOR BOOKS

*Scrapbook of the Sixties* is a collection of published and unpublished texts by Jonas Mekas (1922–2019), filmmaker, writer, poet, and cofounder of the Anthology Film Archives in New York. Born in Lithuania, he came to Brooklyn via Germany in 1949 and began shooting his first films there. Mekas developed a form of film diary in which he recorded moments of his daily life. He became the barometer of the New York art scene and a pioneer of American avant-garde cinema.

Every week, starting in 1958, he published his legendary "Movie Journal" column in *The Village Voice*, writing on a range of subjects that were by no means restricted to the world of film. He conducted numerous interviews with artists like Andy Warhol, Susan Sontag, John Lennon & Yoko Ono, Erick Hawkins, and Nam June Paik. Some of these will now appear for the first time in his *Scrapbook of the Sixties*. Mekas's writings reveal him to be a thoughtful diarist and an unparalleled chronicler of the times.

# On Alban Berg & Anna Sokolow

December 18, 1954

We went, with Elizabeth, to Kaufman Auditorium for an evening of modern dance and music. *L'Histoire du soldat*. Despite the fact that I like this work very much, this tasteless, mediocre production made me almost hate it. I still remember Karl Heinz Stroux's beautiful production, in Kassel, six years ago.

But on the same program there was *Lyric Suite* by Alban Berg, choreographed by Anna Sokolow. It was impossible not to be pulled into its music and dance, its atmosphere of complete desperation, loneliness, frustration. The man here is helpless, a tragic puppet without a will of his own, performing agonizing, hopeless movements to the rhythms of equally sad, agonizing, hopeless music. If this is the essence (and art deals with essences) of the world we live in; if the world of Alban Berg and Anna Sokolow is also our world—and what other world could it be!— ah how sad we must be, deep deep inside!

Elizabeth said that although this production is *true*, it is only partially true; it shows only a small part, only one aspect of reality (truth) and therefore I shouldn't make wide generalizations based on Berg and Sokolow. "There are other parts and aspects to life, more happy, more optimistic," she said.

"There was no protest on the part of man, no struggle against his morbid fate, the struggle which is the basis of all classical moral drama; there was nothing but helplessness," she said. "Yes, but then," I argued, "if this is only one part, then this part must be very big, immensely swollen." I thought about dozens of experimental artists, films made by young artists today, those desperate, sad films of Harrington, Anger, Markopoulos; or those many painters and writers, New Directions, etc. etc.

"But look," I said to Elizabeth, "if we begin to call a particular period black or desperate or lost, or whatever word we choose, this word has two edges: with one edge it cuts into the past, with another it cuts into the present and future, it acts upon us. Words have magic powers, just by their sheer presence, and today when we read them—yes, the words, the names act upon us, they cut into us. That's what I am thinking about. It is not that these works aren't true. They *are* true. What counts, however, is what *we do* about it, once we know the truth. You see, today we are so badly lost that although the truth is shown to us by our artists we are no longer able to act, to do anything about it, to learn anything from that knowledge, from that truth. We are like children. The truth is there, like a rock, but we continue on the same disintegrating road. The terms we invent to describe our spiritual attitudes, states, and conditions when they are correct (even when our analyses are correct) boomerang back at us and we sink still deeper. The words that describe our present (or immediate past) we take as our guides into the future. We confuse words with reality."

"Yes," said Elizabeth, "but isn't then the moral responsibility of the artist to create a more constructive, more optimistic art which, instead of evoking or naming by name a ferocious dragon, would evoke a more hopeful specter of the future? Can we say that Berg is using his moral responsibility? Or is he only a puppet expressing agonies of his generation without any will of his own? Although his music and

Sokolow's choreography really express the spiritual state of a large segment of this generation, and although both artists have recorded and presented it very impressively—as far as their arts go—still, aren't they both performing negative acts toward their contemporaries because of their moral passivity, because of the magic meaning of arts, and because of man's inability to learn from art? What will this do to us, how it will affect us, the unengaged, uninvolved, 'objective' art of this century? And further, are the artists themselves aware of this problem of morality, and the possible consequences of their art?"

"You see," I said, "it's here that the critics, philosophers, and the critic in the artist himself fail. The artist doesn't fail, but the critic fails. I am certain that nobody in the audience took *Lyric Suite* as a critical statement on the human condition today; they were watching it only as 'an art for art's sake,' as 'modern art,' as 'art experience,' without realizing that *this is them*, that they themselves are being mirrored on the stage. It isn't the work of art that fails; it is our attitudes to works of art that must be changed, how we look at works of art; the deeper functions of art have been forgotten, that's the real crux of this matter. We keep blaming the artist. This lack of understanding of deeper meanings of art has contaminated, sunk into the center

THE YM-YWHA

*presents*

## an evening of

## MODERN MUSIC, DRAMA, and DANCE

**MURIEL SHARON**          **ANNA SOKOLOW**          **EMANUEL VARDI**
*Production Director*          *Choreographer*          *Musical Director*

**DORIS S. EINSTEIN**
*Lighting*

### Saturday evening, December 18
### and Sunday evening, December 19, 1954 at 8:40 P.M.

1. EXPLORATION

    Moods ............................................................Macero
    Rose Petals ....................................................Macero
    Mascera ........................................................La Porta
    24 + 18 ........................................................Macero

Teo Macero, *Saxophone;* Lanny Di Jay, *Accordion;* Clem Derosa, *Drums;*
John La Porta, *Saxophone* and *Clarinet;* Charles Mingus, *Bass.*

2. LYRIC SUITE ....................................................Alban Berg

Choreographed by ANNA SOKOLOW

Allegretto Gioviale
  *Donald McKayle*
Andante Amoroso
  *Sandra Pine*
Allegro Misterioso
  *Beatrice Seckler*
Largo Desolato
  *Eve Beck*
  *Jeff Duncan*
Adagio Appassionato
  *Esther Beck*
  *Judith Coy*
  *Laura Shileen*
  *Joanne Vischer*

Michel Gusikoff, *Violin;* Bernard Robbins, *Violin;* Claire Kroyt, *Viola;*
Adolph Frezin, *Cello.*

INTERMISSION

Program note from a concert by Anna Sokolow,
December 18 and 19, 1954

3. HISTOIRE du SOLDAT............................................................Igor Stravinsky

Conducted by EMANUEL VARDI        Directed by MURIEL SHARON

Choreographed by ANNA SOKOLOW

Sets and Costumes designed by PAUL SHERMAN

Costumes executed by HELEN BELLAMORE

### THE CAST

Reader ........................................................Fritz Weaver
Soldier ......................................................John Harkins
Devil ....................................................Frederic Warriner
Princess ................................................Annabelle Gold

Part I

1. Beside a brook.
2. Crossroads at the frontier.
3. An office.

Part II

1. A town square.
2. A room in the palace.
3. The bedroom of the Princess.
4. Crossroads at the frontier.

Michel Gusikoff, *Violin;* Reuben Jamitz, *Bass;* Bernard Portnoy, *Clarinet;* Harold Golzer, *Bassoon;* Murray Karpilovsky, *Trumpet;* Charles Small, *Trombone;* George Gaber, *Percussion.*

The English text used in this production of "Histoire du Soldat" is adapted from the British translation of Rosa Newmarch and the American concert version of Stella and Arnold Moss, both of which are based on the French by C. F. Ramuz.

———————

Stage Manager ................................................Alice Kraus
Lighting Assistant ....................................Elizabeth Stearns
Production Associate ....................................Charlotte Haft

Stage Manager for the YMHA: SPOFFORD J. BEADLE

Assistant Stage Manager: Jan Marasek

of our artists, into their minds and souls, affecting the true meaning and function of their art. If we look at great works of the past, let's take *Prometheus Bound,* or Milton's *Samson Agonistes,* there is always, in the work itself —in the works which are true statements on the spiritual states of their periods ... there is a thought planted in these works, a critical mind is present, a thought that is always a little bit ahead of and above what's being described—a certain consciousness which lets us know, while we are reading, or seeing, these works, that it is *us* there, our natures are being discussed, these are not works for their own sake. Really, there is always something Brechtian in them, but in a more subtle, subliminal, less obvious way than Brecht's estrangement business. It is this element, this consciousness, this inspiration, this realization that is missing in the work of Alban Berg and Anna Sokolow.

And the lack of it, or the lack of clues to it, made us miss the very essence of the work. All that we saw remained an external movement, moods, desperations, with no meaning to it at all. Yes, beautiful, and strong, yes, but empty, like a beautiful shell: a magical work of desperation, a work of desperation acting magically upon us, upon the audience, upon its own creators—our critical spiritual powers were not awakened—the Cerberus is sleeping—a dragon is devouring its own creator by branding him with its flaming tongue right on the forehead with a sign of doom."

# In Defense of Perversity

November 21, 1958

In a bastard, standardized, conformist, sick society, perversity becomes a force of liberation. Horror and degradation for the professors, the guardians of Morality, it is a drop of Holy Spirit, a ray of salvation.

One has to hit it on the very head. The time has come when the action of silent wisdom ... when the truth takes the form of anarchy and exaggeration and negation. This subconscious, in its organic protest against dehumanizing tendencies, sprouts and bursts and spits out its venom.

Angry Young Men are necessary not because they bring a new philosophy. No—others will bring it in due time. Their function is to destroy. They came against their own will, to begin to get rid of the rotten swelling of their age. They are the subconscious of their (our) age.

The Beat and Angry generation is a protest. Not everybody in this generation is angry or beat. Generations get their names from a few people who express the mood of their generation the clearest. They are being forced by the total subconscious of their generation to utter, to shout, to cry, to beat out their truths, suspicions, hopes, loneliness, warnings, and prophecies. They are the true voices of their generations. Those are sensitive voices. They are perverse—they are not normal. Normality is conformist, money-minded, dead, Eisenhowered and Mamieed, and futurized, Harperized, deodorized. To be beat today is to be abnormal, to go against normality, conformity, to be immoral, to be perverse.

Even the sexual pervert today represents an innocent and helpless protest against bourgeois morality and insensitivity. Better a pervert than a businessman. A pervert is an innocent, crying, beating himself, not others.

When society is unlivable, the brave will die. The innocent will jump out the window, cut their innocent veins, soak in their innocent blood, or dream themselves out in the leaves of marijuana. The insensitive ones will survive and become Mamies, salesmen, atomic pirates, Dulleses, professors, Wouks.

Listen to the songs, on the radio, on jukeboxes, cheap songs, true songs. Popular American songs are the saddest thing in America, or maybe in the world. Listen to their sacred sadness. There was never such sadness in the songs of a large, strong nation: they always came from the trampled small nations, poor, beaten on the paths of war, famine. Now it is in America. An anguished sadness, a suicide sadness, a loveless sadness. Or listen to jazz. It is a kind of silent, hidden, sad crying out, for oneself, somewhere very deep. Or look at the paintings of De Kooning. There is the same suicide sadness, the same cry: he paints his heart out, the heart of his generation. The businessmen do not realize that these songs and jazz and De Koonings are also perverse: they demask their dead happy Peale's *Reader's Digest* smiles. Popular art and modern art sing the truth, as all perversity today does.

Isn't it the Mamies, the Eisenhowers, the salesmen and the atomists, the Wouks and professors that are the real perverts?

Aren't they the ones who go against the truth of life, love, and death?
Aren't they the ones who smear their Old Age in Mademoiselle's
fashions and wilt without tasting it, in anguish? Aren't they the ones
who made love into dating and partnership? Life into business?
The true perversity of our age? Aren't we the holy ones?

Isn't Elvis Presley a half saint, who showed the absurdity
of his parents' generation by exaggerating their ideals, by buying
two, three, four cars? All our fathers' ideals and truths become fake
and lie when lit up: rotten, evil, yellow puke.

So let us be beat and angry, and perverse: if that helps to
dethrone the falsity and rottenness of morality and the puked way
of living. It is more honest today to be confused than to be sure (when
the time is for dethroning). It is more honest to destroy than to
build (there is not yet a clean place for building). It is more honest
to be delinquent (and juvenile) than to learn and accept the ways
of living in lies and puke and garbage.

Holy are the delinquent thoughts and deeds and insubordi-
nation, disrespect, and hate for their ways of living, for their philosophies, for all work (for the perpetuation of the dump); holy is beat
and Zen and angriness and perversity.

The perversity doesn't deny the need of moral values.
It only shows the corruption of the existing moral values. It is the first
anxiety in which the new moral values will be born, in suffering and
in angriness.

Let us then deny and destroy, so that perhaps some of
us will find again and keep, until it is needed again, the truth of life,
the spontaneity, the joy, the freedom, exultation, soul, heaven and
hell. Let us free ourselves for perversity, become James Deans
and Presleys and Parkers and Osbornes, De Koonings, Kerouacs,
Bernard Shaws, and Millers, Genets, Villons, Rimbauds—
to learn the dynamics of the holy perversity, not to be cast into
the dump of twentieth-century normality.

Thus I spit on the generation that has produced me, and this
is the holiest spit of my generation.

$1

# BIG
# TABLE 1

THE COMPLETE CONTENTS OF THE SUPPRESSED WINTER 1959 CHICAGO REVIEW

JACK KEROUAC

## OLD ANGEL MIDNIGHT

EDWARD DAHLBERG

## THE GARMENT OF RA

## FURTHER SORROWS OF PRIAPU

WILLIAM S. BURROUGHS

## NAKED LUNCH

AND POWER, ARMY, AND POLICE BY GREGORY COR

# Absolument Moderne

After reading the first issue of *Big Table*
1959

It is Burroughs [W.S.] who is the most modern ("Il faut être absolument moderne") of all American (or all English-speaking) writers.
Writing on independent film-makers, Brakhage and Cassavetes
in particular, I have repeatedly stated that the improvisational method
of working is superior to the technically pure academic method. The
basic vocabulary of filmmaking is already lodged in our subconscious.
The new generation of film poets—if they are ever going to be poets—
can now, for the first time in film "history," begin creating from
"within." The same applies to modern prose. We have had so many
academic followers of Joyce, Proust & Co. The form was artificially
imposed upon the subject matter. The techniques were too obvious.
Joyce was still in the upper mind. Even Kerouac, who in his
other writings is a modern (in my understanding of the word) writer,
is working on the surface in his *Old Angel Midnight*. When a truly
modern, and primarily emotional, writer such as Kerouac tries to
use conscious techniques, spontaneity freezes.

      Burroughs is the first (to my knowledge) to write *absolument
moderne*. All the techniques of modern writing here are perfectly
integrated. Joyce is already dissolved. Hence the unhampered
spontaneous flow, the unpredictability of form, freshness, aliveness—
the nakedness of Burroughs.

      Those who respect Joyce, the classicists and academicians
(what a paradox: Joyce was made into a stick to beat experimental
writing on the head) will cry blood: the "formlessness" of Kerouac,
Ginsberg, Burroughs. "Form, form!" they cry, not realizing that
it comes to more than form. It is always so: when literature becomes
frozen, stale, a fresh wind of youth comes in from some low downtowns
carrying gusts of uncontrolled, wild life, and threatens to sweep
away all the official literature: barbarians of letters. Rimbaud-like.

      And so it is with the new American writing. Blow, ye down-
town winds, blow, blow! The official literature is splitting apart

syntax, words. Writing routines have become so obviously ridiculous (the only time when one feels like laughing at the dead)—and so dated, 1,000 years old!

It is the new content of their lives, new situations, feelings, attitudes, problems—those of a modern man—that ushers in a new literature. A literature that is open, that embraces life completely, without feeling ashamed—these are the voices (at first fragile, inaudible, but always growing) of our time. One must be very open, very listening, absolutely uncompromising—this is the condition of being *absolument moderne*—which means, being *absolument* alive.

This piece was my diary entry after reading the first chapters of *Naked Lunch* in *Big Table* magazine. I remember the occasion very vividly. It was electrical. I ran to Louis Brigante and Storm De Hirsch, editors of a literary monthly, *Intro Bulletin*, and we read it again together, and we got drunk. To us, it seemed like a new beginning in American literature. We thought it was an event of monumental proportions. We could not sleep that night.

*To the Editor*

May 9, 1959
To the Editor
*The Saturday Review*
25 West 45th Street
NYC

Dear Editor:
I found Rust Hills' article "The Big Trend in Little Magazines" a quite outdated piece of literary reporting. How can anyone who is in contact with the living literature of today write an article about "little magazines," talk about trends, make history evoking conclusions without mentioning even once *Yugen* and *Big Table*, each of which IS making history in American letters? *Yugen*, no. 4, an issue to be remembered by poets (the best ones are there already) and literary historians, is a truly blasting issue of poetry—there hasn't been a more important single issue of a poetry magazine since at least Ezra Pound's days, hands down. It blasts open the field

for new poetry, the same way as *Big Table* (with Burroughs's work) opens the way to New Prose. The Chicago *Poetry* magazine, when compared to *Yugen*, seems to be coming out of the Poetry Wax Museum. *Yugen* and *Big Table* are the two freshest and loudest voices in probably three decades of Little Magazine history. And how Mr. Rust Hills could not have heard of them makes one really wonder!

Jonas Mekas

# "Here and Now with Watchers," or Dance as a modern art

A conversation between Erick Hawkins, Lucia Dlugoszewski, and Jonas Mekas
1961

### JONAS

I am not a dance critic. I am a poet and, as poets usually are, I have always been interested in other arts, which are as great a source of inspiration as life itself. Sometimes, perhaps, even more so.

Anyway, I have been going to dance concerts quite often, and I have thought a lot about some aspects of dance, particularly those aspects which help me to understand the changes that are going on in man and the arts today.

I want to talk about dance with you because I think your work is the purest expression of modern dance, be it the end or the beginning of something.

As it is expressed through *Here and Now with Watchers*, which will remain a landmark in the development of modern arts, your dance has nothing to do with little stories, jokes, or pseudo-intellectual symbolism which I see

in so much of modern dance. It has something big and
serene about it, as all masterpieces do. *Here and Now with
Watchers* is a dance at once serious and joyful (who was
it that said the natural state of mind is delight?), at once
abstract and humanly warm. There is sentiment in it, but
there is no sentimentality; there is emotion in it, but there
is no emotionalism. There is meditation in it, but there
is no intellectualism.

It had still more when I saw it, and I haven't seen this
anywhere else before, or I have seen only glimpses of it here
and there: a dance that touched just barely, like a bird's wing,
the very essence of something of which, I felt, the dancers
and their movements and the audience and myself were a
part. In the same instance, as the dancers were dancing and
as we were watching, we were bound up together, touching
something very deep and very real and very luminous.
Kabbalah says: 'Cry, and thy crying will be heard through
the entire universe.' Here, I felt I was witnessing movements of such purity and perfection that they touched, somewhere, the very heart of the universe.

It was a dance that did not leave you sweetly empty,
as the ornamental beauty of classical ballet does; nor did it
tire you inside as the raw emotionalism of the expressive
etc. modern dance does; neither did it put you into a trance,
as the mechanical school of modern dance does. Your
dance left us wide awake, and thoughtful, like after seeing
*Hamlet*—illuminated.

With this deserved eulogy, I want to give the conversation entirely over to you. I ask you to begin anywhere—
for example: Where do you stand in contemporary dance,
how do you think your dance aesthetics differ from
those of other modern dancers?

### HAWKINS

To do this properly, I need to outline some kind of historical
perspective.

While I was in college, I happened to have vacation
in New York and, by chance, saw [Harald] Kreutzberg
dance. I didn't know until then that there was such a thing
as dance as an art. After seeing the first two dances on
the program, for the first time I knew what I wanted to do.

So I studied in Salzburg for the summer with him,
and then, I asked timidly if I could be a dancer. I invited

him to a coffee house, I was so scared of what he would
have to say. "You can be," he said. I said, "How should I proceed?" He said, "No point in studying with me, you are too
different from me. I will be on tour. I will not be able to give
you the necessary training."

So I came back. Kirstein was just bringing
Balanchine here, to start the School of American
Ballet. I remember I had the first receipt for tuition.
I was very ambitious and I worked like a dog. After a while
Balanchine started a series of performances, and my heart
was broken when I wasn't chosen to be in them.

But I was asked to teach. I was the first student trained
at the School of American Ballet to teach there. I had
an idea, and we started a small summer company. I got it
going, and it turned into the Ballet Caravan. One piece
I did was called *Show Piece*. Balanchine saw it and he
said it was the best piece done in the Caravan. I was excited
as one can be. Because, even at that time, I was already
experimenting. I was not doing dance to Mozart's music;
neither was I doing cute, little stories, sort of Yankee
on tour—a piece of American music, a bit of Japanese, or
Balinese, a sort of travelogue—which, of course, would have
been more popular than what I was doing. My *Show Piece*
was—I hate the word "abstract"—pure movement. It was
not telling little stories or going into sentimental moods of
some kind, following music. I commissioned Robert McBride
to write the music specially for this dance, a fact which
later, as we talk, will lead to something very important.

It is at this time that my aesthetic principles began
forming. I saw the early performances of all the important
modern dancers—Martha Graham, Doris Humphrey,
Tamiris, Charles Weidman, and the others—and I
knew that they were breaking away. They were trying to look
at the dance as a modern art. They were experimenting
with the actual movement. They were experimenting with
the compositions of dances, costumes, sets, music. A new
aesthetic principle was developing. Instead of going "I skip
to the right, I skip to the left, I skip to the right, I skip to
the left," they would use a simple Oriental principle of *asym-
metry*. Instead of skipping to the right, skipping to the left,
you may skip three times to the right in such a way that all
at once the familiar arrangement is broken and one sees
afresh and with surprise.

When one looks at Western art, from the Renaissance on, one always finds Oriental influences in it. Whenever it got more excited, it had to include some universal aesthetic principles which Western art had neglected. They are more universal in the sense that they use a more active dynamic of surprise in movement, rather than a steady diagram. The Western symmetrical principle comes from our predominantly geometric conception of the world. A column here, a column there; a door here, a door there; a candlestick here, a candlestick there. It is a theoretical formality, strict logic. As in our Periodic Table of Elements, which is formed by constant increase in the number of molecules in each element, whenever there was a gap in the orderly increase of molecules, we knew there must be an element that hadn't been discovered. It was pure mathematics.

But that is not the only way in which a human being knows the world. The other complimentary and equally important way of knowing the world is through what the philosophers call "immediate apprehension." It's the direct seeing, the direct piercing of the thing itself, without anything coming in between, that is, "I am mediated." We can't grasp the rhythm of the waves with our minds. We know there is a rhythm. We feel it, but we can't grasp it. This is used in all music and dance; there are always intangible elements of the rhythm. But at the same time, in complete contradistinction to the ungraspable elements of rhythm that we see all around us, when you start to make a work of art, you base it on graspable rhythmic organizations—that is the only reality of human awareness, no matter how you fantasize your aesthetic ideas.

After four years with the School of American Ballet, I was going into the mainstream. I saw the people who were making modern dance and I saw some of their principles. I knew that the School, instead of really helping me to grow, did everything, psychologically, to keep me a teenager. Even today, they still speak about the men in ballet as "the boys." That psychology is still continuing. I knew that this was not for me. I watched every rehearsal of Balanchine's for four years. I started a little dance notation. I was writing everything down. I still have my notations. This was my learning in process, through observation. I have seen Balanchine compose from scratch eight or nine ballets, and I was in some of them myself.

Lucia Dlugoszewski, New York, 1961

Erick Hawkins in *Here and Now with Watchers*,
New York, 1961

One day I said to Kirstein, "I want to go study with Martha Graham." She had, at that time, a special four-week course. I wanted to watch her compose, so I asked her, "Can I come and watch?" She was working then on a dance called *American Document*. As I watched rehearsals, I soon saw that she was planning to use me in some solos and duets. After the premiere I did go back for one tour of the Ballet Caravan, but I had an enormous success in *American Document* and I knew I felt at home in being a part of making a new American dance. I felt in *American Document* what it was to dance like a man, and I saw Martha Graham working, creating her own aesthetic, exploring rather than rehashing an old vocabulary.

In 1946 I did a dance about J o h n   B r o w n. I wanted to bring John Brown into focus, to bring out the ambivalence of his words and his actions. It needed a very specific intellectual side, historical side, to put it into perspective. So I started to write a text for this dance in which I, John Brown, would dance and speak his lines, together with an actor, an interlocutor. I used the actual texts, letters, and speeches. I used some lines from Thoreau and Emerson. At the height of the dance there was a little quatrain by Melville, from a poem he wrote on John Brown, which was perfect in the hanging scene. It touched me very much when the beautiful modern composer L o u   H a r r i s o n said, after the premiere, "Erick's 'John Brown' is the first American Noh play."

In 1950 I had a new wonderful flash of insight which made me go into a whole new direction. One day I asked my friend, the concert pianist Grete Sultan, if she knew a composer who might be interested in collaborating with me. She answered, "I know just the person, L u c i a   D l u g o s z e w s k i." Very soon after, when Lucia sat there at the piano, I said, "My God, this girl is bright." She had perceptions that you seldom run into. She had seen my last performance with Martha Graham and she actually was able to remember movements that I had done, and that was almost a year later. Soon we found that we agreed aesthetically so completely that we embarked on a collaboration of five solos, with the overall title, *opening of the (eye)*.

One of the things that—in the early '30s—made modern dance a distinct art was recognizing that the concept of dance in the Western world has always been inspired

by music. There were moments, in Russia and, I suppose,
in France too, when the choreographer would say, "Now
we want to do this number of turns here." So they would have
a sort of hack composer patch something up, and you did
a solo that had so many steps, etc. But nothing came of validity, artistically, because when you hear that music today
it is half music.

The problem is that if you have anything on the
stage, all the elements of the work must be of equal intensity.
And, of course, that takes hard work. You can't work hard
on one special aspect and then bring in some other elements
that are just passable—if you want an intense work of art.

### JONAS
Another aspect of this is that, in most cases, the music
that is being used is not contemporary but taken from the
last century, or the beginning of this century, written for
different purposes and different audiences. When we listen
to it, we hear it in a certain historical perspective. It imposes
conventions and conceptualizations on the dancer and
choreographer.

### HAWKINS
That is exactly what I mean. And practically nobody understands this.

### JONAS
Rimbaud wrote it, *"Il faut être absolument moderne."*
As soon as you begin using music written before your time,
you begin to step backwards.

### HAWKINS
One of the earliest and most important intuitions of modern
dance, as it began to blossom, was to use music of one's
time. The further intuition (about how to archive the freshest
art) was to have the music written for each specific dance.
In those early years, Martha Graham's collaboration
with Louis Horst, in my opinion, was the most beautiful
and successful. Louis told me just the other night, again—
although I knew it—how Martha composed the dances
completely in silence and Louis wrote his score specifically
for them. I don't know if, for instance, his *Frontier* and
*Primitive Mysteries* scores have ever been played separately.

I think it was in 1935 that *Frontier* was first done.
I was in the American Ballet at that time, but, of course,
I was curious, and I went to every dance concert I could.
I saw *Frontier* three or four times, and to this day I remember exactly what I felt like as I sat there in that seat.
That is an extraordinary test.

The two dances, two masterpieces of modern dance,
*Primitive Mysteries* and *Frontier*, I remember seeing
them at different times and knowing that I was
seeing them.

This led me to the awareness of another important
Oriental principle. The Oriental dancer not only dances but
also watches himself while dancing. Western theatre is
generally ignorant of this, and its goal is to make it believe
you are really the character you are portraying—a sort
of naturalistic concept, and I don't think it can ever make
the most exciting theatre. I think the actor and dancer
doing the role, every moment should be watching himself with an inner eye as he does the role. Something like
this can happen when you sit in a seat in a theatre. The
beautiful way is not only to sit in a seat and watch but also
to know that you are watching. It is a compounded level
of observation.

I have never heard anybody say this, but I think it is
part of the new principle of the new image of dance, and
it leads us into what a movement can do, how you choose the
movement, and how music is written for the dance. I am
stressing the new use of music because only the right music
can allow this to happen, music that understands duration. And Lucia is one of the very few modern composers
who understand this.

DLUGOSZEWSKI

I have always been fascinated by this seemingly unsolvable
element of music called duration. The very difficult problem
of the relation between music and dance showed to me
that music and dance can be related only through the element
of duration, no matter what anyone else says. The music
of *Here and Now with Watchers* was a very rigorous experiment with the element of duration. It disciplined itself to
the devastatingly simple and austere bedrock premise of the
heard pulse. In this way it is an absolute, archaic statement,
like the archaic statements of a M o n d r i a n. By using

the heard pulse in this absolute, humble, and austere way
we could achieve a kind of transparency of pure duration. I finally realized the exciting principle that duration
is an image.

## JONAS
The classical dance, when compared with *Here and Now
with Watchers*, looks like a beautiful paper cutout, two-
dimensional, beautiful people making beautiful, plastic,
two-dimensional movements. Your dancing contains
other dimensions. I have heard you using the expression
"cooperating with gravity."

## HAWKINS
Yes, this is one of the principles that started modern dance
and eliminated the two-dimensional conceptions. I s a d o r a
D u n c a n started it. She wanted to move away from ballet.
There was a need for feeling the volume of the body, feeling
that the body is in volume and not in line. You see, most
ballet movements, essentially, are looked at as designs: the
arabesque, the attitude; or the way jetés are done. Look
at the American Ballet—in the advertisement, this Sunday,
you'll find this big jeté in silhouette. That stands for
dancing! If you look at the insignia of the American Ballet—
Kirstein chose it very accurately—you'll find an outline
such as Leonardo would have used in the Renaissance:
the geometrical aspect of the body, in silhouette and in its
geometrical proportions—the straight spine, the straight
legs, straight arms. The most beautiful dancing in the world
never keeps the knee straight very long. When the knee
is straight, it is not using the subtle, rhythmic, effortless flow
in the hinge that the human knee is. You can test it: you
straighten your knee, hold it, and your muscular sensation
dies, and your sensation of constant changing—which
is the essence of movement—dies.

## JONAS
I see what you mean. It is as though this beautiful silhouette
of the classical dance negates movement. What you do,
when you move within gravity, instead of trying to fight it—
enjoying it, the movement itself being the reason (cause),
the idea, and the content.

HAWKINS

I really think that the essence of the revolution called
modern art is that, for the first time in the Western world,
we can use the materials of art, movements, colors, etc.,
in and for their own sake, and not in service of any concept.
They are good in themselves.

JONAS

Thus, consciously or not, through your dance you are clean-
ing the audience of routine concepts; you are bringing
them in contact with an experience that only the immediate
sensing of the materials of art in their wondrousness and
nakedness can give. The plot can mislead, it can be mis-
interpreted. But a pure movement has no obstacles of reason
in its way, it happens on a different plane, as an instant-by-
instant, immediate experience, a direct illumination of what
it is to be alive.

HAWKINS

You are very right. The point is that there is no separation
between ethics and art. The human being doesn't live in
a dozen pigeonholes. It is one unit. Whatever I think about
anything is going to affect every word I say, every movement
I make. Ballet acts as if it were in some kind of hothouse,
absolutely disconnected, not connected with the totality of
human experience. That is why it lost its true basis.

There is so little written about dance, about its basic
philosophy and aesthetic principles, when you compare
it with what's done in poetry or painting. Why? They are
selling little monographs on De Kooning, for instance,
in all the bookstores. But where are the widely distributed
little books on Graham or Cunningham or Limón?
And there is so much to discuss. We can discuss, for
instance, the philosophy of movement in a way it had never
been treated in the West by anybody; we can talk about a
new image of dance, dance as an immediately apprehended
experience as the dancer does it, as the audience watches
it. Dance is still not taken seriously enough. No subsidy
with vision has come to help our really new modern dance
as it does the other arts—painting, for instance.

I remember reading a new book on Brâncuși.
An American lawyer, quite early, started buying his work.
Every year he bought $10,000 worth of sculpture.

So Brâncuşi did not have to worry for the rest of his life;
he could concentrate on his work. Nothing like this has
ever happened in modern dance. So, of course, it is still
in limbo. Its aesthetics are not defined enough. Nobody
talks about it enough.

Much of modern dance has already conceptualized itself into clichés and most of the time it is not quite good
enough. Some of the brightest people have still not thought
far enough, and so it is not yet as complete as it could
be. Instead of using the expression "modern dance," I like
to say "dance as a modern dance," which, I think, immediately places it in a larger context and keeps it open for new
developments.

Classical ballet, and much of modern dance is not good
enough in its vision of movement itself. It is based on an
inadequate concept of the totality of movement, which is
a very important point.

Ballet comes from the idea of the human figure as
a geometrical arrangement and not out of the immediately
sensed, immediately felt prime physical experience of
moving. Many of ballet's movements rely on the virtuosity
that really comes out of the industrial revolution, on
trying to get a great deal of mechanistic movement, like
thirty-two fouettés or the high kicks of fifty roquettes
on an assembly line, whereas a very simple movement
can have much more poetry.

### JONAS
They are always trying to impress the audience with something else, not with the dance itself. In *Here and Now
with Watchers*, however, it was the dance itself that
I saw. All the other elements—color, lighting, and sounds—
were completely subordinate to the dance. I have never
seen dance in which sounds were used so economically,
so aesthetically, so properly. There can not be enough
praise for Lucia's collaboration, as she stood there, besides
her piano, ALL EARS, as Rilke would say, and as she
punctuated, made periods and commas and parentheses
with her sounds, and underlined and italicized, bringing
still more order into the whole, or opening it up, when
necessary, and leading those among us who were still outside of the dance, not yet exactly with the dancers, into
the very center of it, so that we sat there, silently and

engrossed in this huge and almost sacred happening,
an experience which we have been given as a gift.

### HAWKINS
That is very sweet of you to say. Because I believe it is
so. Because I think it is true. Let us speak about the use
of music in dance, for a moment, because it will help
us to understand another aspect of the new image of dance.
What happens when the music has been chosen, and the
dancer listens to it and composes his dance to it? The
dancer is being led by the nose. In its rhythmic feeling,
he may be wanting to alternate four and five meter;
but previously written music might force him to do the movement strictly in fours, and so he has to stay within that
metric framework. But maybe, at that moment, if he is really
following his spontaneous intuition, he won't be content
with the squareness of a meter in four. He will really
want to feel four and five, four and five in the dance movement, just out of sheer freshness of feeling. So that if the
music has already been set, and you compose a dance to it,
willy-nilly, you are being led by the nose.

### DLUGOSZEWSKI
It doesn't even have to be in four … maybe 7/8 … And then,
what does the dancer do? That can be done maybe with
a musical instrument, but it's impossible for the body
to do it, to go into that kind of complexity. What does the
dancer do? It's even worse than being led by the nose:
the dancer then ignores the sound.

### HAWKINS
Ordinarily, when the choreographer takes a piece of music
and dances to it, he has to stay in the prescribed form. In
that sense, what he is really doing is interpreting the music.
Today there are a few people who know that you can get
something more exciting by not doing it that way.
     The other thing is, the mood or feeling of music will
always alter the feeling of the choreography. What we need
is to get out of clichés and to explore a new area of possible human movement. Let the dancer go a little more into
this inner silence and move out of his own body, without
tagging along to some other feeling from some other source.
He just needs to see what will come out of the totality

of our body experience today, find it in the movement first.
When I compose the dance completely in silence first,
I sometimes feel like a spider spinning its web out of its
own body. In that way I hope that the movement can spring
from a deeper unconscious level and therefore have a
chance to achieve richer and fresher poetry.

### DLUGOSZEWSKI

That is a sort of humility that seems to be lacking in art.
It takes humility, I think. The whole Western attitude toward
the body—we always seem to be getting into this East and
West difference—is that the body is insignificant. Significance and profundity come from something and somewhere
else, they think. Yes, it takes humility. Every time I try
to say something about the choreography of *Here and Now
with Watchers*, it's so hard to talk about it unless people
have a sense of poetry. They say: "Oh, that's all there is?
Oh, he is just worried about the sensations and movements?
Oh, that's nothing …" What do you mean, that's nothing!
It's the highest thing to do, because it takes humility
and the greatest courage. Oh, it's like life itself, life itself
is the greatest thing, right? And yet, if you wanted to be
funny about it, you could say: "Why should I say life is
the greatest thing? A bug has it. Am I more on the same
level as the bug?" This is the attitude.

### HAWKINS

Most people, it seems to me, in the West today have forgotten to say thank you for their existence in the body.
We always have to use the body and its movements in the
service of something we think is greater.

### DLUGOSZEWSKI

Profundity …

### JONAS

Culture …

### HAWKINS

But when the dancer starts and stays right in the discovery,
in the new possibilities, new shapes of movements, organizations of movements, dynamics of movements, the inner
feelings and qualities—then, of course, there is no reason for

Erick Hawkins in *Here and Now with Watchers*,
New York, 1961

the music not to happen (be written, composed) at the same
time as the dance is happening. They go along together.
Then, the problem, of course, is to find the composer who
will collaborate, make an exploration of equal intensity
and equal aesthetic interest. And that seems to be the main
problem. Lucia is willing to work this way for the total
collaboration and not, as most composers do today, just
write a piece of music for a dance for which they are commissioned. They write, but they don't care about the dancing,
know little about it, and the music stands alone, and
not part of one complementary whole.

Duncan, who really was the John the Baptist of what
became dance as a modern art in America, rebelled against
the hack compositions of the ballet as it was done by
composers like Adam Minkus, even Tchaikovsky—who
also did hack work—only that he happened to be bright
enough to transcend it a little, and he had big fights. Isadora
Duncan said, "If our dance is going to be important, let's
use the best music." So she went to Gluck and Wagner
and Beethoven and Schubert and Chopin. Unfortunately, that was one direction of modern dance that
America did not outgrow. It was the only way Isadora could
proceed in her time, because we didn't have good enough
American composers. What it amounts to is that some of the
modern dancers really were cashing in on the acceptance
of some recognized composers.

I want an equal exploration in music and in dance.
I say this categorically: if you want a new work of art in
dance, you cannot use music that hasn't been written within
the last five years. In five years the art changes. Going to
Webern or Satie is like going to a museum, getting some
old costumes, putting them on the stage, and calling this
a new dance.

### JONAS

It would follow that all classical ballet is not only unaesthetic
but is also immoral, unless it is done for study or museum
purposes.

### HAWKINS

One might say it is the way: that to compose in a vocabulary
of movement is aesthetically immoral, just as it would
be to compose today like Tchaikovsky. Or, as Gertrude

Stein put it, "The business of art is to live in the actual present, that is the complete actual present, and to express the complete actual present."

Even if you use dance to convey ideas, concepts, narrative—as I did in *John Brown*—if you use any kind of plot, or a myth from previous times: the materials of the art, the sounds, music, colors, the costumes, the form of the choreography, the movements must come out of your immediate experience. The individual cannot make up the myth; what we can do is directly experience it and transform it into our own materials, out of our own experience.

The minute one uses any concept or idea that has a historical life, there is a further obligation: it cannot go against the most up-to-date intelligent knowledge of anybody living at this present time. I cannot make a dance saying that the sun goes around the earth. I cannot do anything in my dance that is false to the most up-to-date knowledge of man. So, when somebody comes along and uses myth, plot, or idea from past times in the dance, if they do not really understand the myth or idea, they are making a work of art that is false to human life, that is, they are infecting the world with false ideas.

### DLUGOSZEWSKI
On the other hand, you could have an inferior idea but be so superb as an artist that you translated this wrong idea into a superb work of art.

### HAWKINS
I disagree with you. You can't do it without changing the idea.

### DLUGOSZEWSKI
Some people say it doesn't matter what the idea is.

### HAWKINS
But I say it does matter.

### DLUGOSZEWSKI
I really know it. But you have to see this dual situation. For instance, Gieseking—or even Wagner—had some ideas that were not very good, but their art was superb. And what do you do about it?

HAWKINS

I don't think that you can say that their art is superb.
You cannot have a false idea, no matter how beautifully it is
embodied in the materials of the art. It will always have to
finally be superseded. It will always be outdated some time.

When the dancer chooses to use as the theme or a subject of his dance a true idea, be it the life of Christ, life
of Buddha, or a beautiful myth—the idea has to be embodied
in brilliant art materials. That idea has to be expressed
in completeness and intensity and brilliance right in the use
of the materials of art themselves. One of the main places
that dance can fail is that it can take an important idea and
not express it with enough depth and invention and completeness in the actual movement itself.

A good example of such a failure is in what we call taw-
dry modern religious art where the spiritual idea can be
an eternally valid one, but the artist's use of the colors and
shapes, say in the painting, can be gross, without imagination and taste.

As I see it, we dancers today have to work harder
at finding movement that has more vividness and intensity.
In the Western world, we still think, for instance, of the spine
as a rigid ramrod. What we have to do, on the scientific as
well as aesthetic level, is to see how human movement in our
culture can be best experienced in its totality. And this is
where morality or ethics come in again. We have to begin to
see what kind of movement we want. I feel that the movement in the West is psychologically and morally inadequate
for the most part. It emphasizes aggressiveness.

Everybody walks, for instance. But many people grow
up with very erroneous ideas of how to walk efficiently
and therefore in a way that is aesthetically beautiful. If one
is careful, one can very easily read the ideas that a person
has of himself just by watching him walk. In the same
way, what happens to the general way of moving in dance
today in the West is not something inevitable. We are
faced with deciding really what kind of movement we think
is most beautiful and expresses the most sensitive norm
of what human beings can be in our society.

One of the important new ideas in the beginning
of modern dance was born when Isadora Duncan began
to intuit that human movement really starts in the pelvis
and spine. She also said you don't have to lift your legs

very high. You don't have to strain to get them up, to make
contortions. She said there is a norm within which the
body will move with freedom and plasticity. But it doesn't
have to go into stunts. That is not at the service of poetry.

### DLUGOSZEWSKI

What you are doing in your dance, I feel, is pinpointing
the prime material of the art of dance—the movement itself.
You say certain movements are immoral because they are
aggressive. But maybe the reason is that those movements
did not come from watching the movement for its own
sake. The aggressiveness in the movement comes from the
fact that it's used to show something else, it serves something else, to show man's domination of nature, for instance.
This is what the male ballet dancer does. The female
ballet dancer, it would seem, is more abstract but the movements again come not from looking at the movement but
from the idea that the body is slightly unworthy, not the most
profound thing. It seems that the woman, generally, wants
to deny the body—she always tries to be ethereal. The inad-
equacy of ballet for us today in the mid-twentieth century
is that the technique and aesthetic is essentially that of the
mid-nineteenth century, when the woman dancer in the
toe shoe embodied the concept that a woman was a disem-
bodied spirit. It seems to me that with Eric, and especially in *Here and Now with Watchers*, the two most brilliant
contributions technically—and I don't see them anywhere
else—are the new use and new understanding of gravity
and a new understanding of time. They both came directly
from this very humble look at the movement itself.

### HAWKINS

Yes, I think the most beautiful way is to accept gravity and
not try to dominate it.

### DLUGOSZEWSKI

The other thing is this business of time. Certain avant-
gardists are making a big noise about it. But again, if you
look at the movement itself, if you are willing to be that
humble and courageous, then you see that this "time" that
everybody is talking about is not sensed time, not immediacy—but that they are again talking about an idea,
something that is outside and, they think, more profound.

But actually, the greatest contribution an artist can give is immediacy.

### HAWKINS

What I would like to do is to see beautiful people letting things happen. The way I try to teach is to show students instead of telling them, "Look at this movement and see if what I say is true." The same in terms of relationships. I don't want to dominate the audience, even though maybe it wants to be dominated. The dance should be like lovemaking, an equal activity and an equal passivity playing back and forth between the two all the time. What I am trying to do is to find in my dance equal active and passive movement constantly. Some early modern dance, some of the early techniques, teach beginners that you have to trust every movement—the muscles, tight. That is completely wrong. There must be a constant interaction of activity and passivity. The centering of the body is in the pelvis, with the legs as tassels and the arms as tassels. It is this that I don't see anywhere, except in Oriental dancers.

About aggressiveness: if we say that the person knows how to yield, we say that he is not stiff-necked or stiff-kneed. The most beautiful dancing comes from the bent knee. The knee is never held straight. I think that this idea could revolutionize our dance by itself, if understood.

### JONAS

I already said earlier that your movements, although seemingly abstract, are very concrete. There is something very basic about them. There is somewhere a point where the utmost abstract becomes the utmost concrete. And that is the most difficult to achieve in art. Like the amazing simplicity of G o e t h e. I don't want to go into mysticism, but I believe, as the ancients believed, that you can give birth to a star by the right movement or the right word (which is a movement, too). God's movement—WORD— preceded the creation of the world. That's what gets me thinking when I watch *Here and Now with Watchers*.

### HAWKINS

I think it is the difference between what is called existence and what people mean when they say, "I want to live."

When they say, "I want to live," they are really talking about
having many emotional satisfactions. But then, there is
the other existence, on a higher level, the immediacy of the
moment-by-moment existence. Those who are wise enough
realize that just to exist is about the nicest thing that could
happen.

### JONAS
It is in the sense that one could say that naturalistic art
is really an abstract art—it doesn't have anything to
do with the essence of life. De Kooning or K l i n e or you,
on the other hand, are the true realists ...

### HAWKINS
It is here that we are touching the real meaning and
essence of art. It also indicates where modern art should
go. F.S.C. N o r t h r o p, in his book *The Meeting of East
and West*, speaks about art in its first function and art in
its second function. I think that he presents the most basic
aesthetic formulation in the history of Western thought.
He shows the two ways of knowing the world. The Western
mind works through what he calls the theoretical component. In the Orient, to know the world means to know
it through aesthetic components, through the immediate apprehension. When he came to the first performance,
he said to me—and we never met before—"H a w k i n s,
this is tremendous." I said, "Northrop, on reading your
book, for the first time in my life, I didn't feel like a fool
to be an artist."
     Northrop shows that the way of art is to use the aesthetic
component of things primarily, and that is the primary
way of knowing in the Orient. It is the way of immediate
apprehension. This is contrasted with the predominant
Western way of knowing, which is the theoretical component,
the way of knowing which produces our science. Naturally,
what I meant by what I said to him was that for the first time
I understood that the way of knowing in the Orient is analo-
gous to the way artists must work primarily. The artist's
primary concern is with using his senses, and valuing the
materials of art: colors, shapes, sounds, smells, and movements in and for their own sake.
     Art, in its second function, is to use those various mate-
rials of art to convey an idea not in the materials them-

selves. And it takes these two functions of art to make the
totality of art. Both ways have always been used. But in
Western art, until the revolution of so-called modern art,
the artist valued and created primarily in the second
function of art.

   Last spring I read a quotation from Mallarmé about
his friend Manet: "Manet understood that painting is
made with oils and colors. Manet understood that white
is white, before it is a white cloth." The real revolution that
would lead modern dance to another stage, a deeper exploration, is really to stay in its first function, in the concrete
experience of body and movement. I would like for dance
to catch up with the other arts. Mallarmé was writing
in the 1890s. But in dance, even today, if you do a movement
in and for its own sake, so many people ask: "What does
it mean?" Put it in words! What I would like to see is a
poetry of movement that is pre-conceptual, one that cannot
be verbalized in any way.

"For people thus trained to separate immediately experienced fact
from theoretical inferences that transcend it, the standard for
measuring achievement in the dance may well be something in addition to, or quite other than the theoretical combination of ancient
Greek geometry and the physical culturalist's muscle building, always
fighting gravitation, which, beautiful though it be, is the traditional
ballet. The dance and music of Erick Hawkins and Lucia Dlugoszewski
will be appreciated also as the much less muscularly artificial and
the more immediately natural and beautiful standard of artistic mea-
surement in the domain of the aesthetically immediate which it is.
In short, concept by intuition contemporary dancing *as well as* the
anti-gravitational Greek geometrically ordered dancing of medieval
of modern Soviet bourgeois society will flourish." (*Philosophical
Anthropology and Practical Politics* by F. S. C. Northrop, New York:
Macmillan Co., 1960, pp. 312–13.)

# "Totentanz" Bread & Puppet theater of Peter Schumann

May 15, 1962

*Totentanz* at Judson Church. It could be called a "happening". A young man, Peter Schumann, is behind it, I found out later.

None of the participants were dancers. They were painters, just anybodies, nobodies. And it worked. It worked as an experience of anti-dance, anti-ballet, anti-theatre, a cleaner of the mind. Moving freely, playing music, without knowing music, without knowing dance, or if knowing, forgetting it, beginning from scratch.

This is not art, someone said. What is this business of looking for art everywhere? Can't one even spit without someone declaring that spitting is not art? Sometimes I wish I could burn down the theatres and art galleries. I think we should introduce an annual day on which we'd perform ritualistic burning and destruction of established works of art.

Anyway. We are opening ourselves, we are loosening up, everywhere, little by little. Did the man who asked about Art give any thought as to why something like *Totentanz* is being done? At this place, this time? Or what it means, how it reveals us, our needs—I mean, the needs of our souls, a need for still more opening, more unpretentiousness, humility, almost humiliation?

It is not for the sake of effect that *Totentanz* was performed. The reasons were more real. It was a spontaneous, inevitable action, like a movement of the hand that betrays something inside or a word that slips out, in sleep. It was a necessity and fact. And don't ask for the reasons. To understand the reasons, we know, may help us to understand ourselves. But perhaps it is too early; we are not ready to understand the real reasons for what's

happening today, both in life and art. Let it happen by itself a while longer, before we put our clumsy minds to it, before we begin to analyze it. For our lives in this decade (and, possibly, for one more) are mysterious, uncontrollable happenings. It's not our rational, intellectual, bookish inquiries that will reveal the path (philosophy, religion, ethics, etc.) which we will take or are taking; rather, it is in the happenings such as *Totentanz* (which come from nobody knows where and which say and express something nobody knows yet what or why) that the seeds and the keys of/to our future are hidden, sometimes more, sometimes less open to the eye of the outsider, or for that matter, to the insider's eye, too.

These strange voices, the actions of *Totentanz*—these men and women coming in, walking out, these masks, clumsy movements, fragments and hints of trance states, bodies and voices, falling, mingling, or sitting

BREAD AND PUPPET THEATER

quietly—are reaching out for new inner states and motions, a part of the inner revolution which is beginning to release energies and truths that we have in ourselves. There is sacredness in this foolery.

# A note on Jean Genet's film, "Un Chant d'Amour," and Harold Pinter

The year was 1964, early January. From Knokke-Le-Zoute Experimental Film Festival, where B a r b a r a   R u b i n and I created a scandal when they forbade us to show J a c k   S m i t h's film *Flaming Creatures*, we proceeded to Paris, where we spent some time with R o m a n   P o l a ń s k i as our driver—we had a car, a tiny car but a car. Eventually he gave up when Barbara decided to go swimming in the Seine. We could not persuade her not to do that. So we left her by the Seine and went to La Coupole.

It was during that trip that I revisited N i c o   P a p a t a k i s. I had met him some years earlier, during the reshooting of Cassavetes's film *Shadows*. In 1950 Nico helped J e a n   G e n e t make his only film, *Un chant d'amour*. It was a legendary film, which few people had seen, even in Paris. The censors did not allow it to be shown in the theatres. So I asked Nico if I could take a print of it to New York. Nico wondered why I wanted to take that kind of risk, but I was very determined about it. So now we were at Café de Flore and in my huge raincoat pockets I had the film. To make the transportation safer, we divided the print into several rolls.

Since the travelers from Paris to New York usually were checked very thoroughly, I decided to go first to London for a day and *then* arrive in New York from London instead. You have to know that Paris in 1964 was considered by the customs people a smut city. On my previous return from Paris to New York they confiscated two Olympia Press books I was carrying in my bag. London travelers were not being checked so carefully at customs. That was the advice given to me by Brion Gysin, in whose home I was staying in Paris. So that's what I did. On the plane from London to New York I got into a conversation with my neighbor, who happened to be Harold Pinter. He was on his way to New York for the opening of one of his early plays. As we were talking, we discovered that we knew some of the same people, including Nico. So I told him what I had in my pockets. We discussed the best strategy to deal with the customs guys. The plan that we devised was that he would go first, since he had more stuff. I usually travel very light. I was to follow after him.

And that's what we did. He got his huge suitcase down from the running belt and we moved toward the customs guy of Pinter's choice. I followed him almost like a servant. The customs man surveyed us and asked Pinter to open his suitcase, which Pinter did. The customs man peeked in and his face went strange: there was nothing in the suitcase but some thirty copies of Pinter's play.

"What are these?" asked the customs guy.

"It's my play that is opening on Broadway next week," said Pinter, calmly.

You had to see the face of the customs guy! He lit up, his eyes lit up, he went all gaga. Here is a real Broadway playwright, a celebrity, a suitcase full of plays! All excited, he motioned to a couple of other customs guys:

"Come, take a look: this guy has a play on Broadway. No joke."

They all surrounded the suitcase staring at it in an *awe* that I *cannot* describe to you. And since they seemed to ignore me completely, and I had no suitcase, I just walked through. Then I turned around and waved to Pinter. I could see from his face that he enjoyed the way the affair went.

I proceeded toward the exit with the print of *Un chant d'amour* in my raincoat pockets.

# On John Cage

January 2, 1965

Music (sound?) evening at the 92nd Street "Y."

Stockhausen's *Kontakte* (for piano, percussion & electronic sounds), played by Max Neuhaus and James Tenney, John Cage's *Atlas Eclipticalis with Winter Music* (a version for kettle drums & piano), played by Max Neuhaus and Philip Corner.

Stockhausen dramatizes the sounds, melodramatizes them. It's still Wagner etc. It bothered me all evening, and I tried to understand why. The piece was masterfully executed and rich in sound, etc.—but it bothered me, it seemed almost a misuse of sounds; one wanted to hear the same sounds just as sounds, separated by pauses and placed in space with no dramatics.

After the first few moments of Cage everything became immediately clear. What a difference! Here we have pure sounds, or almost pure (execution sometimes seemed to dramatize them, but not enough to destroy the purity and nakedness of the sounds)— the beauty of sounds left in the world by themselves is enough to keep you in suspense, yes, almost in suspense, because of

the tremendous tension created by the silences, because of the tensions between the sounds and the listener. I never realized until this evening the greatness of Cage, the purity of Cage & how old-fashioned and impure and melodramatic Stockhausen is when compared with Cage! I sat there in absolute suspense, completely caught by these sounds, sitting on the edge of my seat, and I was myself like an instrument on which he seemed to work now. Things were happening inside, stirred and touched, things that were dormant for a long time, never touched by other art (or half art). It was an experience so rich and so overwhelming. An experience equal only to La Monte Young's Second Avenue concert that we went to with Andy four weeks ago: there, too, I was sitting on the edge of the seat for two hours, and I wasn't the same man when I left the place (or perhaps, more truly, I was awakened to myself, I was more myself). I felt the same way now, listening to Cage's music. My own life became clearer to me somehow, illuminated in a new way. That is the secret power of all real works of art, that instead of enslaving you, instead of enveloping you in a dream, they wake you up to yourself, they open you up, they make you free. That's what Cage's music did to me. Later, I was wondering—really, not even wondering, but just noting it down sort of, the fact that only art which is as intensely structured and as pure as that of Cage (there are others) can reach our true depths. No impure art, no half art, no bastard art can do that—it stays on the surface, it stirs some emotions but never reaches beyond them, into the deepest crevices of mind-body-soul. Cage does it, P o u n d does it, R i m b a u d does it, Homer does it. I had a feeling that art is either GREAT or it's NOTHING. There is NO place for *almost* ART. To jump a hurdle *almost*, means that the stick (barrier) fell down. To swim across the river, *almost*, means that you have drowned.

# A salute to Cardee Schneemann: In Praise of Surface

March 1965

So much has been said about the "essence" of things and men that you'll forgive me if I say a few words in praise of the surface.

I was provoked by this sentence: "Schneemann abstracts, removes all social context, alters and distorts reality instead of moving toward its essence." (Michael Smith, *Village Voice*, Nov. 26, 1964 in his review of *Meat Joy*.)

Arts have always rebelled against prescribed "essences," against "social significances"— for those terms mean and imply either the old (comfortable) essence and significance (a trick to protect oneself from anything that may upset the status quo) or they simply mean nothing (or nobody knows what they mean). So the artists junked everything that had been known as essence and significance and began searching for it, from scratch.

In painting, in sculpture, for a decade now the artist has been exploring new textures, materials, surfaces, junk, garbage, things around us, putting them in/on canvasses until they swell (and smell), until they are no longer paintings, but things— striving, hoping this way to escape the prescribed meanings, forms, perspectives, contexts.

In cinema: Smith, Warhol, Brakhage, Markopoulos, Rubin, and Jacobs go directly to the surface (impactness) of things, of people, textures, faces and bodies, and exploring the eye that sees it and the means and ways by which it sees. Things that surround us ... the human body itself has become invisible during the last two centuries. Two centuries of industry, rationalism and materialism succeeded in making the material world invisible to our eyes. It was Warhol who demonstrated to us that a Campbell's soup can can be visible, that the Empire State Building can be seen. Smith, like a

*Meat Joy*, Carolee Schneemann's performance at Judson Church, New York, 1964

magician, opens to us the world of color and texture in the simplest materials around us, colors we keep looking at every day without seeing, without perceiving them. Brakhage and Markopoulos are demonstrating to us that there is LIGHT, and that we have eyes, and that there is a human body. Ken Jacobs shows us that shadows exist. Nam June Paik even shows that DUST exists and falls on everything, including film. Nothing can be taken for granted: we are basically blind.

Music: La Monte Young goes beyond all melody, his music becomes one uninterrupted sound, all sounds fade into one, and then you listen to the very surface of sound and you discover the most fantastic harmonies, you hear the sound for the first time, you hear the music of the spheres.

# Jim Dine's "Natural History (the Dreams)"

May 1, 1965

In a large TV studio, far in the back, like *The Magnificent Ambersons*, crouched in a chair, really with his legs stretched in a fauteuil, Jim Dine sits and thinks. Gets up, walks around a few steps, sits down again. He has big shiny boots. His thoughts, various private moments, memories, are recorded on tape; we hear them on tape. The place is cold and empty on weekends.

We got in, it was dark. We sat down, in darkness, with flashlights blinking. The "piece" started with the lights (regular studio lamps with reflectors) going on and off irregularly, in five spots. Dine sitting. On the left of the studio: four girls sitting on a bench, tightly, side by side—they look like cutouts from *Harper's Bazaar*, and with their purses on their knees, constantly taking out and

Program 1     TV Studio, 81st Street and Broadway    May 1-3, 1965; 8.30 pm

FIRST THEATER RALLY:  NEW YORK

Steve Paxton and Alan Solomon

present

Jim  Dine's

"NATURAL HISTORY (THE DREAMS)"

with

Jim Dine

Nancy Fish                                    James Silvia
Bob Brown


Judith Hidler                                 Joe Raffaele
Colleen Bennet                                Peter  Hujar
Constancia Calderon


NO INTERMISSION

***

STAFF FOR THE FIRST NEW YORK RALLY

Steve Paxton & Alan Solomon: Production    Jennifer Tipton: Lighting Design
Nancy Fish: Manager                        Dick Robbins: Sound Consultant
Toiny Castelli: Production Assistant        Bill Mayer: Technical Assistant
Frank Konigsberg: Counsel


***

SPONSORS OF THE FIRST NEW YORK RALLY

Robert Rauschenberg
Pocket Theater
Surplus Dance Theater

passing a handkerchief, going
through this action all evening
long, a nonsensical action. Further
to the right: some kind of steel
table—it could be a baker's
table—and a man and a woman,
dressed in a white night shirt
and shorts, working all the time
on a piece of dough, with plenty
of flour thrown into the air
and around the table, often like
a cloud. They fool around, the
woman pulls him by the shirt, a
couple of brief embraces; but they
keep working—work we must—
then they wash the table. Further,
in the center: Dine sitting and
thinking. Further to the right:
a man, in a white longish dress—
looks like some kind of shirt—
with a butcher's or baker's cap or
hood on, cutting with a little saw
little five-inch pieces from a long
steel pipe. He managed to cut
three pieces and almost the fourth
one, but not quite. His sound
provided the music for the evening. Not too sharp, a small thin
handsaw. On the extreme right,
a table, a TV set, and two young
men, playboy types, in white
sport shirts and pants, in summer
dress sort of, like dressed for
tennis, but also could be for the
night; they sit or stand, watch
TV, talk silently, a few snatches,
we don't really hear them, and
they keep having their meal,
I mean, they eat all the time, they
have some bread, some salami,
mustard, they make sandwiches,
watching TV all the time, quite
casually, and keep eating.

Now, these actions go on all
the time. One hour, approximately.
The lights keep going on and
off, now lighting up one action
now another. Sometimes we see a
glimpse, for two seconds, or a split
second of one action, then of another, or two or three actions
at the same time. Really, I kept
looking, and so did the others,
now at one, now at the other. It
became, really, like a movie: very
clear, very simple, with a soundtrack on tape. No sudden and
rash movements, no big excitement, very peaceful, almost
abstract. Your eyes go from one
shot to another, brief shots,
separated by darkness (black
leader). Most of the cutting was
done with the lights, but you
could do some cutting yourself,
by choosing this or that action,
this or that spot to look at, then
move your eyes to another, and
wait for the light to come on,
or go off, then move your eyes
toward the boys with the TV, then
again back to the bakers (bakers
really provided the most visually interesting point of attraction
for the eyes, it was very pleasant, really).

The mood of peace and
whiteness pervaded everything.
Also, the element of darkness,
and space. Each little action
was concentrated in a comparatively small area, like six feet by
six feet; and each action area
was separated by plenty of dark
space or gray space; so that
each was like a thought, hanging,

moving in a space, independent from each other, but nevertheless all five were tied together by darkness and space so that there was a feeling that they all belonged to Jim Dine, to the man who sits and thinks there, or at least they threw a reflection upon him, in one way or another. I mean, there was a unity in all this, everything hung together, none of the actions ever really became an action in itself, independent from the totality, despite the space. It all made one; a melancholic, meditative, little bit lonely reminiscence of a man thinking, remembering, reflecting in some dark corner of his mind as the world—it could be also the night—continued around him, really, a small, middle-class, small life, small thoughts, petty preoccupations, and no real tragedies, and therefore a little bit decadent, and middle-classy, and in a sense uptownish, just like the place itself, on 81st Street and Broadway—all emotion and life, energy really, reduced to surface actions, nothing that would involve deep or subtle emotions, or dramatic clashes. It all happened, remained on this surface plane, Pop plane, like the bread next to a TV, BIG bread, the label said; or salami sandwiches, tomato—yes, this was the Museum of Natural History of Life; that's how life would look, if you could just put it there, in one of those glass windows.

I think Jim produced a masterpiece in this work. But now it's all gone. I am sitting alone, this late night and writing this down—but it's only a memory now.

# Notes on shooting "The Brig"

Movie Journal
June 24, 1965

Since it's summertime and there isn't much else to do, I'll give you the full account of *The Brig*. I thought this should be done as a supplement to the recently published book on *The Brig* and the Living Theatre.

Late in February 1964, I went to see *The Brig*, the play, the night it closed. The Becks were told to shut it down and get out. The performance, by this time, was so precisely acted that it moved with the inevitability of life itself. As I watched it, I thought: Suppose this was a real brig; suppose I was a newsreel reporter; suppose I got permission from the US Marine Corps to go into one of their brigs and film the goings on: What a document one could bring to the eyes of humanity! The way *The Brig* was being played now, it was a real brig, as far as I was concerned.

This idea took possession of my mind and my senses so thoroughly that I walked out of the play. I didn't want to know anything about what would happen next in the play; I wanted to see it with my camera. I had to film it, not knowing what will come next, like real life.

As I sat outside, waiting for the play to end, I relayed my thoughts to Judith and J u l i a n   B e c k. They were as excited about the idea as I was. We decided to do it immediately. Actually, we had no other choice: they had to leave the theatre the very next day. David and Barbara Stone, who came to see the play with me, realized that they too had no choice: They got stuck with another production. "I suspected it before coming," said Barbara. "We'll never take you to another play," said David.

Next day I got the film and equipment. The theatre was already locked up by the owner. We got the cast and the equipment into the theatre through the sidewalk coal chute, late at night. We left the place the same way at three or four in the morning. We found part of the sets already taken down. The cast put it all back into place. There was no time for any testing of equipment or lights. The lighting remained the same as during the regular stage performance. I placed two strong floods on the front seats of the theatre so I could move freely around without showing the seats. I had three 16mm Auricon cameras (single-system, with sound directly on film) with ten-minute magazines. I kept changing cameras as I went along. The performance was stopped every ten minutes to change cameras, with a few seconds overlap of the action at each start. I shot the play in ten-minute takes, twelve takes in all.

I filmed from inside the brig, moving among the players, constantly stepping in their way, disrupting their usual movements and *mise-en-scènes*. My intention wasn't to show the play in its entirety but to catch as much of the action as my "reporter" eyes could. This kind of shooting required an exhausting concentration of body and eye. I had to operate the camera; I had to keep out of the cast's way; I had to look for what was going on and listen for what was said;

## THE BRIG

with The Original Cast of The Living Theatre
Stage Production by
JUDITH MALINA-JULIAN BECK

A Film by JONAS MEKAS and ADOLFAS MEKAS
Produced by DAVID C. STONE

Written by
KENNETH H. BROWN

I had to make instantaneous decisions about my movements and the camera movements, knowing that there was no time for thinking or reflecting; there was no time for reshooting, no time for mistakes: I was a circus man on a tightrope high in the air. All my scenes were stretched to the point of breaking. (I had the camera, the mike, and the batteries on me, a good eighty pounds of equipment in all; the size of the stage didn't permit any other people than the cast and myself; I envied Maysles and Leacock their lightweight equipment.) I became so possessed by what I was doing that it literally took me weeks to get my body and all my senses back to normal.

One of the ideas that I was pursuing—or getting out of my system—was the application of the so-called cinéma vérité (direct cinema) techniques to a stage event. I wanted to undermine some of the myths and mystifications of cinéma vérité: What is truth in cinema?

In a sense, *The Brig* is an essay in film criticism. *The Brig*, the
play, was perfect material for such an experiment; the performances
were so automatized, so perfectly acted, that the play moved like a
ballet of horror. I threw myself into it, and I used it as a raw material,
as it happened, as if it was a real event—which, in truth, it was.
My approach wasn't too kind to Kenneth Brown's play: I was
a parasite sucking his blood.

　　　　The editing followed the same principle. Now I have seen the
play, I said to myself, now I have ideas about it; now I can't edit this
footage without dragging in my post-considerations. But there were
passages that dragged, I knew, as far as the camera work and the
play went. So I said to my brother, Adolfas: You haven't seen the
play; you haven't seen the shooting (he was in Chicago at that time,
editing Goldstein); so now you come and edit it as a total stranger and
without any pity (my brother is a sadist, a very cruel man, and has
no heart). I treated Brown's play like a piece of raw material, with
no attempt to get into its "true" meanings. Judith Malina almost
cried whenever I missed some of her beautiful and subtle touches—
they were happening on the left of the stage when I was on the right;
and some of the lines were gone; but I said: Don't worry, Judith,
don't worry—just think how much we miss in real life. I'll catch
what I catch. (Really, I should tell you that a week later, persuaded
by Malina and Brown, we went through great pains and risk to get
back into the theatre once more. We rebuilt the set and shot the
missing bits. But when I saw the new footage on the screen, I realized
that it didn't have the spontaneity of the first night's shooting.
I already knew the action, I knew the movements, and even against
my will, I began anticipating the action. It turned out lifeless, so I
threw the footage out.) Now you take this footage, I said to my brother,
and treat it with disrespect and cruelty; cut out whatever isn't worth
looking at; forget there was a play—we both hate plays anyway;
do unto me what I did unto Brown and Becks.

　　　　So that's what he did. We screened the footage and my
brother made notes and he cut chunks out of the film. Really,
it was more complicated than that. During the shooting, two cameras
out of three conked out. Sometimes the film was running thirty
frames per second, sometimes twenty. The sound came too fast, or
too slow. During the editing we often found that the distorted sound
was more effective than the "real"—so we often left it that way;
in other places, where lines were important, we used the "protection"
sound track, cutting it into little pieces and then "tape dubbing";
in other places, again, we overlapped both sound tracks at the
same time. (Two soundtracks were recorded during the shooting;

## THE BRIG

with The Original Cast of The Living Theatre
Stage Production by
**JUDITH MALINA-JULIAN BECK**

A Film by JONAS MEKAS and ADOLFAS MEKAS
Produced by DAVID C. STONE

Written by
**KENNETH H. BROWN**

one directly on film, magnetic; another separately, on a beat-up
Wollensak machine.)

And there I lay, that morning, on the floor, exhausted,
waiting for Pierre to come back with the truck, to pick up the equipment. Everyone was gone. The theatre was empty and dead now.
This was the last time the Becks gave a performance in New York.
It was suddenly so sad. I thought I was completely alone. But then
I opened my eyes and I saw a girl, seventeen, I guessed, or sixteen,
or she could have been fourteen or twenty—I was too tired to figure
it out—and she walked around in the empty theatre and I asked her
what she was doing there, and she said, "I live here, I am an actress,
and this is my home." But the theatre is closed, I said. "I know how
to get in," she said. And she showed me her things, in a dark corner,
in the cellar, a suitcase, a blanket, and a few books. Then I fell asleep

and when I opened my eyes again I saw her sitting there in the dim light of the empty theatre and reading a play. She looked like a stray cat, alone, sad, and small.

Then the truck came, and we got out and the rats came back and everything was over. The girl stepped into the street—we decided to have a coffee—and it was spring slush and she wore thin summer sport shoes and the water came in immediately and took possession of her feet—but she said nothing, she was all part and blood of the Living Theatre, she was the last one to leave it. Watching her there that night I suddenly understood why the Living Theatre survived all these years and why it will survive again: they were as mad as I was; their devotion to their art and their work was fantastic and beyond reason. As far as I know, that girl taught me that, and so far as I know, she may be still living there, underground, or in the sewers—she may not even be real, she may have been the underground angel.

Next day, the literary agents got all upset: Why didn't you ask for our permission, they said, you can't do things like that! Film unions jumped on me: how do you dare make a movie without unions! Oh, hell, I said. If anyone still wants to make a "real" movie out of Brown's play, to "adapt" it to cinema—let him do it. Brown once told me he had an idea for a million-dollar production of *The Brig*, with thousands of prisoners. It should be done. The point of cruelty done by one man to another can never be overstressed. I, myself, I am not interested in adapting plays, I always said so and I am repeating it here again. *The Brig*, the movie, is not an adaptation of a play: it is a record of my eye and my temperament lost in the play. And then, in the first and last place, *The Brig*, the movie, is my gift to the Becks, those two beautiful human beings. My own share in all of this, really, is the pain in the neck, which every cinéma vérité filmmaker feels most of the time—and I can tell you, pains in the neck can be as bad as those of the heart.

By the way, the film cost me $1,200 to make.

Jonas Mekas during the filming of *The Brig*,
New York, 1964

# The Living Theatre: From the Conversations with Judith Malina and Julian Beck

This conversation took place in August 1966 at the house of
Jerome Hill, after the performance of *Frankenstein* at the Festival
of Cassis, which Hill had organized.

*On Prisons*

### MALINA

Outside of the seven prisons in the United States, we have
been busted—let me see—in Paris, in Stockholm, Italy,
Holland ... Do you want to know the crimes? In Paris, it was
for rehearsing. We rehearsed *The Maids* in a hotel room.
They said we violated the *domicile*—because there were
three men in a room rehearsing *The Maids*. The Parisian
police were the most quickly brutal I have seen. Unbelievable. They came in and they began to beat Bill Shari
immediately. We were all sitting, and we said, please, we are
only reading, you know, you can see we are having a quiet
reading, you know ...

*On Audience Participation*

BECK

We want to collaborate with the public.

MALINA

We want to collaborate, to work with those who are on stage; with those who are in the auditorium; with those who are outside of the auditorium: with the entire world.
We are utopists.

There have been places in which the entire audience joined in. When there are more students, particularly with *Mysteries*, there is a tendency to come back for the second and third time and, being familiar with the piece by then, they sometimes enter the proceedings in a very provocative way to test our ability to cope with them, and so far we always have. It has sometimes posed problems, not because of the participants but, as always, because of the law. In Vienna, some students from the acting class got up and played with us, and it was very good for them, but the police absolutely panicked at the idea of members of the audience coming up on the stage of the Theatre of Vienna and the mayor closed the performance.

*Reception in Different Countries*

BECK

I think we have been received well everywhere. The audience everywhere was interested in our presentations. It is difficult to say where—in Rome, Berlin, Munich, Stockholm—we have received the most receptive audience.

MALINA

One of the wonderful things that happens to us is encountering the differences and similarities between the different cities. In every city we find those people who are closest to us and who represent, from where we can see it, a very close international community. In cities where there is a very lively youth, in a city like Amsterdam, there is immediate contact, immediate communication. In cities where the underground movements are more suppressed, like in some Italian cities, where there is a certain reservation toward

the young people—the contact is also immediate, only
it's more underground. But I don't know whether it's better
when there is already an immediately responsive group
or when there are three people we can really influence in
a city where they felt dead and buried.

*In Germany*

MALINA

In *The Connection*, you know, we always wait for a certain
cue until the audience is in. Before the audience is let
in, there are people on the stage, they goof around, they sit
and talk, smoke, and begin to feel free on stage, as the
audience comes in. Usually, backstage, we gauge the beginning of the actual performance by when the audience is
actually assembled—then we begin. But the audience didn't
come to Berlin! We couldn't hear anything. And Julian
peeks out—and there is a full house sitting there! Because
the actors are on stage, so they are sitting there observing the actors, in their seats. Eight hundred people and not
a peep! We were astounded. It's marvelous in its own way.

In Berlin, after *The Plague*, a woman got up and started
shouting: How can you do this disgusting thing! And she
started to hit one of the actresses. *The Plague* upsets people
in Berlin very much, because they are very strongly divided
politically. They are either saying, "Horror, horror!" or they
are saying, "Why are you bringing out those old guilts?
You are trying to arouse our guilts, the guilts of our fathers.
We are not guilty, why arouse it?" Guilt. They go into that
bag of "Why do you bring up the concentration camps
to us as if to accuse us, you Americans? Why don't we learn
to love each other?" It was a great scene with the porter
of the theatre coming and showing a number tattooed
on his arm by the concentration camp and saying, "NO, NO,
SHE IS RIGHT!"

In Essen, we played *The Brig* opposite a church, and
in front of the church, which is in the middle of the square,
there was a statue of Alfred Krupp. After the performance, all the students came and said, "You brought us
a real disarmament message." And we said, "Then why
do you keep that statue over there!" There is a big statue,
four times life size, of Alfred Krupp and there is such

a feeling of veneration in the city of Essen for this statue
in front of the church, it's unbelievable.

## In Italy

### MALINA
You want to know about Italy? The Roman audiences are
there to show disdain: if you can distract my attention from
myself and my neighbour, you are very good. Now let's see ...

### BECK
The Roman audience says, "Show me that you are more
important than I am. If you can do that ..." In Venice, it
was tremendous. I have never seen such an audience. After
every piece there was tremendous applause. I thought it
was unbelievable. We were very afraid of that show. We had
just come from a very successful Milan engagement and
everybody told us that the Venetians are very difficult.
That was the summer international audience.

## In Austria

### MALINA
In Vienna they took *The Plague* for an erotic orgy and
the mayor closed the theatre. Next day, the front pages of all
Vienna's newspapers said: SCANDAL IN THE THEATRE
OF VIENNA. The Theatre of Vienna is a national monument.
They had the premiere of *Die Zauberflöte* and the premiere
of *Fidelio* there, it's like a holy shrine, and there were
people running on and off the stage, and they took it all for
an erotic orgy. In Germany they take it for the gas chambers.
In Italy they take it for the plague, although all the meanings
are perfectly correct. It's whatever you see. And if you see
the gas chambers, it's the gas chambers. In Milan we played
to a very elegant audience. A titled lady ran screaming
up the aisle and said in absolute agony, "Oh, Malina,
how wonderful!"—and completely destroyed it ... I'd have
preferred it if she'd said, "You shit, what are you doing
this for?" I'd have played with it. But we had too elegant an
audience. We really got caught. It's a very high class, but
it's very beautiful to play for that.

*Yugoslavia*

### MALINA

In Yugoslavia, we played in Sarajevo. It was an avant-garde
theatre festival which had all the Yugoslavian intellectuals.
Like intellectuals all over the world, they sat and discussed
it with us for hours, the Theatre of Cruelty, other theories.
And then we made a little tour through towns like Zenica,
which is the wild west of Yugoslavia. It's a steel-mill town,
and it's in the middle of a totally futile situation—with big
cranes pulling up very modern buildings—it's in the middle
of a complete mix-up by this very technocratic organization. We were the first—in Banja Luka also—the first foreign
company that ever played there. They had had concerts
but they had never had a theatre company. And they came
to see the *foreign* theatre. They saw *Mysteries*, and said,
"Mmm, *foreign* theatre is very interesting." You see, they
had no reason to think this unusual because the entire
situation was unusual. "This is what they do ... this is American theatre ..." And they accepted it and loved it and
grooved with it and said, *"Wonderful*, yes you have a very
great feeling of theatre in America. When you do *Mysteries*,
that is a very good example." You know? And they took
it as absolutely standard and dug it, too. It was a very good
audience. A workers audience, not sophisticated. It was
wonderful to play for them. They completely accepted it;
everything that we did they accepted as natural. That is,
it wasn't shock theatre, it was merely good theatre for them.
It was good theatre without the sensation, without people
saying, "Oh ..."

In London I'd rather show *Frankenstein* than *Mysteries*.
I think, for London, *Mysteries* would be a harder act—
in fact, impossible, because, you know, they would simply
say, "That's not theatre, that's a hoax." You know, in
that British way, and just dismiss it—and they can't dismiss
*Frankenstein* that way.

*Living Theatre Company, Actors*

### BECK

There are some who have been with the company for eight
years. Then, there are others who have been with us for

a year or even only six months. Most of us, however, we came
together from New York two years ago when we arrived
in London. I think fifteen of us. It's a very hard life, to
be traveling all the time, without a home, and we live most
of the time with one meal a day.

*Discipline and Anarchy*

MALINA

One of the things that we pride ourselves on at the Living
Theatre is that we try our hand at anything. It's that
big split in our personal lack of discipline, for which we are
notorious, in the sense that we are undisciplined and that
we have no rehearsal discipline, no formal discipline—
that we are impossible to live with. Every hotel all over
Europe throws us out because we don't keep hours, we don't
keep times, we don't keep the radio down, we play music at
all hours of the night, we refuse to be social creatures, we
break every rule, we cannot have a meal in a restaurant without getting into trouble. We are completely and totally undisciplined and a messy bunch of people who can get on stage
and do a superbly disciplined piece of work. But this is
where we want to stay. We want to draw a line not between
our work and our life, but between this possibility that,
when we play *The Brig* about the Marine Corps, we can be
as disciplined as marines, and at the same time not to have
to go through any of that shit in our lives. That is, to live
outside, to try to live—just to try to present the anarchist
point of view, the anarchist point of view being that we
can live together as family without the cohesive limitations
of rules and regulations. Because we are basically not
disciplined creatures but harmonious creatures—we can
make a harmony that is not necessarily based on sterile,
acceptable preformulated arrangements. This is what we
are trying to prove, and we are trying to prove it in our work
and in our lives. We are trying to produce very disciplined
performances without becoming in any way disciplined creatures—rather, to be undisciplined creatures on one level,
and on another level, every rehearsal I tear my hair out
because someone did not come to a rehearsal. And if you
don't come to a rehearsal of the Living Theatre, the discipline
we practice is not to scold and not to shout. That's very

The Living Theatre, constructing the Stage for Frankenstein, on the French Mediterranean coast, Cassis, 1966

hard. To be permissive is *very hard* when your work is all
screwed up because somebody didn't arrive. What we
are bound to express is to say: What happened? You wanted
to lie in the sun? All right. All right. It's fouled me up,
but you have that right and I want to give you that liberty
and it makes me C-R-A-Z-Y. But I want to give you that
liberty. That is, we tear ourselves apart on that level, rather
than on the other level. We are taking it upon ourselves
to practice such permissiveness, and that's terribly difficult
to be permissive about somebody that fouls up your work,
your project.

There is a whole theory, which I believe is basic to our
entire civilization, which believes that punitive measures
are educational, that is, instructive. It is instructive to punish.
Now, this is a very basic question about our whole civilization. But I believe that evil has its own punishment.
I believe that. Therefore, I think that the person who has
done anything that I'd say is evil needs all my help and aid,
because he's already punished. I did slap my son's hand
once. And I always thought that I was wrong, there must
be another alternative. It was the only time I ever slapped
my son, and I always thought about that. He is seventeen now.
And if I don't know anything better than to slap his hand,
that's my problem. There must be a better way to teach a child
not to do something. There are educational processes which
are not punitive. I think we should instruct. Not all education
should be punitive. You see, I am basically against what
I did in this case, I think there must be better ways.

We all have our particular crosses and mine is that
I often face the people who do not come to rehearsals,
and I say, "You, you really destroyed my work, but you know,
it's all right, it's cool." It hurt me personally, actually, and
I know perfectly well that what I was saying to the actor
is only another form of punishment, and I don't admire myself
for that, and I wish I could get over that trait, of this "look
what you've done to my things ..." because I could do
something that would be more than this immature thing.
I think that we have to help people get over their faults,
not by being angry about it but by inspiring enthusiasm;
not by saying, "Oh, you are always late! This is the fourth
day in a row we haven't been able to start because you
haven't been there," but to inspire them with the work
so much that they get there in time because it's so groovy

at the Living Theatre, Cassis, 1966

to be there, and if I haven't made it so groovy for them to
be there, then all I can say is, well, I didn't make it, I didn't
make them want to be there.

But then, we have been working with exceptional people
who have exceptional devotional attitudes toward their
work up front, or they wouldn't really be here. So we are dealing with people who are already readier to be disciplined
simply and solely for the sake of what we want to do together.
The point is to bring work to that point where that is
enough. If they miss a rehearsal, that's enough punishment.
All I can say is, "Gee, I am sorry you were late to the rehearsal." But really to be sorry, not with a sarcastic edge
of "sorry" but really to feel it: "Gee, I know, you're sorry you
missed it." I know you are with it, I know you are with me,
and I don't distrust you to the point of saying, "Eh, you don't
really care about the work," because that's where I often
get hung up. Because they really do like their work, and I
am accusing them of something false, I throw at them a false
accusation. It's hard, our living together, and we are finding
out how to do it.

*On Improvisation*

                    MALINA
In *Mysteries* and *Frankenstein* there are fixed forms within
which the actors improvise. On the one hand, the actors
are very free; on the other, they are extremely disciplined.
Both plays are improvisations within fixed forms.

*The Case of the Third Act of Frankenstein*

                    MALINA
The third act in Venice was very different from Cassis.
Only the intention was the same. What we have now in Cassis,
we have these fifteen boxes—if you can see them as boxes—
in which, every night, each prisoner plays what we call
"his world action." It is a total improvisation on the part of
each actor, and each actor completely free to take any trip
that he feels he wants to take at that moment, short of going
out of the box, short of using words. It's different from
one box to the other, from one moment to another, the actor

has no idea what he is going to do next. When the lights go on, he does it. In Venice, our intention was exactly the same. But we played scenes from I b s e n's plays; each of the boxes played a different scene from a different Ibsen play. We had *The Doll's House, The Enemy of the People, The Wild Duck*, not one after the other but all playing simultaneously, all the time, fifteen times, with all of them whispering, and one of them playing loud. And we went fifteen times through all these Ibsen scenes and the fifteen scenes were the climatic scenes of each play. I played the Mrs. Alving, mother-finding-son scene; Nora played the "here I'll give you back the ring" scene. But it didn't work.

BECK

The initial idea, the initial moment, was a total ignition. But after forty minutes it was really boring. It was theatrically boring—not as a mistake.

MALINA

And the monster from the second act keeps going through each scene and killing various members of the cast, killing Nora, killing Hedda Gabler, all these killings.

BECK

The master builder climbed up to the top and kept falling; he climbed up and fell down fifteen times ...

MALINA

... at the end of each of these fifteen sequences ... but it didn't work.

BECK

Everybody who walked into rehearsal and saw one minute of it flipped out with excitement. But during the performance it became unbearable. It became an idea, but as a theatrical experience it remained essentially a literary game.

*The Theme of Frankenstein*

MALINA

In *Frankenstein* we have the central idea of Ibsen's central theme: which is, again and again, the crushing of the

individual by the social structure. Which is exactly what
we intended to say, in both, in the first version in which
we actually used Ibsen, and in this version in which we use
prison for the same end—to show the individual crushed
by the social structure, attempting to assert his individuality
but again and again stopped by the whistle that says: This
is the end of the scene, now you move onto your next scene
but you are still bound by this prison, so that the theme is
the same. Only that here the free improvisations of the actors
are so moving, the way they manage to fit such incredible
variations, flights of fancy, and whimsies, and these incredible
torments—through which they express their rage ... Also,
there is a strange magnetism of spectator as performer. One
spectator is going to be attracted by Karl Enhorn's myth-
ology; and one person will be more fascinated by Howard's
variations. This is the glory of our company, because
there isn't one person in it who does not have a fantastic
individual contribution to make. And this is why this
is the most astonishing group of artists. Each person has
extraordinary karma to emit, which is why the miracle
of the Living Theatre is its company and not ...

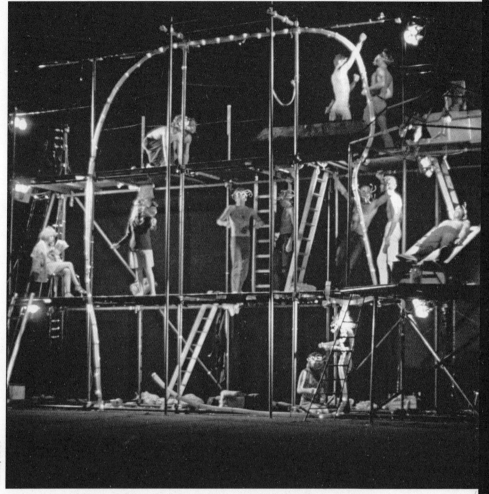

So often Julian and I are given credit for the power of the Living Theatre, but it's a fantastic community that's managed to work together and who need each other. These are tremendous egos looking for a non-egocentric center which is so rare in the world.

What we are trying to do is to find all the factors that make it possible. Beck's and my simple task is to make possible the functioning of tremendous egotistical forces together, to solve the conflicts, to set the stage for the movements of these strange forces, instead of the easier choices. A theatrical manager would choose people who easily work together.

*Religion and the Living Theatre*

### MALINA

Religion at the Living Theatre is a whole subject. We are
the most religious and heretical group of people that you can
find. For instance, everyone in our company is an ordained
minister of the Universal Church of Life. This Universal
Church of Life is an organization which allows for anyone who believes in universal life to join it. It bestows a clerical standing upon all those who say: I preach universal
life. We are so totally bound up in our ritual, in our circumstances, ceremonies—we live a ceremonial life. Even in
our passports it says "Reverend Jimmy Tieroff," "Reverend
James Anderson." We have six reverends, in perfectly
authorized clerical standing, and we are often able to
use this to our advantage, to aid and assist us with certain
problems. For instance, if someone is incarcerated, it's
easier to get in if you put on a collar and show your creden-
tials as a reverend—this is of great practical value. And
I see no difference between one ordination and the other,
because the sincerity and religiosity in our group is as
great as in any group. The pagan aspects of it are to be
admired and condoned.

I speak as a Jew, and many others speak as convinced
Christians or Catholics—there is no dichotomy between
such an overall embracing religion and the individual religious attitudes contained in it.

### JEROME HILL

The other day you said to the Marseilles correspondent
something which I thought was very true: you said, we
are creating something that we want to be so beautiful
that people will say, if it's that beautiful, it must be
true. There is no other better defense you could possibly
make concerning your work.

### BECK

It's what Paul Goodman says about the *Song of Solomon*:
the songs are so beautiful they must be true.

### HILL

It's true of the Bible; it is true. I am not a Catholic, but
it's true about the Catholic Mass: it's so damn beautiful.

And I wish they would have the faith in their own
Mass and not run around doing their financial things.


*Art as Torture and Art as Playfulness*

MALINA

In a way, *Mysteries* is our attempt to express a religious
conviction. Insofar as the Living Theatre is a group,
it expresses a religious conviction.


BECK

At first, we had a chorus saying certain things, but it was
too direct.


MALINA

It went directly to "We must love one another or die," and,
unfortunately, if you say that in the theatre, nobody believes
you. If it were simple enough to say that, then we wouldn't
need art anymore. As F r e u d says, art would be antedated
by life; we wouldn't need art any more, we would work,
we'd break into that free world where art would be nothing
but playfulness instead of the profound torture that it is for
everyone today. And that would be another world and that
day will come and art will be unnecessary, or it will become
another kind, another part of life, it will become playfulness. But now it's not playfulness, now it's torture, ordeal.


BECK

The function of art is essentially that it alerts the senses
and the intelligence. Once your senses and your intelligence
are alerted, then we won't need art anymore.


MALINA

The pain alerts the body that something is wrong, that the
intelligence must come to its aid.


BECK

If your nerves are dead, you could lose your arm, because
you would simply let it burn.


MALINA

Pain is a warning signal. Art is the same kind of pain.

BECK

Like dreams, too.

HILL

But then—the body attends to its needs ... Dreams are also
warning you that psychologically and physiologically you are
already being prepared. The body's ability to repair itself
is just unbelievable. It's like the itching of the healing wound.

BECK

The same is true when you have a group of people. Whenever
you leave a group of people in trouble, a group of people
who are aware of the fact that they are in a state of
emergency, you have the group attending to its needs—
in a flood, or soldiers in a war, anybody ... or a shipwreck—
people help each other, people do something about the
problem. And our great problem today is that we are in
a state of emergency, every minute ...

MALINA

And we are behaving as if we are not.

*Toward the Glow Play*

MALINA

The Living Theatre has tried for years now to create what
we call a Glow play, a play that glows. A play that expresses
our glow, our hope, our joy. We have tried in this way, in
that way—we have not yet succeeded. There are moments
in *Mysteries*. Yet *Mysteries* is seen by so many people
as a total horror play. There are moments in *Give and Take*,
there are moments in *Chorus*: the breathing, the sound
movement, the song. What shall we say of Taylor Mead's
very understandable dislike of *Mysteries*? He hates it.

HILL

I know he likes *Mysteries*. But then he dislikes certain things.
It's something personal, you tread on something personal.

MALINA

We tread on his cool, on his cool. We stand there and we
scream. And he won't do that. He doesn't dare to do that.

And we are saying to him: scream with all your guts, baby,
or you aren't COOL. And he says, NO. And he spoke during
the play, and how pertinently, and how rightly he expressed
himself. He was wrong, but he expressed the wrong point
correctly. He said, Viva Death, Viva Syphilis, Viva War!—
Now, why did he say that? He said: Down with the intellectuals! He said it because it was insupportable to him to stand
in the middle of the street, to walk and scream out with
his real guts, real balls. [She screams.] He can write a cool
letter to the *Herald Tribune*, a good letter too, and other
important things, and of course, he stands for the same things
we stand for, he is on no other side—I don't call him the
opposition. The point is that *Mysteries* brings out not our
enemies but our friends, those who are with us, but who say:
This is insupportable to my cool! And we are saying: Give
up your cool and go all the way. Either scream until you glow
or glow until you scream and change it. We are still looking
for the Glow play. And we'll do the Glow play one day,
and when we do the Glow play, it will be the greatest thing
we've ever done.


*Looking for the Word and Art without Evil*

HILL
The other day I saw Chaplin's daughter. She came here
before going to jail—it's incredible, one of those Italian
things, it was for nothing, and it's very difficult to explain—
and she was very down and worried. But she had a wish
to come here, because the Living Theatre was here.
I have never seen such a reaction in my life. She went home
saying, "Oh, what I am worrying about?" She saw both
*Frankenstein* and *Mysteries* and absolutely collapsed and
went home happy.


MALINA
Good God, if we can do it for one person, isn't it worth all
the damn trouble? If *Frankenstein* can do this, how much
more will *Paradise Now* do!
    It's a terrible struggle to find the words. You know,
Berdyaev said it for us so perfectly, as perfectly as he
could. He said that perfect phrase—he said: The problem
of the artist is to make good look as interesting as evil.

That really is the ultimate crux of the whole problem,
to make good as interesting as evil. The fascination
and glory of evil is so great. It's very, very difficult, because
the whole twist of our brain is against that: it's toward
the darkest, toward the sinister, toward the left side,
the evil side.

*Searching for the Glow Sound*

MALINA
I don't want to say that *Frankenstein* is an unfinished
work, but perhaps it is something that, over the years, has
to change until its final word, and we have to take time—
a production here, a production in Berlin, in Venice—until
it breaks through to its final sound. What I am hoping for
is, when the monster is walking forwards, to create a sound,
just one ringing sound ... That will be what we have been
talking about: a sound. That's how it happens. We talk about
it for a long time, each person develops his aspect of the
sound, and then we put it together, and then it becomes
a sound, some of the sounds that you hear in *Frankenstein*.
We want to create a sound that will be what we call terrible
and beautiful, so terrible and beautiful that it will imply
all that despair and that when the monster at the final countdown begins to walk toward the audience (we have begun
to work on this, but we haven't finished yet—I know we
can do it), with the countdown that terrible and beautiful
sound will still be ringing in our ears with an equal propor-
tion of despair and hope. Despair and hope will be the
sound ringing in their ears at the point of countdown, at the
point of their zero, when they have to make their decision.
Their decision will have to be between the despair aspect
of the sound and the hope aspect of the sound. This is
very subtle, and very complicated, and it will certainly take
us a few weeks of trying sounds. And how we work to get
these sounds—incredible—the actors are fantastic in
supplying contributions of noises, sounds. By the time you
have the sound together, all twenty actors together with
their own sounds, you get an incredible symphonic thing
in which each person is putting action into the stove.
It's an incredible kind of amalgamation that's like a string
quartet plus ...

In the chord we do some special things. In the chord
we'll get a certain kind of breathing, and anybody who
has to make a sound listens to the sound of the person next
to them, on either side of them, and follows that sound
and it goes around. We all listen to each other. The chord
is nothing but the result of listening. The chord is not
sound making but it's listening and responding to what
you hear. And it's a very beautiful experience.

### A JOURNALIST
Maybe you did not intend it that way, but really, at the
end of *Frankenstein*, I felt—and it's perhaps a very personal
thing—I felt very, very down and it agreed exactly with
my personal belief that everything in this society, everything
is in its own prison and therefore every individual is
imprisoned and that's the end of the whole thing.

### MALINA
Because we haven't yet found the way to say to you: It's
not so at all! We'll have it that way, and we'll find that sound,
and I am sorry that we haven't found it yet. Sorrier than
you are.

*Prison and Frankenstein*

### HILL
Also, don't underestimate ... the fact that nobody who is
really inside himself finds any restricted area in prison ...

### MALINA
For that reason, the actions inside each of the cells have
to be free improvisations by the actors. Because in prison
the first thing you notice is that incredible liberation—
when everything is taken away from you, when you are
totally, totally bare, stripped of all freedom, you suddenly
realize, "My God, I am totally free," in a whole new way
that you never thought.

78

*Mysteries*, performance by
the Living Theatre, Cassis, 1966

*Paradise Now*, performance by
the Living Theatre, 1968

*Toward Glow: Exorcising Evil through Art*

JONAS

What message should I take to your friends in New York?

MALINA

Tell them we are looking for the Glow play. So far all we got
is HELL. We don't even really know yet what evil is; we only
play it. We play it as if our playing evil would eliminate it,
almost like a ritual of exorcism. You know, we play *The Brig*
as if our playing *The Brig* would make the whole Marine
Corps disappear. We really do it. It does, it does. It is very
important.

*Living and European Youth*

MALINA

The fact is that those six, eight, ten—one, two, ten people
that we can touch in the audience—that is our audience.
Everybody else in the audience is only so much superfluity.
I am not interested in them, I don't care about them.
People ask: Did you find that your plays were successful
in Yugoslavia? How were you received in Paris? What
was the audience in Amsterdam? I am not interested. I am
interested in the four kids, I am interested in the ten boys,
I am interested in the one kid in Yugoslavia who said:
Wait a minute. That's the whole audience. I am not interested
in the others. They aren't important to me, they know how
to make money. That's all we work for, for those few, and when
they come to us and they say, "Man, you did it to me," I feel
oh … And, you know, it could be some little kid that decides
he isn't going to go into the army, or he could be your friend
who said: Now I'm not afraid to go to jail. Because of this
experience I know that my theatre is successful and I
don't care whether we make money, whether we get other
engagements, whether they throw bombs under our cars,
whether they say we aren't geniuses, whether they say
we are phonies—it doesn't matter. This one person is relieved,
and that's the one who was suffering, and that's the one
I care about—and that's who the whole thing is for. As far
as I am concerned, the Living Theatre is a success when
that happens.

*Theatre as a Group*

BECK

We also think that it's a success that our group, despite the
caliber of its work on the stage, as long as it manages to
sustain itself and continue as a theatre, this is our important
message to the world.

MALINA

And you have no idea how difficult that is. Because they are
thirty people, or twenty-six people as we have now, it's just
a miracle how we are together over two years. About money:
we agreed that for each engagement, that all the money
we made we divide among ourselves. To sustain a repertory
theatre this way, I don't think there is another theatre in
the world like it.

BECK

You can't imagine what a revolution for each person it
was, to suddenly take whatever money there is and divide
it. And if there are wives in the company, mothers or
children or mistresses, we are going to split with them, too.
And it doesn't matter if someone is playing the leading
role, managing, or is hanging around doing nothing—it was
a very far-out moment …

*Undergrounds of Europe*

MALINA

It's a very crucial period that we are all involved in. These
are important areas that we are touching internationally.
There is a great breakthrough when people can begin to use
informal forms in the countries where formal forms are tight.

It's very … I'm German enough to find it unbearably
difficult to speak, to say DU in German to somebody. Even
my parents, they are people who'd never say DU. Their
closest, who are not family, they call SIE. Now look at people,
like in Rome and Amsterdam and Berlin, who totally
refuse SIE. It's such a great breakthrough for them.

These are basic forms, and so deep. I find it so difficult
because I know if I say DU to the waitress who waits on
me in a restaurant in Berlin, then she thinks I'm insulting her.

*Mysteries*, performance by the Living Theatre, Genoa 1966

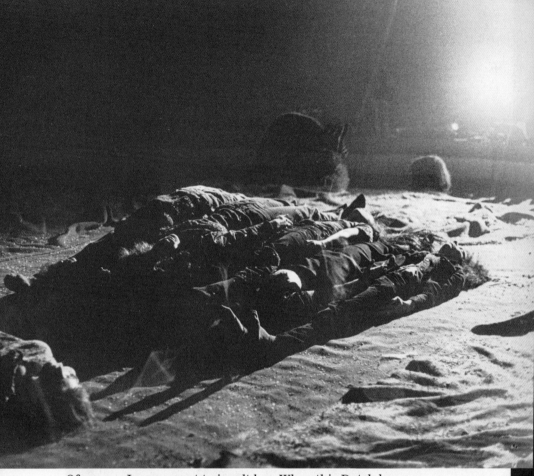

Of course, I never want to insult her. When this Dutch boy
did this, it was so beautiful, when he said JE T'AIME,
to the cop, and he said it three times, and the cop hit him.
It was was a whole breakthrough for the cop too. Because
the cop realized that it was an insult to him on many
other levels of his existence, that line, I LOVE YOU. Do you
see how difficult it would be for anybody with a German
accent to say DU to everybody? Now, Carl, for instance, says
that all the young people now are saying TU and DU and
I'm going to do it. I say it's easy for you, and it's very hard for
me. And he doesn't know why it's hard for me. He doesn't
know why it's really impossible for me to say DU to a
German whom I meet casually. And I'm fighting it, because

Judith Malina and Julian Beck, founders, directors, and performers at the Living Theatre, New York, early 1960s

*Mysteries*, performance by the Living Theatre, Cassis, 1966

it shouldn't be. Because here is one place where this
whole rigidity can be attacked. Here is a rule we can break
now, immediately. Just by saying DU to somebody, the
walls crumble.

   Because if you say DU to somebody you're already living
in a real relationship to that person. It's very hard, especially
when they think you're insulting or putting them down.
It's a fantastic revolution. Provosts also say DU, in Amsterdam,
I understand. They are refusing the other form, that's one
of their big ways of insulting. It's so beautiful, because it's
so simple. But it's hard to follow.


*E. E. Cummings*


                          MALINA
Do you remember, Beck, do you remember when we visited
Cummings on Patchen Place? Oh, that was a fantastic journey. We were two young people, nineteen years old, and we
wanted to start a theatre, and we know nobody, and we have
no means, we have no money, and what to do as a teacher,
adviser, honored person, and artist, what do you advise us?
Can you spare us a few minutes to talk about this? We
only want to know what you have to say to two people who
are willing to take a step into the abyss. Help, we don't
know where to go. Because this is 1947, there is like wartime gray gloom. Where shall we go? And one of the people
we went to was Cummings. And he invited us over there.
And I was scared! We were both scared. And I said, Julian,
don't leave me alone for a second because I am scared
to see him. And we knocked on the door, and it was pouring,
and I said: All my hair will fall out—I will be terrified,
don't leave me alone for a second. And we came to Patchen
Place and we rang the door bell, and it was pouring rain,
and I had this rain kerchief around my hair which made me
very ashamed, but I had to keep my hairdo or something,
and I was very scared, and Beck was very bold and brazen
and ...


                           BECK
I knocked on the door ...

MALINA

... and Marian opened the door and said: Oh, you are Becks.
And she said to Julian: Hm, look, run down to the bakery
and ask for Mrs. Cummings' cake, you run down. And to me:
You come in ... And I came in, and she said I had to go
to the kitchen, You sit here. And I sat down and Cummings
came in and took my rain kerchief with my stringy hair
and I said ... eh ... ehhh, ehh, weee ... we ... at ... the ... ehh ...
theatre ... ehm baaaa ... Julian come back with his cake!
I don't know what the hell I said to him.


BECK

It was a bakery that has since disappeared, to the left of
Suters, where there is some boutique, it was a very divine
cake, and we stayed for hours and hours.


*About "The Brig"*

BECK

[Talking about Germans in Berlin building that served
as a stage for filming a version of *The Brig*.] I really became
more and more panicky and finally I said, "Let me see
the plans," and they certainly had planned the stage, which
was off by a meter and a half.

   They shot *The Brig* for TV. And it was very interesting
and amusing. They picked out every correct moment.
They picked out every significant detail. They went over
the script and said: Now, prisoner no. 8 speaks—so the
camera is on prisoner no. 8; now prisoner no. 2. The exact
opposite from what you [Jonas] did, with your jumping
around and dancing around. They did everything so exactly
precise. It's a beautiful performance, it's fantastic ... it
has something to do with the Marine Corps in a funny way.
It was filmed in the spirit of the Marine Corps, the Germanic
spirit of the Marine Corps. And what didn't come across is,
of course, the protest against the Marine Corps, which your
film has and which our production has. That was left out
entirely and that's why it's a wonderful pro–Marine Corps
film—I think you could use it for recruiting. It's a terrible
thing, which you should really see, because it's interesting
to see, the exactness—every image, every face, exactly—
except that you miss what really happens, which is that

each of these poor people, each of these actors is playing his own life. And that's what doesn't come through, and that's what Jonas has. They didn't have it all. And it wasn't good, because it didn't have the protest in it. Your version I think is a masterpiece, it's miraculous.

HILL

I saw it first in the basement of the Museum of Modern Art and I came out and I was no longer in New York. I just flipped. Not that I wasn't in New York any longer but I realized that New York was exactly that.

MALINA

The white lines were clearly drawn ...


*About Faith and Miracles ...*

JOURNALIST

Do you believe that your work, your plays will change some people, today, tomorrow? Are your plays made, performed so that the knowledge of what they are about comes slowly, like in a year or two, without the person knowing it?

MALINA

We are asking for immediate comprehension.

JOURNALIST

But that is rarely possible?

MALINA

But we have the belief, the faith in the possibility of a miracle. *Mais nous avons la croyance de la possibilité du miracle.* Those are other words for the "word," "engagement." *Je suis vraiment ici. C'est à dire, j'ai la croyance de la possibilité de changer toute pour le meilleur instantanément.* That is our faith. We select certain forms and we play with them in front of you so as to change you.

# Interview with Gerd Stern and Michael Callahan: USCO

June 1966

### JONAS

First, I should like a brief introduction to where USCO
works and when it started; that is, the historical background.

### GERD STERN

The first performance was in November 1963 at the San
Francisco Museum of Modern Art. Actually, this was probably
the most ambitious thing we've ever done because we were
not aware, as we are now, of the problems. It wasn't until
1964 that we started thinking of ourselves as USCO. The
first performance we did under that name was in Brandeis
in 1965.

### JONAS

When did you settle in Woodstock? And who were the
original members?

### GERD

It's rather confusing, because we were in Woodstock even
before we went to San Francisco. It's been a continuous
movement back and forth. We've never all been together
at one time.

    Let's get into this whole name thing—it seems to me
that the trend toward a traditional society in Coomar-
swarmy's terms or McLuhan's ... that is, if we're going
back to the role of the traditional craftsmen who did it,
fine. I think maybe we're some small part of that being to

happen. It is happening all over. On the other hand, we
live in this world where there is a fantastic focus on status
and orientation (and I don't want to get into the fetishistic
situation of saying: No, I'm not going to tell anyone my name).
There are some people in the group who say, "Well, no
names, no names, no names, no names, no names." It doesn't
matter whether it's positive face paranoia or negative face
paranoia; it's just as bad. Anyhow, Steve Durkee—who
is basically the painter and the architect and the vision-
creator—and I knew each other and had worked with each
other as early as 1961, maybe even 1960, in the east. Then
Michael Callahan and I met when I went back to San
Francisco and worked there in 1962 and 1963. So we worked
together in California and then up in Vancouver, where
we did our second performance. Then he came back east
in August of 1964. Judy, my wife, and I had made a cross-
country trip back here and performed along the way.
The first performance in California involved sixty-four
people and about eighteen channels of mixed media.
We really didn't know what we were doing. We started
with a kind of a chaos and we worked our way slowly ...

JONAS

Was there any thought behind you that pushed you to do
what you were doing, or did you just work with materials?

GERD

The ideas were very powerful in the beginning. The ideas
may have been more powerful in the beginning than they
are now in terms of motivation for the performances;
the materials grabbed us more strongly as we went along.

JONAS

By ideas you mean ...

GERD

For instance, I started out in poetry. Michael came out of
electronics. In about 1960 F. T. Richards gave me McLuhan's
Report to the National Association of Educational Broad-
casters, which he had gotten from John Cage, which
was the basis of McLuhan's book *Understanding Media*.
It was just about that time that I was starting to work from
written poetry into collage poetry.

The idea that you had to look at media in terms of
their effect rather than their content took me on an immense
jump which wound up with poetry, with lights, and sound
and film. That work was first exhibited here in 1962 at
Allan Stone's. When I got to California, Michael was working with the San Francisco Tape Music Center.
He designed and constructed their original system. It was
the idea of hybridizing various media and the invention
of Michael's circuitry in relation to making these ideas
possible (that is, controlling, programming, and randomizing,
to a certain extent, multichannel operations) that made
it possible for us to start working on this.

### MICHAEL CALLAHAN
Electronic music was one of the first things I'd done at the
time I was in high school and starting on collage. It was just
a very easy jump for me to make.

### JONAS
What effects are you trying to create, if any, with your show
at the Riverside Museum?

### GERD
All of our performances and exhibitions have had, somehow,
a concentration which is focused in the title we use, "We
Are All One." It is very hard to sense at any one moment
to what extent that statement applies. At any moment,
the two of us, or the thirteen of us that live in the church,
may not be capable of that ideal. It seems to me that, in
terms of the performances and exhibitions, the paintings,
the lights, the projections, the environmental media-contact,
it becomes a question of human beings sharing time,
of making the material productions in this world into an
environment in which this becomes feasible. We've all
been in the art world before, and since. It's been a tremendous source of dissatisfaction.

### MICHAEL
We've all hung separately; now we're all hanging together.

### JONAS
How would you compare your work to what other people
are doing in the area?

GERD

We go to the museums and the galleries and we see these
works hanging and they're hung basically so that what
you can do is you can pass by. I'm sure that very few people

Down by the Riverside, performance,
New York, 1966

USCO, advertisement for USCO, mid-1960s

make things to be passed by. I mean, most works of art in our society end up by being objects of meditation, but the way they're used in the world is rarely as an object or a thing to live with. They're hung there or they're standing there, and there is no place to sit, there is no place to stay. What you're invited to do is to go on to the next, and the next, as if it were a book that you had to walk through with the works of art representing the words. It's pretty disillusioning. It doesn't matter whether it's your show or anybody else's show. The first idea we had when this space became available was to try and create the kind of situation that we had at home, where the church is filled with things that we and other people—us, in the larger sense—have made; and we can spend time there. I think to a certain extent we have managed to make that happen in the Riverside Museum and we managed to have it happen at the San Francisco Museum a couple of years ago. There's a situation

USCO, poster for the performance *Hubbub*, MIT, Cambridge, Massachusetts, mid-1960s

in which people stay for an hour or two hours or three
hours, rather than come in and go out.

At the World we came into a given situation. It was
strange. You know, it came right out of the Cinematheque
showings. At first, our arrangement was simply to build
a piece of equipment, a console which controlled twenty-one
slide projectors. It was very interesting to us because
up till then we hadn't been able to afford punch-paper tape
and all kinds of equipment for our own controls. After a
week, Myerberg, who had been up to the church, called
us and said that his arrangement had fallen through: Could
we make all the film and slides? I said yes. We wound
up making two and a half hours of film and fifteen hundred
slides in three weeks. The situation was given: there are
actually nineteen screens. Each is individual and they
are dotted around the room. We didn't design the concept.
Myerberg comes out of *Fantasia*, which is, to me, kind
of a triumph in program music. The world is a contemporiza-
tion of *Fantasia*; it is another piece of contemporary program music, because the tunes and slides and the films
all go together. It has very little to do with the kind of work
we've been doing where we try to merge all the channels,
make them yield to each other, and go in and go out.

The surprise to us has been that it worked. Most of
the press who have come there to look at it, stand up in the
gallery and look at the thing happening. You can't understand what's happening from that viewpoint. But once you're
on the dance floor and you're turning around, moving ...
Of course it doesn't matter whether the images merge or
yield on each screen, because your motion gets them going.

### MICHAEL

I've seen all the slides. I run the console sitting up there
for five hours or whatever. The other night I got down there
and was dancing. It was just totally different.

### GERD

Your own motion takes you out in this case. That's a completely new area for us. I don't know how to handle it and
I don't think any of us do at this point. The integration of the
audience follows. Again, what McLuhan talks about is the
integration of all the media. The participation of the human
being in terms of ritual makes a lot of sense. He says what

the teenager does is from overload. When he gets overloaded, he looks for myth. This ritualistic aspect is very myth-making —the slides, the images become symbolic; they become archetypes rather than individual. It doesn't matter whose face it is anymore; it's a face, a mask.

JONAS

Why do you think there has been such a general trend toward media mixes?

GERD

The tools are really becoming available.

JONAS

But this kind of research has been going on for at least ten years. Why suddenly all of this?

GERD

In terms of civilization as a whole, the idea of simultaneity is the seed idea of our time. We use that line: "In a world of simultaneous operations, you don't have to be first to be on top." It is the possibility of seeing your activity as a part of a wave ...

I think if we can hang on for another decade, it's not going to be the people marching in the streets for peace (although I think that's beautiful), but these ideas and this movement in society which will make peace a possibility. Maybe a decade is too optimistic. It seems to me that when the kids (I'm in my thirties now, but most of the people I'm working with are in their twenties, and Michael is twenty-one) get to be a powerful majority, the kind of status and power play we have now just isn't going to mean anything anymore.

JONAS

Do you mean to say that the art of escape is being replaced by an art of meditation?

GERD

I mean it is the end of the literary political era, in which you have to pass through the whole alphabet to get from A to Z, the end of the era in which in order to get from Washington to Moscow you have to construct a fourteen-page docu-

ment, which, when it gets to Moscow, has obviously turned
into a paranoid drama; it will be the era in which you
can pick up the phone and look at the other person on the
line, in which you have instantaneous transmission of
information, in which you can use a computer to process
a whole bunch of new data and come out with something that is real, where you are not dealing with the illusion of the investment of one man's career against another
man's career. That's true in the arts too.

For instance, I feel sorry for A n d y  W a r h o l  when
I see him down at the Dome. I don't think he knows the
eventuality of what he is dealing with. He seems to think it's
the same old game of putting the serial image of the movie
actress heroine up on the wall, that it's only being played
now with different tools, but I don't think it's the same game
at all. I think it's an entirely new potential and I don't think
it has anything to do with being Andy Warhol, what-ever-
your-name-is. That's the kind of loneliness I see in that scene.
I would characterize it by saying that in our scene you see
a person approaching the other person and you see people
throwing their arms around each other. The hug is a per-
sonification. In that scene I see a great distance between
everybody. I see the same long hair and the same clothes
and the same tools. I see a tremendous fear too, which
I don't see in our group (I don't mean our little group but
throughout the country; like out in Colorado there are
kids that have built a place called "Draff City"—they built
it with two-by-fours and tar paper, but they are geodesic
domes not two-by-four frame houses).

### JONAS
Do you consciously make certain colors predominant with
the intended meaning?

### GERD
You should talk to Steve Durkee because he's very central
on that level.

### JONAS
Let me insert that when you read certain books from
Kabbalah on, you find a meaning ascribed to certain colors,
the colors of auras, etc.

GERD

We're working with the rainbow. We've been very involved
with the diffraction grating, which splits up light into
the rainbow. I worked with Kabbalah so many years ago
I shouldn't even say I worked with it: it seems like a fantasy
in my past, or out of it; but when you see the oscilloscope
we use (and this is one of the areas we want to get into), you'll
see that it's dealing with frequency, whether it's color or
sound or the visualization of the wave form and the multi-
plication of that wave form, there's some secret of the mystery,
for me, of the space-time continuum. It's in the rainbow
and it's in the sweep of the audio-oscillator and it's in the
visualization of the wave form as phosphor on the cathode
ray tube that it becomes most apparent to me as mystical
reality. To try to put it into words, either with technical or
mystical vocabulary is the task of the next few years. In
understanding the tools—here the tape recorder: the voice
recorder, preserved, echoed, mirrored, magnetized—what
do we understand about it? We grew up in a world where the
understanding of it was not what we were taught. At the
time we grew up, people were just beginning to develop these
things. To understand the motivating power and the basic
energy, in terms of fire, water, earth, air, and ether, or
electricity, is an area in which art and education have potential. The medium mix leads us into seeing something of
what this power or energy does.

We were doing the pieces at the New Theatre. According
to Tim Leary, we were having some sort of simulation
of the psychedelic biochemical experience and, according
to us, just doing what we do, but here we were with ten
or fifteen projections of electric light and electric sound
on the screen. He got up in the midst of all this and said,
"Of course, the only good kind of light to use in a session
is natural light, the light of a candle or the light of fire."

I think that's the wobbling pivot of Confucius: it's
ambivalent—is it natural or is it artificial? Of course electricity is natural, but not to us, who were educated before
electricity was our natural environment. I grew up in Europe
and I remember that the telephone was a real ritual object
(it isn't now) to my father. It certainly was a stranger in
the house. My eleven-year-old daughter takes more naturally
to running our equipment than I do.

GERD

One of the early pieces which was shown in San Francisco in early 1963 was the large octodome. The name of it is "Contact Is the Only Love." At the time it was our most ambitious piece: it contains sound which circulates through eight speakers; it has neon florescence; it has sixteen inter-locking rhythms from 480 flashes per minute down to things which happen in a cycle of once per minute. It uses the highway as a metaphor. In a sense, it was a great revelation because all the messages are "Go On, Go On, Go On, Turn Ahead," and it was characterized at the time by the press as a Stop sign. Still this seven-foot yellow octagon in the mind of people who were actually present is a Stop sign although it doesn't have the word "Stop" in it. I was interviewed on television in front of it, and the man says, "You folks see this big Stop sign here." You see the power of a classic situation like driving down the highway. You've been imprinted for a number of years with the small red Stop sign, and a seven-foot yellow octagon which says "Turn Ahead, Go On, Go On, Go On, Go On" and is called "Contact Is the Only Love" becomes a Stop sign. There is a room of Sakti paintings; one of them is S h i v a; one of them is S u k t a; one of them is Shiva Sakta. In the center is a fountain with a rotating light column. The whole is very dimly lit. But the light passes from one to the other. Basically in terms of painting it is a very low-definition experience. McLuhan says that in media where all the details are visible, that is in high definition, you accept it but you don't really integrate with it, you don't really fill in. With the low-definition experiences which are very contemporary, for instance television, you get into it—you feed a lot of yourself back and forth into the images. Much of what happens here is input rather than output from the paintings; I don't imagine that one out of two hundred people that come into that room see the dancing Sakti in that painting. It doesn't bug us. It works; that Sakti's there, vibrating out of that painting. Who cares whether they are arms and legs; they're part of the vibrational universe.

Michael has been working for several years on circuitry. When I met Michael, I was flashing lights. I was using sign machinery, pure digital on-off, on-off material. It didn't matter whether it was once a minute or four hundred and eighty flashes a second. It wasn't until he came along that I under-stood the whole contemporary preoccupation with whether a

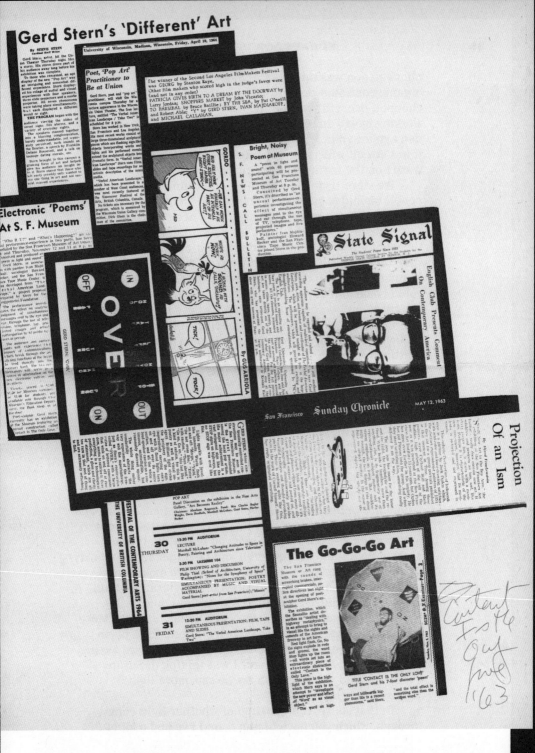

phenomenon was digital or analogue, whether you had this organic continual process curve going on or whether you chopped everything up in terms of clock time. Now we're working mostly in terms of lights and analogue. The lights don't go on and off in that room; they pulse phenomenon. It is a circuit which uses an element called a triac which wasn't on the market six months ago.

We were trying to create an environment in which people should communicate more with themselves than with anyone else and in which there was a period of, in John Cage's terms, "silence." I didn't understand for a long time the whole idea of "silence," but then it occurred to me that, in music, silence is simply a rest. We're trying to create a situation here in the Riverside Museum in which people could come and instead of using their analytic functions, simply go out. It seems to me that's what's happening. You look on those couches and people are flaked out for an hour or two at a time. The Museum is amazed. It is a little museum, as you know, and they don't generally have shows of this nature. They were used to getting about five or six people an afternoon. Not only that but they were used to getting schoolchildren brought by their teachers or a middle-aged crowd; now there is a crowd of teenagers and people in their early twenties. It is also obvious that a lot of it is just word of mouth.

To get back to the nub of it: What about the religious nature of this experience? What about the religious nature of the media experience? It's funny because the media are being used by the orthodox religions as a means of propaganda the same way they are being used by other organizations of our time. When you forget the literary content potentials of the media and begin using them fairly straight as experience, I think you begin to experience the religious reality which resides in the vibrational universe, in the nature of light, in the stroboscopic flash— in the sense that when G o e t h e was dying, he said, "More light!" I had used that line as a takeoff point for a poem a few years ago. All that time I had thought he was asking for more light. Some time later I was talking to Susan Firestone and she said, "Oh no, he saw more light." The light was there.

In that sense, the question of whether light comes through, which you have in film ... and I've had a lot of

questions in terms of Judaism, for instance, in terms of the
graven image. What does it mean, "Thou Shalt Not Make
a Graven Image"? But in film you take this image and you
throw the light through it. In our performances we had a lot
of through-light, but in this show almost all of it is through-
light. You also have light on. The light which you throw
on something then reflects and bounces back. It seems to
me to be the confrontation between the window and the
mirror. In the end you have to find some hybrid of the two,
because in terms of understanding humanity and understanding the possible relations with God, the way is not either
by looking in a mirror or by looking through a window
but by being able to see in the window the mirror and in
the mirror the window. Then the reality becomes possible.

The line we have been using for the last couple of years,
"We Are All One," comes out of Meher Baba. We have
all been profoundly influenced by the image of Meher Baba.
Again it's basically a media image. It's not his words on
paper (at least, I speak for myself; his words on paper don't
mean that much to me), it's his image, the image of his
face photographically and the image that I've seen of him
on film. It is the experience of another human being. Then
I see his words; I read him saying, "I am the avatar and
each of you are also avatars; but I know it and it is through
my knowing that I bring the knowledge to you." It's not a
new message or anything, but the fact that he's alive in this
world ... One of our ambitions is to go over there and record
Meher Baba on film. There's no knowing who or what he
really is, but it's the first time in human history that it is
possible to get a good recording, visually and orally of a
person who has made his claim. Next December he is going
to appear out of seclusion for some Westerners. If it is possible to raise some money to take equipment and people
who can handle it over there at that time, I think it would
be an invaluable document.

It also seems to me that here's a perfect potential for
a multiscreen 360-degree environmental situation. This
face which causes everybody to see someone else in him.
It's the kind of face that could be you, Jonas, or, as some
people who've come into our house think, Tennessee
Ernie Ford or Sammy Davis Jr. or Humphrey
Bogart. There was this guy who came to our first Brandeis
performance in '65, Bob Dreyfuss. He saw the face

of Baba which we flashed on the stage. Then he came and asked us, "Who is this man?" We told him. Within six months he had left for India to see Baba. He was the one who came back with Baba's message to America about no drugs. They are an illusion. It can cause great harm, he says. The whole last section of the performance that we will do at the Berkeley LSD conference will be based on stills of Baba's face.

### JONAS

How do you reconcile the fact that the majority of the people who find value in your show have taken LSD? Maybe it's because they think, for them, that's the only way out?

### GERD

How to get out of this world! The power in our civilization of the everyday, of the mundane, of the ubiquitous is stronger than it's ever been. Although God knows how long we all will still be into them, I think drugs are passé. We've been working our way out of it. Our problem today is, we need more Stations of the Cross. We need places to go, all over. The Riverside Museum is just a little hole in the wall.

# On Expanded Cinema

Selections from Movie Journal

February 6, 1964

Is our eye dying? Or we just do not know how to look and see any longer? The experiences of LSD show that the eye can expand itself, see more than we usually do. But then, as Bill Burroughs says (I quote from memory), "Whatever can be done chemically, can be done other ways."

There are many ways of freeing the eye. It comes down more to removing various psychological blocks than to really changing the eye. We never really look at the screen directly; we are separated by the misty ocean of our inhibitions and "knowledge." Experiments which Brion Gysin is doing in Paris with his "flicker machine" (read *Olympia* magazine) show that without the help of drugs, with a light flicker (even with your eyes closed) you can see colors and visions you were not able to see before and the memory of which (as with LSD) remains after the experiment. A series of blocks has been removed. As Professor [Gerald] Oster, who is conducting similar experiments in Brooklyn, says (again from memory): "The eye is inhibited. In some cultures more, in some less. We do not properly use the moiré patterns of the retina, because we think it is not practical. Our practical culture has reduced our vision." Salvador Dalí believes that "the Greek and Arab artists had this training of the eye for releasing the inhibitions of the eye. Only after the burning of the library of Alexandria was the education of the eye gradually neglected."

We say the single-frame technique in Markopoulos's film *Twice a Man* bothers our eye. People have told me that, after seeing Robert Breer's film *Blazes* or after Stan Brakhage films, they have head-

# MOVIE JOURNALS BY
# JONAS MEKAS
## as they appeared in the Village Voice
## Subject: Expanded Cinema.

aches, which is very possible. Others among us, those who have been watching these films more often, feel that the movements are too slow—we could take so much more. Our eye has expanded, our eye reactions have quickened. We have learned to see a little bit better.

But still our eyes are so limited! Some people can still see sprites and pixies. I saw an item in a recent issue of *New York Times* about a woman in London who can read colors with her fingers. Brion Gysin writes: "What is art? What is color? What is vision? These old questions demand new answers when, in the light of the Dream Machine (flicker machine), one sees all the ancient and modern abstract art with eyes closed."

Stan Brakhage (in *Metaphors on Vision*) writes, "Imagine an eye unruled by manmade laws of perspective, an eye unprejudiced by composition logic, an eye which does not respond to the name of everything but which must know each new object encountered in life through an adventure of perception. How many colors are there in a field of grass to a crawling baby unaware of Green? How many rainbows can light create for the untutored eye?"

*Blaze of Glory*
Ian Sommerville (in *Olympia*) writes, "I have made a simple flicker machine: a slotted card-board cylinder which turns on a gramophone at 78 rpm with a light bulb inside. You look at it with your eyes shut and the flicker plays over your eyelids. Visions start with a kaleidoscope of colors on a plane in front of the eyes and gradually become more complex and beautiful, breaking like surf on a shore until whole patterns are pounding to get in. After a while, the visions were permanently behind my eyes, and I was in the middle of the scene with limitless patterns being generated around me. There was an almost unbearable feeling of spatial movement for a while, but it was well worth getting through, for I found that when it stopped I was high above earth in a universal blaze of glory. Afterwards I found that my perception of the world around me had increased very notably. All conceptions of being drugged or tired had dropped away ..."

All these loose thoughts concern the new film language that is developing, a new way of seeing the world. Louis Marcorelles, one of the editors of *Cahiers du Cinéma*, wrote me a week ago, talking about the new American cinema: "Suddenly, I can't look at the ordinary cinema any longer, even when it's signed by Godard." Yes, but even critics are blind for the most part. We have a number of talented men and women creating a new cinema, opening new visions— but we need critics and an audience capable of seeing those visions. We need an audience that is willing to educate, to expand their eyes. A new cinema needs new eyes to see it. That's what it's all about.

---

February 27, 1964

"Fantastic Gardens," the E l a i n e S u m m e r s evening presented three times last week at Judson Memorial Church, combined a number of experiments that have been going on during the past few years with multiple projectors and the participation of live actors. One of the earlier and still most memorable experiences in this area was R o b e r t s   B l o s s o m's evening at the Living The- atre three years ago, where he attempted to combine his personal appearance on stage with movies, slides, and sound tapes. There was one piece on his program (I don't remember by whom), in which a number of boxes were stacked onstage simultaneously with the sounds, which all together created an unusual surreal audio-visual-spiritual experience.

There may have been many other experiments in this area. S t a n   V a n d e r b e e k did some weird and effective things at the AG (Fluxus) Gallery three years ago and, later, at the Maidman Playhouse, using multiple projection and multiple screens. Other attempts, more limited in scope, have been tried at Judson Church. Iolas and Wise Galleries had shows which, in one way or another, were connected with the exploration of movement and light. One could see a very effective use of slides and movies in R o b e r t   W h i t m a n's happening "Flower."

*Entire Presence*
Anyway, I don't intend to give a complete historical report on the subject here—I would have to go back far into the '20s. What I saw at Judson Church last Wednesday was by far the most successful and most ambitious attempt to use the many possible combinations of film and live action to create an aesthetic experience. Specifically, one could see here a huge ballet-happening, often involving the entire audience and using the entire presence of the church itself, its walls, its columns, balconies, ceiling. Mirrors were distributed which the audience used to catch the beams of light crisscrossing the church. When one looked at the audience, it seemed to be dancing too, going through the variety of flattering, floating moments, hands moving in the air as if they were chasing and following the light beams, in a strange ritual of light.

There were screens at both ends of the auditorium and three or four projectors, with the images being projected at various times, singly or in a chorus, the church, the ceiling, and the columns, and on and around the dancers and the audience. Superimpositions were created right there by throwing two or three images one upon the other; and there on the screens, on the walls was a man working a handheld projector like an image gun or a light-brush, swinging it the way he felt like, in images of color and black-and-white, changing their size and background.

*Split Screens*
Fantastic effects were produced by using a split screen, a screen made of several dangling strips of white material which moved and separated, and there were human figures appearing through the partings, moving into and out of the screen, submerging, disappearing into it, participating in it, so that at times you didn't know or knew only vaguely what was the photograph and what was the real live presence. The action of the images overlapped or repeated or extended the actions of the dancers and people—the same figures, often appearing on the screen as in the dance arena or around the balcony. Etc.

All this worked as an artistic unity—at least there was a conscious attempt toward it, and it often succeeded—and it had nothing to do with merely technical trickery. What that experience really was isn't easy to describe. One thing I can say, it had little in common with the experiences of C i n e r a m a or D i s n e y's C i r c o r a m a, where one is either too conscious of technique, where there is always a circus feeling (which is an experience too), or just simply a huge and overwhelming physical involvement in a visual sensation. Here, though, there was a more spiritual use—or perhaps, more correctly, an attempt to achieve or reach more subtle levels or areas or depths of audiovisual experience, beyond the simply (or just merely) physical sensations and involvements; there was an attempt here made to produce an aesthetic, soul experience consisting of a variety of feelings, motions, and emotions. It came close to an audiovisual spatial symphony that moved us and involved us in strange and beautiful ways, new ways, never before experienced ways, something that contained amazement and glimpses of not yet familiar beauty.

June 25, 1964

There are very strange things happening in cinema. And

the strangest thing is that there is really nothing strange in it.

First, there was the static image of a train pulling into the station (if we begin there). Then there were filmed plays. Then there were stories and slapstick fantasies. Then the poets did away with plots and continuities and stories. The poets of the '60s did away with the representational image itself. The camera now picks up glimpses, fragments of objects and people, and creates fleeting impressions, of both objects and actions, in the manner of action painters. A new spiritualized reality of motion and light is created on the screen, as in the work of Brakhage or Jerry Joffen. In *Dog Star Man* Brakhage abandons the frame itself. He plants bits of color film in the very middle of a black-and-white frame; his frames become mosaics. Gregory Markopoulos introduces single-frame editing. Commercial TV introduces subliminal, repeated single-frame images. The flash-and-glimpse reality that we see through the windows of cars and jets has become our daily visual experience. Our eye is undergoing physical changes. Gysin is creating visionary images with the dream machine.

You have heard about the destruction of the screen, about the experiments you can see even at the New York World's Fair: multiple screens and multiple images. You have seen multiple and handheld projectors, multiple screens and the fusion of live and screen action at Judson Church during the "Fantastic Gardens" evening. Those who have been especially lucky have even had a glimpse of the work of Harry Smith, the greatest wizard working in animated cinema since Méliès—his multiple images, slides and projectors, his magic, cabalistic space cinema.

Film stock itself has reached its limits (and I am not really talking about the images on tape). Brakhage made *Mothlight* without a camera. He just pasted moth wings and flower petals on a clear strip of film and ran it through the printing machine. Storm De Hirsch even got rid of the film: she made her film *Divinations*, at least two-thirds of it, on 16 mm tape, by punching, carving, and painting on it, by working on it with tiny instruments that she carried out from a surgical operating room.

Naomi Levine painted and scratched and put so many things on her movie strip that it cannot be printed, although it runs through the projector. It will remain the only copy, no prints will be made. The same is true of Barbara Rubin's movie *A Christmas on Earth*—it too will remain in its original. It is the same as in painting: no reproduction can ever recreate the original. The filmmakers are no longer interested in making dozens of second copies. They feel that the original strip is the only true film and no print can ever match the original. Markopoulos,

Ken Jacobs, and Jack Smith do not even edit with work prints: they work with their originals (and it is not only a question of money).

Going still further: Nam June Paik, Peter Kubelka, and George Maciunas have made movies where they did away with the image itself, where the light becomes the image. Kubelka's white light film has given me my strongest visual experience.

Going still further: Reports have reached me that Brion Gysin and Antony Balch and Barbara Piccolo in London or Amsterdam or somewhere— it doesn't matter where—got rid of film, projectors, and cameras: they are working with smokes and vapors. Dalí is working with contact lenses which will throw color images on our retina while we sleep.

*Absolute Cinema*
It is from here that we are only one step away from the absolute cinema, cinema of our mind. For what is cinema really if not images, dreams, and visions?

We take one more step, and we give up all movies and we become movies: we sit on a Persian or Chinese rug smoking one dream matter or another and we watch the smoke and we watch the images and dreams and fantasies that are taking place right there in our eye's mind: we are the true cineastes, each of us, crossing space and time and memory— this is the ultimate cinema of the people, as it has been for thousands and thousands of years.

This is all real! There are no limits to man's dreams, fantasies, desires, visions. It has nothing to do with technical innovations: it has to do with the boundless spirit of man which can never be confined to prescribed screens, frames, or images: it jumps out of any manner of dream imposed upon it, and seeks its own mysteries and its own dreams.

*An Interview with Naomi Levine:*
Sheila Bick: "Do you want to be in a movie, Naomi?"

Naomi Levine: "No, I am a movie."

---

July 9, 1964

*Movies at the World's Fair*
*To Be Alive* (Johnson Pavilion), by Alexander Hammid and Francis Thompson. Uses three screens separated by narrow partitions (no intention to merge the three images completely).

Images photographed and edited to demonstrate that people can be happy everywhere, quite an original idea. Smiling faces; children; flowers; more children; people "looking" happy. In New York, in Africa, even in France! Commentator quacking all the time, selling happiness. Filmically, a few bits of effective editing can be seen, a few seconds of kinetic experience. Moral of the movie: the world is cute.

*Information Machine* (IBM Pavilion), by Charles Eames. An audiovisual lesson on how information is being collected (by men and machines); it teaches absolutely nothing. Uses at least six motion-picture projectors, four or five slide projectors, and a live announcer appearing now on the right, now on the left, now in front of us. A very busy performance confused, overcrowded, perfectly unfunctional, and, I would dare to say, silly.

*Lasting Impression*
*To the Moon and Beyond* (KLM Pavilion), Cinerama production. Images projected on a round "planetarium" ceiling of quite huge dimensions. The forming of galaxies is shown; a few man-made vehicles cross the skies. Nothing much happens, no great information is given; however, the visual kinetic experience is overwhelming. From what I have seen at the Fair (movie-wise), this is one show that leaves a lasting impression.

*From Here to There* (United Airlines Pavilion), by Saul Bass. People saying goodbye; babies smiling; kisses; more kisses; plane taking off; the screen expands from normal to cinemascope; aerial shots of rivers, fields, deserts; the plane lands;

more kisses; more babies smiling. A few stock shots beautiful in themselves. Bass likes to divide his images with lines, horizontally and vertically, in three, in six, in nine. Moral of the movie: travel by air is cute.

*The Searching Eye* (Kodak Pavilion), another Saul Bass "experimental" movie; more stock shots on an expanding screen. More flowers, more birds, time-lapse photography à la Disney (blossoms opening). Two or three beautiful shots.

*Wonderful World of Chemistry* (DuPont Pavilion), directed by Michael Brown for Elliot and Unger. The story of DuPont products. Uses three screens on wheels: the screens slide on and off the stage as needed. Combines live actors (fashion models and announcer) and actors on screen (perfect timing); projectors used; also slides and lighting effects (brilliant job). Live actors conversing with actors on screen (perfect timing); a rose is passed by one of the live models on stage to a model on screen, who in turn passes it to another live model, who in turn passes it to the third model on the third screen. A perfectly timed, slick advertisement, the most perfect from the six I have seen so far, with no art pretensions— pure Madison Avenue. (Haven't seen yet the Circorama—screens around the auditorium—and the USA Pavilion "travel through the screens" show.)

*Small Wonders*

As a rule, movie theatres themselves were more effective than the movies. The Johnson Theatre is a small wonder: a fattened egg in the air, sitting on six light columns in a pool of water; a theatre that looks like it's for a hundred but which seats five hundred. The IBM Theatre is another small wonder.

Multiple screens and multiple projectors have been used much more effectively by Kenneth Anger, Stan Vanderbeek, Harry Smith, Roberts Blossom, and Elaine Summers

(not to mention Abel Gance); nevertheless, a trip to the Fair is worthwhile—there are a few moments of kinetic experience (like the KLM show) that cannot be produced unless there is big money behind it. Sheer bigness is sometimes a part of the quality and the content of the experience, and it is beautiful.

I noticed a great number of trees and plenty of water at the Fair. But if one could tear down the pavilions one could make more space for water—I figured. All the youth of New York could then come and make love there.

---

August 27, 1964

*Laterna Magica* opened in Prague almost four years ago. For its time it was an advanced experiment combining stage and cinema. By the time the show reached New York, its value had become purely historical. Everybody's doing it now; the World's Fair is full of *Laterna Magica* shows. Elaine Summers's Judson Church show early this year remains the new, and hardly surpassable landmark in this "total cinema" form.

*Laterna Magica*, like most other "firsts"—like Cinerama or "three-D"—has more to do with showmanship than art. Even as a show, the only excitement in *Laterna Magica* comes in the last five minutes. A roller skater on stage is moving (at least such

is the impression) along a street on screen (a street filmed from a fast-moving car). The moving screen (street) image is flashed against the roller skater on stage (he swings his legs and arms and jumps right and left to avoid the cars but never leaves the spot really), and the effect is one of a neck-breaking ride along the busy street—an effect matched only by the early Cinerama shots of the Coney Island rollercoaster rides.

*Mainly about Green*

*Ingreen*, a twelve-minute film by Nathanial Dorsky, was screened at the Washington Square Gallery last weekend. It's hard to tell what it's all about, but I would say it is mainly about green. It is made of beautiful greens. There are glimpses of figures, of images that are recognizable, but the aesthetic experience is created by the flow and play of superimpositions.

The superimposition is coming back to cinema. It hasn't been used effectively since the early days of Man Ray and Watson. The work of Brakhage remained the work of a lonely giant. In New York, the superimposition came back permanently with Ron Rice's *Chumlum*, with Barbara Rubin's *Christmas on Earth*, Carl Linder's *The Devil Is Dead*, and now Dorsky's *Ingreen*. There is a whole school of younger filmmakers working with superimpositions— Dove Lederberg, Abbott Meader, even Bruce Baillie. One-image cinema has become too slow for the quick eyes of some of the new filmmakers. Brakhage has done his work.

I got so bored with *Laterna Magica* that I walked out of it long before it reached midway. After swallowing one Gorky at the Russian Tea Room, I decided to go back to see what I was missing. The show looked much better. Alcohol made my mind and my eyes (on an empty stomach) go blank at moments—there were blank spots in my consciousness and my eyes were not so intense in checking what was going on.

Life became more "interesting." That's why Chekhov characters always drink—from boredom.

*More about Green*
I remember another time when I watched *Marienbad* and *L'Avventura* doped with pot. There, just the opposite occurred. My perception was increased. I could see more than usually. The movies became tedious. A shot of ten seconds seemed to last ten minutes.

The small point I am making here is this: The cinema of superimpositions is created by people whose perception— by whatever process—has been expanded, intensified (Brakhage is opposed to the use of drugs for the expansion of the mind and the eye's consciousness). Their images are loaded with double and triple superimpositions. Things must happen fast, many things. Lines, colors, figures, one on top of another, combinations and possibilities, to keep the eye working. All this is too much for an untrained eye, but there is no end to how much a quick eye can see. So here we have these two extremes: the slow and the quick, Andy Warhol and Stan Brakhage. There are many faces to cinema.

---

June 3, 1965

Since I sadly remain the lonely historian of the new cinema,

I should report here on the various uses of movies at the recently concluded First New York Theatre Rally, organized by Steve

Paxton and Alan Solomon, which took place in a huge television studio on Broadway and 81st Street.

One striking use of cinema was seen in Carolyn Brown's dance piece *Balloon*, with Barbara Lloyd and Steve Paxton (performed May 11 to 13). In the back of the studio was a balloon of approximately 20 by 20 feet, around which and in front of which the dancers moved. The immense balloon served as a screen on which images (newsreels, etc.) were projected. A weather balloon was used, and I was told it took three days to fill it with the air from a vacuum cleaner.

On the same program, in his piece "Spring Training," Bob Rauschenberg used a portable screen tied down to the back of a dancer on which slides were projected.

*Tent Happening*
For Robert Whitman's happening "The Night Time Sky" (May 14 to 16), the studio was transformed into a huge tent. There were openings here and there in which certain happenings took place. The audience had to lean or lie down on the ground and look up or uppish. On the entrance side of the tent and on the entering audience images were projected—mostly harbor images, ships, people, with harbor and crowd noises on the soundtrack. The feeling one

got was of embarking on a journey on an ocean liner. Other images were projected inside the tent. One series consisted of factory images, furnaces, in color. On the top of the tent (inside) were reflected colored jewels: elongated, hallucinatory shapes. At various times, as the people lay down and watched the "sky," the canvas tent was illuminated blue and green from outside. The television lighting facilities served here perfectly. The feeling was lyrical, quiet, poetic. The climax of the evening was a projection from the center on the "ground" into the tent's inner peak (dome) of a man sitting on the toilet and unconcernedly going about his crap business, pulling his pants off, relieving himself, pulling his pants on, flushing the water, washing the crap down. Everything was seen as from inside the toilet (under a glass, really), so that the whole messy and unaesthetic (at least until now) and crappy business was performed right on the audience's heads. By some this was taken as a critical comment on what has happened to the happening theatre in general. Others giggled and laughed, some comfortably, some not.

The most amazing use of cinema, however, was in *Shower* (May 24 to 26), another piece by Robert Whitman. The piece is just what the title says: there is a shower box and there is a girl in it, naked naturally, taking a shower. The whole thing is so beautiful and so real that people kept coming back and peeking into the shower box to see if the girl was really there. The amazing effect was achieved by projecting a color film of the girl taking a shower onto the back of the shower box which was made of plastic glass, on the other side of which water was running down. It is really a further extension of what Andy Warhol started with his *Sleep* movie. And it contradicts and dismisses (for good) the statements that the real thing, or something that looks real, cannot be beautiful or cannot be art. It is the old nonsense of the aestheticians. Whitman has used plenty of ingenuity in building this simple box and getting the amazing tridimensional effect (probably because of the haziness and thickness of the glass). The end result is amazing and it pushes cinema into another field of unexplored and new possibilities.

There was another piece, really a fragment of a piece, from May 24 to 26, as a part of Tony Holder's *Lightweight* (unless I am confusing the pieces), which provided a very strong kinetic experience. A dancer moved around in a small circle in complete darkness, but with a spotlight flickering on and off, with dark and light flashes at possibly one-third of a second gaps, the motions of the dancer weren't seen and when we saw him next, after another fraction of darkness, his hands and the position of the body were slightly changed. The impression created was like a normally photographed (twenty-four frames per second) movie projected at eight frames per second—sort of staccato movements, a kinetic experience of strange power.

*Expanded Cinema*
Later this summer the Cinematheque is organizing a huge survey of the various new uses of cinema. The leading artists of these new uses of cinema (expanded cinema) will take part. As I have said quite often before, cinema is only beginning. Don't go to Cannes to look for new cinema—come to New York.

---

July 1, 1965

Coming back to New York: I would like to say something about one very small film which I think is a minor (or maybe even a major) masterpiece. It is George Landow's loop film called *This Film Will Be Interrupted after 11 Minutes by a Commercial* and which was screened at the Cinematheque last Friday. Loop film is a comparatively new film form and the best film loop

I had seen till now was Dick
Higgins's *Invocation of Canyons
and Boulders*. Landow's loop
consists of one foot of black
leader and one foot of a medium
close-up of a beautiful girl
blinking (one blink). It was shot
on 8 mm and printed on 35 mm
(four 8 mm tracks) and then split
in half (for 16 mm projection)
with one image track fully visible
and the other one half cut off,
and with sprockets printed in the
middle, with a few edge numbers
visible—really, it would be easier
to reproduce the film here in full
than to describe it. The kinetic
and visual experience produced
by Landow's film is even more
difficult to describe. In the first
half of the loop the image slides
(because of the special way
the loop was spliced together);
the other part is sharp and
in registration. The loop runs
(is supposed to run) twenty-
two minutes. There is humor
in it (the blink); there is a clear
Mozart-like, Mondrian-
like sense of form; there is the
richness of image, about the
richest frame I have seen in
any film when you take into consideration all the movements,
lines, the beautiful whites,
the reds and blacks. It is quite
safe to say, with all that we
know about the cinema as an art,
that Landow has created here
the first film-loop masterpiece.
His earlier film, *Fleming Faloon*,
is a master's work in its own
right.

One thing about Landow's
and Higgins's loops is that there
is nothing unnecessary in them;
every aspect and every detail
is made to work for the whole,
beginning with the photographed
image and ending with the physical presence of the celluloid
itself. Splices usually are never
seen, not to mention felt. Splicing
is considered a boring craft;
splices should never be seen.
But splice is coming back and asking for its own rights. (Read Stan
Brakhage's essay on splicing in
*Film Culture*, no. 35.) The texture
of the film, the grain of the film
comes into an existence of its
own through Brakhage's and Ken
Jacobs's 8 mm work. In Landow's
loop you can see and feel the film
sprockets, the splices, and even
the running of the film through the
projector—really, it is a particular
characteristic of this new film
form that it pulls you into a total
film experience, all its aspects
included. The special difficulty
of this form is the fact that the
loop is repeated continuously and
that only the richness of visual-
kinetic content can sustain the
eye and the film in time. Film loop
is a form—and Landow's loop
is a supreme illustration of it—
in which nothing superfluous can
be tolerated; whatever is on film,
including the splicing glue, should
be made to be seen and felt as
a part of the whole.

By the way, the film was
booed at the Cinematheque and
it was cut off before its proper

(twenty-two minutes) time. Someone shouted, and he meant it as a joke: "Another genius was born tonight at the Cinematheque!" But I mean it here in all seriousness.

---

July 22, 1965

Monday, July 12: *Psychedelic Explorations*, at the New Theatre, East 54th Street. Timothy Leary opens the evening as "a psychedelic session without chemistry"; Jackie Cassen projects polarized "light sculptures"; acrylic and aniline projections by Don Snyder; automatic analogue projections by Richard Aldcroft; polarized glasses and prisms; slides fade in and out and dissolve into each other; color filters; moving polarized sculptures superimposed over the slides; vague organic and inorganic forms glide across the screen; slowly shimmering mosaics; voice (Leary) reads from ancient Chinese scriptures; electronic music; assorted sounds; stroboscope light flickers upon the screen; Edith Stephen dances in the stroboscope light; a box, a compound of prisms, with colors blinking on and off; Woodstock group (Gerd Stern) projects random movies and some more organized highway footage; two movie projectors, three or four slide projectors, analogue projections; the screen becomes a moving, flickering collage; a collage sound track; radio, music, voices, nonsense speeches, bits of this and that, at blasting volume.

I liked the part which preceded the program proper— I mean, when the projectors and slide machines were being tested, lights arranged; flashes of unusually beautiful whites; fleeting glimpses of an imperfectly placed slide; the empty slide frame full of light. Like that Oriental musician who went to a Western music concert, I preferred the instrument tuning period to the real concert. I remember liking a number of movies (both of the Hollywood and "underground" breed) in their "rushes," in their chance order, with the different "takes" growing into strange symphonies—but I saw little in them when they were "completed": the non-art of "rushes" had more power in their chance state than the "artistically" organized end result: materials were organized into clichés of art.

*Slide Level*
The first half of the program, the slide and aniline show, although sometimes pretty, remained on the level of slides. The feeling prevailed that somebody was trying to sell something with these slides. They did not exist for their own sake. It was the soundtrack, the voice, which made the images illustrative, forced a meaning upon them, which wasn't there.

The voice did not leave our eyes alone to follow the flow of shapeless colors and forms as they came, but forced the mind to look in them for something else, even if that something else was vague; the mind was never left "at the mercy of the eye," as Robert Kelly has said about the films of Stan Brakhage. The intention, or the hope, no doubt, was that the words would act upon consciousness (and the unconscious) magically, subliminally. That would have been the effect under LSD. But the audience wasn't on LSD and the words came in all their distracting superfluity.

The evening made me appreciate Brakhage's work anew. Later in the evening, Dr. Gunther Weil mentioned that the Chinese —or Tibetans—know how to construct rooms lit and proportioned in such a way that anyone who is left alone in such a room is affected the same way: the room makes them cry. The work of an artist involves similar precisions. We saw colors, pretty slides, but they remained pretty slides. An artist's temperament and intelligence was needed to organize them in time and space into "life-sustaining forces" (again using Kelly's expression).

*Life in Collage*
It was the chance and the lack of "artistic" control that gave some life to Gerd Stern's screen collage. The chance meetings and groupings of images and lights on the screen produced a kinetic experience that was new, more by the force of science than art. A physical fact, a visual force/ fact was there on the screen and we could not ignore it, we had to wrestle with it or leave the place, and it did something to us as we wrestled with it.

The purest kinetic fact of the evening, however, was the projection of the stroboscope light on the screen—the play of white light on the eyelids, the purity and directness of light experience.

Strange, though, that two filmmakers who have reached the furthest frontiers of new vision, who have explored the light and the eye most—Stan Brakhage and Peter Kubelka—have never used drugs. More than that: recently both have taken a clear stand against the use of drugs for the expansion of consciousness. The place of an artist in a society can never be clearly defined. The artist remains above the dailiness of the experience and above the work of the scientists— even if his work has much to do with the science.

*No Pretentions*
The Psychedelic Theatre has no great artistic pretentions. Its aim remains expansion of our consciousness—whatever that expression means. I was sorry, therefore, to see that whatever was gained last Monday was consumed and nullified by a small incident. During the

first part of the program, which was contributed by the C o d a G a l l e r y, a young man was standing by the wall and shooting his own 8mm movie. During the intermission, the Coda Gallery confiscated the young man's film. They did not want, they said, any footage of Coda Gallery art to be seen in his little movie, because a big movie company was coming to make a real movie about them. Suddenly, on the human level, everything became petty and all kinds of B o s c h creatures began creeping into the open. The dreams and illusions of success, possessions, fame, money—these old forces engulfed all other energies and I left the place in a hurry to get some fresh night air. What is the real interest of Coda Gallery, I asked myself as I walked. Expansion of man's consciousness?

Yes, drugs expanded consciousness! Sometimes, I am afraid, consciousness is confused with the ability to see more color images, with the expanded eye, with the quickness of the eye. But as the quickness of the hand can be used to thrust a knife into one's heart, so the quickness of an eye, the simultaneity of seeing can be used by both Devil and God—as the consciousness and the soul remain sleeping.

---

November 11, 1965

Not all that's happening at the Film-Makers' Cinematheque this month is or can be called cinema. Some of it has no name of any kind. The first three programs of the New Cinema Festival—the work of A n g u s M a c L i s e, Nam June Paik, and Jerry Joffen—dissolved the edges of this art called cinema into a frontiersland mystery. Light is there; motion is there; the screen is there; and the filmed image, very often, is there; but it cannot be described or experienced in the same terms as you describe or experience the G r i f f i t h cinema, the Godard cinema, or even Brakhage cinema.

The medium of cinema is breaking out and taking over and is going blindly and by itself. Where to—nobody knows. I am glad about both: that it's going somewhere, and that nobody knows where it's going. I like things out of control. At some point, the artist will ram his feet into the ground, will stop the medium, and will start taming it, using it to plow the fields of his own imagination— but the bull is still running. People who watch the avant-garde cinema keep asking me: What's new? Who is doing new movies? And it's difficult to answer. For they expect to see or hear more about the same, but what's happening isn't the same. The currents that are moving within us, and as externalized by the artists, are ripe with impulses and they spurt out in uncontrollable and unfamiliar gushes. So the avant-garde artists them-

FILM-MAKERS' CINEMATHEQUE
434 LAFAYETTE ST.          AL4-4060

SPECIAL ANNOUNCEMENT

FESTIVAL OF EXPANDED CINEMA

New and startling developments have been taking place in cinema during the last two years. The peripheries of cinema have been expanding in a number of new directions.

Film-Makers' Cinematheque will be devoting the entire month of November to an extensive survey of these various experiments and developments. The programs will include multiple screens, multiple projectors; multiple imagery; changing screen and image shapes; merger of live performers and screen action; multiple exposures; moving slides; kinetic sculptures; hand held projectors balloon screens; videotape; video projections; various light and sound experiments; etc.

The Festival will consist of thirty evening programs. Each participant will be responsible (in whole or in part) for an evening program. We hope to have at least twenty different programs.

Among the artists participating in the Festival will be:

| | |
|---|---|
| Kenneth Anger | The Once Group (Ann Arbor) |
| Roberts Blossom | Nam June Paik |
| Robert Breer | Larry Rivers |
| Jackie Cassen | Beverly Schmidt |
| Milton Cohen | Jack Smith |
| Ken Dewey | Don Snyder |
| Ed Emshwiller | Gerd Stern |
| Al Hansen | Elaine Summers |
| Dick Higgins | Aldo Tambellini |
| Alfred Leslie | Stan Vanderbeek |
| Angus MacLise | Andy Warhol |
| Klaus Oldenberg | Robert Whitman |

Special announcement for the Festival of Expanded Cinema, New York, 1965

selves sit in the audience, surprised and repeating, "What the hell is happening?"

*About Mystic*

Now, this current gush, as much as one can generalize at this early (not so early, though) stage, is marked by an almost mystic drive toward pure motion, color, light experience. It has much to do with other arts, painting, sculpture, happenings, environment, music, but the cinema aspect, light, screen (in a number of different forms), image (filmed or produced by other means), and motion dominate these works. The surge is wide and intense. Half-a-hundred different artists are represented in the November (Expanded Cinema) show alone.

So the avant-garde artists, who are working in a more classical tradition of cinema, are asking themselves what this new gush of light-motion art will do to their work. Have no fear, cried the captain! No good "old" art is ever invalidated by the "new" art. What it will do, it will help to separate the genuine and intense "old" art from the shallow and half-felt "old" art. In creation, in the present, everybody has his chance. But in time perspective, only art remains.

For a number of years now, the avant-garde artists (in cinema, and in other arts) felt, and publicly insisted, that they are creating something so different from the traditional art that their work, they felt, could be defined as anti-art. And they were right. They had to take that attitude. The artist is always right, even when he is wrong. That attitude was his liberating acetylene wedge to bore into the heart of the always-new reality.

But now, with a five-, six-, seven-year perspective, these far-far-out and anti-art works begin to fall into the same thousand-year-old treasury of all art. I realized this suddenly when I watched Nam June Paik's evening. His art, like the art of La Monte Young, or that of Stan Brakhage or Gregory Markopoulos or Jack Smith or even (no doubt about it) Andy Warhol, is governed by the same thousand-year-old aesthetic laws and can be analyzed and experienced like any other classical work of art.

*Edges Blurred*

Still, there are aspects that remain ungraspable, unfamiliar to the uninitiated. Take, for instance, something that could be called the "period of emergence." It has become a part of the new art experience and is an essential part of a great many happenings. Beck-Malina theatre, environment, music (sound), and light-motion art. The edges of where a specific work of art begins and where it ends are blurred out. Really, one could say that a happening of Ken Dewey or the cinema of Jerry Joffen

or a "ritual" of Angus MacLise
fades in slowly into the world,
sustains there for a while, glows,
and then it dissolves out again
imperceptibly.

This causes some annoyance
and sometimes anger to those
uninitiated into the experience
and aesthetics (they are always
the same but differently dressed
up) of the new art. A great part
of the audience walked out before
Jerry Joffen's work revealed itself fully; they walked out during
the period of emergence, before
the work came into its glowing
equinox. Being accustomed to the
traditional (what they think of
as traditional) art, the audience
was annoyed that there was
no immediate art "experience,"
no immediate aesthetic shocks.
Those who remained, however,
and surrendered themselves and
sat into the evening, witnessed
(or grew into) forty minutes of the
most beautiful, spiritual, almost
heavenly cinema experience.
Then again, it slowly faded out.

This art was born from a
new attitude to art, which in turn
was born from a new attitude to
life. We are beginning to meditate.
Meditation was out of the western
world for about 1,500 years. It
is interesting to note, here, in this
context, that when you go to some
Chinese or Japanese monasteries, where some of the great works
of art are kept you have to go
through a one-week period,
sometimes longer, of preparation,
waiting for that specific work

of art, learning about it, thinking
about it, so that when you finally
face it, you are completely ready
for it and you see it in its full
glow. That is the direction some
of the art in America is taking
(it's the Beat revolution that did it).

The first three programs
of the New Cinema Festival
represent three different and
basic groups of artists. Nam June
Paik belongs to the purists, to
the "intellectual" wing; Angus
MacLise is the emotion; Jerry
Joffen is at home in both. Paik's
program was perfectly designed,
constructed, and executed.
There was an almost classical
simplicity and purity about it.
MacLise, with all his visual mystic-
ornamental flair, and the beauty
of texture (in image and sound),
like all emotionalists, didn't
give much attention either to the
general structure or the details
of the evening, and his work,
despite all-pervading lyrical qualities, had much of the distracting
messiness of a dress rehearsal
about it. Jerry Joffen, however, has
so much personality and artistry
that even those parts which failed
became somehow integrated
and worked perfectly in the total
structure of the evening. In the
past, it has always been that Jerry
Joffen's failures were more interesting than some other artists'
successes.

Jerry Joffen is a master
of destruction. I mean it in a good
sense, in the sense of spiritu-
alizing the reality, dissolving time

and space. A scene is filmed in two or three superimpositions; then the screen spiritualizes this superimposition reality further (the screen consisted of several layers of silky and colored materials); this is dissolved further by lights and mirrors. At the very end the reality becomes pure light, pure color, pure motion, pure air. But the amazing thing here is that the presence of image and motion, the feeling of cinema remains in the consciousness of the viewer, whereas in the case of MacLise one vacillates between the theatre, music, and cinema experience.

The same could be said about the use of words. MacLise's words, recited as part of the ritual, hung heavily and with a sentimental theatricality upon the stage; Joffen's words were pronounced without any emotion, abstractly, each word parted by time-space. The sentence, thus, was spiritualized, dissolved (similarly to what Markopoulos did in *Twice a Man.*)

---

November 18, 1965

I will continue with the report on the New Cinema Festival at the Film-Makers' Cinematheque.

The Jack Smith and the John Vacarro evenings had little to do with cinema. Both pieces were exercises in the Artaud theatre. Cinema was used only as an auxiliary of the theatre. We know, however, that the theatre of Artaud is a theatre of kinesthetic violence, something that, as experience, dissolves into cinema experience.

The Jack Smith piece, *Rehearsal for the Destruction of Atlantis*, as one would expect, was an orgy of costumes, suppressed and open violence, and color. The center of the piece was a huge red lobster, a masterpiece creation of costume and character. Vacarro's piece, *Rites of the Nadir*, was a theatre ritual, less decorative. Vacarro has a first-rate theatre sense. He is a showman, with a sense of timing and pacing. Smith's piece was loose and relied on chance, on coincidences, on conglomerations.

Although the Smith and Vacarro pieces were presented as part of the New Cinema Festival, they may be—historically speaking—the first successful fusion of the Artaud theories, the happenings and environment experiences, and traditional theatre (through the spoken word) into a new kind of theatre.

*Expanded Theatre*
Roberts Blossom's program was an expanded theatre (not an expanded cinema). Two pieces, however, *Duet for One Person* and *Poem for the Theatre* (both danced by Beverly Schmidt), fused the two mediums and produced something, we weren't

sure what—Blossom calls it "film-stage." Blossom used the dancer, color slides projected on the dancer and the background; and a motion picture of the same dancer projected on the stage (as the dancer danced).

Arthur Sainer's piece, *Untitled Chase*, was a theatre piece with a film loop projected on the left side of the stage. The loop showed a man chasing another man; a girl in a red dress leaps, like a dancer; the man is beating the other man; girl leaning by the man on the ground; man sitting on the ground, looking ahead, "thinking." After three or four minutes of the loop, the same three people come on stage (as the loop continues) and perform what we already saw in the loop, now in more detailed form, with a few emotional splashes of dialogue (they "think," they "worry"). The attempt tended to go downhill, perhaps from lack of form, pacing, or imagination.

Standish Lawder's piece, *The March of the Garter Snakes*, effectively demonstrated that a slide can produce kinetic experiences. He began with something that could be called an old-fashioned slide, and ended with a "moving slide." The motion was produced by inserting drops of color paint between two pieces of glass. After a few seconds, from the heat of the projector, the paint began to melt, to spread, to travel, producing unpredictable

and often beautiful (although too "pretty") patterns, strikingly affective as "abstract cinema."

*Demonstrates Possibilities*
However, it is Don Snyder who is the master of the slide art. His show, *Epiphany of Light* (which was a part of the psychedelic theatre, three months ago), demonstrated numerous possibilities of slide dissolves, black and white, and in color (synchronized or counterpointed with sound). Images gradually grew into color symphonies (two slide projectors were complemented by a motion-picture projector) that kept one in surprise and amazement. There were attempts at subliminal images, planted occasionally (usually some Buddhist images).

Snyder's slide art merges completely with the medium of cinema. I should say something about the "prettiness" of some of Snyder's images. Although, like all nature-produced patterns they are more pretty than they are art, they nevertheless, when seen on the screen, and in motion, produce a kinesthetic experience, a shock or color and motion that should be judged not by the design of a single slide (frame) but by the patterns of visual impulses.

The most dazzling pieces of "expanded" cinema, in the true sense, were provided by that old Barnum of Cinema, Stan Vanderbeek, in his three motion picture compositions: *Movie-*

Stan Vanderbeek in front of one of his film installations, 1964–1967

Stan Vanderbeek's film installation, 1964–1967

*Movies* (a choreography for projectors)—four movie projectors, three slide projectors, and a flashlight were used, and projectionists walked on stage in a ballet of handheld projectors; *Pastorale: Et Al* (a film and slide study for dancers, with Elaine Summers); and *Feedback No. 1: A Movie Mural.* In this last piece, the theatre became a huge movie mural, with a battery of five projectors— a sound and image experience so unusual and so full of motion and visual impact that we all suddenly said, "Yes, IT WORKS! IT WORKS!" meaning the multiple projection cinema. The moviemural was followed by one of those applauses which, in the newspapers, are usually called "half-an-hour applauses"—there was so much excitement. The feeling was that we had witnessed something very new, and very beautiful, something that could neither be described nor explained. It acted upon us with its multiplicity of images, associations, memories, eyes. The impact was both on our retina and a physical, kinesthetic impact, on our body—and it wasn't Cinerama, where it is the vertigo that does it. Here the impact was produced by something that was more formal; it came from the organization of visual, kinesthetic materials and that's where art comes in.

Piero Heliczer's evening, "The Last Rites," was a ceremony, a ritual—really, the most successful (as ritual) of the six rituals presented at the festival. This was not because Heliczer had the New Testament for his script; not because of a certain unfaked directness and immediacy that he produced. Although he was "acting," there was something very real about it. Angus MacLise's music helped a lot to sustain this mood. At the center of this ritual was Cinema, the tiny 8 mm image projected on a large screen in front of which, on the stage, a ceremony of watching the image and blessing the image was performed. There was something ambiguous, inexplicable in this blessing of the image, in this playing of the bishop, in this watching of the image. Later in the evening, Weegee (of *Naked City* fame) brought some of his latest work, and it was projected as part of the ritual and beautifully destroyed and incorporated into the whole by Heliczer.

*More Human*
Much of the evening was just fooling ("acting") and just nothing —as most of what Heliczer does, is. But that is where, as far as I can see, the originality and beauty of his work and its essential difference from all the others, is. His work has none of the ambitiousness and artistic struggle of the others, none of the wanting to be impressive, or shocking, or ugly, or violent, or grotesque—something that is so much part of contemporary art. Heliczer's art

I find more human—if not more beautiful.

Above all, however, I should stress here the ambiguity of his work, the mystery of his work. The art of Vanderbeek, Smith, Vacarro was a direct, almost physical assault on the retina, on the senses, with nothing left unsaid: you get it all or none at all. Nothing is concealed. In Heliczer's evening (and it's more proper to speak about it as an evening than "a work of art") was mysterious, ambiguous, suggestive, indirect. And it is here that the kinesthetic experience begins to connect with the poetic experience—which, for me, is a higher and more subtle art than just a pure kinesthetic experience—as far as my thinking and feeling goes.

---

December 2, 1965

The unusual festival of film happenings at the Cinematheque is continuing. When they are bad, they are very bad; when they are good, they are almost great. Last week, Ken Dewey, Dick Higgins, Ed Emshwiller, Gerd Stern, Ken Jacobs, and, less intensely, Jackie Cassen, Aldo Tambellini, Elaine Summers, and Ray Wisniewski continued the series of new visual discoveries.

Ed Emshwiller remains the craftsman and the scientist of the avant-garde cinema. His piece *Body Works* may be not only the best piece he has ever done, but also the first successful attempt at cinema ballet. Whereas most of the other filmmakers who use multiple projections leave a lot to chance, Emshwiller presented a completely controlled and almost scientifically planned work that was dazzling in its visual effects. He played tricks with our eyes, with our vision, with the depth of field, with the long shots and close-ups; right there before our eyes he snapped his fingers and the dancer changed into a skeleton or became a huge hand or became two dancers.

Gerd Stern's evening was less dazzling but it was more beautiful for the eye. Here again was a planned presentation of multiple imagery (defraction boxes, strobes, carousel projectors, live action) but with enough holes for chance so that the effect wasn't as scientifically abstract as that of Emshwiller. Stern is more attracted by the soft and pictorial conglomerations of light, color, and motion. He admits being greatly influenced by Marshall McLuhan. Their complete trust in McLuhan permitted them (Gerd Stern and his collaborators, Michael Callahan, Brian Peterson, and Jud Yalkut) to abandon themselves completely, not to bother about what art or cinema is, and work on this sensuous sea of color, motion, and light that seems to surround us completely and we swim in it almost bodily, and it is like going through the most fantastic dream.

I state here openly, I admit that I have experienced subtle aesthetic illuminations during Dick Higgins, Gerd Stern, Ken Dewey, and Ed Emshwiller shows, and my aesthetic senses are not easy to please: I have spent thirty years of my life doing nothing but perfecting these senses. I realize perfectly that there are many questions to be asked here concerning this festival, and I will be asking them later, at the end of this by now revolutionary festival —questions that will begin with What Is Art? What Should Art Do? etc. etc.—but at this time I would like to remain chronicler, albeit an emotional one.

Ken Jacobs—who, with his ten unfinished (money, money, money) films, is probably the least known, although one of the most productive (creative), beautiful, and influential of modern filmmakers —gave us a strange piece, as part of the festival, a political romance performed as a shadow-and-light play (and some color prisms).

Ken Dewey's piece wasn't a shadow play, but it was shadowy from somewhere deep, or far, repeating and overlapping itself, and there was light going on and off, and when it was on, you could see four or five women standing on a white stage, all white like milk, five women in milk and in wedding gowns, like in a store window on a misty morning, with streets

still empty, in Williamsburg, Brooklyn; and it was a sad piece. The voice said, and repeated in a thousand different ways and shades and phrases: "I." "That's not you." "It's me." ("I have great respect for an artist who is as nervous as he is," said D a v i d B r o o k s, and he has studied more F r e u d and psychology than I.) And the movies were running along the ceiling, the most perfect use of the inside of the theatre I have ever seen—Dewey used the ceiling beams as screens, breaking the image into four or five depth levels. He also defracted light through the carefully placed and angled mirrors on the sides and the back of the theatre and they caught, at certain moments, glimpses of light and images creating an almost ecstatically beautiful pure crystal light experience that sounded like Mozart; I could almost write down the notes.

But the thing I wanted to say at this point is really this: Ken Jacobs, by making his show into a shadow play, pointed out, intentionally or not—and he has always been right—the direction most of the artists at this strange festival have been moving in, many different directions and through many different and complicated side routes: the art of the shadow play.

Permit my insane head a few heresies: Isn't it possible that CINEMA is really nothing new? Isn't it possible that the art which we thought was Our Art, the twentieth-century art, isn't our art at all? Isn't it possible that the shadow-and-light artists of Persia, of China, of India were the real masters, the real magicians of the art of light, motion, and image? How little we know about it. Aren't we coming back to it, though, closer and closer to it, as the least naturalistic, as the most stylized, most controlled art of telling stories and creating magic through light, motion, and images?

When I watched the shows of Ken Jacobs, Gerd Stern, Don Snyder, Stan Vanderbeek, Jack Smith, Emshwiller, Tambellini, or Jackie Cassen, I suddenly saw them as the new shadow play magicians. I felt that there was practically nothing that couldn't be done by a shadow artist. The motion-picture camera can be eliminated from most of these shows with new gains for the creative imagination. I am exaggerating now, no doubt, to make my point, but what I saw with my dazed head was the rebirth of this forgotten art of the past, the art of shadow play that will become, during the next few years, the controversial challenger of cinema as we know it today, and a new source of inspiration. Not that it will push out the cinema as we know it today— but it will make it look like only one, and perhaps not the largest, part of the art of motion, light, and image. The ground is shaking and the cinema we knew is collapsing, the screen, the projector, the camera, and all. Suddenly, and without any bang (I am the only bang) the entire so-called Underground avant-garde cinema has shifted in time and space and has become a part of classical cinema, for our own and our children's enjoyment. The new avant-garde of cinema (light play) has moved ten years forward, into new explorations, and, if you'll permit me to contradict Marshall McLuhan, what the artists are doing ... their dreams are so much farther advanced than the rest of human activities that it will take at least another ten years to catch up with the artist and create proper tools to enable him to put those dreams into reality.

---

December 23, 1965

In my last column I did not have time to report on the closing program of the New Cinema Festival I at the Cinematheque, but I should mention it now since it was one of the most successful programs of the festival. (It was repeated last week.) Each of the artists—Oldenburg, Rauschenberg, Whitman—came with beautifully conceived and executed pieces. Oldenburg's *Movie House* piece was performed in the seats of the theatre, while the audience stood in the aisles. A group of performers sat in the seats watching a movie (light without film, projected from a low angle, so that the heads of the "audience" often came on the screen); they moved from place to place, restless, as people do, smoking a lot, carrying packages and bundles and shopping bags; a man tried to drag a bicycle across the seats: a colorful medley of people from various walks of life. It was all pure Oldenburg; a Movie House poem of sorts, like all Oldenburg happenings usually are—poetic essences of very concrete daily realities; a look at the familiar from a poet's distance.

*Perfect Clarity*
Robert Rauschenberg presented a motion-dance-objects piece, *Map Room II*, with images, objects, compositions, and symbols reminding us of his work in painting, but also different—I thought it was more like seeing his very personal autobiography put here on stage, everything executed with perfect precision and clarity that contained a certain classical D a V i n c i-like beauty.

Robert Whitman's show combined live action with the filmed image. He played his performers against the images, for humor and for surprise (the same performers appeared in the film on the stage). Like any good magician, he had a good bag of tricks ready; as an artist, he let the tricks fail, sort of, and used their imperfections as a formal quality. Still,

Whitman's show, very often, came close to being just a display of virtuosity; it was more on the slick side than any other of his shows I have seen—I mean, it was less ambiguous, more one-dimensional. But it was beautiful, nevertheless, and something completely new in movie-theatre experience. Only Emshwiller matches him in the effective and planned use of cinema for surprise's sake. That is also the main weakness of both artists, perhaps, this surprise effect—for once it is gone, much is gone.

I couldn't say it about Rauschenberg's show, though, and particularly about one, and the most memorable single, image (or moment) of this—or any other—festival: his "neon stick" walk across the stage which amazingly and ingeniously combined formal beauty and richness of meaning. As an image it can never be erased from one's memory. In this walk, in this image, Rauschenberg has created one of the richest visual metaphors I have seen in all my movie-theatregoing experience. What that metaphor exactly means ... it could mean many things, and a different thing to each of us—but none can remain unmoved by it.

February 3, 1966

For some time now a visiting
Englishman by the name of
John Jones has been spying on
American arts. He has been
studying art galleries, coming
to see the Underground movies,
getting to know the artists themselves. He even persuaded Claes
Oldenburg to collaborate on
a movie called *Claes Oldenburg
Hangs a Picture*. Since so many
other painters, sculptors, and
even playwrights (LeRoi Jones,
for instance) are setting up
studios with lights and cameras,
ready to move into cinema—
I got interested in what kind of
thinking is going on in their heads.
Here are some notes I received
from Claes Oldenburg on … *Hangs
a Picture*.

"This film is an effort to
translate my happening aesthetic
into film. My happenings are
usually concerned more with
the objects that occur than with
events. (In fact, object worshipping
is how I understand the happening.) Time is drawn out in order
that objects appear more clearly.
This is done by repetition, use
of slow motion, and producing
a container of stillness which
includes the spectator.

One effect I have been able
to do only imperfectly in happenings is the close-up, which is an
extremely suggestive technique
in exploring the object. In Chicago,
during the happening 'Gayety,'
by means of an opaque projector
on the screen. I cast giant close-
ups of actual objects in motion
on a screen over the spectators,
a sort of concrete movie. The
film gives me the use of intimate
close-up—to me it's the most
important substance of film."

*Rotating Viewpoint*
"Film also gives me the rotating
viewpoint in this film—the viewpoint in this film (*Claes Oldenburg
Hangs a Picture*) is to be absolutely free and not have to explain
itself. Of course the time is easily
controllable and the concentration
space is established by the dark-
ened theatre conditions. It amazes
me that in film it can take so
long to document (or rather reveal)
a simple thing. A happening
lasting twenty minutes would take
a year to explore (I mean not
the act of filming, but the resulting
detail on film). The effects are
in fact wasted in a happening (as
in daily life) which remains in the
memory as a vague impression.
I would like to create an absolutely
clear memory from all sides,
in all imaginative dimensions,
of an utterly simple object.

As it turned out the subject
of this film, the hanging of a
picture, is much more complex
than John or I imagined. This film
might be regarded as a potential
still to be filmed. I certainly
felt the epical fatigue as I stood
on the shores of the floor repeating that long, long journey
to the wall, my Hercules hammer
in hand. Anyway, the driving

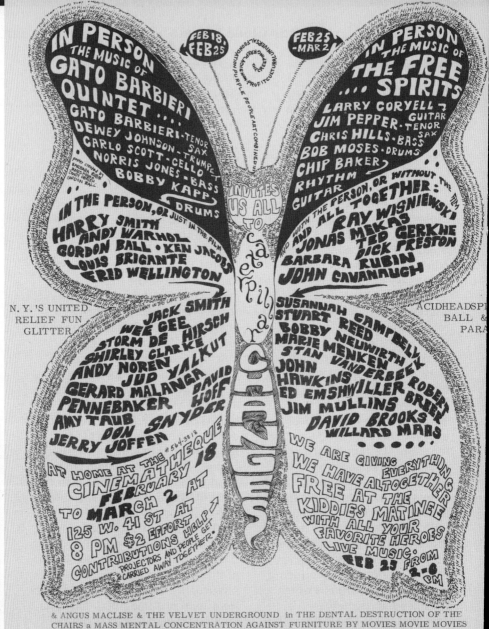

of a nail would have been suf-
ficient, or the turning of a door-
knob for the twenty-minute
length."

*Film Removed*
"The sound in this film is supplied
by a magnification of the projector sound, an attempt to draw

the act of the film showing into the documentary revelation as was done in *Movie House,* in which the film was removed, the better to concentrate on the details of its projection and its audience."

As you can see, there is some new excitement coming to cinema, from new people. As for the others, you should try to see more of the current Andy Warhol productions. After traveling across the entire history of movies—after going through the silent movie period (*Sleep, Eat, Blowjob*), the early sound period (*Harlot, Juanita De Castro*), and after making some of the best "cinéma vérité" examples in this country (*The Poor Little Rich Girl, Screen Test, My Hustler*), Warhol has now entered into no man's land. His two latest works, *Paul Swan* and *Edith Sedgwick* (double-screen projections), are among the most important new works I have seen anywhere. Basically, both films are portraits. Warhol may be the greatest portraitist living. The portrait of Edith Sedgwick, with four faces (and four soundtracks) projected at the same time (a combination of rear-screen projection, video-tape, and actual filming) belongs to the best cinema made today, and, it is also possible, marks one of the climaxes in Warhol's creative work.

Stan Brakhage, too, has been making film portraits (on 8mm) for some time now. What Warhol and Brakhage have in common (besides being great artists) is the incredible amount of work they manage to turn out without losing quality. The new form, the portrait in cinema, has lately inspired them to produce an amazing series of irreplaceable documents of our times. The air is full of excitement! French newspapers are full of headlines about the crisis of cinema.

SUGGESTIONS: See the animated film series at the Museum of Modern Art this and next week; *Claes Oldenburg Hangs a Picture* this Saturday and Sunday matinee at the Cinematheque; also don't miss Bruce Baillie's *Quixote,* his most beautiful work to date, this Friday and Saturday at the Cinematheque. Buy the English edition of *Cahiers du Cinéma.*

---

February 17, 1966

A few months ago, when writing on the Psychedelic Theatre, I stated, or I thought, that what some of the drug users take for an expanded consciousness is only an expanded eye, an increased ability of seeing.

Since then, I had other occasions to think about this subject. One day, a young avant-garde woman playwright, after looking at some of Stan Brakhage's movies, walked out muttering that "these films do not increase man's consciousness; they are only for the eyes." It was the typical reaction of someone used to thinking and seeing in literal, not visual, terms, one who confuses cinema with literature. "You mean," I asked her, "that your vision, your eyes have nothing to do with your consciousness? Does your consciousness exist separately from your eye? And what about music? Is music only for your ears? Is your consciousness connected with your ears?" What is consciousness really, that big word? Every one of our many senses is a window to the world and to ourselves. The eye, liberated from the inhibitions of seeing, gives us a new understanding of the world. This liberation of the eye can be done by drugs, or by an education through the mind—this is really Gerald Oster's subject. A good deal of research is being done these days in this neglected area.

The other day William Vehr screened his new film, *Brothel*. Something bothered me about this film. It seemed to be so rich in textures, in colors, that at some point I had to walk out. Then I came back again and I watched some more. I told this to Bill Vehr. "For over a year now I have been studying the arts of India," he said. "I found there something in common, spiritually, with what I want to do. I conceive, or I make my films like tapestries. They could be watched like Oriental tapestries. My film is an ornament in time, a film tapestry woven with bodies, close-ups of materials, drapes, costumes, and blotches of color, joined together by the continuous movement of the camera. I never stay too long on one detail or one face. This face, this figure, never becomes a character, a person— the camera keeps floating in and out, it goes up the shoe, up the leg, up the hand, across the eyes, and on the bracelet—this tapestry has really no end and no beginning, it could go on like this for ever and ever. Isn't it legitimate in art to do something like this?" "It is perfectly legitimate," I admitted. God hasn't written with fire on the sky that cinema (or any art) is only this or that. Only history is finite, not the future."

How do we look at a piece of tapestry?—I reasoned further. Do we look for more of the same, or do we rest our eyes, turning from one kind of design or color to another? There is a rhythm, a spacing, that we do with our own eyes (plus, nature has provided us with blinking). Now, this film is in front of our eyes all the time. Brakhage told his audience while introducing *The Art of Vision* (which runs over four hours) that they are welcome to walk out at some intervals if they feel like doing so—he has done so himself—and then come back and watch more. It could even be projected (as he has done) in one's own home, in the evening, as you do some other things at the same time. Like looking at a piece of tapestry, then looking at somebody in the room, or at the window, then looking again at the tapestry. Can we appreciate cinema that way? It seems it's possible.

```
                    PRESS
                    FOR IMMEDIATE RELEASE


        The Underground will present a festival of movies, slides, film
loops, jazz, rock, et al.  The artists, led by Barbara Rubin, plan to
topple the current concept of theatre and movie house by placing the
musicians in the middle of five screens (one on the floor!) and seating
the audience on large palettes instead of the conventional rows of seats.
Featured are top jazz saxophonist Gato Barbieri and his quintet and the
exciting new rock sound The Free Spirits, plus films by leading under-
ground movie-makers; among them Andy Warhol (responsible for "The Chelsea
Girls"), Jack Smith, Ed Emshwiller, Jonas Mekas, and Miss Rubin.
        It's all part of the radical new programs being presented at the
Film-Makers' Cinematheque, 125 W. 41, under the title "Catepillar
Changes".  There will be shows nightly at 8 p.m. from Saturday, Feb. 18th,
thru March 2nd.  Tickets, priced at $2, will go on sale each evening
one hour before the performance.
        On Saturday, Feb. 25th, there will be a special matinee (the
"kiddie" show),from 2 to 6 p.m., for which admission will be free.
(Attendance is limited to 200.)

                For further information, call 564-3818 after 3 p.m.




TO THE PRESS
        ON FEB. 18th to MARCH 2nd at the CINEMATHEQUE 125 west 41st STREET
FROM 8PM ON WE ARE HAVING NEW YORK'S FIRST UNITED ACIDHEADSPEED RELIEF
FUN BALL & GLITTER PARADE.  IN THE DENTAL DESTRUCTION OF THE CHAIRS
A MASS MENTAL CONCENTRATION AGAINST FURNITURE INSTIGATED BY THEIR
PRESENCE BY ANGUS MACLISE & THE VELVET UNDERGROUND WITH THE CONTRIBUTIONS
OF THEIR MOVIES, SLIDES, LOOPS, PROJECTORS, & MADNESS OF HARRY SMITH
ANDY WARHOL RAY WISNIEWSKI JONAS MEKAS TED GERHKE STEWART REED GORDON
BALL LOUIS BRIGANTE KEN JACOBS FRED WELLINGTON MATT HOFFMAN DICK PRESTON
JOHN CAVANAUGH JACK SMITH PIERO HELICZER SUSANNAH CAMPBELL BOBBY NEUWIRTH
DAVID THURMAN AMY TAUBIN RICHARD FORMAN GERARD MALANGA STORM DE HIRSCH
WEE GEE ANDY NOREN SHIRLEY CLARKE JUD YALKUT PENNEBAKER DAVID HOFF DON
SNYDER JERRY JOFFEN MARIE MENKEN JIM MULLINS ED EMSHWILLER STAN VANDERBEEK
HOHN HAWKINS ROBERT BREER JERRY HYLER WILLARD MAAS DAVID BROOKS BARBARA
RUBIN PLUS IN PERSON THE MUSIC OF GATO BARBIERI QUINTET & THE FREE SPIRITS
& JUST ABOUT ANYONE ELSE YOU CAN THINK OF FOR 12 DAYS IN THE MASS LOVE
CONTEST "SMOTHER ME".  WE EXTEND AN INVITATION TO YOU GLADLY THOUGH I
SINCE OUR LAST MEETING AT THE EVENING OF NAM JUNE PAIK & CHARLOTTE
MOORMAN WE WILL HAVE TO MAINTAIN BETTER THE er THE ER OF THE BUILDING
& THE FIRE & THE LICENSE DEPARTMENTS SUGGESTIONS THOUGH AGAIN  WE CAN
NOT GUARANTEE WE WILL COMPILETE THIS SHOW EITHER.  & PLEASE BRING YOUR
WIFE GIRLFRIEND CHILDREN FRIENDS & ALL TO OUR MATINEE PERFORMANCE ON
FEB. 25 th STARTING AT 2 pm love & kisses   ALL OF US
```

Barbara Rubin's announcement for her Expanded Cinema / Mixed Media Caterpillar Changes show, Film-Makers' Cinematheque. New York, 1966

We are only begging to find out these things. These are all new aspects of cinema. It is perfectly legitimate, as an aesthetic experience (or, simply, as an experience) and as cinema, to have screenings in open rooms in which you wander in and out, where movies, Bill Vehr's or Andy Warhol's or almost anybody's, are being projected continuously. We cannot measure or judge, evaluate all cinematic creations according to the established theatrical motion-picture viewing conditions and traditions.

When U S C O had their show, not very long ago, at the Cinematheque, they stressed their anonymity. "In a world of simultaneous operations, you do not have to be first to be on the top," said the program note. This is another idea that is floating around lately. It is no great surprise today to see a college literary magazine with no names of the authors printed next to the poems. Andy Warhol doesn't sign or title his movies—the idea that there is no art, that everything is craft, and that all art is bourgeois (says Fluxus), is becoming more and more prevalent with the spreading of psychedelic drugs and with the dissemi-

nation of Oriental philosophies. What we do existed before us; we have seen it in our dreams or in other lives; identities can be exchanged; nothing new is created or added to what already exists; everything is an illusion; there is no beginning and no end, no top and no bottom.

However, even if the word "art" is replaced with the word "craft," we end up at the same place: the best craftsman is the most honored man, the most sought-out man—whether he makes a painting, or an everyday utensil, a vase, a Brillo box, or a chair. And then, every great craftsman at a certain point loses his awareness of how he does it: he just does it. The good thing about this is that, once the name of an artist is dropped, once the works of art begin to float freely as pieces of craft not attached to any name, we'll be forced, gradually, to acquire a truer, a better knowledge of what a good craft (art) is: we'll have to make all the choices ourselves, there will be no name mystique or prestige attached to the artifact to help us. In other words: no more snobbery. The general level of taste, the appreciation of the beautiful, should, therefore, increase.

---

May 26, 1966

Suddenly, the intermedia shows are all over town. At t h e  D o m (Jackie Cassen and USCO); at

the  C h e e t a h; at the Martinique Theatre (Robert Whitman); at the Riverside Museum (USCO); at the Cinematheque ( K o s u g i). There were artists working with sound-light multiple projections for a good ten years (USCO gave its first performances in SF in 1959)—but they remained in experimental, semi-private stages until the Expanded Cinema survey at the Cinematheque last autumn. When I first planned the survey, the idea was to pull out these artists, whose work I had followed privately for years, into the light of day, and see how they will hold. I felt that without such an exposure they were beginning to lose the perspective of what they were doing. Thus Pandora's box was opened.

The Plastic Inevitables (Velvet Underground, Warhol and Company) performances at the Dom during the month of April provided the most violent, loudest, most dynamic exploration platform for this new art. The strength of the Plastic Inevitables, and where they differ from all the other intermedia shows and groups is that they are dominated by the ego. Warhol, this equivocal, passive crystal, has attracted to himself the most egocentric personalities and artists. The auditorium, every aspect of it—singers, light throwers, strobe operators, dancers—is screaming at all times with an almost screeching, piercing personality pain; it could also be called desperation. In any case, it is the last stand of the ego, before it either breaks down or goes to the other side. Although there are intermedia shows, the Plastic Inevitables remains the most dramatic expression of the contemporary generation—the place where its needs and desperations are most dramatically split open.

At the other, almost opposite end, is the USCO show (at the Riverside Museum)—the show that sums up everything that USCO has done till now, and one of the shows that I ask you not to miss. The Riverside Museum show (as was the USCO show at the Cinematheque and the current Long Island show) is a search for religious, mystical experience. Whereas in the case of Plastic Inevitables the desire for mystical experience is subconscious, USCO is going after it in a more conscious way. They have arrived somewhere, and gained a certain peace, certain insights, and now they are beginning to meditate.

Nevertheless, I often get the impression that the mystical, meditative mood of many of the friends that I meet in psychedelic circles is really not the beginning of the new age or new cosmic consciousness but the sunset peace of the Age of Pisces, of the Christian era—the sunset meditation. At the Plastic Inevitables, however, the dance floor and the stage are charged with the electricity of a dramatic break just before the dawn. There is emptiness with ugly stuff oozing out just before the dawn. If at the USCO show I feel surrounded by the tradition, by the past, by the remnants of the Oriental

religions, at the Plastic Inevitables
it is all Here and Now and
the Future.

The Dom, after the Plastic
Inevitables left for California, was
taken over by women. Although
USCO has a hand in it, it is practically run by Jackie Cassen and
her team. The show falls somewhere between USCO and the
Inevitables. There is the ego and
a touch of perversion coming
from the performers; and there
is the mystical tendency on
the dance floor and in the visuals
—the kind of color abstraction
and pattern play that by now
has come to be known as "psychedelic." Although much frantic
movement and color and light
play is going on, the show is
peaceful, ornamental, and femi-
nine, most of the time.

The Cheetah provides the
most curious use of the intermedia. Whereas the Dom and
USCO shows are restricted (or
became restricted) to the in-circle,
Cheetah was designed for the
masses. An attempt was made to
go beyond the personal, beyond
the ego, to reach the impersonal,
abstract, universal. The smoky
color patterns, the hugeness
of the place, the shiny aluminum
reflector sheets create an impersonal, metallic feeling—as
opposed to the sexuality and
emotionalism of the USCO shows.
One could say that the feeling
at the Cheetah is one of being
OUT—beyond both, USCO and
Warhol—in those regions where

both the mystic preoccupations
and the ego are abandoned, where
you disappear and become zero;
no more empty body moving to and
fro to the rhythms of the amazing
Chambers Brothers in the
grey twilight of the dance floor.

Very often while watching
these shows, I ask myself: What
are all these lights doing? What
is the real meaning of the strobes?
Where is all this coming from
or going to? Do any of the artists
know the meaning and effect
and power (both healing and dam-
aging) of colors and lights? I have
noticed, very often, how suddenly,
during certain surges of colors
and lights, I become electrified,
my nerves become jumpy as
if somewhere deep inside I were
pierced with a knife; or, at other
times, suddenly the peace surrounds and takes me over. The
same with the new sounds.

Yes, but that's partially what
this is all about: we are over the
first, experimental, private stage.
Now we are thrown into the open,
to find out what this is all about,
what it's doing to us. Man will find
out soon what the light is all about;
what the color is all about; what
the movement is all about. The
Pandora's box of light and color
and motion has been opened
because the time was ready for
it. There are moments, at the
Dom, and at the Riverside Museum,
when I feel I am witnessing the
beginnings of new religions, that
I find myself in religious, mystical
environments where the cere-

monials and music and body movements, the symbolism of lights and colors are being discovered and explored. The very people who come to these shows have all something of a religious bond among them. Something is happening and is happening fast —and it has something to do with light, it has everything to do with light—and everybody feels it and is in waiting, often desperately.

---

June 16, 1966

A few weeks ago, I raised a question: What is the strobe light all about? The strobe has been on my mind for some time now, as it has been on the minds of many other people I know. Last week, while talking with Steve Durkee, who is responsible for much of the USCO show, a few new thoughts came on the subject.

### JONAS

We keep asking this question, "What's the strobe all about?" because in a sense, the strobe dramatizes the intermedia, the light shows. One could even say that it dramatizes the light itself.

### DURKEE

Strobe is the digital trip. In other words, what the strobe is basically doing, it's turning on and off, completely on and completely off. You can't do it with incandescent light, you can only do it with gas. It goes on and off, on and off. It creates a discontinuance so that it looks like the flicks. It's real, no question about its reality; but so far as what it's doing—we know little about it.

### JONAS

Since there is nothing but white light in it, it represents —as some people feel about it—the point of death, or nothingness.

### DURKEE

Death? Yeah. We live in a world of magicians, really. What humans have learned to do is to tap into the fifth element, or ether, into this fantastic energy source, and they draw from it for their own use—that's what we see manifested in electricity. I don't think about it either as negative or

positive—just an energy that is all around us. We use strobes,
and they turn a lot of people off. A lot of people think
about it as about DMT: a very metallic, harshly synthetic
type of thing. But, then again, it is perhaps only a question
of acclimatization. Fifty years from now, everybody may
be living with strobe lights. These things are hard to tell.
But that death thing is certainly part of it. The On and
Off. Actually, almost all electric lights go on and off sixty
times a second anyway, that's how they operate, the cycle
alternation. But the incandescence itself—the filament
in the bulb holds the light so that you don't get that harsh
on and off. What do you think about strobes?

JONAS

I am still thinking about it.

DURKEE

Do you like them?

JONAS

They don't bother me. I have met a number of people who
have, they say, gained much from various aspects of the
intermedia shows. But the strobe always bothers them. Some
of them feel that there is something almost evil about it.
But how could the light be evil? But then, when we talk about
light we usually think about the sun, and there is warmth in
the sun. The strobe is cold. But it's always there, at whatever
intermedia show you go to—it's always there, in one form
or another—sometimes for rhythmical reasons, sometimes
to create the illusion of motion. Maybe it's something that
joins cinema and whatever else it is.

DURKEE

The best use I have seen of strobes was at the Trips Festival
(at the Dom) where they had them hung up on wires, and
something that looked like shower curtains, and people would
go inside and dance, under the strobes, and you could see
the incredible scenes of these people, inside. And I began
thinking about them as showers, electrical showers. You
go inside this thing and you go through the whole thing and
you come out.

JONAS

On the dance floor, under the strobes, very often you lose
the sense of the musical rhythm, you pick up the strobe
rhythm, instead—you can't even hear the sound, you lose
the sense of sound ...

DURKEE

... or who you are—because all you see are fragments
of yourself. It's really like being in a movie.

JONAS

You become a particle, a grain of the movie. Maybe that's
what it is. We are cut by strobe light into single frames,
to eight frames per second or whatever the strobe frequency
is, on and off ...

DURKEE

... like movies become real ...

JONAS

Maybe only now some clarity is beginning to emerge about
what cinema is all about. Or, perhaps, the matter's about
being confused completely. For eighty years now all we hear
and see is cinema, cinema, cinema, but we know nothing
about why it came into existence, from what deep human
or cosmic necessity, and why it came at the end of the
Piscean Age. What's the meaning of our becoming single
frames?

DURKEE

It is hard to understand the meaning but it certainly seems
to be what's happening.

JONAS

Spirituality? Dissolving all the points of hard resistance,
both of matter and mind? So that every reality that is here
like a rock is being atomized? You know, we started with
a simple screen and one-long-take images; then we started
superimposing images; triple superimpositions; then two,
three, eight screens; single frames; superimpositions were
further atomized, spiritualized by silk screens and colored
veils and soundtracks. Now we've left the screen, the film,
and we come down to ourselves; with strobes we cut our-

selves into single frames, like some symbolic or magic
gesture or ritual. Is this a desire to reach other dimensions,
to go beyond our skins? Or just the opposite?

DURKEE

Still, some people are really turned off by strobes.

JONAS

But it's very possible that those are the fears of something
incoming. We are going into a more spiritual age and there
is a fear of losing the old bag with all the junk that's in it
—a fear of death of the old. So it's evil, they say—that's how
big the fear is. But light shouldn't create fear if you're open
to light. It creates fear only if one holds out against it. To
me evil is, in art or life, only what keeps us rotating in the
same place like the record that gets stuck in the same groove.
But in the intermedia shows, the strobe opens us. In any
case, I don't see how it could set any aspect of us back, even
if it's just one day back. I see our understanding and knowledge of it only opening, like the very fact that we are talking
about it, and thinking about it, and reacting to it—and not
only you or me, but everybody. That means we are going
to find it out, that's all. It helps to see ourselves in a new way.
Again, like Andy Warhol's movie *Eat*, where you see a man
eating a mushroom for forty-five minutes. Now we are beginning to see ourselves in a different perspective, or in no
perspective at all, perhaps—in the simultaneity of distances
—like looking at ourselves from outside and inside at the
same time, out of our own body—learning again everything
from the beginning. Or something like that. In any case,
it's exciting. Like going to the first grade.

---

June 23, 1966

Last Thursday I was watching
the Beverly Schmidt *Moon-Dial*
piece at the Bridge Theatre.
     It was often a breathtakingly
beautiful performance. But that's
not what I really wanted to write
about this time. It's something
else. In the middle of the performance, during one of its most
culminating passages, I turned
around for a moment and looked
where the slides were, and the
projectors were set behind the
audience's backs. And I saw this
amazing, almost phantastic thing
happening: I saw both Tambellinis
immersed in a deep dance of
their own, moving, with handheld

projectors and slides, shaking, and trembling, no longer conscious of themselves. And when I looked at their faces, they were going through similarly fantastic changes and it seemed that the things on stage were directly, physically connected with their fingertips, their face movements, with their very flesh—and it went deeper, through their flesh to their souls: every light trembling, every motion that took place on the stage was produced directly, by this fantastic action-reaction.

And I remembered how, just last weekend at the Philadelphia College of Art, Sol Mednick was saying that he felt that one of the things that cinema will probably never have is that tactile feeling, that energy that sparks when a painter or a sculptor presses his brush or knife against his materials—the tactile interaction which produces a very direct relationship and enables him to completely transmit his temperament and his feelings through that brush or that knife into that canvas or that wood.

And I remember Stan Brakhage telling (and I think he writes about it in *Metaphors on Vision*) how, in his earlier years, he used to spend hours every day, moving in his rooms with an empty camera, and how those who come to the Cinematheque often watch with amazement as John Cavanaugh goes through his strange performances in the lobby with an empty camera.

David Brooks used to do that, and Jerry Joffen, and Ron Rice. And I have seen Barbara Rubin going through an entire evening of shooting with an empty camera; or the amazing performances of Ray Wisniewski during his multiple projections.

*All That Horror*
Here is another aspect where new cinema differs from traditional cinema—in this direct relationship between the artist, his tools, and his materials. I have said before that the camera has become an extension of the artist's fingers and the lens, his third eye. I remember, after shooting *The Brig*, walking for weeks, trying to get out of the trance into which I was pulled during the shooting —I absorbed with my body all that horror myself. Judith Malina thought—or was it Miss Hecht who said it—that I wasn't really shooting but performing one of the strangest dances they ever saw.

The essential point here is that this is not one-sided activity: it's an interaction. The camera movements are reflections of the body movements; the body movements are the reflections of the emotional and thought movements—which, in their turn, are caused by what came in through the eye. A circle between the artist's eye and the camera eye is established.

None of this is entirely new in arts. All that I'm saying is that it's new in a different way. One can imagine D. W. Griffith standing beside his camera during the take of a scene, and, while the camera grinds, going himself with his face and his body and hands through all that's happening in front of the camera, becoming almost an electrical cable connected with the camera—although it doesn't touch it, it's there, objectified, removed, transposed. It's what one could perhaps call an epical removal, as compared with the direct contact of a more personal creation. Both are eternal.

*First Time*

No, this isn't new. But for the first time we were seeing it happen in cinema in such an intense manner. There was always this personal relationship—but the frequency, the intensity, was different. Through the intermedia projections it has come out. Really, what's happening is that some of the work of Harry Smith, of Jerry Joffen, or Robert Whitman or Barbara Rubin or Andy Warhol cannot be shipped and shown in a film can: their projections have become extensions of their creative work, the film in the can isn't really the thing by itself.

This spring, the Cannes film festival wrote to me asking to suggest what new American films they could show in the critic's section. Could I ship some films to them, they asked. No—I wrote to them—your thinking is all wrong: you are still thinking, that all that's good and new and exciting in cinema can be wrapped up, canned, and shipped to you for "previewing": those days are gone. Some of us are making "film evenings," not "films," and you have to take to Cannes not only the "film" but the filmmaker, all the equipment and, perhaps, technicians. I suggested to them a few programs to take that would shake up Cannes. My suggestions were, naturally, ignored, and Cannes had another of its "worst" years.

That's what's happening.

That's what I thought in that one second just before I turned back from the Tambellinis to the stage where Beverly Schmidt was moving, surrounded by a web of light.

# Texts on Ken Jacobs

June 25, 1985

Dear Ken:
I don't think I'll have time to decently sit down, relax, take time, and write about your last show at the Whitney (*Making Light of History: The Philippines Adventure*). I have to give up such an idea. Until the Courthouse is done & open, I won't have such time. I dream luxuries of time ...

So I'll drop you a few stenographic notes, instead. To begin with, what you're doing is so uncompromising, and so pure—pure cinema, I mean—actually, probably, whatever is pure as cinema is also pure in every other way, too—the visual, kinematic activity achieved, created with an absolute minimum of image material is truly & absolutely incredible, when I begin to think of it. I saw something I've never seen before. The intensity of the experience of seeing it still vibrates within me. Like that other time, when I was seeing *Tom, Tom* for the first time.

A river of images, or maybe an ocean, irrationally/ it seemed/controlled, as they rolled and rolled and swerved and grew in intensity, swelling, swelling—and when I think that it was all achieved only by manipulation of two slightly different frames. You have prevailed, persisted, been driven to & by & gone through many searches, trails & trials, versions, pieces—to arrive at diamond cutter's perfection, in this work, in this stage of your, again, pioneering and ecstatic—no matter how lonely, misunderstood, and unappreciated—art—Ah? How does it feel to be a pioneer for the second, and third time?—in these days—years!—of miserable film wares, commerce, grant & foundation & NYSCA & NEA films—& fashions, vogues, vulgarity, pedestrianism—misery of images that we have on all "independent" and "media" screens—

To see your work was a feast which even now, after many days, weeks, yes, two months! is still continuing, deep, in my visual, sensual, kinetic memory—

I'd say, in this connection, that there are works that one likes and that survive in you, but they survive as some memorable bits, pieces, images, scenes, or maybe ideas—and then there are others which remain in you totally, as total experiences that change you, that remain in you as standards, measures of experience, cinema experience—and they totally change your perspective of what you see & how you see it, ever after—such was, for me, the experience of seeing your work that day at the Whitney—as the vulgus came in and walked out again and yapped & chewed cud—

      Jonas

*MONDAY, MAY 13, 1985*

## *Philippine Insurgency: No Easy Task*

Post Photo by Don Hale

Brig. Gen. Jaime Echeverria of the Philippine Army addressing residents of a village in Mindanao.

Collage by Ken Jacobs, 1985

Notes for Myself: First Draft

Ken Jacobs, *The Winter Footage* (1964)
(preamble to *The Sky Socialist*)
16 mm, silent, 24 f.p.s, 50 min, color. Edited 1984.
Viewed February 1986: seen twice.

Notes:
... about the human predicament ... people in some sort of predicament ... state of predicament ... like the beat. Ken may not want
to be associated with beat, but this work—and his early work in
general—contains some sort of quintessential beat ... the poetry
of the beat, the daily dregs. Poetry of the dregs. About people stuck
in loneliness ... the city ... feet walking the street, not exactly sure
which direction ... hesitations ... in some search for what? For the
answer to the predicament? ... in a way, lost, happy but lonely and lost
... fifty minutes of a huge epic ... back to the essence, to the roots ...
to the feet ... in between, there are shadows and patterns and
light play, between the people and the Dreg World ... and what Ken
films and the way he puts it together, some of the details, sometimes you think, ah, how could this ever work? But it works! It always
works, when Ken does it. Ultimate victory of art! The staged, the
invented and the real in perfect unity. Taking chances, always taking
chances ... feet in the snow.
    People don't play for the audience, they relate only to
the camera, they do everything for and with the camera, not with
or for the audience.
    Beat Surrealism??? Bob unfolding the pink stuff ...
and absurd ... broken umbrella ...
    ah, the loneliness of the '60s ... Storm and Louis by the
fire on some dreg street ... and so much love, so much love, or rather
loveliness ... this film is pure loveliness ... not in a candy cheap
way, but abstract, pure, uplifting, cleansing loveliness.

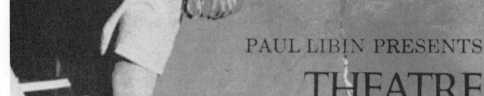

PAUL LIBIN PRESENTS

# THEATRE
# HAPPENINGS
## BY ROBERT WHITMAN

EVERY FRI., SAT. & SUN. AT 8:30   $2.50
MARTINIQUE THEATRE, 32nd & BROADWAY, PE 6-3056

Ken Jacobs: Star Spangled to Death

> 1957/2004. 6 hrs 30 min
> New York Film Festival 2003
> Rotterdam Film Festival 2004
> Anthology Film Festival May 2004

Organic, living organism that grew and grew over a period of forty-seven years.

Ken says, "The film is done; it weighed on me all those years." But I wouldn't take that for the last word. Maybe the only film I know is *Artaud: Monumental Song of Despair & Hope*.

Of epic proportions, incredibly complex in meanings. It's an absolute masterpiece that will be seen differently by every viewer. The greatest found-footage film. No found-footage film can be made after this one; add to it Joseph Cornell, Bruce Conner, Julius Ziz, and Bill Morrison. A film that contains some of the most cinematic and grotesque film material from the first hundred years of commercial cinema.

A film that is not about avant-garde. A film that is not like Brakhage or the last Bruce Elder, who create their own worlds of their own making. This one creates a world according to Ken Jacobs out of bits of the banal, clichéd, grotesque, vulgar, dripping sentimentality that is being sold to the people as real food and everybody feeds on it and even enjoys it and then dies.

Ken Jacobs: "It is a social critique picturing a stolen and dangerously sold-out America, allowing examples of popular culture to self-indict."

So Ken takes a knife and cuts it all open. Irreverently and lovingly and with the skill of a good surgeon, he reveals it all to us from the inside, and we do not know whether to laugh, cry, run out screaming, or applaud.

And there is Jerry and Jack wrapped in it all, trying to live in it, to exist one way or another—you have to be Jack to still dance through it all at the same time as you cry and starve. Yes, this is a film that sums it all up and you almost hate it, but at the same time you know it's all true, it's all true, this is all the America we live in, our home, the official America of the twentieth century, here it is on the plate, so eat it and then vomit it all out.

Luckily for me, this is not my America in this film: I live in another America, the America of my dreams.

Sunday Evening, September 3, 1995

Dear Ken:

I just heard, on the radio, a very exciting organ piece from the fifteenth century: an organ piece that has to be played together with the church bells, the bells of the church in which the organ is located. And the piece was played on the same fifteenth-century organ— because the little town, I think it's in Austria, has no money to replace the old organ with a new one. Supposedly, there were many pieces written for organ that are supposed to be played with the church bells ... Of course, this is nothing new to you, but it was to me ...

But the real reason why I am writing this little note is your *Marriage of Heaven and Hell*. I have several things to say about it, all of little importance, but I still have to say them:

1. I saw your piece without knowing its title and without any background information about sound or image. I have this weird habit not to read any program notes or ask any questions before I see anything. I just want to see the THING with no info.

2. I did not know Lucas was playing it live and therefore I thought you had it on tape ...

3. What I saw and heard was so incredibly magnificent, so powerful, and most deeply moving. Since I did not or could not iden-tify any images, I saw only shapes and fields of light and darkness, and I was trying to figure out what was happening and what was what. But I could not. So I gave it all up and just went with what I saw and what it did to me. And I had a very disturbing perception, feeling, of an incredible, Miltonian fight or struggle taking place right there on that screen there in front of my eyes, and intensified and underlined by Lucas. The struggle, the fight was almost painful. There was some-thing ominous in this fight, in the rhythms, frame struggles, and ocean-like recedings and swellings, it was Miltonian, it was. I think I find, or rather, I found, as I was sitting there, and later, walking home along the dreary streets, I thought I had just seen, experienced one of the greatest pieces of screen art, projection art, cinema art. Its uniqueness, its depth, its dramatic impact, its mystery, and its incredible reality!—how can I put it, I am running out of words.

4. I found out, after the show was over, that Lucas was making it all up right there, improvising, so to speak, going with it. I found that quite an incredible fact. He did an incredible job. That guy is an incredible musician.

5. Yesterday, at Anthology, I found your fax about the Knitting Factory show. I read the title of your piece: *The Marriage of Heaven and Hell*. Again, I could not believe what I read. Because

---

Review of *Thirties Man*, a mixed-media show by Ken Jacobs at Film-Makers' Cinematheque, May 1965

what I saw there, that afternoon / August 27th / was just that, just what you suggest in your title. I felt, when I saw it, I felt both Heaven and Hell there on the screen. What I did not read, or rather did not read literally, was the marriage. I saw it rather as a titanic struggle. But, of course, every marriage is a titanic struggle, and especially, that of Heaven and Hell, it must be, it must be—and you showed it, you showed how it really is—so thank you, Ken, thank you, Flo, thank you, Lucas!

Jonas


Evening—as usual—of April 10th, the year: 2001
(... now morning of 11th)


Dear Ken:
My nose is bleeding. So I thought I will write you this little letter. Because you are my nose-bleeding friend. I remember you told me that. I even filmed you showing your bleeding nose in Binghamton.

Anyway, as far as I can remember, age seven, age ten, age twelve, fifteen—my nose was always bleeding, once a month or so. I used to sit on a stone, in the fields, watching the cows, shepherd that I was, and the nose used to start bleeding. It was always so upsetting and mysterious because there was so much blood and I used to run home to my mother who did everything to stop the blood running, with cold water, pails and pails of bloody water, I still see those pails.

light theatre experimental

program 1  1967  final performances
the proliferation of the sun by otto piene
blackout by aldo tambellini
thursday april 20 at 8:30  10  11:30 pm
friday & saturday april 21 & 22 at 8  9:30  11 pm  $.

Show announcement of *Black Gate*, a theatre evening with plays by Otto Piene and Aldo Tambellini, Bridge Theatre, New York, 1967

Or lying on my back. Or stuffing the nose with cotton or some other stuff. But then it ran into my mouth. Ah, the smell of blood, I can still taste it in my mouth.

Anyway, it happened again and again.

All the blood I've left in the fields of my childhood, and in all the travels over Europe, wartime—not blood of war, but blood from my own nose, how pathetic …

Then it stopped. Maybe for three decades.

But now for the last few months, my nose decided to get back at her bloody works, and today, I was walking down Mulberry Street, and it started again. I tried to keep my head sort of up—people looked at me, they thought I was weird—but it kept running. I had a napkin in my pocket, now it was all bloody, and the people looked at me, they almost made a circle around me, who knows, this may be contagious, AIDS or something—but then it stopped. By the time I arrived at Anthology it was sort of OK.

Later I asked Hollis, do you know why my nose is bleeding? She thought, all her teachings tell her that there must be something in my nose that demands more blood, or too much blood, run into it. But when I was a child I don't remember anything being wrong with my nose except that bloody bleeding.

So I thought I'll write you this note, brother in bloody nose, brother of bleeding nose. Do you have any theories and explanations for why your nose used to bleed? Is it still bleeding, sometimes? Things like that. We just have too much blood, somehow. Why? Why? Why? Why aren't we like other normal human beings? It would be so nice …

Jonas

# 39 Notes on Dance

Summer 1967

1.

"Almost immediately a large moth fell at my feet, fluttering wildly. I said to Jane: 'What's that?' in a stupefied voice to which she immediately replied: 'It's a death dance.' It fluttered for fully twenty minutes before our dog ate it."
(Stan Brakhage in *Metaphors on Vision*)

2.

One could say: a line moves across the frame. Look, how
that line, how that leaf, that light, that woman moves
across the frame. Choreography of the frame. Everything
that moves has something to do with dance, has dance
in it, without really being "a dance."

3.

We have films entitle *Dance Lines*, *Dances of Machines*,
*Dance of the Inner Voice*.

4.

Rhythm in a film has more to do with music than with dance.

5.

Plastics (cineplastics) has something to do with dance.

6.

If I see one more film with a man or a woman in a black or
white leotard "dancing"—always a symbolic representation,
always a bad dancer—I'll reach for ...

7.

Dancers in movies should be naked.

8.

The subtlest dance qualities of a film come through the soul
of the director and the cameraman and only in the second
place through the actors.

9.

The movements of a filmmaker with the camera is a
dance. Stan Brakhage used to practice camera-dancing with
an empty camera every day. So do Jerry Joffen and
Barbara Rubin. Ray Wisniewski's performance with
handheld projectors at the Cinematheque, October 1965,
gave me one of the most memorable dance-watching experiences.

10.

"It was a dance, I was watching it like a dance,"
said Jenny Hecht after watching me shoot *The Brig*.

A still from Maya Deren's film
*Ritual in Transfigured Time*, 1946

### 11.

Dance-music-poetry-drama-sculpture-architecture-song-cinema are all different and separate art categories. Each of them expresses a different aspect of our soul. Dance has nothing to do with cinema, cinema has nothing to do with dance. Formally, I mean, as an art; otherwise, they all come from the same soul.

### 12.

Dance-music-poetry-drama-sculpture-architecture-song-cinema is going through a transition, its parts intermixing so as to rediscover their own true identity anew; all arts have become mixed media. We talk about expanded cinema, kinetic sculpture, three-dimensional painting. Cinema has everything to do with dance. Dance has everything to do with cinema.

13.

Dance is the human body in motion, "as the dancer
watches it" (Erick Hawkins). The material of dance
is the human body.

14.

The material of cinema is light in movement.

15.

Some filmmakers have attempted to create "dance films"—
films based on the principles of dance, those principles
understood (or misunderstood) as rhythm. Maya Deren
was much concerned with it. A few others are. Such films
always look like "films with dancers," films in which people
dance, or films in which pieces of film "dance."

16.

Brakhage in *Interim* didn't intend to make a dance film,
but the movements of the film, of the camera, of the protagonist are invested with dance feeling. There is a feeling of
dance created here without anybody really dancing in it or
wanting to make a "dance film."

17.

Homework: Observe how the film dances through the gate
of the projector.

18.

There are filmmakers who have filmed dances and who
wanted to remain "pure." Pure cinema, I mean. The
dance, usually, was destroyed. Many films, which could have
been useful and irreplaceable dance records for the film
student, have been destroyed by pretentious filmmakers not
humble enough to just film what they saw in a humble
Lumière-Chaplin-Warhol manner. Let the camera
be a loving tool, cinema a loving brother or sister to
the older art, the dance.

19.

Chaplin said that dance should be watched by the camera
with love and respect, as if from the audience seat. He did it
in *Limelight*, and it was beautiful.

20.

Some of the mixed media shows are really dance shows.
Mixed media is an "expanded cinema" if the cinema predominates; mixed media is a dance show if the dance
predominates. Elaine Summers's *Phantastic Gardens*
show at Judson Church in 1964, Ed Emshwiller's
mixed-media show at the Cinematheque in December 1965,
Robert Rauschenberg's mixed media show at the
Cinematheque in December 1965 were mixed-media dance
shows.

21.

Two most unique and most memorable and most perfect
pieces of mixed-media film dance were given by Beverly
Schmidt at the Bridge Theatre in July 1966, and by
Ed Emshwiller at the Cinematheque in December 1965.
The cinema medium was most perfectly, most ably, most
ingeniously harnessed to create original dance pieces
inconceivable without the assistance of cinema; light
projections were used to create a new kind of dance that
was both illusion and reality, shadow illusion and body
reality.

22.

I shouldn't forget to mention the work of Angus MacLise
and Jack Smith—their light-dance-sound-movie rituals
performed at the Cinematheque in 1965.

23.

The Jack Smith and Mario Montez dance sequence
on the roof in Bill Vehr's movie is one of the best pieces
of humorous dance I've seen in cinema. Also, Taylor
Mead in Paul Morrissey's *Taylor Mead Sings and
Dances*; also, the Jack Smith and Taylor Mead dance
sequence in Ron Rice's *The Queen of Sheba Meets the
Atom Man*.

24.

*Chumlum* has a feeling of an Oriental dream dance.

25.

*The Brig* has a feeling of a Dance of Death.

### 26.

We also say: He danced his life away.

### 27.

We also say: This piece of sculpture is poetry (it evokes
a feeling of poetry.) Some films evoke a feeling of dance.
The films of Ernst Lubitsch and the early films
of René Clair dance.

### 28.

Or Marie Menken. Her camera dances. *Arabesque
for Kenneth Anger*, or *The Bagatelle for Willard Maas*.
Brakhage and Menken, and perhaps Jack Smith: three
camera dancers.

### 29.

Also Ken Jacobs: the sequence with children in *Little
Stabs at Happiness* is one of the most beautiful pieces of
film-camera-choreography. If we want to talk about dance &
cinema, this is it.

### 30.

To watch Barbara Rubin shooting is like watching a
mysterious ritual dance—"It's fantastic," says Ken Jacobs.

### 31.

And then there are the Jackie Cassen and Andy Warhol
(Plastic Inevitables) stroboscope dances where we are
atomized, cut into film frames, where we become light atoms
in motion.

### 32.

"... in the making of *Mothlight* ... I have always had sense
enough ... to follow The Dance rather than take over
as I was often tempted ..." (Stan Brakhage in *Metaphors
on Vision*, referring to the creative act.)

### 33.

Len Lye's kinetic sculptures dance gracefully, singing.

34.

16 mm & 8 mm cameras have become extensions of
our fingers and they move to the beat of our hearts, to the
flow & rhythm of our emotions and, hopefully, our souls.
They are extensions of our body moving, dancing. Whatever
man expresses through dance, whatever part of his being—
a particle of it, of that essence—is transferred to the movie
through the movie camera dancing as the extension of our
fingers—which is our body which is our emotions which
is our mind which is our intuition which is our soul.

35.

But what is it, really? What is that particle and what
does it do and where does it come from? We don't exactly
know. It must be a reflection of Heaven, our memory
of how we moved or how our spirit moved through Heavens.

36.

The origin of dance, the origin of film that dances must be
in Heaven. The origin of dance in film, of "dance film," is
on Earth—our own small doings. But a filmed dance, when
filmed by a filmmaker whose soul dances, could, again,
become Heavenly.

37.

If you'll hit me on the head, the stars will dance in my eyes:
it's the dance movie of my nervous system.

38.

Go, little naked and impudent songs,
Go with a light foot!
(Or with two light feet, if it please you!)
Go and dance shamelessly!
Go with an impertinent frolic!
Greet the grave and the stodgy,
Salute them with your thumbs at your noses.
Ezra Pound, *Salutation the Second*

39.

Our blood dances through us; three steps forward,
one step back.

Pier Paolo Pasolini in his Rome apartment, 1967

# A conversation Between Pier Paolo Pasolini, Jonas Mekas, and Gideon Bachmann

July 1967

### BACHMANN

Mr. Pasolini, if I understand your most recent statements
on the subject correctly, you maintain that the camera,
when it shoots, always operates in the present; that what you
have in the camera, always IS the present, but the minute
you cut, or edit, and you put all those "presents" together,
you create the past.

### MEKAS

I see no basic disagreement between this view of Mr. Pasolini's
and what I believe, or even what Brakhage believes.
We all work with pieces of reality by editing. The question
is, how, and where, one edits. Many of us begin to do
it during the shooting. All painting is edited, all poetry
is edited, but it's edited during the process of painting,
during the process of writing, not after. Many poems are
destroyed by post-editing. Some are also improved, of
course. The accusation is often made that that we no longer
edit our films, but the people who accuse us in this way
simply don't see that cinema has become more mature, that
like other arts the editing is in the creation, takes place
during the shooting, intuitively, automatically, in the
shooting. Of course, I'm talking mostly about poetic cinema,
not much of this is taking place in narrative cinema yet.

But when I say editing, I don't mean only editing
between shots, as, for example, my single-frame shooting,
but also within the shot: the camera edits by moving, within

one single shot. You can take Douglas Sirk or John
Ford: the camera edits inside of their single shots, too. There
is montage in their cinema when you don't "cut" the scene;
it's in this sense that I say that there is no disagreement
with Pasolini's view.

### BACHMANN

Basically it seems to me that you are considering editing
to be more of an emotional act than a logical one, as Pasolini
does, and that you edit the "past," or rather, you fix the
definite expression (which may be the same thing) intuitively
in the act of creation, uniting ALL the creative act in the
single moment, thereby making the "present" of the act
into the "past" of the work. In short, one would say, putting
your and Pasolini's ideas in one pot, that the creative act
makes past out of present or, rather, stops time.

### MEKAS

As cinema advances, editing techniques will continue to
change, will become more and more automatic. Painters don't
usually make a logical choice, saying, "Now I've got to move
the brush to the right, now a bit up," etc. They feel where
the brush has to go. That's what I mean by editing becoming
automatic. And I don't think it's a matter of how good an
artist you are, I think it's a basic idea. It's a matter of feeling.

For us these are not new ideas, but coming to Europe
one is confronted with the fact that our films are still "new"
to large groups of people. So if you don't mind, I would
like to ask, in this conversation, what is considered "new"
over here? You have a festival of "new" cinema, weeks
of "new" cinema, and when you go to these things you
find people there arguing about the meaning of the adjective itself.

The dangers of overstressing "new," of course, are that
it leads critics to saying that something is NOT new, when
they look at a body of work; they expect that something
"new" must be totally new, a different animal, which it cannot
be, because of all the roots. So I say that the "new" in
cinema means bringing up the language, sharpening the
language, the syntax, the grammar, the rhythms, the methods
to express the contemporary possibilities and the changed
realities. That doesn't mean inventing; the vocabulary stays
practically the same. Only one or two words are added.

After all, Rilke used the same language as Hölderlin,
but with changes. The change of rhythms take place in
all arts. What I'm talking against is people like Aristarco
looking at our films and saying, "Oh, Dziga Vertov used
the single-frame technique already, cubists did this before,
Buñuel did that before, that isn't anything new, what
you are doing."

PASOLINI

Well, let's not worry about the professors! Anyway, for me,
everything is always new.

MEKAS

Some form of consciousness, however, about what is "new"
is necessary, probably beyond what you say. Because there
are dangers. When life around us changes, when reality
around us changes, when our inside reality is changing, some
artists have the tendency to reduce the new content to
the old forms that they know by using the same old rhythms
of twenty years ago, the same syntax—they squeeze into
that Procrustean bed the new sensibilities, and therefore
the content is distorted. That's the real problem, and
the reason why one has to be aware of the concept "new."
It's not that everything that is being done today is new
if the reduction, this squeezing, occurs.

PASOLINI

Beyond the fact that everything is always new, because
we see it ANEW, I don't want to define "new" or agree
to the establishment of norms of this kind. Obviously everything is new in the sense that all occurrences are eternally surprising, and thus no statements about occurrences
can have validity when made before.

MEKAS

I agree that "new" shouldn't be defined, but I do want clarification. Because there are, already, so many who are
clubbing our new cinema—or rather cinema—on the head,
using their own definitions of "new." These definitions,
which aren't usually even definitions, must be destroyed,
these vague biases. Maybe what we need is a very OPEN
understanding of "new," so that they couldn't use it to club
us on the head. Otherwise there will be more and more

surrealists, Dziga Vertovs, and cubists to club us on the
head. I know it's on its way.

PASOLINI
The only way is not to listen and not to pay attention to these
people. The only relationship to them that you could have
is one of disdain. I don't feel I have time for imbeciles.

MEKAS
I'm not worried about myself. But wherever I go, this question
comes up. You don't have to face the practical aspects of
it, but I do. We have a travelling exhibit of four film evenings
traveling in Europe now, and every evening, without fail,
in the discussions that follow the screenings, somebody will
get up and ask this question. It's not because it's called
"New American Cinema," but really because they are
confused by the concepts that are being planted on them
by the professors.

BACHMANN
So your desire for clarification is largely pedagogic: to avoid
misconceptions you want to clarify, more for others than
for yourself. Wouldn't it be more important to research the
phenomena themselves, which are CALLED new?

PASOLINI
This is something I always do. To place myself in front of
phenomena that call themselves new and analyze them.
I agree to using your criterion of "new sensibility," but this
new sensibility is something abstract. It obtains meaning
when inserted in specific histories, concrete situations. After
all, every artist, when he invents those few words of language
of which you spoke, in order to adjust his language to
the new sensibility, does so while inserted in a very specific
culture, in a very specific social and linguistic context.
Thus when I ask myself the question of how to analyze the
phenomena I find myself confronted with, I try to find the
social, political, and historical roots of that newness.
    In that sense, I think that the complete, total novelty
of the, let's call it the American, experimental cinema, is
the spirit of the New Left, which is a new political, social
phenomena. On the level of forms alone, the professors
may be right in defining the derivation you cite, but in terms

of spirit, the New Left is an entirely new thing. I'm not
even saying that your films necessarily belong to the New
Left consciously and willingly, but in the historical sense
they are a different expression of its spirit. Your new forms
are new contents of opposition to American society.

### MEKAS

I always ask that our travelling programs be announced as
political programs of films, but often the organizers of local
manifestations fail to do this, and in fact this demand of
mine is the one that usually arouses the most discussion.
It's very simple: politics to them is still a very super-
ficial thing.

### BACHMANN:

Perhaps it would be practical, at this point, to clarify
(not to say "define") in what way this anarchic cinema has
a political function.

### PASOLINI

That seems very obvious to me. It's the same as the reason
the director of the Pesaro Festival didn't want to stress
the political aspect of your films. He is, of course, a socialist,
and thus a traditional Marxist by training and education,
by morality. Thus for him your films are non-political because
they come from the midst of the middle class, and thus they
do not reflect the Marxist experiences. It's difficult for him
to accept that they are political, if they aren't Marxist.

### MEKAS

I guess ours is a Marxism that has gone through F r e u d,
W i l h e l m R e i c h, Beat, and LSD ...

### PASOLINI

Sure, but besides that, American knowledge of Marxism
is learned, not a lived experience. There has never been a
revolution in America that could be called Marxist, and
thus Americans have no direct experience of it. Nor do
Europeans; Marxism is a living experience. Thus I consider
your fight a political fight outside of the Marxist fight,
outside of the Marxist scheme. Therefore I love the young
American new cinema and do not love that of Italy. I do
not like the young Italian cinema, because it is *qualunquista*.

Like much of avant-garde Italian literature, by the way,
is *qualunquista.*

### BACHMANN

That word, of course, cannot be translated. I'll have to give
an approximate explanation. The *Uomo Qualunque* ("Any
Man") was a political party in Italy shortly after the war that
pretended to be sort of an "Everyman's" party but, in effect,
hid neo-fascist tendencies. Today *qualunquista* has become
an adjective in the Italian political dictionary that could
be vaguely identified with our use of "reactionary," but
it has the additional significances of the refusal of societal
responsibility and of totalitarian leanings, a sort of Hell's
Angels attitude. It's very hard to explain; anyway, it's a dirty
word in progressive circles. If you recall the list of accusations that Orson Welles, in Pasolini's film *La Ricotta*,
throws at the idiot journalist who has come to ask him
for an interview, it includes *qualunquista* ...

### PASOLINI

... and *rasista* ("racist").

### MEKAS

European political movements are always very politically
conscious, based on the experiences you described. But
in America we have very little political experience. Artistic
movements, and even political ones like strikes and student
movements, did not start as a very conscious political
movement but as a very personal reaction, and only later
gained a larger political leaning and consciousness, and
now it is approaching, sort of, Marxist thinking, in a sense,
but it started as a personal reaction, first, as a not wanting
to stand for the situation as it is. We say, "We don't want
to be where we are; we don't know what's ahead of us, but
we don't want to be where we are." That may be the major
difference between the American younger generations and
the European younger generations, with the latter always
wanting to have, at the beginning, a political purpose before
they act.

That is always the question that meets us in Europe:
"What is your aim?" We say, "Our aim is to get out from where
we are." That's why they often call us anarchists.

PASOLINI

In Europe, too, however, there are similar experiences.
The "Boheme" poets of the nineteenth century, for example,
let's call them R i m b a u d ians, have lived this experience.

MEKAS

And the Provos, now ...

PASOLINI

Thus there exists this third force, this alternative, in Europe,
too. But the Marxists, of course, accuse this movement of
the third alternative of being *Borghese*, anyway. To be born
from the midst of the middle class. It's a sort of love-hate.
It's not a normal, unexpressed love for everything there
is, but a hate for it, a hate for this establishment, a hate
that largely resembles love. Let's call it disappointed love.

MEKAS

A few weeks ago I tried to explain the meaning of anarchy
in America today to the representative of *Pravda*. It took
hours. It was the first time that I felt one of them understood
the meaning of actions that have no precise aim in fact.
Actions that have as their only aim the destruction of
the situation in which we are now, so that we would be free
to go somewhere else. It was the first time that a Soviet
communist, a man of that kind of orientation and education,
really seemed to understand it. That, I thought, was progress. And he understood, also, that our attitude can have
a useful political function.

PASOLINI

You mean that Russian understood it? As a communist, he is
an empty man ... maybe filled by a little bit of desperation.

BACHMANN

To be empty, and filled only with a bit of desperation, doesn't
seem to me to be a communist prerogative today. In fact,
it seems to be that the great danger of the Third Alternative
lies in the fact that the industrial age has accustomed the
youth of every country to being led along a certain path,
a certain hope, and that the ideas of anarchy may be coming
too late for them, because they could disorient them completely. Once you lose independence of spirit, thought, and

action, you hardly know what to do with the liberty of spirit, thought, and action when you are offered it. Is there any action or attitude that is consciously undertaken or cultivated to counteract the great indifference?

### MEKAS

We know that in America today there are seven million cameras in the homes, seven million 8 mm and 16 mm cameras. We will take cinema away from the industry and give it to the homes. That is the whole meaning of what's called *underground cinema*. By taking cinema away from the industry and by exaggerating, by saying that EVERYONE can make films, we are freeing those seven million cameras. Any child who grow up in a home and sees that camera, he could already do something else with it than take tourist movies, he could do something with it to work toward consciousness of his own position. I think that eventually these seven million cameras can become a political force in one way: that all aspects of reality will be covered— eventually it would go into the prisons, into the banks, into the army, and help us to see where we are, so that we can go out of there and go somewhere else. We want to give these seven million cameras a voice.

### PASOLINI

I've got my doubts ... How many typewriters are there in America? I don't mean to ridicule your hope. On the contrary. But I'm trying to find out why you find the cinema a better road to liberation than literature?

### MEKAS

Because with a typewriter you write your own fantasies, you reflect your own distortions, your own dreams. Good; you write poetry. But the camera shows reality, bits of reality, faces and situations. Because this is not Hollywood, Cinecittá filmmaking, which is staged. But these seven million cameras will be used to film reality in quotation marks as it is. Nothing can be hidden behind a face that you actually see.

### BACHMANN

Largely unlike your films, your ideas resemble those of Pasolini in defining reality and in defining film. In a recent

essay, Pasolini has said that the basic unit of film is not
the frame but the photographed object. You both, in your
work, have a much lesser faith in the capacity of the camera
to reproduce reality, or to show reality, than in your words.
But much more important is the faith that you have in the
people who, according to you, will use those seven million
instruments of consciousness. Who has so far done
any work, or what steps have been taken, to implement
your plan?

### MEKAS

At the moment we are collecting money for a project which
we are calling "Shoot your way out with a camera," whereby
two hundred cameras will be given to negro children and
young people, including film and free development and
technical advice, but without any strings attached—no need
to show us, what they will shoot, and no suggestions as to
what they should shoot. The project is intended for negroes
between the age of sixteen and twenty. Underground
moviemakers in all the cities will help with practical advice.
We have a four-page instruction sheet in which we stress
that this is not an educational program, or an anti-poverty
program, but that it is an underground cinema program,
and they can do with this material whatever they want.
We think these two hundred cameras will start something,
but we don't know what, of course. But we are giving them
without asking for anything in return. We very simply
want them to find joy in filming. The program has already
started in Washington, DC, and in New York. It will be
operated directly; we won't give these cameras to any
organizations, churches, groups, or centers for distribution,
but our film makers will go into the areas, meet people,
largely by chance, and give the cameras by personal selection. The problem is that the people who could benefit
most from this plan are used to refusing everything from
white people, because of the atmosphere that has been
created over the years, of total distrust of any "good" that
comes from white to black.

### BACHMANN

How will the films be shown, or will they? You must ask them
for the films ...

MEKAS

Yes. The films will be shown, in each of the cities where they
are made, and then they will travel. This will be arranged
through the Film-makers Cooperative. But the film-*making*
has to come from them. We cannot make films for the black
people.

PASOLINI

This seems to me to be a beautiful project, completely
revolutionary, completely new, and typically American.
That is "now" cinema, I guess.

BACHMANN

Could you imagine going down to Calabria and distributing
cameras among the poor people there?

PASOLINI

It should be possible, yes, except that we never think of things
like that.

BACHMANN

In every country, I suppose, people think of the things that
touch them most closely. And then there are the things
that touch everybody, everywhere, like wars, like emotional
death in our age, like the disappearance of the natural.
But each artist in each country, operating in the specific environment of concrete preoccupations that you spoke of before,
obviously is primarily concerned with the preoccupations
that for him are the most urgent. In fact, when you, Jonas,
were asked at the press conference in Pesaro, why you were
claiming that your films were political, you said because
they were concerned with the most urgent preoccupations
of the people in the USA at the moment; the concrete clarification of that statement, however, was lost in the rhetoric
of that evening. What I would like this conversation to turn
to, then, is a clarification of what that means, to each one
of you in your countries, "the most urgent preoccupations."

MEKAS

I'm not sure that there is much big difference between the
national and the international "urgent preoccupations." Take
Vietnam. That touches everybody. Now Peter Gessner
made a film about it. And at the moment some twenty

other filmmakers are each working on making two-minute
films on Vietnam. They will be put together as a sort of
collage anti-war film. But of course there are other problems
we have in the USA, which are not the problems of Brazil
or Italy. Let me put it all in one sentence, one question:
"Do you think that if today America stopped the war
in Vietnam, that it would thereby change as a country?"

Of course, this isn't a question I'm asking Mr. Pasolini,
because he would agree with my view; it's just a statement
I'm making in question form, BECAUSE SOMEBODY HAS TO
CHANGE AMERICA, OR ELSE THERE WILL BE ANOTHER
VIETNAM WAR! That is the root of it all. If nobody changes
America on a deeper level, tomorrow there will be an-
other, similar explosion like Vietnam. That's what I'm saying.
But these are obvious things.

BACHMANN

What do you personally and as a group of filmmakers and
as a group of conscious individuals living in America today,
feel you can do toward this aim?

MEKAS

It's already happening. The artists are establishing small
cells across the country; and not only the artists, but
all those, who through the beat experience, or drug experience, or other consciousness-changing experiences are
freeing themselves from the patterns of living, of feeling
in contemporary American society, are building small cells
in various places of the country, which are already based
on different ways of living. That means, cells of "beautiful"
people. It's from these cells of beautiful people that the
change in America will come. Their motto could be phrased
thus: "PARADISE NOW!" Because what you have to do, you
don't postpone it to tomorrow. You do it now. The "tomorrow"
engagement is right now. And when I say paradise, of
course, it's just an idea, it's just an idea. But these, too, are
all obvious things. Just like the fact that America wouldn't
change by stopping the war in Vietnam. And to say "beautiful
people" is also just an idea, a simple idea. But it includes
this: none of them approve any of the existing political or
social alternatives that exist or are advances in the USA.
Sometimes, and I think this is such a time, one has to accept
the action itself as a purpose.

PASOLINI

You are right, of course, in saying that if the war in Vietnam
ends through a miracle, that isn't going to mean a change
in American man. But if it ends because of a civil war in
America, in which the "beautiful people" win, it would
be a different story. I am waiting for civil war in America!
It would be the salvation of the world!


MEKAS

Something is happening. The contrast, the clashes are
becoming sharper. Less than a week ago, a whole group
of friends of mine who were singing in the park were arrested
for singing in the park. The movement is spreading, and
they are feeling it. The conflict is between those small cells
and the big body, and it is becoming so sharp that I believe
the rumors that concentration camps are being built for
all the drug addicts, and all those beautiful people, I believe
it is true. In fact, this has been discussed in the United
States Senate.

The protest that started about ten years ago, toward the
liberation of the negro, against war, against various political actions of the government, is now going on in universities
and has reached the public, is continuing on its own momentum; nobody can stop it. So now the function of the artist,
of those who are in the avant-garde of humanity, is becoming
different. They now have to look and see what is necessary
on a deeper level. So when we are talking about what Allen
Ginsberg is doing, or Snyder—that is already something
else. We are not walking with posters anymore, because
the nation is walking with the posters. Our work is different.

It's an enormous responsibility, when you consider,
that two million teenagers across the USA are waiting for
guidance. Who is going to give them that guidance? Who are
the leaders? It's there that responsibility bounces back
to us, to Ginsberg or Snyder or to myself, and to a few other
people, and then we have to work on ourselves, make
ourselves better people, because otherwise we cannot give
guidance.


BACHMANN

That takes us back to the question, or rather I should
say, fear, I expressed before: that the teenagers of today,
used to receiving packaged guidance, may be unable
to utilize the freedom of choice you offer, unable to digest

anarchy as an expression of liberty. You are almost stuck
with the need to do something that is, it seems to me,
in direct contrast with your own ideas: to be educational.

MEKAS

Nevertheless, in whichever way we approach it, this remains
the biggest task of the artist today. This is the answer to
your question about our most urgent preoccupations, this
worries us very much. To give guidance, and what guidance,
and how?

PASOLINI

I can see exactly where your problem lies. Up to this point,
the American revolt has been a stupendous thing, the thing
I admire most in the world today. But in essence it has
always remained basically irrational, having always found
its motive inside of America itself, in the authentic part
of America, in the authenticity of that which is democracy,
that is, the truest example of pure democracy. But at this
point, of course, what is necessary IS guidance, but this
guidance can only be an ideology. America isn't awaiting
guidance, it's awaiting an ideology.

MEKAS

We hope that something in this direction is already
happening. The latest thing in the USA now are the be-ins.
They take place in San Francisco, in New York, various
other places, also in small towns, where people gather on
Mondays in the parks—all those who may be called, maybe
very vaguely, the beautiful people. They gather, in thousands,
sometimes two to four thousand, or ten thousand of them,
and they just sing, dance, or do nothing, just so that there
is some communication between them, a start. And since
they have no guidance, they can grow only by being together,
and out of this something may develop—we still don't
know what.

BACHMANN

You mean in ideology?

PASOLINI

If an ideology can be born, you will have the civil war.
And if you have the civil war, the world will be safe
for maybe three hundred years. If all this can crystallize

itself somehow, because that's how man is made, into an
ideology, that would give people the force to make the
civil war, like the negroes would, if they had an ideology.

MEKAS

I think that some form of ideology is in the making, and
you can see it by looking at what is happening. For example,
I think some elements will come from Thoreau, which
is a very strong influence, and Buddhism and Zen ...

BACHMANN

But these are all movements or rather thoughts that touch
the individual strictly on the inside ...

MEKAS

Yes, but these thoughts cause forces that in another two
or three years will begin to develop toward something
like an ideology, maybe even a political one. The merging
of all the forces, for example ...

BACHMANN

Unfortunately, it seems to me, all these movements finally
become social movements—become too big not to be
social movements. All ideologies which are built on the
principle of making the human being a better human being
are fine, but they will not create an ideology for a civil
war. Anyway, as you know, any war, even a civil war, always
unites, but it also makes everything come down to a pretty
similar level, it nivellizes. Anyway, all these movements
are pacifist movements, and I don't think civil war is what
they are plotting.

MEKAS

This is an area that one still has to research ...

PASOLINI

But also pacifists are actively pacifists ...

BACHMANN

There are doubts about their intentions. I think all of us,
in our areas, have absolute consciousness. In America it's
the absolute consciousness that things can't go on as they
have been going; it's not just a matter of research, it's a matter

of being sure. But it doesn't seem to me matters can develop
toward "ideologies," because these, too, are concepts that
are based on other concepts, like the one, for example, that
the majority idea is a good thing. It seems to me that this
idea can too easily bend with every wind that is blowing,
depending on how conscious a mass your majority is. It seems
to me further, that the great thing about the Third Alternative, is that it is NOT a social movement, does NOT have
an organized ideology but is built precisely on the tenet
that every man seeks to return to HIMSELF, in order
to find peace. But today "peace" can be found only socially,
and there is thus the constant danger that the movements
will destroy themselves because their nature is not to
be "movements," or that they succeed in *being* movements,
like a civil war, for example, isn't the thing that they
would ideally WANT to achieve.

### MEKAS

The people of the Third Alternative, as you call it, realize
that they can grow only by working with others, of course.
That's the reason for the be-ins. The next stop, in fact, is the
consolidation of this being together into some more concrete form. For example, in the last six months, the population of San Francisco alone increased by about 200,000,
most of them teenagers that came searching for guidance. San Francisco exploded. Snyder and Ginsberg and
Leary have spent much time there, advising them in small
groups of two hundred or so, to leave the city and form
small communities. And this is happening. There are already
some villages, for example there is one in New Mexico,
the population of which was only about two thousand people,
but which about ten thousand teenagers are swamping
and camping there this summer. They will create a city,
slowly taking over the government and everything in
the city. In maybe two years, this development will create
concrete civil centers for the Third Alternative.

### PASOLINI

It may be true that an ideology isn't the only thing that can
unite people and simplify their liberty, there is also religion.
Maybe what you are creating in the USA is a mystical-
religious movement? Maybe even such a movement can
bring about a civil war.

MEKAS
Those civil wars are the bloodiest ...

PASOLINI
In any case, it is eminently clear that if this civil war doesn't
happen, America will assume the heredity of Germany,
becoming the country of Nazism carried to its extreme.

BACHMANN
The great totalitarian systems, like the great cultures,
have always traveled west ...

MEKAS
This is the one area in which we cannot give you answers;
we just have to intensify our work and search for the answers.

BACHMANN
Is there anything positive about the Italian situation that
would interest the USA?

PASOLINI
No. I am saying it to you in a very simple manner: no. I have
just returned from Morocco, where I shot my latest film,
and upon returning I was tempted to drop everything, drop
the films, drop my previous life, and return to live in Morocco.
And not because I love Morocco. But because my arrival
in Italy was so terrible, so shocking, it was unbearable. There
is no sign of hope, no light, no nothing. It was like arriving
in a madhouse of REAL mad people, that is, calm madmen.
I had passed ten days of terror; it was as if I couldn't live
in Italy any more. There were ten days when I considered
leaving Italy. And the worst thing is that the Italians don't
notice anything. And after what you tell me about New
York, maybe I'll give up everything and go live in a desert
in Morocco, where the problems are simple, known, pre-
industrial: laziness, retardation, poverty—things we have
learned to cope with.

MEKAS
Naturally I cannot judge whether this desire stems from
a kind of mystical drive, because the whole thing in America
IS very mystical. But it touches all our actions every day.
Everything one does connects, every step counts, and all the

steps that make up the day are connected with the individual
having to make his momentary decisions. The clash is born
here: in their daily, simple experiences they have to clash with
the social and political realities around them, and this
is how our struggle becomes political. Right there it becomes
political. That's why they have to form those villages and
undertake actions together.

There is no compromise. That's why I say that they
must build those concentration camps, because there
is no way of merging the two, no way of coming together
between our people and the concrete political realities
of today's America. There is no merging of the generations.

### BACHMANN

But this struggle exists in other countries, too. Only today
I read in the newspapers that the police in Milan were very
proud to announce that they—in a "completely legal action"—
have completely destroyed the "village" of Barbonia, which
had been a sort of place like you describe exists in New
Mexico, except that the *capelloni* (which is a derisive term
in Italy, which comes from the fact that the people of the
Third Alternative wear their hair long, and *capelli* means
hair) here in Barbonia were only about seventy, who were
chased, imprisoned, "restituted to their parents," and generally cleaned out. The article carried the same old accusations, of how they had advanced vague theories of freedom
without having any concrete answers or programs to offer.
I ask you: Where the hell are they supposed to get clear
answers and ideas from if nobody in the so-called "normal"
world has any clear ideas? Isn't it enough that people of
fourteen and sixteen and twenty years of age have the consciousness to know that things can't go on the way they
are? Isn't it enough that they take the risk of avoiding the
benefits of middle-class life? That they were willing to throw
their lives and their comforts and their reputations in the
balance, in the vague hope that somehow, somebody, somewhere will help them find the answer? I get sad when
I read these righteous reports by the police lieutenants,
amplified by newspaper reports to the effect that "the police
were assisted by the population of the area, who shouted,
'Throw them out, burn them out, burn the swine alive!'"

I'll tell you one thing: Pasolini is right. You can't fight
with consciousness against stupidity, and you can't say

limpidly, OK, this is the problem we've got to work on. Before
you get a chance to work on this problem, they will have
eaten you up, and all your fine beautiful people will be working on Madison Avenue or for Finsider or Olivetti. Nobody
has ever wanted a war, but when one is flung on you, you
can't fight it except in the terms that it knows. Unless you believe that by osmosis the people of the Third Alternative
will become more numerous in the whole world than all the
other people put together, these who have the guns and
the ammunition and the fine words and the comforts. Your
people exist everywhere, call them Provos in Holland or
a million different names in Prague and London and Rome
—the only consciousness they have is the consciousness
of revolt against nothing. Nobody has a revolt FOR something,
because the aims cannot be defined. "Paradise Now!"
—what paradise? Where paradise? With what values? What
would it offer? How would it solve the problem of over-
population?

### MEKAS
Aims are for tomorrow. Ideologies are for tomorrow. We say
"Paradise Now!" because we don't want to wait for tomorrow.

### PASOLINI
That is a typically religious attitude. In religion you never live
your life tomorrow; that will be another life, the promised
life. But all human ideologies are always ideologies for tomorrow, yes.

### BACHMANN
That, of course, is the origin of hope.

### PASOLINI
Hope is a strictly human sense of a belief in a better kind
of tomorrow that man can set up himself?

### BACHMANN
No, more *spes ultima dea*. Instead of saying to himself,
I'll have to commit suicide today, man invented hope. Now
he can say, I don't have to commit suicide, I'll live better
tomorrow. In fact, I would say, in that sense, suicide and hope
are the same thing. This is how the sense of time is born,
exactly in the same manner as you have explained when

talking about film editing: the continuity of time begins
to exist when the past begins to exist, that is, when man puts
together his awareness of the present, which would lead
him, normally, to suicide, and instead decides to invent some
other system of continuation, hope is the simplest method.
Hope, like suicide, is the giving up for today.

PASOLINI
The flight ahead, is an old established method ...

MEKAS
... in the name of which the worst evils have been committed.
The whole handling of the negro cause by the whites, for
example. Before, the white man, seeing ahead, always wanted
to go into the house of a negro and solve his problems for
him. Today the situation is changed, the negroes are solving
their problems themselves. The negro doesn't need our
leaders and guidance any more, they have enough leaders
themselves now. We know that there is a lot of violence
brewing in New York this summer, for example, and we are
not helping to create it, but neither are we against it. We
say, if the negroes want to blow up those buildings, good,
let them blow up those buildings today, let them make their
war today, we won't be against them, but we cannot HELP
them, we cannot do it FOR them. You have no idea how much
antagonism was created over the years by the fact that
the whites have always wanted to do the work of the negroes.

PASOLINI
I understand your position very well; it's a position of total,
absolute democracy.

MEKAS
What other thing would you suggest? I think that if there
were a civil war, this younger generation of whites would
probably support the negroes when it came to fighting,
I don't think there is any doubt about that, but at this stage
they can only give moral support. In the manifestations,
however, we are all together. In the "be-ins" there are whites
and negroes together, in the large-scale demonstrations,
like the big anti–Vietnam War demonstration, in which
200,000 people participated, the negroes were together with
the whites. It was the first time that the movements were
really united.

PASOLINI

I can understand your position very well of not wanting
to make their decisions for them and letting things develop
democratically as they must. But the problem is, I feel, that
the negroes, a bit like Israel today, are developing nationalist
forms. And I can understand them too; they are right to
think that way, probably. But this is the point, where ideology
is lacking. Even on the basis of Marxist ideas, it would be
simple to demonstrate that this was not a racist but a social
struggle.


MEKAS

But this whole situation, this strange relationship between
white and black, is only the found product; we came and
found this situation already messed up by the previous generation. To solve this mess of the previous generation, to
leave them alone is about the only thing one can do. Perhaps
then, at some later date, we will come together as equals.


PASOLINI

Together, maybe later, but now it's going ahead in this quasi-
religious way, which none of you know where it can lead.
It starts mystically-religiously with the whites and mystically-
ethnically, or I should say racially, for the negroes, and
I don't really see how these roads could lead together. Because
religion and mysticism are centrifugal forces, and they
may separate. That the negroes will free themselves by force
seems to me natural, because they are now in an abnormal
state. All your ideas are good at the start, but I feel you must
face the realities that you provoke. After all, the negroes
have nothing to lose anymore. But you still have many
things to lose: all your middle-class privileges, as you said
before. In fact, what you have to lose is the privilege of
being "beautiful people," which is still a form of privilege.


BACHMANN

Then you are saying that an ideology must be found, even
if an ideology itself would again reduce the amount of liberty
of the individual? Even while the lack of a central ideology
is in fact part of their being? I mean, you are saying that they
must have an ideology in order to win, even if ideologies
are against their nature. That seems to me to correspond
to what I said before.

When you talk of cinema, making one of your grammatical analyses of this art, even while you say that everything up to now is always new, you are in fact contradicting yourself by making a rule which says that one shouldn't make a rule. And the same seems to me to correspond to what I said before.

Every ideology, therefore, carries in itself the germ of its own death, even if only through the fact of its own proper establishment, which is another paraphrase of your filmic theory of montage. And then you have to remember this business of the group spirit: when you talk of concentration camps ... well, you know that in concentration camps there is almost always a much better group spirit than in free cities! You come down to the fact that the concentration camps and those New Mexican villages are in some form one and the same thing, or, in fact, that these villages are *voluntary* concentration camps! Wars and revolutions have always created art and spirit, but well-being has never created anything. Thus as long as man is relatively well off (and he is getting progressively more so), he won't free himself. It's an old conversation between us: whether the biological need of man is to express himself more in a time of hardship than in a time of easy life. All the historical experience, despite the theories of M a r x, points to the first.

### MEKAS

I think our "Paradise Now!" slogan includes these possibilities, and that with it we can forge ahead, because first of all we are conscious that the times aren't good, despite the well-being that surrounds us, and secondly it helps us to function in an atmosphere of optimism.

### BACHMANN

I think that the only optimism of this time is an absolute pessimism; only that can help you continue—to know where you stand, to feel who and where you are. If you are conscious of the reality that surrounds you—of the fact that man on earth has a limited life span, then you can live, because you live within reality.

### MEKAS

We only know one reality and that reality is two facts: the first is that we consider the world around us completely

distorted and corrupt and that we don't want it, and
the second is that there exists another reality of those
few people who lead completely different lives, and we say,
eh, if all the world were like that, it would be beautiful.
So we are not pessimists; we say it would be beautiful, but
we also take that for granted. Because nothing worse can
happen than that which exists. And we think change is possible. We say we are with these forces, not with these. All
that without theorizing about the past or the future, without
saying that's how man developed, these are his rules, all
that ...

PASOLINI

I'm told there is, in America, still the problem of the poor
whites?

MEKAS

Of course, and in fact, the poor whites and the negroes
are the only two groups in America today that want
revolution, now, for the first time. And then there are
always personal things, problems of one group not liking
another, etc.

BACHMANN

I think this conversation can have a value only if we go
beyond the problems which are common, daily ones. These
are wars already begun: Vietnam, negro liberty, poverty,
freedom of expression. All these are expressing one fact: that
man today can no longer be man because he is completely
surrounded by the group, completely systematized, whether
in the good or the bad sense, in a delicate, concrete, social
situation. The real problem is what can man do, as an individual, in order to be.

So far in history, we have always been HELPED by
the hunger, by war, by the badness of man, and all these
things have helped us to think that the real struggle is
on the outside of ourselves. But these struggles—the one
for the negroes, the one for the New American Cinema,
the one for comfort, these resolve themselves. But nobody, no situation, has helped us to solve our INNER
problems, the problems of becoming ourselves, of being
ourselves.

### MEKAS

Probably I agree, when I say that we must change America from the inside, or China from the inside, or Russia from the inside, when we want to tackle the problems that are those of finding a new way. I try to stay away from historical theories, and to stick to that which I see around me, close to me.

### PASOLINI

All religions have always said this, that the problems are not the outside ones but those inside of man. In this sense, the hunger of the Chinese, which helps them to keep away from their inner problems, and their well-being, which is a dream that also keeps them away from reality, are the same thing; thus both hunger and well-being are reduced to being similar: they are both external things.

### MEKAS

But you cannot dismiss the outside manifestations; for example, the Vietnam War works on Americans on the inside. But the Vietnam War is also creating the young generation of America pacifist. It works both ways. But we all know that the ideology is important, that it has to come, that the road has to be found.

### BACHMANN

Do you think that out of your Third Alternative an ideology will ever grow, one that could be defined, and in accordance with which man will be able to live more happily?

### MEKAS

It always happens. So there will be one. We cannot put it in words yet, but there is *something* developing, in America right now, that could be called ideology.

### PASOLINI

But, of course—and I think it exists, and it is what is called the New Left. They do have an ideology, a bit eclectic still, a bit unconscious of itself, a bit in the stage of formation.

### MEKAS

Yes, maybe our ideology will come from there. It will take another two or three years, but ...

PASOLINI

To me the ideas of the American New Left belong among
the most revolutionary ideologies in the world today. Perhaps
along with the Chinese, anti-Soviet ideology. Those to me
are at the moment the two great, living ideologies that are
really exceptional. Because in China the problem is, of
course, that in the no-longer-hungry country socialism won't
get to be a bourgeois movement, so that Chinese socialism
won't become a society of well-being, too, like in Russia
or America, because the civilization of well-being is the same
everywhere.

MEKAS

The only groups in America today where negroes,
for example, find connection are these of the New Left.

PASOLINI

You must arrive at precise definitions. It's a human need.
Otherwise you end up in spiritual well-being, which is even
worse than material well-being.

MEKAS

You must understand, of course, that I am using the concept
of "Paradise Now!" a little like an agitprop mechanism.
I want them to get interested in films and to begin asking
questions. It's a good slogan against the professors. The
discussion always leads to more interesting areas. At one
of the most professorial discussions I had with our groups
about films in Italy, I proposed a resolution, which read:
"We have found nothing new in American Cinema, and thus
we propose that Italian cinema, too, remain where it is."
That got them excited. Objections make people talk. And
often think. And finally, that's all we want to cause at this
moment. And I think, in some small way, we are causing it.

# Theatre of Richard Foreman

A conversation between Richard Foreman, Amy Taubin,
Michael Snow, P. Adams Sitney, Ernie Gehr, Jonas Mekas,
Joyce Wieland, Ken Kelman, and Margaret Ladd
March 15, 1969

### JONAS

I thought—now that Richard's third production is over,
and I see that it probably won't be reviewed, like the other
two were not reviewed—I thought maybe we could make
this into a group conversation concerning all three productions. Because this is a theatre that interests me. I think
this is a very important theatre. The other night, somebody
at McGregor's mentioned that this is the most important
theatre since Beckett, and I jumped a little bit. I jumped
because, although I have no intention of denying the importance of Beckett's theatre, I never really cared for it.
To me, his theatre remained a theatre of emotions and Fate.
Foreman's theatre, at least the aspect of it which interests
me most, has abandoned the emotional field and has
entered into the mental sphere. This mental aspect interests
me most. It's no accident that Richard himself calls his
theatre "ontological" theatre.

### SNOW

It's a good point to start with, that you think it's mostly
mental, or one of the emphases. I think it's very concrete
too, and it's very much using the materials, arranging
the materials of theatre. Some of its implications are mental
or philosophical, but the thing that moved me about it is
just the way it is composed and the displacement of things,
all the stuff there is to use—speech and action.

JONAS

It was all very formally arranged—or should I say structur-
ally?—the few elements that there were. Because what
is Richard's vocabulary here? Jokingly, the vocabulary was
like fifty words. The English language wouldn't survive
with this playwright.

SNOW

But then, they're given a certain use which I would say
is concrete. I'm just approaching it from that point of view,
to go on from the point of being mental. The arrangements
are made from those elements, like the words, which
have different kinds of senses and are, in their implications,
ontological. But one of the things that's beautiful is
that they are almost sculptural arrangements of things.

JONAS

What's important to me is that we—all of us in this room—
we stopped going to the theatre, and we have seen some
of the better work, including the Living Theatre and
a number of local experiments. And they are a little bit
like five years ago, or more. They are back somewhere.
And here, suddenly, we face something that interests us,
that stirs us, provokes us, pulls us in. Now, why?

SITNEY

Well, what has there been since Beckett?

JONAS

The Theatre of the Absurd, the theatre of improvisation,
The Theatre of Cruelty, the theatre of the Actors Studio, and
the theatre of the ridiculous & camp. Plus, the happenings.

FOREMAN

In America today, and it seems to be true in Europe also,
the advanced theatre is simply very much into very physical-
ized and emotional attempts to use ... essentially to use
the body as an expressive mechanism, and responding
truly to the fact that language and ideas don't work in the
theatre any more and are attempting to get past the mind
through really intense work on the body. I think it absolutely
doesn't work.

Richard Foreman, in his 491 Broadway Theatre, New York, 1976

SITNEY

This is a really interesting point for me. The Living Theatre
as an example of expressionist dance, OK. But how do you
feel about your direction in terms of Kenneth King's work?

FOREMAN

I think it's much closer to a lot of that area of dance—
Kenneth King and ...

SNOW

Yvonne Rainer.

FOREMAN

Yes, Yvonne Rainer. Because those people ... well,
they certainly are not coming out of abstract expressionism,
and basically I think all the advanced theatre is.

SITNEY

One does look at it as theatre learning a lot from dance
in different ways.

FOREMAN

Not that I have seen very much dance.

SITNEY

I don't mean personal influence. I mean in the sense
of a Zeitgeist. But it seems to me that if the Living Theatre
comes out of an area of dance and a certain extreme
of erotic dance, the Martha Graham School ...

FOREMAN

I don't know if that's true.

SITNEY

I think it does. I think to a very great extent that dance
has set a pattern of stage work in this country. Dance,
like film ... I am very much involved with contemporary
dance, especially in America. I think it's very important,
I think the theatre has learned from it indirectly or directly,
and the Living Theatre through the European mode of
dance, which is Béjart to a strong extent, and it wouldn't
surprise me if direction—I'm not talking about playwriting now—did learn a lot from the experiments of
Yvonne Rainer, etc.

SNOW

One of the strong influences has been happenings—
Kaprow especially. It seems the whole audience and
actor relationship is being ... Everything is merging
more. And the whole thing with the sight ...

SITNEY

Well, that's the expressionist principle. But there is another
dance principle of formalistic dance, principle made out
of everyday life. The Living Theatre is going in the happening
direction, but this theatre seems ... the reason I could
look at it ... I ordinarily can't look at a play. The reason
I could look at Richard's play is it had that sense of reality
—a gesture of reality that this other area of dance has.

SNOW

It's a very traditional setup: the stage is there, and you
back there, you're the audience. That's one of the beautiful
things about it.

SITNEY

I'm thankful.

SNOW

It does something new to that relationship. It really does.
Even though it is a traditional thing, that's one of the things
I really like about it. You're really given something and
not coerced. You're still left to do what you will.

FOREMAN

Yes, the one thing that I hate—I mean, I can't stand anything
in the theatre any more—it used to be that every year I'd
see two or three things that I liked a lot, but it's really been
a few years since I've been able to endure anything. I just
no longer see any justification for manipulating the audience
for putting them through certain preconceived emotional
changes that I think only deepens their habitual responses,
which are the things that louse them up in life. I think
I'm at least beginning to *not* try to do that, whether there
are certain emotional effects or not. But I think all the
experimental theatre—and the regular theatre in this
country that I've seen that I can't buy into—is essentially
trying to put the audience through those emotional
changes that they've decided will be good for the audience.

JONAS

That includes the Theatre of the Ridiculous.

SITNEY

Oh yes.

SNOW

And the Living Theatre especially.

SITNEY & FOREMAN

Certainly, yes.

Kate Manheim in *Total Recall*, a play by Richard Foreman,
New York, 1970

*Total Recall*, a play by Richard Foreman,
New York, 1970

FOREMAN

And some of them are better than others. Some of them
are worse. But just as a premise. I find it a totally useless,
almost a bad thing to try to do.


SITNEY

Do you mean even ... I don't mean in the flagrant sense
of really going out in the audience and violating it—
but how about in a more old-fashioned sense of presenting
an object which is moving? Let me give you an example.
I saw your play a second time, and I was very careful
to observe certain things, and I paced myself differently,
very easy in the beginning—since I'd seen it the other
night—to have all the energies in the end, and I noticed
in the last scene, in the beginning of the last scene, there's
just Hartman and Ida, and there's the kind of moment
for me personally that reminded me of Chekhov and
reminded me of that moment when the stage is quiet and
the two characters who have gone through so much are
together, and I felt that very strong theatrical presence
and I was really moved by, grabbed by that. It was a quiet
moment, and it had thousands of years of theatre behind
it, and I didn't mind that at all. This made the play.


FOREMAN

I think the task is to deny nothing like that. You know,
in classical playwriting you're aiming at things like that.
You say, how do I achieve things like that? But if they
arrive as found objects in the course of the other work
that you are doing, that's fine.


SITNEY

That's an interesting point. Did others feel that moment?


SNOW

Yes. Would you say that applies to the humor involved too?
I thought it was a by-product, in a sense. There are things
that are funny. But all I can say is they seem to be
a by-product of the things that are done and happen.


FOREMAN

It's very interesting for me because I started getting into
the theatre when I was very young, in high school, and I used

to do these gigantic productions ... and a couple of months
ago I was thinking, what's the difference between the way
we were working then, which is the way I think people still
work in the professional theatre, and the way I'm trying
to work now? And I really think the difference is that in those
days, and generally in the theatre, you're sitting there and
you say, like: What will *work*? What can I do to produce
predictable effects that I then will, say, *work* into the theatre,
and ...? That simply doesn't seem very interesting. It seems
to me much more interesting to choose various almost ethical
rules of procedure and put them into operation, and if the
rules are beautiful and right, then, by definition, what
you get by observing those rules has to be very important.

### SITNEY

This is your application of the basic postwar aesthetic
to theatre. It just hasn't been dealt with before.

### FOREMAN

I don't think this theatre is particularly ... I don't think
this theatre is anything but in the mainstream of the
advanced arts in other areas. I don't think that for various
very practical reasons the theatre has been able to exploit
all kinds of things that have been going on in other arts
because the theatre is ruled by all kinds of other practical
considerations. I've always felt that Gertrude Stein is the
major literary figure of the twentieth century. For various
reasons I haven't really studied her plays too carefully—
but, as opposed to someone like Artaud, and everyone
now is influenced by Artaud ... I first read Artaud about
ten years ago when it was first translated into English and
it seemed very nice and sort of self-evident and, of course,
everyone would agree to it; but Gertrude Stein's theoretical writings on literature and on the theatre I have
returned to at least twice a year and continually ponder
and am as troubled by and led by and ruminate upon.

### SITNEY

I would say one advance over her practical situation is that
Gertrude Stein was so pleased whenever any conventional director wanted to do any of her plays. She'd just give
it to him and say it's jolly.

KELMAN

I consider myself here in the function of being. After I
noticed the other people here ... I at least could consider
myself as being here in a very specific function—that
is to say, as a member of the cast and crew of *Angelface*.

SITNEY

But you're also here in the function of being one of the
other people professionally involved in theatre and writing
for theatre.

KELMAN

Well, professionally, not commercially, but yes, professionally.
But that doesn't qualify me to speak about this point any
more than being a filmmaker qualifies Kubelka to speak
on Bresson or Brakhage on Jack Smith. I mean,
not necessarily. Now if I were famous, I would make a statement on behalf of this play because if I were famous, I'd
be in a position to give testimonials. I respect this play,
*Ida-Eyed*, and the one I was in too, *Angelface*. I had great
difficulties with it because I considered myself a romantic
and I considered the plays to be about something else.
And they are very difficult for me, but, at the same time,
it seems to me that there is a precision, a style in them that
is completely clear. It can't be missed. And this is always
admirable. It indicates a clarity of vision. So when I
see it or when I'm in it, I know what's going on. I was closer
to the core of the play when I was in it. And I must say—
speaking of the kind of thing you are mentioning—that
is the found thing which may occur, which is not particularly
premeditated but which comes out of the structure, what
happened during *Angelface*, where I think I played the title
role or one of them. What happened there was the only
time I wasn't on stage, when I was sitting not worrying about
missing a cue, but listening, I got a tremendous sense of
what I should do, which I only realized yesterday, when
I began to think about all this. But I got that sense of the
theatre, which had nothing to do with that theatre there,
but something ... But at the same time it was there because
I encountered it. It was the use, which was an expedient,
of using that tape along with the voices, which was ...
I suppose largely just because, as you said, we couldn't learn
all those lines. But it had its effects and its powers, and

when I heard all those sounds going through the air, it made
me think quite a bit. I became devoted where I had been
before only somewhat on the way. I became devoted to a
theatre of echoes. And that was, I think—it must have been,
although I wasn't in the audience—a theatre of echoes,
a great deal of the time, or maybe even all of the time.

SITNEY

But so was *Ida-Eyed*.

KELMAN

Well, yes, but …

SITNEY

… in essence.

KELMAN

Yes, but you see, there's the difference between what
I perceived there and what had to do with me. The kind
of echo that you perceived in *Ida-Eyed*, which is more
like the echo in the script, which is written there, which
is a kind of serial echo and has to do with structure
and form, whereas what I became concerned with then,
apart from the other question, was the physical echo,
the voice going through space as a spiritual manifestation.
But that this kind of thing should happen indicates to
me the richness of what's going on. I have to speak from
this level. I can't really say anything in a very critical or
objective way, but it did mean a great deal to me. And of
course, *Rosencrantz and Guildenstern Are Dead*,
which amused me more than this, which was certainly
more of an entertainment—I knew to be an emptiness from
the first two minutes on, and I got nothing out of it except
I was able to say humorous things about it for some time
afterward and to do imitations. I would have to work much
harder to say something funny about *Ida-Eyed*. Or do
imitations or anything like that—it isn't set up that way.
I think other people in the cast could say something maybe.

GEHR

Well, I find it difficult to use the word theatre with Richard's
work. I've been involved in two productions. I've seen the
third one. There is a big problem when we deal with theatre.

Same way as when you use the word motion picture, or
cinema—generally people associate it with stories being
told, people moving in front of the camera—and I find
it hard to talk of Richard's work as theatre. I think it has
to do a lot with life ...

JONAS

What do you want? This is a *vital* theatre ...

GEHR

Yes, but ...

JONAS

There's a stage. It's real. There are people. They are real.
They are pronouncing certain words. They are real. Things
are happening there. You sit. You watch. In front of you
there ...

GEHR

Well, I realize ... I'm not saying it is life. Obviously it's
an abstraction and everything, and it's performed as an
abstraction, but ... I find it very inadequate to use the word
theatre, because you have to think of what has been done
before. I've stopped going to the theatre for the last two
years. The last play I went to see, I went to see the Open
Theatre, *America Hurrah*, and I walked out. I'm tired
of theatre ...

SITNEY

But the reason you wouldn't call it theatre ...

GEHR

... is not a connotation I like ...

SITNEY

... is because theatre has fallen so low.

GEHR

It's become a pure cliché.

JONAS

So when you see good theatre, suddenly you don't want
to call it that.

GEHR

The trouble is you go to see a play and you have to sit
through so many clichés to hit on one second that maybe
is real. Everything is done in a certain way.

FOREMAN

But you did go to see the Living Theatre. I saw you there.

GEHR

Yes, well, I walked out too, didn't I? I mean, it's fine for
some people.

JONAS

I went, and walked out, and I am almost the mother
of patience.

FOREMAN

I … When I go to see things that are done in the theatre—
even things like the Open Theatre & the Living Theatre—
it just doesn't seem real to me. And one thing that I was
trying to do is—I don't know on what level I'm talking,
but the gestures, and the things that happen, be they acts
that are being done, words that are spoken, just the way
they are—try and make them really, really be THERE.
And that's really all I'm interested in, almost, having all
the things that are there REALLY be there.

SNOW

Yeah, that's an interesting thing. I feel it's very real and yet
it isn't naturalistic and has a terrific reality that's just …

FOREMAN

Well, naturalism just doesn't seem real.

SNOW

Yes, there's some kind of thing that's turned over there.

SITNEY

Well, this is a true point. I would like to add something
here just for the record. Not all of us here are disenchanted
with the Living Theatre. I consider *Frankenstein* a major
experience. *Paradise Now* is something equivalent
to the lower rungs of purgatory. But *Frankenstein* I think

is something valid. But then, there is a difference between someone who is in a completely different discipline just looking casually at an area and seeing things about it, and someone who has absolutely committed his life to it, so I understand perfectly your point.

### SNOW

*Ida-Eyed* has reality on a lot of levels, and I wouldn't want to compare it, and I think we are making a mistake in trying to be so contextual. I don't think you have to clarify *Ida-Eyed* by talking about other theatre. You can talk about it specifically without saying it's opposed to this or that. To return to that whole thing about it being real, it's real on so many levels rather than being real only on an almost documentary level. It's real on levels that have to do with the way the mind operates.

### MARGARET

That's what I think, that that's what was great about it to me. I mean, I was in it. Rehearsing and performing it. I never got bored with it. In fact, I'm sorry it's over because I feel that I must have had a better experience …

### JONAS

You are an actress. You are disqualified … OK, we'll accept you, since there aren't many of us. I felt like you did. Once you went in, you were like in another world. We were watching Ken Jacobs's *Tom, Tom, the Piper's Son* and we said, this is it. And Richard said, if I had to go to an island and only take one movie, this is it. Now, when I was watching *Tom, Tom*, it was also a very abstract experience to me, and it pulled me in, and I had to use some effort to get into it and stay with it. And as long as I was in it, its gravity pull was so strong. It kept me all the way in, and I knew if I allowed myself to fall out of its gravity, I'd be *completely* out, as happened a couple of times when people interrupted me, and I looked then at the screen, at *Tom, Tom*, and it had no meaning at all to me—until I blasted myself again into its orbit. Once you are in, it becomes a very exhausting, very rich experience. And the same here. It happened with *Angelface* and it happened with *Ida-Eyed*. I went into your play, and I had to use some effort, some force to get into it. I blasted myself into it—and

most of the theatre today is so thin you don't need to blast
yourself into it, it's like water—and I stayed with it from
beginning to end, and I was leaning forward in my chair.
The same with *Angelface*, the same with *Ida*, I was with
it, from beginning to end, like being completely somewhere else, on some very abstract, very formal, on
some *mental* plane, or elan, completely somewhere else.
No doubt, B r e c h t would put a curse on it: where is
the *Verfremdungseffekt*? He will, from his grave: Wake me
up, wake me up!

   Anyway, it was not like anything else in the contemporary theatre that I know. I don't want to confuse one
artist's, in this case Richard's, personal world with *direction
in theatre*—but really one's fully and clearly expressed
world is like a direction itself. I repeat again, as I said in the
beginning of our ramble, that to me, it's this mental aspect
that is a special uniqueness of Richard's theatre. I don't find
that quality in any other theatre I know. And he achieves
it through a very, very formalistic, very controlled staging,
so formal that it's almost the opposite of formal: it's reality
itself. And when those details become very real, they become
very real only because they are hanging, each of those
little details, on those frames that are very carefully worked
out, constructed. Reality, to be really seen as real, has
to be properly lined up. We have sometimes rambled
on, Richard, Amy, and myself—on some occasions, drinking
coffee somewhere—about how Jack [Smith] used words
in the *Lobster*, four years ago, on Lafayette Street ...


                        SITNEY
*The Rehearsal for the Destruction of Atlantis.*


                        JONAS
Yes ... where words already had a presence. Each word
was treated individually. And then I went to the Living
Theatre, in Brooklyn, to *Paradise Now*, and I thought they
are running around shouting that they hate this or that
or that they love this or that, and I thought: Oh if they
would only use mikes, powerful mikes, right there, and they
would speak very close & softly. Because they are, they
*were* trying to be very honest, very sincere—*Paradise
Now* and all that—and when you begin to shout, it just
becomes something else. And I thought: Don't they know

that they are speaking *words*? Don't they see the *space*,
the actual space between them and *me*? If they would only
use mikes, and come very close to us, very personally use
the words which are being pronounced as the messengers,

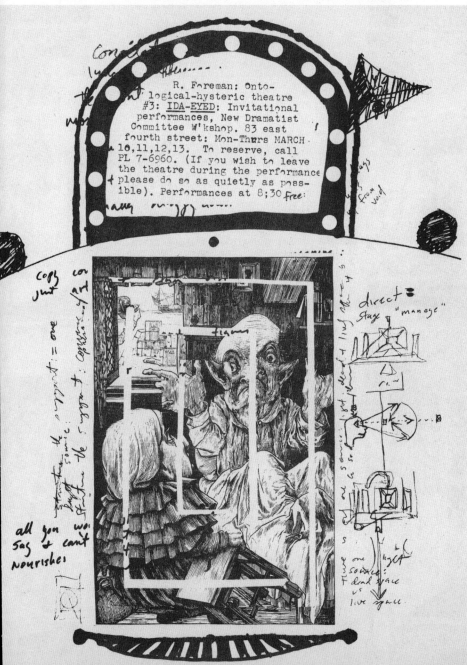

Performance announcement for Richard Foreman's
Ontological-Hysteric Theatre, New York, 1969

transmitters, the words and the quality of the voice.
But they didn't do that. They just shouted. So I walked
out. I hate markets.

The New Dramatist's Committee presents a workshop performance: ☐

1) Ontological-hysteric theatre: R. Foreman:
IDA-EYED (#3) An Intelligent Revelation.

2)Performance limits: 1 hr. 15 minutes(minimum) 1 hr. 40 minutes (maximum).

3) Ontological-hysterical theatre is/is-not
of benefit to all potential spectators.
Therefore if the individual spectator finds
at any point during the performance that his
perceptual resources have been so exhausted
that he feels compeled to leave the theatre,
he is asked to do so as quietly as possible--
causing a minimum of interfergrence with the
work still being done by performers and/or
other spectators.

4) Cast: HARTMAN=Duane Rivers: IDA=Margaret
Ladd: OTTO REINMAN=Albert Amatau: GERTRUDE=
Diana Davila: NURSE=Elsa Raven: DOCTOR+=
Matthew Lewis:        Stage production by Mr.
Foreman:        Crew: Peter Schifter, John
Pryor,Gintare Sileika, Max Brandt, Rich
Kleenschmitt.

5) Clarification: Ida is Hartman's wife.
Otto is Gertrude's uncle. Hartman is working on himself, whatever the external circumstances.

6) Plot: (Scene by scene) 1: Otto comes to
Hartman's apartment and asks him to allow
Gertrude to live there. 2:  The Doctor and
the Nurse come (to care for Ida? is she ill?)
and, fidding Gertrude asleep on the couch,
kill her. 3: Otto returns to see how things
are going between his ▮ niece and Hartman.
4: Hartman is concerned with demonstrating
to Otto that Gertrude is dead. But she is
only sleeping. 5: Ida returns. Otto enters
carrying a big light in front of his face.
6):Hartman comes to terms with life and
learns to accept everything.

7)Noteworthy stage events: Scene 1: Chair
that vibrates. Scene 2: Chair that collapses.
Scene 3: Chair that collapses (repeat). Scene
5: Chair that rolls to the light. Scene 6:
Gertrude and the Doctor are carried out like
pieces of furniture.

NOTE:  During the performance there will be
approximately 300 units of silence.
              ▢ ▢
New Dramatist's Workshop. 83 East Fourth
Street (Between Bowery and Third Ave.)
Mon.-Thurs. MARCH 10-13: 1969.  8;30p.m.

SITNEY
The point you are making is very close to mine. It's really
against some of the theoretical points you say. For me
personally—as I hear you speak, Jonas—I think I had a
really different experience of the play, *Ida-Eyed*. For me,
personally, what the play was ...

JONAS
... it was probably different for each of us ...

SITNEY
It worked! It worked in those traditional ways, in those
traditional ways in which I ask the theatre to work. And,
as Richard said, the things that worked, they may have come
sort of ... like a billiard shot, off the cushion, rather than
by direct manipulation. I think that's probably the only way
to work today, but what I was seeing moment by moment
was such things as an entire erotic presence of Gertrude,
an entire diabolic presence of the doctor and a culminating
scene between Hartman and Gertrude.

JONAS
It wasn't on any other level?

SITNEY
No, let me make a point. Now the only reason I could
even bear to watch this sort of thing is because of those
other levels, those other levels of form made it possible,
after theatre had really died for me, to see it. But the experience for me was not in any way the experience I have
of similar technology—for example, dance or film. Not
at all. But an experience of those things that theatre can
do and the means were other than that, the means certainly
weren't geared to that, but that was the experience I had
of these moments. The normal means of creating these
moments are those hard-hitting dramatic technical things
that you can learn at the Yale Drama School, where Ken
and Richard went. I assume that's what they teach there,
how to build up tension. Obviously these things weren't done
in *Ida-Eyed*. The mechanism of the play, the moment-by-
moment perceptions were on a very high, abstract, formalistic level. But what was there, I was feeling, was almost
a play that I could describe as very simple—it may almost
seem ludicrous—which is a couple, and another woman.

A sexual presence enters the house and, at the same time,
conjoined with her is a diabolical presence of the doctor.
And the final scene, which to me is of terror, is again
a confrontation of the man and the woman after both the
diabolical male and the sexually potent female presence
have left. Now this is like ... this could be Chekhov.
This could be Broadway in 1930. But here it was real to me
in a very potent, solid way and what I felt coming out was
the theatre experience, in a completely different way than
I would feel after a dance evening. This really gave me
that theatre experience. This must be very far from your
whole view of the play.

FOREMAN

No. What aspect do you think would be far from mine?
I mean, I don't, especially at this point ...

SITNEY

What I have described in a very conventional play.

FOREMAN

I can't see the difference any more. I say to people,
you know, is this really any different from normal stuff?

SITNEY

Well, it works. That's the difference. And I have a number
of criticisms, and the criticisms I have revolve specifically—
I mean ... Really, I wish I had seen *Angelface*, so I would
know the difference between the relationship with found
people and the problem about using actors.

MARGARET

Now, you see, I disagree with you. What I want to say is this:
that this play can be experienced differently, that I think
the reason Jonas reacted to it as an intellectual thing is
because he was allowed to. I mean, Richard did not make
him react in any way he didn't feel like reacting. I think
that's what the great integrity of the play is.

FOREMAN

Could we just clarify something? We've been using the
word "intellectual." I think there could be some confusion
as to what that means.

JONAS

Yes ...

FOREMAN

Because I think that what we really mean is something that
has almost more spiritual overtones rather than—like
people would say, I b s e n, you know—let's go back to the
theatre where you deal with ideas and use your mind.
I don't think that Jonas means you use your mind the way
that you use your mind in G e o r g e  B e r n a r d  S h a w's
theatre, but rather an emptying of the mind so that the
mind is more alert, more awake—I would hope. And
that's what happens to your mind in the experience rather
than having it filled with good ideas that you can really
chew on.

JONAS

Right. It's here also that we come to your own notes, and
it says: "Ontological-Hysteric Theatre." Why do you put
it that way?

FOREMAN

At the time that I wrote it, I remember it was for *Angelface*
and I remember I was trying to think of something because ...
that, er, Austrian cutting up animals was just here. He
had a fancy name [H e r m a n n  N i t s c h]. But as time has
passed, it's like one of those quirks of destiny because
I really again and again think what a lucky choice it was.
     It really expresses what I think is going on in the plays.
Ontology of course in philosophy is the study of being as
opposed to beings, and what I'm really interested in is taking
whatever is going on and just like ... putting enough space,
putting holes in it. Informing it, with the beingness of it
just coming through and almost swamping it and obliterating
the specific beings. And that's the pauses. There are
like three hundred pauses in the play, and the reason those
pauses are there is because ... one has to collect one's
thoughts. Then you start out with certain objects or certain
gestures or certain words, and then just ... The *being*
underlies them, sweeps through ... like, clears them out,
then you stop, and start again with the next group of things
that you're going to let the being-that-sustains-them-all
sweep through.

MARGARET

But the way you speak about found objects: I think that
you either consciously or subconsciously must have planned
that the relationships between the people were—well,
to you—were moving.

FOREMAN

Oh yes.

MARGARET

They seem to me to be moving for you and therefore they
were for me.

FOREMAN

I start out with a very ... with a naturalistic scenario.
I'd like to feel that I'm starting out with what we all inherit
as a standard, normal everyday vision of life and then ...
airing it, letting it out on the line to air. Instead of sunlight,
just letting *beingness* get in there and knock out all the
modules of habit and ...

JONAS

The more you clean out all those emotional, all kinds
of psychological details, one is open to all kinds of new
experiencing ...

SITNEY

What surprises me is that these very same constants came
across so clearly.

FOREMAN

I just want to make something that if people have the
inclination to do so, they can go there and ... they can really
feel good. It just amazes me that so many people don't
seem to feel good ...

MARGARET

When you were speaking about non-actors doing it, just sort
of interesting people doing it rather than actors, in a way
I think it would be the ideal thing to have interesting actors
who were trained very specifically in this kind of theatre.
Because I really think that there is an acting problem, which
I don't feel I conquered and which is a completely new

problem from anything I've ever faced in my acting work,
which is really incredibly exciting. I mean emotionally
exciting—whatever exciting is.

#### SITNEY
But see, the word that I would have to offer there is ...
and Richard knows it as well as I do, that this is a problem
that has been faced by film directors. And from what
I know of the solution they've ... this is a parallel solution.
That is, there is a way. The traditional way of describing
it was that, well, because it was film—the cutting and the
taking of shots—it's possible to have a non-actor play the
role. This would start with Rossellini, or Bresson, and
almost all of the best people who direct "actors" in films.
And I conceive of the possibility of doing this in theatre.

#### MARGARET
I don't ...

#### JONAS
As it happened, unfortunately, none of you two saw
*Angelface*, in which this principle was put into practice,
and where it worked brilliantly. It was a great theatre,
with fantastic "actors," all non-actors.

#### MARGARET
Maybe they should become actors then.

#### JONAS
[jokingly] Aren't you, perchance, a secret agent of the
Actors' Guild?

#### MARGARET
I just mean that they have to be people who truly love
theatre because I think that in the play there's something
about loving theatre.

#### JONAS
They loved *Richard's* theatre.

#### FOREMAN
I also think that working in this way ... When we did
*Elephant Steps* last summer, I was working with opera

singers. Now opera singers are notoriously awful on the
stage and the first thing Stanley said, months before we went
into rehearsal, was, "Oh Richard, what are we going to do?
We're going to have terrible people. It's just going to be
awful." And I said, "Stanley, don't worry because we're going
to be working in such a way that I really think that we're
going to be able to find, to *use* whatever we find in them,
and it's going to be OK." Now, I really think that it worked
out wonderfully. They weren't as good as the people in either
*Angelface* or *Ida-Eyed*, because they were opera singers,
which means something special as far as acting goes,
but I really think that some of them were more incredibly
beautiful as opera singers on that stage than any opera
singers I've ever seen. And I think it was because of
the specific way they were allowed to work, which I think
relates to the way people like Bresson work with non-actors,
because in essence opera singers are ... you know, they're
worse than non-actors, because they're horribly trained
actors. But working with anybody in that sort of way ...

MARGARET

But ... just like everybody has rejected most playwrights
in the theatre—and I certainly have—I think people
have rejected most actors because most actors have had
to work for those playwrights and have really become
perverted in their whole perception of the way to behave,
and most of them are lousy. I mean, mostly it's going
to be, you know ...

JONAS

Maybe, for the purpose of informing those here who
didn't see *Angelface*, Richard could say something about
how *Angelface* was performed—what was the procedure—
because it's pertinent here.

FOREMAN

There was a tape recorder. The lines were broken up (as
in *Ida-Eyed*) into three, five, or seven lines per unit with a
pause in between. The actors recorded all the lines monoto-
nously, at a fairly quick speed. They read through the
play with the pause. In performance the tape was played.
The actor, as soon as he heard one of his own lines coming
over the tape, would start to repeat that line as soon as it

began, but whereas the recorded line was spoken at normal speed, in repeating it he would delay after each word so that he never got to finish the line. And if, on the tape, he started another line in that same unit, he could either continue his original line or pick up the new line ... The only rule was that when they got a pause, wherever they were on stage when the tape stopped, all of the actors stopped.

### SITNEY
Now this isn't in the script. I read the script.

### FOREMAN
No, it's not in the script.

### SITNEY
I mean, this seems like a brilliant idea ...

### JONAS
How many rehearsals did you have?

### FOREMAN
Two weeks, two and a half hours a day.

### SITNEY
I'm curious as to how the tape recorder came about ...

### FOREMAN
I don't know. I remember I sat there for weeks before rehearsal talking to Amy about how we could do it—I can never get non-actors to memorize the lines. And we just thought of all kinds of technical procedures and tested them and experimented with them, and this seemed all of a sudden very interesting. And now, for instance, *Ida-Eyed* was written to be performed exactly that same way, but it seemed sort of dull to go through the same thing. So we sat around trying to figure out something else, which I think is much more interesting. I think there *should* be two separate creative processes. First you get the text, which then becomes the found object that you go to work on.

### JONAS
There were pauses between the lines, here and there. Were they controlled? Did you control them?

FOREMAN

Pauses between every five or six lines. It would vary,
but I did always control the length of the pauses. I would
stop the tape recorder in the preset pause on the tape
and hold it for as long as I thought was interesting.

SNOW

Yes, the sound was fantastic.

JONAS

Then, the pauses, the pacing of the play, could be different
every performance?

FOREMAN

Yes, it was always different.

MARGARET

Richard, you knew what was going on in the play, right?
I mean, specifically. Steve came one night. He came twice,
and he said he knew much more what was going on the
second time. Therefore, he said, it was ten times more exciting for him because he knew.

FOREMAN

Well, it's no joke that I print the synopsis. Maybe it should
be more detailed. I don't know what to do about it.

SITNEY

I thought it was very discreet—the printing of the synopsis.
I thought it was discreetly done. Because I saw the play
twice and they were two different experiences. I tend
to go to plays and concerts—not so with films—with a great
deal of energy and to fade as it goes on. It's my personal
thing. So I saw it once with the absolute high key of energy
all the way through Scene Four. The second time I dozed
through Scene One and by the time I got to Scene Six,
I was ready to take on even the waiter at Ratner's. To me
there were two experiences, but in terms of theatre they
were exactly the same experience. The point was there.

JONAS

That's the strangest way of looking at a play I've heard yet.
Since we are so frank, I'll make a confession too. I saw it

by Richard Foreman: onto-
logical-hysteric theatre:
(live) Cinematheque: April
9-10-11 and 14: 8:30

twice, *Ida-Eyed*, and I don't know what it's all about. I know
nothing and I'm not interested in knowing what it's all
about: I was not interested in what it was all about when
I was watching it. Same case as with Gregory's *Twice*

*a Man.* Later I read the synopsis and I didn't care what the
synopsis was all about. I liked it as a thing in itself, but
I didn't connect it with the play. Now I'm reading it [reads
program notes]. Same when I read Gregory's synopsis.
I said: Really! That's what it's all about? And I had completely liked what I saw ... [laughter] It was like in music, all
that formal music, and the same thing here ... That's why
I say I got pulled into that formal and ontological world
and it was fantastic. I was with it ...

FOREMAN

I don't print detailed notes because I think there is something wrong if people don't ... I only mean that in the
sense that most people get so upset if they can't figure out
what's going on. I also love to see things where, on that level,
I don't know what's going on. But this is an important point.
I specifically start out in my own mind with a naturalistic
scenario and with essentially realistically conceived characters, and the whole point is to reach people, no longer to
be blocked by seeing those aspects dissolve. So really the
whole point is to dissolve. You do start with that ... but to
dissolve it ... not to end up knowing about it, because I think
knowing about it is getting fixated on it, is getting refixed
in all the grooves of association and habit and so forth that
get us into all kinds of trouble in life.

JONAS

Now, you worked on *Angelface* with non-actors, and in
*Ida-Eyed* with actors. Do you think *Ida-Eyed* would have
been stronger if you'd done it with non-actors?

FOREMAN

I almost don't want to answer that question from the so-called
aesthetic point of view. I didn't feel that I could ask non-
actors to learn it. For me, that's an excellent reason for not
using non-actors. A practical reason like that is just as
beautiful, as pleasing, as an invented aesthetic reason.
Now I found that I was ... I seriously meant that I have no
opinion.

JONAS

They were two different productions, that's all.

FOREMAN

Yes, because different things are fine in their own circumstances. And what I do next will depend on all kinds of circumstance, and I'll just let the decisions come from them.

[Pause]

JONAS

Since we're sort of stuck, why don't you talk about something as trivial as your own growth as a "young theatre man in New York."

FOREMAN

Coming out of college I came to New York, and at that point, I guess, we were just moving out of abstract expressionism in art, into pop and op and so forth, and I thought that was very dull. And I thought of myself as in this very vigorous, viciously intellectual European tradition, and accidentally I happened to see some of the early screenings of the various original classics of the New American Cinema, and, well, for the next two or three years, I guess, I saw just about everything and it was certainly a major influence that changed the way I looked at art. It was interesting to me because it seemed to me—I was thinking about this the other day—at that point the films were an art that were in a specific place that allowed me to place myself in a specific way, very healthy. A few years later I had the same experience with hearing for the first time some of the new music that was going on in New York around people like La Monte Young and Terry Riley. And then recently—in the past couple of years—I have thought that painting and sculpture, with all the minimal people, are kind of ... falling into line. And the first thing that I was aware of that, at least for me, was sort of "placed" in the same way was New American Cinema film, and I think that there are a lot of other arts now that are starting to be in the same sort of place. They do the same kind of thing to me when I look at them.

AMY

It seems to me it has to do a lot with what Jonas is talking about when he says "the mind," "mental." It is a particular kind of use, allowing something of "mind." It is what

annoys people who don't like what you're doing. I think
you get closest to it when you say you want to baffle
the mind.

### FOREMAN

Yes, well, the avant-garde theatre in this country generally
says, "We want to exploit the body, and release the inhibitions of the body, because the mind, is no longer of any use,"
and the tradition of the mind that we have up till now—
certainly there are problems. But in emphasizing the body,
and coming out at the audience and caressing you and
hitting you and having the actors do all kinds of physical
things, my experience is just that the mind takes another
violent step to defend itself. And I think the only way
to transcend the mind is really to find a way to confront it,
to baffle it. You must deal with *it*, if you want to get past
it. You can't get *past* it by turning to another sensory thing
more strongly, because that's just going to make the mind get
stronger in response. You have to deal with the mind to get
past the mind. And I, too, think you have to get past the
mind as it is now. The way we are using it now. And I think
that the New American Cinema films were the first things
that I saw that were starting to do that sort of thing. And it
interests me because I remember that one of the few, like,
accepted critics today, well-known critics, of anybody
who liked the New American Cinema, was Susan Sontag.
I remember reading her article about *Flaming Creatures*
and she liked it a lot. But I remember her saying how, well,
it's wonderful and all that, but of course Jonas Mekas says
it's something new and different, and what's the matter—
doesn't he remember the stuff that Buñuel and Dalí
and Cocteau and all those people were doing back in the
'20s and '30s? And I think she's incorrect. I think there
really is something very different going on, first with these
films, then with the new music and now with the painting.
And I hope that my plays are the beginning thing in that
same tradition for the theatre. Obviously there were people
who felt similar things, and in other ways similar things
were going on previously. I mean, someone like Gertrude
Stein obviously was doing all kinds of things we haven't
even caught up to yet. But I think we're in a wonderful time.
I think incredibly great art is being produced today that
very few people know about or understand.

SITNEY

I'm shocked at the small number of people who'll show
up for art on any level, except when it's at the Billy Rose
Theatre, and then you get Clive Barnes ...

FOREMAN

I was really thinking of specific people that I care about
who seem to have difficulty believing that things like
this aren't just putting them on, at least to make those
people understand that they weren't being put on.

MARGARET

I think they will.

GEHR

I think the notes you had for the last play helped, although
they should have gone more into it. It's the same problem
that you find in films. You have a lot of people who come
to see new films—if you can call them that—but they aren't
prepared. And you're throwing this stuff at them, and
they expect what they always expect, and there's always
somebody in the audience that will react, you know, loudly,
that will not sit still. And unless somebody prepares
the audience at least in some way, this will happen whether
you see films or theatre. And when you prepare them
wrongly, it is also dangerous. This is like what happened
with *Elephant Steps* at Tanglewood, at one performance,
when there was a sort of a pre-introduction. If anyone
was sincerely trying to approach the thing, that pre-thing
would put people off, because it was approached in the
wrong way. I really don't know what could be done; maybe
you could talk about it, to introduce it.

FOREMAN

I have the feeling that doing that always sets people up
to think, "Oh well, we're going to have to use our intellects
for this," even if you tell them precisely, "Don't think
about it in an intellectual way"—

SNOW

It seems sort of didactic, turns it into a classroom. It's
true that preparation helps, but there's something wrong,
it just seems ... It does help a little bit, but there's some-

thing strained about telling people what we are going to
show you. It's in the work.

GEHR

I'm not talking about describing the play or the film. It's
like ... well, the reaction that Jonas had, which comes closer
to mine than would Sitney's reaction, which is twofold.
I really don't care about the description, the synopsis of the
play, because my reactions to the play have nothing to do
at all with the relationships between the characters ...

SITNEY

Mine does, completely. Ultimately. I mean, not moment
by moment, but ultimately, when I think about it and when
I experience it on the deepest level, it does.

GEHR

Well, I've seen it twice, too, and I don't ...

FOREMAN

Well, it seems to me that all of this art ... all of this stuff that's
going on is really, in a certain specific sense of the word,
a gesture toward, at least, a kind of spiritually oriented
art in various ways. And maybe we should speak within those
terms more, because then it wouldn't seem too important
whether or not it was enjoyed in quotes, in the terms in which
they are telling themselves they must enjoy. Much of this
art is concerned with things in similar areas, in placing the
spectator in such a way that he can at least connect with
those energies.

JONAS

You could mention light, the use of light in *Ida-Eyed* ...

SITNEY

Recently, there are a number of attitudes I've been encountering, more and more attitudes where religion—among
hard-core intellectuals—where the idea of a religiously
oriented art is horrendous ...

FOREMAN

I don't think we're talking about hard-core intellectuals.

SNOW
Who are all these hard-core intellectuals?

JONAS
I said, to me it was a *mental* experience. I mean on some
mental level. I don't mean intellectual experience.

SITNEY
I mean precisely that. It seems to me the kind of play that
might well ... I really wish a couple of people had seen it that
I encouraged to see it ...

JONAS
Then we would have found out what stuff the intellectuals
are made of these days.

FOREMAN
I think about a year ago, I had a discussion after I did
*Angelface*, and I got into a long argument with a playwright
who shall be nameless but is certainly one of the well-
known avant-garde playwrights in New York, who writes
articles for *The NY Times*, etc. And we were talking and
somehow we got into the area of ideas and she said, well,
what ideas are in your play, and I started talking about how
I really didn't want "ideas" to be in my plays because "ideas"
got in the way of reality—you end up with concepts of
things rather than the things, and she really got so angry
when I refused to say that there were any "ideas" in my
play that she stormed out of the room and said, "Well, that's
idiotic."

JOYCE
That's it. That's the limit.

[Pause]

FOREMAN
It seems to me really, the interesting problem in the theatre
—and I think it may be stronger in the theatre than anywhere else—is really the problem of language. I suspect that
in the Elizabethan era somehow—in a sense that's not true
today—the crucial moments in people's lives really did
turn upon confrontations of one person and another, vis-à-

vis the use of language—and you really had the feeling
that your life was a series of saying things to other people
and things happening because of that.

SITNEY

But this also must have been true of drama at the end of the
seventeenth century.

AMY

But I don't necessarily think that is, in effect, drama.

SITNEY

You mean Congreve and so on?

AMY

I think some Restoration and Jacobian drama is extremely
good.

SITNEY

Also, I mean, like ... Is Oscar Wilde ...? I mean, there were
times in history when people really lived in terms of what
they said, and these times were not necessarily times of great
drama.

FOREMAN

Even if that's true, the point is that people seem to generally
have the feeling today that it isn't true now that language
is a prime mover of life, and as a result, in literature, there's
a difficulty in using language. Look at all the books written
that discuss the breakdown of language in today's literature. The narrative theatre does not face up to that, but
the advanced theatre does. But again, most of the advanced
theatre tends to deal with that problem by cutting out
the words, having the actors use animal noises, improvise,
all kinds of physical things, which again, I think, is no
answer to the problem. If the problem is with the language,
you have to confront the language.

KELMAN

I don't understand the whole thing, actually. Because
first of all, I don't think I believe it. I don't think I believe
that this problem exists now. I think we still do what
the Elizabethans did.

SITNEY

Our situation here tonight certainly tends toward Ken's point.

KELMAN

Well, that's a parody of what I'm saying ...

FOREMAN

No, it doesn't tend toward Ken's point. Because what are we doing here tonight? I don't know if this really means anything crucial to anybody here.

KELMAN

Yes, *this* tends to negate what I'm saying [points to the tape recorder], its very presence, in a way. But I wish you would pursue it a little to the extent of clarifying not exactly what you mean by the—to put it simply—noncommunication but what forms have replaced it, for instance.

FOREMAN

Replaced speech?

KELMAN

Yes. Do you think ...

FOREMAN

It's very strange, but the only thing that makes any sense to me is like the ultimate play which would capture the image. The ultimate play would be like you have these people on the stage, and they're sort of milling around mumbling to each other, and about every five minutes suddenly the whole stage goes *click* and turns a little—click!—you know? And they get shaken a little, and they go back to mumbling, glub-glub-glub-glub.

JONAS

Cut-ups, blurs, single frames on stage, shaking the "camera," actually done during the production.

FOREMAN

It used to be, when a king would say, "All right, we're going to war against Italy ..."

KELMAN

But isn't this really into the aspect of the idea of causality?
I mean, as much as language? That is to say that drama
has traditionally functioned as a very cause-and-effect
thing, more than any other art. One thing happens, another
happens, this thing builds—and now, our concept of the
world is not that.

SNOW

Then you do agree with what Richard says about the use
of language?

FOREMAN

I don't say that the difficulty with language is the
root phenomenon. I think the difficulty comes from other
things.

KELMAN

Ahh, this is the knot for me because I think ... I'm not
sure that I feel the difficulty of language as being the direct
and crucial function of the other difficulty.

SNOW

You mean not the product?

KELMAN

Oh, I prefer to say function, I think.

FOREMAN

I guess I just don't agree. And I see the theatre as the
medium which uses language in a very specific physical
sense, and a language which has now been eaten away
at by termites. That's why the problem of language
bothers me: not because I think the problem starts with
language.

KELMAN

Yes, of course. Right. The ways of thinking, the language ...

FOREMAN

But it manifests itself most problematically, for me,
trying to deal with the theatre, in trying to write language.

KELMAN

Yes. This is true for me too, but I think it's only because
it's through the language that the play exists.


JONAS

But when we speak about theatre, when we say: Our theatre
today is in bad shape, we always come to the directing.
I think that's basic. Plays are there—and playwrights have
their own problems, be it language or something else—
but when the theatre dies, it happens again and again, and
it always comes down to the direction. The theatre dies
in the actual production. Maybe that's what killed the
language. You can revive the language through the production.

SITNEY

Since Strindberg at least.


[Laughter]

KELMAN

Strindberg?


SITNEY

I mean, one of the great sad experiences for me was seeing
the Berliner Ensemble. A theatre which lived motholog-
ically in my imagination and fell flat on its face in my eyes.
At least, as far back as I can go is the Strindberg Theatre,
which produced his plays, and he called it the Intimate
Theatre. I mean, it doesn't seem to me so outrageous
and so laughable, in the sense that ...


JONAS

How large was Strindberg's theatre?


SITNEY

I gather it seated about sixty people.


KELMAN

Oh, you're speaking about the physical theatre now, not the
playwright.

SITNEY

Well, no, a playwright working for a theatre. The relationship
between playwright and theatre. I mean, I like your own
work very much, as written …

KELMAN

Well, I like Lorca …

SITNEY

I mean, I have no idea, after having spent a few months
in Andalucía, how Lorca could possibly be done. But since
1910, 1915—when was Lorca—'32? It is still a lean time.
It's a time of picking one man fifteen years later who was …
it really is. I mean, theatre is slightly more productive
than opera has been.

JONAS

I am not too sure we are speaking about the same thing …
And then, I don't know which I like more really, Richard's
plays or his productions. You see, what we have here
is a playwright who stages his own plays. If I just read
them … it's exciting, but the productions themselves hit me
right between the eyes. Because the same lines could be
staged by director so-and-so and they could disappear there.
But in Richard's productions, in all three cases, the words,
the written words, were treated so royally that they became
like objects, each of them …

SNOW

I think we're passing over really interesting implications
about what Richard said about language. And something he said about causality, or feelings, or ideas about
causality …

FOREMAN

Ken said that.

SNOW

Yeah. Well, I think that's really very important to what
you're doing. Your use of language is really … it investigates,
I think, like, all the implications of where language is in
relation to actions, in reporting it, or announcing it. And it's
really much more nuanced about the possibilities and the

causes of things than any other language that I can think
of offhand in an artistic way except for ... well, I'm thinking
of J o y c e. Am I making any sense? This has some kind of
connection with the contemporary feeling for causality.
At least, I respond to it on that kind of level. How things get
to be what they are. The form that they take. And it becomes,
as I said, religious, because it relates to some kind of idea
of a first cause even as a degree.

### KELMAN

I think that what happens is that when we encounter a use
of language that begins to, in some way, come up against
causality, when this happens in a medium where we expect
a causal relationship, which was always dependent upon
this, it manifests itself very strongly. And, of course,
what happened—and now I'm able to say something which
indicates I know something (a little) about modern theatre—
the theatre of absurdity is a theatre which began to play
with causality, and things would happen that one would not
ordinarily expect to happen considering what plays have
been, but this was kind of like the classical formulation
that clergymen might have used when speaking to others
or themselves of someone who denied their religion,
which is to say, well, if he's an anti-Christ, he really does
accept Christ because he merely speaks of the same
thing in negative terms. And this is kind of what's going
on in absurd theatre.

### SNOW

That kind of thing has been going on in all kinds of theatres
that you're not dignifying with the names of theatre like
the English music hall and all that kind of thing.

### KELMAN

Yes, of course, this goes back as far as ... But this is also
comedy ... this is the root of comedy too. But it begins
to come forth in a serious artistic presentation—and I put
this in quotation marks—more or less with the Theatre
of the Absurd.

### SNOW

*The Goon Show* ... I don't know that too well. But it
seems to me that something that Richard is doing is really

dealing with this problem rather than just playing around
with it, and I mean the problem of causality and all of
its implications.

FOREMAN

Yes, I think that's true. You know, there are all those pauses
and like each of those pauses is an attempt to return to
the first cause.

SNOW

It's set up like a philosophical discourse. In a way it's
Wittgensteinian. Like you set up this thing, and then
you contemplate the problem, and it often has to do with
relationships between a word and what it represents.

FOREMAN

Yes, I couldn't agree more. But I have the feeling when
we are describing it this way that anyone who hadn't seen
the plays would get the impression that they are, er …
well, not like they are, because at the same time they are
very, very real. The only thing I'm concerned with is making
them physically real, not just language games.

SNOW

Yes, I think they're very real.

FOREMAN

I guess people who don't like them do feel that they are
just that.

SNOW

I mean, they could be a kind of fantasy. That's another aspect
of what you are saying.

SITNEY

They seem eminently real. In fact, I feel like maybe I mis-
interpreted, because to hear Ernie and Jonas, I mean …
to me Richard's plays seem concerned with those very basic
problems that most people are concerned with.

AMY

But now you're talking about narratively real.

SITNEY

No, no, they're obviously not narratively real. Imagistically
real. The image, they create. The situation they create ...

JONAS

Usually, what's really real on one level is really real on
all possible levels.

FOREMAN

But in every play I have seen over the last ten years,
the character comes out and any line he says, just stop it
at any point ... whether he's having a deep emotion ...
no matter ... what he's doing, I *don't* think it's real. I don't
know why. And somehow I do think that if a character
says, like, "I'm looking at my hands," that's real. I don't
know why.

JONAS

The others aren't real because they are formless.
In the truest sense. There is no mise-en-scène. It's formless.

AMY

I think what Jonas was starting to say before about production, how you [Richard] do it—is terribly important. Because
it seems to me that maybe the difficulty ... I don't know ...
You talk about mind and you talk about emotions or theatrical things that are recognizable forces at work in it. But
the thing that no one talks about—because it's the hardest
thing to talk about, and it runs parallel to what Jonas
talks about when he talks about mind—is a specific, aesthetic
emotion. I mean, I'm moved emotionally which is what
most people who go to the theatre want; they want to have
the emotions that they go through in life, which are faulty, not
real, simply reproduced or reaffirmed in the theatre ... to
be able to say, "Aha, those people are feeling the same thing
and here now I feel it again." The thing that is the aesthetic
emotion of the theatre, specific things that can happen within
the theatrical form which cause specific aesthetic "emotions"—for lack of a better word—to arise, are simply not
dealt with. And I think that's what is most extraordinary
about Richard's productions. Just elements that are unique
to the theatre, like light is unique in the theatre in a certain
kind of way, someone coming on wearing wings is unique

in the theatre. There are certain things that are *in the tradition* of the theatre ... doctors and angels and, you know ...

JONAS

Now take this last scene of *Ida-Eyed*. In both viewings of *Ida-Eyed* I was caught by the form, by the pacing, by the formal aspect of Richard's theatre, the contemplative state into which I was pulled in. But both times, toward the end—like the last two minutes—when they just sit there and the other two have been carried out, there at that moment, both times, I began *getting out* of it, descending to the ground. And from that half-descended state, I watched them, sitting there, very real. It was a cathartic experience. Like I went somewhere, completely somewhere else. I went through the space, and now there I am. I came back, but the catharsis that I felt was not emotional and not psychological—to the great disappointment of the psycho-analysts—but again, a mental one. As I looked at them, sitting there, onstage—so beautifully, so sadly ... And that's where Chekhov comes in too. Everything comes in there. That's great theatre, and a theatre that works. A great scene.

SITNEY

It worked because of the whole play that went before it, before that scene. Because of this kind of distance.

JONAS

Obvious. But I came back to myself there, always there, in that scene, somehow, both times.

FOREMAN

I'm certainly glad you feel that way because that's certainly intentional. It's like bringing people back to earth.

JONAS

You have been somewhere. Now you're back. But there remains a touch of light on your forehead.

[Pause. Then Jonas turns off the tape recorder.]

# A conversation with Susan Sontag

Movie Journal
October 30, 1969

### JONAS

I met you on my way to *Duet for Cannibals* at Lincoln
Center and you said, "I don't think you'll like the film."
Why did you say that?

### SUSAN SONTAG

I don't know why I said it. I think I was putting myself down.

### JONAS

I knew it was one of those casual remarks. But then, I
thought, a remark like that could also be an "aesthetic" slip
indicating that you perhaps see cinema as two cinemas:
one in which I work, and another one in which you work.

### SONTAG

No, it was just an intuition. But it also could be just my own
defensiveness. Because even when some people told me
that they liked the film a lot, my first reaction was: You do?
And you, certainly you like so many different things that
I don't have a stereotype of your taste.

### JONAS

So now I'll try to tell you what I thought. I saw the film again,
yesterday, just to get closer to it. I think the film is very well
made. At the same time, I found myself disliking the film,
although less than the first time. To say I disliked it is not
too correct. There are aspects of it that I like. The film
is well structured. It's executed with clarity and precision.
But I sit and watch and I ask myself: Why did she make
this film? It's a very stupid question, but it keeps coming.

SONTAG

Now, when you say that, I begin to see why, when I met you,
I thought you wouldn't like it. Because it's true. I don't think
this film had to be made. What I mean, I could tell you why
this film was made, but I don't feel this film is necessary. This
film exists because I always wanted to make films. I do want
to make films. I want to go on making films. The opportunity
came out of the blue, like a miracle, an invitation, *carte
blanche*, from a Swedish producer, to come and make a film
in Sweden. I have been looking around at how to start making
films for a long time, talking to people in France and Italy,
I have been very cut off from the film world here. In Europe,
writers, artists, intellectuals, they all meet each other,
you meet them naturally, there is much more exchange there.

JONAS

The equivalent of that atmosphere you find here in the
underground where there is the same kind of exchange.
Only that you have been in different circles.

SONTAG

I spent a lot of time out of the country during the last few years.
Anyway, this chance came up, without even trying. And I
was grateful that I was given this chance, because the hardest
thing is to make your first film, just to prove that you can.
I wanted to make a film that was relatively inexpensive and
had a small cast. It cost around $160,000, which was rela-
tively inexpensive. I made the film with Swedish actors and
with a Swedish film crew. I wanted to do something there
that also could be done someplace else. From necessity it had
to be some kind of abstract story that happens to take place
in Stockholm, but it could just as well take place in Paris
or Rome or London or New York. And that's why I thought
you wouldn't like it. It's not connected, it's not really rooted
in social reality—it borrows from a social reality but it's
not really rooted in it. And it's one foot off the ground in some
way. There is something abstract about it in perhaps even
a negative sense. The film is very private. Then, in a way,
it's not private enough, it's very detached. And this was a kind
of film that I thought I could make, I could do this film and
wouldn't fall on my face. I wanted to do something that I knew
I could do and do something else after, with the experience
that will come from this one. I would never have made this

film if I had been making a film in America. The story
would have been a very different kind of texture, the types
would've been more intimately connected with the people.

JONAS

When your film bothered me, I reasoned: You have been
a writer till now. Steeped in the writing craft, in words.
I find your presence in your books. Reading, like every other
art, is a step-by-step process. You go sentence by sentence,
paragraph by paragraph, and there are certain movements
of meaning and language, of syntax, etc., that keep you going,
keep your interest. But now you translated yourself into
another medium. And when I go through your film, second
by second, step by step—I see how everything's well made,
calculated, structured—but I feel something is missing,
something got lost in translation—it's too plain, too bare.
While in your writings you are there totally, every curve
of your thought, every emotion is transmitted through words.
In your film, I felt some of the subtleties got lost on their
way out, got stuck in the technology, in the equipment, etc.

SONTAG

I don't think that's true. There may be something wrong with
the film, but I don't think it comes from the fact that I was
translating myself from one medium with which I was familiar
and into one with which I lack familiarity.

JONAS

But if you are a writer, and let's face it, you are one—your
thinking, your whole being is directed by it. Don't you think
that affects your being totally?

SONTAG

No, because I have got a feeling that maybe I should have
been making films all this time instead of writing. I actually
have more doubts about my fiction than I have about my film.
Because the film is very much conceived as a film, I never
would have written it as a novel or story. I had this film
in my head which I saw from beginning to end. The writing
of the script was very easy. I just closed my eyes and I saw
all the shots and where everybody was moving. I saw it as
a sequence of shots. I felt less struggle, as an experience ...
less struggle than in writing. It seemed more comfortable.

JONAS

Yes, but maybe it's that struggle that produces certain
dynamics which ...

SONTAG

But it felt very natural. In some ways more natural than
writing.

JONAS

Which only proves that what's natural is not always ...
hmm ... hmm.

SONTAG

I can't convince you to like this film, obviously.

JONAS

I don't really dislike the film. It's only that it bothers me.
I am trying to get closer to it. Usually we say that certain
avant-garde movies are for limited audiences. But we don't
usually say that about a narrative film. If it doesn't pack the
houses, we say it's no good. But when I was watching your
film, yesterday, I thought that there is a narrative film which
is only for very limited special audiences with certain sen-
sitivities, certain intellectual directions. At present I happen
to be in a different group, in a different climate, so that
I am not that close to your film. Some day I may shift, for
a change, or by chance. And I may come to like your film very
much. There are films about which I wouldn't say this—
there are films which are simply bad. But when I was trying
to put my finger on something where your film really
failed, I couldn't put my finger on it. That's why I take this
as my own problem.

SONTAG

A lot of different people like it, and for reasons that I can't
even understand. But I find that, generally, I can predict
who is going to like the film and who not. And certainly it's
not only people who are involved in film. I don't think about
my film as a filmmaker's film.

JONAS

I was trying to look at it symbolically. But then again ...

### SONTAG

No, there aren't any further meanings. My film is a machine to produce certain experiences during one hour and forty-five minutes while watching it. In some way it's self-contained, hermetic. It's something that in the watching should produce a number of different emotions. When I say hermetic, I mean the characters are sealed off. It's the formal relations of these characters that induce this emotion or that emotion, this anxiety or that anxiety. Viewing this film produces certain kinds of anxieties and also certain kinds of fascinations and a funny kind of laughter—it produces these experiences with these means.

JONAS

I see all that. But still I keep questioning myself. I even went
as far as to say to myself: Now, it looks like it was made in
the '30s, the film has certain qualities of mood and image
from the '30s ... I couldn't pinpoint any stylistic differences.
I know, the film was made a year ago, but its style looks
like it's from years ago. I thought, maybe it was the Swedish
crew.

SONTAG

No, no. It's all in the script. The crew only followed it.

JONAS

So it's exactly the way you wanted it to be. Which baffles
me still more. Because in your writing, there are certain
movements, certain groupings of words and ideas which
immediately testify that, say, *Death Kit* was written in
the '60s and not in the '30s. And you aren't a Burroughs
or a Kerouac: your prose style is very conventional.
Nevertheless, there are certain dynamics in it that I find
very contemporary. But I don't see that in your film.

SONTAG

I don't feel that in my writing either. But I don't think,
for instance, that my film could have been made, say, before
Straub. [*Nicht versöhnt* showed at the New York Film
Festival four years ago.] Straub was very important for me.

JONAS

The formality of your film, yes. Did you edit the film yourself?

SONTAG

Yes, I edited it myself. Maybe I was not ruthless enough,
that is possible. In Sweden it's not that you are free to
do it yourself, but they expect you to do it. What I was saying,
this film wouldn't be what it is, if I hadn't seen Straub's
film. That's why I feel it's a film made in '68 and not
in '38. I don't know if that shows in the film, but I experience it.

JONAS

Yes, now when we are trying to understand it by discussing it,
yes, I see certain formal qualities that are certainly there

and that are contemporary. There are certain ellipses there. What I like about Straub is his staccato. I didn't like Straub on first viewing. But I came to like *Nicht versöhnt* with second and third viewing. I like his staccato. And that's why I am waiting now for your next film, because only your next film will place *Duet for Cannibals* in a clearer perspective. The third one will again add something else. So that the windows will begin to open.

### SONTAG

It's not for me to defend my film. Either one trusts the artist or not. The film is an experience. Of course, one can refuse it—maybe there is something personal, maybe it's in the film. The only thing that makes me uneasy is a lack of necessity in the social sense. I know that if I had worked in America, it would have had a social dimension. But it was made abroad. This is not a film about politics, though it assumes a political milieu.

### JONAS

Would you show this film in Hanoi?

### SONTAG

Ah ...

### JONAS

This is an unfair question. Hanoi is at war.

### SONTAG

No, the Vietnamese certainly don't need it.

### JONAS

Who needs it? You?

### SONTAG

I needed to make it. And I think there is a place for it.

### JONAS

These are not fair questions.

### SONTAG

The films that are made in Hanoi, you can't see them as films. They aren't films. They are part of a national consciousness,

which is struggling heroically. When I was in Hanoi, I went
to their film studios and I was watching what they were doing
and they were making film posters. They are instruments
of national consciousness, and I completely approve of that
kind of cinema. I don't think people in Hanoi can afford
anything else right now. But our situation is more complicated.
Art that is interesting to us is an art that disturbs people,
changes their heads in some way.

[After a telephone interruption.]

... There is this question of sensibility, though. It's very
interesting to me that you say, for instance, that the first time
you saw *Nicht versöhnt* you had a resistance to the film.
I don't say that my film is like Straub's film. But it certainly
may help to explain my sensibility. When I saw Straub's
film I practically fainted. I was so taken by it, I wanted
to go and kiss the screen. It was like an answer to a question
that I didn't know I had. But when I saw the answer, then
I knew that this question, the problem that the film was
dealing with, the stylistic problem was solved. I knew it within the first ten seconds of the film. So there is this question
of sensibility. Obviously, my film is very different, but he
wasn't the final step in my film education. I think after I saw
Straub's film I said: Now I am ready. He answered the last
question that I had in my mind and so I started working
myself. You had to come to like it, but to me it was an immediate response, the sensibilities touched. Earlier, a film
that had a similar effect on me was R e s n a i s 's *Muriel*.
Another one was B r e s s o n 's *Les Dames du Bois
de Boulogne*. And certain films of Ozu. Those are the films
that spoke to me as a filmmaker. That doesn't mean that
I liked them the most.

### JONAS
Our rambling here leads us to certain keys to your work.
There is nothing wrong with the keys. There are groupings
of sensibilities to which we need a key. And certainly,
during the second viewing of your film I got interested in
precisely the qualities to which all the keys from this talk
seem to lead now, to certain formal abstract qualities.
And I am wondering now what will happen with the viewing
I intend to go to. I am going to report back to you.

# A Conversation with Emile De Antonio

Movie Journal
November 13, 1969

This week I saw two films on Vietnam. One was made by the Newsreel group. It is identified as Newsreel's Hanoi Film. It's about
forty minutes long and is available through Newsreel, 322 Seventh
Avenue, NYC. Norman Fruchter and Robert Kramer
went to Hanoi to shoot the film. The film concentrates on the people
of North Vietnam, on their resistant spirit. It is an unpretentious,
direct film, like a letter from Vietnam. A letter which should be read
by everybody.

The second film is Emile De Antonio's *In the Year
of the Pig*, which opened at the New Yorker. It is a much bigger film.
It concentrates on the political folly, on the speeches of the politicians and the generals. In collage form it traces the American involvement in the war. As such, it is an important and unique document.

I visited De Antonio in his editing room where he
is putting together a film on McCarthy's presidential campaign.

### JONAS

You have become a specialist and authority on a kind
of political documentary where the filmmaker is involved
with huge amounts of material which he then reduces to
a presentable length. In all such films, there is usually this
question of credibility. You have all these bits of film,
this 100-minute collage, but every bit is out of the original
context. You have edited them according to your own
political stand.

### DE ANTONIO

I considered this problem, obviously, very seriously. It's really
a philosophical problem first: Is objectivity possible in
the kind of political film that I do? And my answer is that
objectivity is impossible. Because I begin with a set of

Institute of Contemporary Arts
Nash House  The Mall  London SW1

Every Thursday Friday Saturday
and Sunday at 6:00 and 8:30pm

ICA members and guests only
Box office  WHI 6393

Emile de Antonio's

Opens Friday 22nd Nove
A new film about Vietnam

# in the
# year
# of the pig

MAKE WAR
NOT LOVE

Poster for the film *In the Year of the Pig*
by Emile De Antonio, London, 1970

passions and feelings. I don't think you can be objective
about the war in Vietnam.

### JONAS

Obviously. It's also obvious that the saying "the camera eye
doesn't lie" is just a saying. The camera eye will lie as much
as the filmmaker behind the camera will lie. My question
was more directed to the ways of presenting already existing footage.

### DE ANTONIO

I aim for a kind of collage where, by the way you make it,
you achieve an element of reality which is more real than
the real material you started with.

### JONAS

I will tell you about one slightly different usage of such
materials as yours. I have been dreaming about it.
Your materials always seem to me to be perfect materials
for my own dream document film. I would use the same
footage, or almost the same footage as you did. Only I would
make neither collage nor montage with it. I would simply
string the pieces together, very scientifically, with an
introductory frame, the way D.W. Griffith used to
do, giving the name of the speaker, place, and date. Then
we would have a collection of irrefutable bits of historical evidence, almost like notes that could go with text-
books. As it is now, the film can always be dismissed
as propaganda.

### DE ANTONIO

Yes. But I am more interested to work the way I am working.
And then, Vietnam exists in history. And all other films
on Vietnam leave that out. They may have more passion,
more emotion. But I am interested in the political theories,
in the mass of facts. I am interested in establishing a line
of thought. You can't arrive at the sort of linear factual
explanation in a film that you can in a book. Not even a single
book contains it in any intelligible way. But I think that
because of certain peaks within the film that sort of point
at what happened, you have revelations, the film reveals
what really happened.

### JONAS
I liked the materials. I watched the film from the first frame
to the last. And I had only two hours' sleep last night.
It's all very real. And some footage is funny gallows humor.
The generals for instance. I have never seen such a bunch
of morons. You see them, in the film, they are there for real,
and you know they are there in charge of this war, and
you see their faces, you listen to them, and my God, they are
morons, they are murderers and morons. My personal opinion
is that DDT has destroyed people's brains. Why else would
people entrust their fate to morons?

### DE ANTONIO
Most of the people I interviewed have seen the film and
they agree that they have been used in a straight way.
The film has been screened for Asian scholars; it played
at Harvard and similar places and nobody objects to
its history aspect.

### JONAS
How much footage did you have to begin with?

### DE ANTONIO
You see, you can only work by compression, with collage and
technique. In all cases I had so much negative material that
I was almost at the point of going insane. Usually, I make
two selections. I saw some materials in Prague, some in East
Germany, the American Broadcasting Company footage
here in New York, I saw everything the National Liberation
Front made in film and everything that Hanoi had on film,
etc.: I look at everything they have and while I do that I make
the first selection. From the thousands of hours of film I
ended up with a hundred hours. Then I started shooting
interviews and getting other materials. The form starts
evolving as I go.
     Most of the films on Vietnam have little meaning
for me, because I am not interested in refugees and staged
battles. We had too much of it, so that we almost became
desensitized to it, it doesn't do anything to us. What I was
interested in was the intellectual line of what happened,
and it tells us more about what happened, I think. I am
not interested in demonstrations or anything of that kind.
I am interested in the establishment side, because that's

the important side, frankly, that's the side we hope leads
to demonstrations.


JONAS
What's the McCarthy film you are working on?


DE ANTONIO
It's not so much a McCarthy film as a study of why the
campaign failed. Is it possible to work within the system?
The assumption of the film is that McCarthy was the
last best hope of working within the system in a national
election.

When you said you were coming here, I remembered
one of the first times we met—because I don't see you
any more very much. But we were together when the New
American Cinema Group was founded, ten years ago.
We all went in different directions, which is fine. But it
was a very curious beginning. I think it was a very important
moment in film because nobody was really confronting
Hollywood or the big phony European companies, and most
of us had never even made a film yet. Shirley was preparing
*The Connection*, and you were shooting *Guns of the Trees*,
and it was in reaction to your film that I started *Point
of Order*. But some very good works came out of the period,
and it's almost time for some theatre to come up with
a retrospective of the entire period of the New American
Cinema, ten or twelve works, the earlier ones, because
I think—and you know I am interested in history—I think
it's terribly important.


JONAS
To look back, to survey, to sum up, and then make another
step forward ...


DE ANTONIO
Because when we started there was very little happening
and there was very little hope at the time.


JONAS
You said we all moved in different directions. But on the
other hand, if you look, you'll discover that basically
we are all connected, we are all dealing, trying to deal with
certain realities.

DE ANTONIO

I think the connections would become clearer with such
a retrospective. Because everything that has been done since
then was done outside the existing system, I mean, politically,
financially, artistically, every aspect—and there was no
underground yet—but now you know that the underground
no longer can be contained in that concept. Because
some of the underground people are playing now in regular
theatres or at universities. So we are at some point of another beginning now.

# Jack Smith, or the End of Civilization

Movie Journal
July 23, 1970

It all started when Ken and Flo came to pick me up, around eleven
o'clock. While they were waiting for me in the lobby, someone
completely blocked their car. Someone parked a huge car in front
of Flo's car, right to the bumper. Flo said she'd pushed her car
back enough so that if another car came, it would have enough space
to get in and to get out. But what this other car did, the man had
no consideration of any kind for the one who was behind him,
for Flo, and pushed back as far as he could, with a totally useless
overdose of space in front of him. He bottled Flo in.

As Flo was struggling to get out, inch by inch, we noticed
that the car behind us showed some life. There were two men
there, they got in, and obviously they were going out, and obviously,
we thought, they see and they understand Flo's problem, so they will
pull back to permit her to gain some space and get out. We watched
them. They pulled back a little bit, and as Flo was almost ready to go,
the two men in the back started going forward, to get out. They got
out. It suddenly became clear to us that they never had any intention
of assisting Flo: they just cared about themselves. Probably they
didn't even notice Flo's problem. They were simply oblivious to other
people's problems.

So we were driving, and talking, and trying not to be ironical. Ken told about walking with Stan, during his visit five years ago, somewhere downtown, and showing him this and that, and how Stan walked with his eyes down, on the street, and when Ken pointed out something, Stan just lifted his eyes for a split second, and down his eyes went again, as though, if he were to look longer at the lights, buildings, and signs, all the civilization of New York, it would get stuck on his eyes, and through his eyes in his memory, his very being, like some disease—so he was guarding his eyes from really seeing it. And Charles was telling me yesterday how he and B r u c e   B a i l l i e— on his last visit, two months ago—were driving to the Museum of Modern Art, and Bruce was holding a scarf over his face, to keep some of the fumes and dust and smog out, and when they were only one block from the museum—where he had to pick up his films from the screening the day before—he told Charles, turn back, turn back, let's go back, let them mail the films, and he turned back, to Brooklyn, and he left New York.

We stopped at some Italian place, had some antipasto and some wine, regained some strength, looked at some of Ken's stereo slides, and went to Grand Street. It was about half past midnight, the time when, we guessed, Jack maybe was ready to start his show. Because that was really the reason we met. This was our theatre evening, our evening out, we said, and Jack had this theatre thing going every Saturday midnight at his loft. But Richard had warned us not to come too early, because Jack is never on time, and if we come too early, we may end up by being in the play—he has actor problems. So we arrived around 12:30 and we walked up the four floors and into Jack's studio, and the studio was about the same as I saw it last time, with Jack's living "quarters" in the front [entrance] part of the loft, and in the center area a couch and four or five assorted chairs, and the whole north end taken up by a huge, fantastic garbage dumping ground, human wreckage set, Jack's stage. Seven other people were there. So we made ten altogether. Jack was there, on the set, lit with spotlights, picking up things, and placing them down again. In his hand he held the pages of the script. A phonograph was playing a Latin tune. It seemed that we walked in just when he was about to make his decisions about the evening. He stood there, in front, on the left side of the set, for a moment, and he said some-thing to the effect of, "Should we just listen to the records? It's a kind of night that I think is just for listening to the records. Shall we play some records, shall we?" He spoke slowly, and casually, with the usual J a c k   S m i t h slowness, and with a tone of voice that came from somewhere very deep. "Does anybody want to be in the play? Maybe

Jack Smith at the Film-Makers' Cooperative,
New York, 1962

we'll just play the records." After this little announcement he re-
sumed his busying around the set. He changed records, he fixed a
thing here, a thing there. He climbed to the second floor and changed
the spotlights—the whole ceiling to the second floor was missing,
but he had left part of it, for the lights and other mysteries which
we didn't see. So he disappeared, for a moment, upstairs. Then he
descended the rusty old brown steel ladder again. A few script pages
fell from his hand and settled on the set.

   Meanwhile, a fluster was going on in the "front row."
There were three very young men, and a boy of twelve or thirteen.
They kept joking that they wanted to play, they kept poking
fingers at each other and giggling. Nobody else seemed to be interested
in becoming an actor. Jack stretched his hand and pointed at one
of the older boys, and at the young boy. "You, and you, you come here."
"No, I don't want to act," said the younger boy. The older one went
to Jack. At the other end of the set was a contraption made of boards
and lumber which looked like a huge coffin standing on its end
(and which, as I later found out, it actually, or symbolically, was).
A second young man stepped on the set. The "actors" disappeared
behind the coffin, where they could hide—that was their "dressing"
room or space. Jack disappeared too. Then he appeared again,
to change the record. Now the record was Richard Strauss's
*Salomé*, I think, and he played it at slow speed, so that it dragged
unevenly. He disappeared into the "dressing" room again and
one could see him holding the pages of the script and hear him
talking. The slow dragged-out music enveloped us all into a post-
midnight unreality that seemed to become more and more real.

   The set was a huge arrangement of, I have no other word
for it, human wreckage: cans, bottles, containers, signs, bits and parts
of things, a toilet with a doll sticking out, dirty underwear on the
line, a huge red sign which said ALL DAY $2 (later Jack placed
a burning candle under that sign, and he used the candle as a ciga-
rette lighter throughout the night, and the audience did the same).
Another sign, half covered by junk and litter, said FREE GIFTS,
and still another said EXOTIC FRUITS—it was part of some fruit box;
still another sign, half buried in the garbage, said BETTER LIVING.
There were feathers, two or three old, dried-out Christmas trees,
an assortment of paper boxes, containers, and cans and bottles, all
meticulously arranged, and ropes and things hanging from the ceiling
and the walls, and pieces of plaster on the floor, and a large plastic
fish next to it. Can you imagine a huge house, a living room maybe,
of a large family with all kinds of things, and this house suddenly
caves in, and you find it here, in Jack's loft, all of it, a huge pile, with

all the middle-class home utensils, and things, and lumps of plaster—
the entire caving-in of a middle-class capitalist culture, TV culture,
A&P culture, Macy's culture. So it was all here. Or the essence of it,
and it was sad and miserable.

As the small activity around the "dressing" room continued,
and Jack kept changing records and touching this and that, slowly,
very slowly, one began to see, to realize, that there was nothing, absolutely nothing, almost not even a piece of dust that was there by
accident, by chance. It was all very carefully distilled and arranged.
One had a feeling that it was the result of many years, of ten, of fifteen
years of distilling. With the music filling the space in between, often
at slow speed, and garbled and scratchy—the music seemed also
to become part of the set, it just fell in, into the whole, became part
of the set, or grew out of it. One slowly began—having nothing else
to do—to study the set, segment by segment, area by area, and
discover how every part of it was a small masterpiece of perfection,
a small masterpiece of human wreckage, and how all the small
masterpieces of the set made one huge set, one huge masterpiece.
More than that: As Ken later remarked, there was absolutely
nothing that hadn't to do with the essence of the human wreckage.
One slowly began to perceive that this was not just a set for some
kind of theatre piece that was coming up, a background, a crutch for
it: No, this set, this arrangement was already the content and the
essence of the whole thing, the content of the evening, of the play,
it was there and it spoke already to us, and acted upon us, and it was
all structured just so; and slowly, around 1:30 or thereabout, it seemed
to us, to me and Ken, that it didn't really matter, it was no longer
essential what would come or should come, that the content of
Jack's huge work was already beginning to gain power and sink into
us, this set, and Jack walking there, like a night watchman (or was
he a grave keeper?), picking up this and that, and whatever he did
or didn't do, and whatever his "actors" did, by doing almost nothing,
or by doing something—everything seemed to fall into the set,
to enrich it more and more.

It was around 1:30 or so that one of the "actors" came
from behind the coffin contraption. He had strokes of red makeup on
his face, and one leg of his trousers was sort of pulled up, and an
old brassiere was on top of his "Puerto Ricano" jacket (I heard the
"actor" in the dressing room keep repeating, "Should I be the village
fool, village idiot?")—so he came out, and there was some kind
of water pool, small as it was, behind the wreckage, or in the midst
of the wreckage, and the idiot began washing his feet in it, but
unbelievably still wearing his desert boots, which he then took off,

emptied of water, put back on. Later he picked up an empty can from Jack's set (later, Jack put it back exactly where it was before) and started picking up water and pouring it out, picking up and pouring out. Jack brought him a chair, so he could sit down, and he kept working, splashing around the water and in water, and he wasn't sure what he should "really" do, he kept asking Jack, whenever Jack passed by, and he kept whispering to his boyfriend who was still in the "dressing room," and it was all so right and absolutely idiotic and proper and beautiful to do, that it went perfectly with the set and the play. Jack stood by the phonograph table (on the set) and he was working it, and he told the idiot to start reading lines, "Shout, as loud as you can, each separate word," as soon as the "telephone stops ringing." And the telephone on the record or tape started ringing and the village idiot came up front with the pages of the script in his hand, and he started reading the lines, and Jack came to him and told him to go back, because "the telephone didn't stop ringing yet." And there was the twelve-year-old boy, who kept walking all over the set, and talking to his two "actor" friends, and going back to his seat, and back into the set again, throughout the "performance"; and he became totally incorporated into the "play," like everything else was. So the idiot waited until the telephone stopped ringing, then he walked up front again and started reading the lines, and he read them fast, the lines that went something like, "Good evening. Welcome to the plaster foundation ... a juggernaut ... Christian civi- lization ... [or was it a Christian juggernaut?] ... Atlantis ..."—and Jack came to him and stood behind him, and told him, angry by now, to read it reeeallly sloow and look carefully at what he was reading. Jack told him to hold his pages in the light. "You can't do things on stage you can't do in real life," he told the boy. "Can you read without light? Can you?" The boy kept reading judgment instead of jugger- naut, and Jack had to stop him three times, and told him to read it loudly, "to fill the room." The boy became angry and shot back at Jack, telling him he had a sore throat and couldn't shout, he would read "regular voice," so Jack went back to operate the phonograph, and the boy read the lines. When he came to the word Christianity, Jack told him that now he should look "at the plaster on the floor," and since the "actor" didn't seem to understand what Jack meant, Jack pointed with his hand at the plaster, lumps of plaster scattered in the foreground of the set, on which a large plastic fish was sitting, and Jack said, "Now he looked at the plaster."

Jack described to the boy his next action: while he played the next piece of music, the boy should go to the pile of stuff and pick up a copy of *Time* or *Newsweek*, whatever it was—there

was a reference in the script to the effect of "my favorite magazine"—
and there was also a line to the effect of orchids, dusty and old,
dust falling on orchids hanging on the vines, and the boy read the
lines and went and picked up the magazine, and Jack told him to point
with his finger at the individual letters in the magazine, to the
rhythm of the music, which the boy did beautifully.

Now it was past 2 a.m. and as I watched, as we watched
this fantastic show, I had a feeling, I was suddenly very conscious
that it was 2 a.m. in New York, and very late, and most of the city
was sleeping, even on Saturday night, and that all the theatres had
been closed and over, long ago, all that's called theatre, all the
ugly, banal, stupid theatres of the world, and that only here, in this
downtown loft, somewhere at the very end of all the empty and
dead and gray downtown streets, was this huge junk set and
these end-of-civilization activities, these happenings, this theatre.
I began getting a feeling, it resembled more and more the final
burial ceremonies, the final burial rites of the capitalist civilization,
competitive civilization—these were the magic burial grounds
and the burial rites of all the corruption, comfort and money and
good living, and free gifts of the world that was now asleep, at
2 a.m., only Jack Smith was still alive, a madman, the high priest of the
ironical burial grounds, administering last services here alone and
by himself, because really the seven or eight people who were now his
audience (the other three were on the set) were really no audience
at all, Jack didn't need any audience, he would do it anyway, and I
had a feeling that he did it anyway, many nights like this, many Satur-
days, by himself, audience or no audience, actors or no actors, he
re-enacted this ceremony, the last man who was still around and
above it all and not part of it but at the same time conscious of it all,
very painfully conscious of it all, the sadness himself, the essence
of sadness itself.

The other actor came from the "dressing" room, he
was coming out for some time now, coming out and going back again,
dressed up as a woman, but the only thing one could really see
was a fantastic plumed bead garb she (he) had on, and she (he) stood
there next to the town idiot, whom Jack by now had sent back to the
water pool, to work with a huge spoon, pouring water—and then here
my memory lapsed for a moment, I may have skipped some important action, I was carried away by some other study or preoccupation
or thought for a few minutes, or maybe I closed my eyes. Jack gave
the idiot a big sign, in red letters, or black letters on a red background,
picked up from the street, and the sign read UNITED STATES
GYPSUM, and they danced for a moment with the sign. Then Jack

told the "actors" to carry the sign up front and show it to the people, and the "actors" couldn't keep the sign straight, so Jack kept fixing it, and then he disappeared into the back of the room, behind the "audience," looking for something and the actors by now were really fed up with it all—they kept asking the audience, "What time is it, What time is it?" and Ken and I kept telling them, "OK, there is plenty of time, it's early, and it's Saturday night, relax, it's early." Every time Jack disappeared for something, the actors dropped their actions, whatever they were doing, and they cuddled together and giggled and whispered something. But whatever they did, script or no script, private or instructed, it all fell into the set, into the play, against their own will, hilarious at the moment it all became part of the huge sadness of the burial grounds, the end-of-civilization sadness, part of the plan, part of the human wreckage, all prearranged by Jack, the Madman of Grand Street, who seemed to know it all, to know the corruptions and weaknesses of men, and the problems he'll face with his art, so he preprogrammed it all, so that now whatever anybody does to destroy his art falls into his art, becomes part of the huge collage, no matter what they do. He prearranged the music and the whole set so that it absorbs everything—exactly like the end of civilization itself, which it seemed to portray—yes, this set became like this culture that seems to absorb everything and everybody—a huge dumping ground, an open mouth of graveyards ...

So Jack told the two "actors" to put down the UNITED STATES GYPSUM sign and he put a large teddy bear on it, and they picked it up, like a casket. Jack himself led the procession, walking slowly around the whole set, and the two actors carried the "casket" with the teddy bear. Under his arm, and very close to his heart, Jack was clutching a large red valentine heart. Did he betray with it his last love, hope for man? Was it his silent message for humanity, for the dregs of humanity? As Jack was walking, he kept interrupting the procession to fix up a detail here, a detail there, a can, a box, a sign, a feather in the set, which his two actors kept slightly disrupting. I don't know what Jack needed, but he interrupted the burial procession and climbed up the black steel ladder, up to the second floor. It was at this point that the actors decided to make a dash, and after a small fluster they dumped the teddy bear into the Christmas tree and disappeared into the "dressing room," from which they appeared a few seconds later, without the makeup and without the plumes. Jack descended the ladder as the actors were leaving the set. Jack engaged them in a small argument, trying to persuade them to stay. He said only one more scene was left: they had to put the teddy bear into the coffin. But the actors insisted

they had done that already. "We dumped him into the pile," they
kept saying. "No, no, into the coffin," Jack kept saying. The younger
boy came from the audience and joined the argument, so Jack got
hold of the boy and told him to wait, as the other two left the set,
and Jack disappeared again for something into the "dressing" room.
As soon as Jack had gone, the boy took his chance and dashed from
the set. Before anybody could see, all three of them, the two actors
and the boy—the entire cast, that is—were gone from the loft. Jack
came out from behind the contraption and looked at the set. He
stood there for a long, long while, very sad. Music was playing, an old
record from the '20s, and a collage of street and car noises. Finally,
he moved his hand and pointed at a man sitting behind me, and
he motioned him to come out on the set, which the man did without
any resistance. So Jack told him to take one end of the GYPSUM sign,
and he took the other, and he put the teddy bear on it again, and
he began a slow march toward the back part of the set where the huge
coffin-like contraption stood. Jack laid his end down, helplessly,
and stood, pointing at the phonograph. He had to change the record,
the music was wrong, he said. It was clear that Jack needed help,
and that the play had to be completed, no matter what—so I got up
and walked into the set and picked up the other end of the "casket"
and Jack put on the right music and came to us. As soon as the music
starts, we should begin to walk, he told us, "at ridiculously slow
speed," and so we did, and we walked, at ridiculously slow speed,
the three or four feet to the coffin; it took us five minutes or so to walk
the distance, and Jack told us to put the casket into the coffin, there,
and walk off the set, and we did walk off the set, through the left side,
as Jack stood there, very tall now, against the structure of the coffin,
leaning against it, in the very center of the set, smoking, and very quiet,
and very much himself, and very sad, but also serene, somehow, as
he looked at us, and at the set, or somewhere we didn't know where
or into what—and there was a huge cross against the coffin structure,
and Jack was next to it, and below, some kind of Arabic castle ...
    And then Jack said, feigning slight embarrassment, some-
thing like, "That's it," and he walked across the set, and to the ladder,
and he slowly climbed up the ladder, probably to cut out the spotlights, and we stood there for a moment, five or six of us, and hesitated,
whether to wait for Jack or not, but we decided to go, it was close to
three o'clock, and we all went down to the street. I turned around as
we left. Jack was still upstairs. The place, the set now was there by
itself, completely empty and alone, the whole place was empty, and I
thought for a moment I should shout to Jack, GOOD NIGHT, JACK,
but I didn't, I thought it wouldn't fit at all somehow, and we left ...

We walked, five of us, down the long, dark Grand Street, without any words, several blocks, we walked silently and without words, and we knew, we knew that we had seen one of the greatest and purest theatre evenings of our lives, and we knew Jack was there alone and by himself in his loft, the keeper of the graveyard of the end of civilization, and one of the last and most uncompromisingly great artists our generation had produced, and somehow everything stood clear inside us, a standard for our lives and our art was re-established, for a moment, this night, in Jack's loft, here, downtown, this late hour, as the city slept. Somehow there was a new hope and life in the black street again, as we walked, silently.

# The invisible Cathedrals of Joseph Cornell

Movie Journal
December 31, 1970

How to write about the movies of Joseph Cornell? Where can I find such lightness and grace and unpretentiousness and directness? My typewriter is here, in front of me, very real. The paper, the keys. I'm searching for words, letter by letter. To pay a tribute to a unique artist.

One amazing part of Joseph Cornell's film work—and he is the first one to stress this and remind us of it—is that a number of other people have been involved in the making of his films, either in photographing them or editing them. But when you see them (nine were shown at the Anthology Film Archives the weekend before last), the same unmistakable Cornellian qualities mark them all. I spoke with Stan Brakhage, who did the camera work on a few Cornell movies, and he said: Yes, I held the camera, but I was only a medium who followed every indication, every movement, every suggestion that Cornell made. Cornell didn't touch the camera, but he directed my every movement, he took every shot. Rudy Burckhardt, who photographed a good number of other Cornells, relates the same experience.

Yes, this invisible spirit of a great artist hovers over everything he does; a certain movement, a certain quality that he imposes upon everything he touches.

*Film stills from Children's Party
by Joseph Cornell, 1938*

When in contact with people, this quality rises again from the work, like a sweet mist, and it touches us, through our eyes, through our mind. Cornell's mist (art is the opiate of the people), Cornell's fragrance is at once unique and at the same time very simple and unimposing. It's so unimposing that it's no wonder his movies have escaped, have slipped by unnoticed through the grosser sensibilities of the viewer, the sensibilities of men who need strong and loud bombardment of their senses to perceive anything. What Cornell's movies are is an essence of the home movie. They deal with things very close to us, every day and everywhere. Small things, not the big things. Not wars, not stormy emotions, dramatic clashes or situations. His images are much simpler. Old people in the parks. A tree full of birds. A girl in a blue dress, looking around, in the street, with plenty of time on her hands. Water dripping into the fountain ring. An angel in the cemeteries, the sweetest face, under a tree. A cloud passes over the wing of the angel. What an image. "A cloud passes, touching lightly the wing of an angel." The final image of *Angel* is to me one of the most beautiful metaphors cinema has produced.

Cornell's images are all very real. Even when they are taken from other movies, as in *Rose Hobart*, they seem to gain the quality of reality. The Hollywood unreality is transported into Cornellian unreality, which is very, very real. Here is an evidence of the power of the artist to transform reality by choosing, by picking out only those details which correspond to some subtle inner movement or vision, or dream. No matter what he takes, be it totally "artificial" reality, or bits of "actual" reality, he transforms them, bit by bit, into new unities, new things, boxes, collages, movies, with no other thing on earth resembling them. I have seen some of these movies in the process of assembling themselves in Cornell's studio during the years, as they were put together, or maybe as they were putting themselves together from earth's dream matter, from things that people usually either throw away or don't pay attention to or pass by without looking, taking them for granted —be it a flock of birds, or an angel's wing, or a melancholy looking doll in a store window— people are always interested in important matters ...

Ah, but do not get misled, either by my writing, the way I'm writing about Cornell's little movies, or by the seeming simplicity of the movies themselves. Don't assume for a moment that they are the work of a "home" artist, a dabbler in cinema. No, Cornell's movies, like his boxes and his collages, are the product of many years of work, of collecting, of polishing, of caring. They grow, like some things of nature grow, little by little, until the time arrives to let them out. It's like all things that Cornell does. Like his studio, like his basement. I stood in his basement and I looked in amazement at all kinds of little things in incredible number, frames, boxes, reels, little piles of mysterious objects and parts of objects, on walls, on tables, on boxes, and on the floor, in paper bags, and benches and chairs—wherever I looked I saw mysterious things growing, little by little. Some of them were just at the stage of birth, a detail or two, a fragment of a photograph, a toy's arm; other things in further stages of growth, and still others almost completed, almost breathing (on the table there was a pile of objects a little girl who was visiting the studio months ago spilled out, and he didn't touch them, he thought the creation was perfect)—the entire place looked like some magic hothouse of buds and flowers of art. And there was Joseph Cornell himself, walking kindly among them, touching one, touching another, adding some detail, or just looking at them, or dusting them off—the Gardener—so they grow into their fragile, sensitive, sublime, and all-encompassing perfections.

Once I was foolish enough to ask Cornell about the exact dates of the completion of his movies. When was *Cotillion* made? When was *Centuries of June* made? No, said Cornell, don't ask for the dates. Dates tie things down to certain points. Yes, when was it made? Somewhere there ... many years ... So there I was, a fool, asking a foolish question. The dates! Cornell's art is timeless, both in its processes of coming (or becoming) and in what it is. His works have the quality—be they boxes, collages, or movies—of being located in some suspended area of time, like maybe they are extensions of our "realness" into some other dimension where our reality can be fixed. Our dimensions come and go, Cornell's dimensions remain and can always be touched again by the sensibilities of those who come and look at his work. Yes, spaces, dimensions. No great surprise to find in Cornell's work so much geometry and astronomy. It has something to do with retracing our feelings, our thoughts, our dreams, our states of being on some other, very fine dimension from where they can reflect back to us in the language of the music of the spheres.

Or like the girls, the timeless girls of Cornell's art, they are either angels or children—in any case they are at the age when time is suspended, doesn't exist. Nymphs are ageless and so are the angels. A girl of ten, in a blue dress, in a park, with nothing to do, with plenty of time on her hands, looking around, in a timeless dream.

So where was I? I was talking about the movies of Joseph Cornell. Or at least I thought I was talking about them. I will be talking about them for a long time. There aren't many such sublime things left around us to talk about. Yes, we are talking about cathedrals, civilization. What's his name? Professor Clark? The cathedrals of today, wherever they are, are very unimposing, very unnotice-able. The boxes, the collages, the home movies of Joseph Cornell are the invisible cathedrals of our age. That is, they are almost invisible, as are all the best things that man can still find today. They are almost invisible, unless you look for them.

# O. M. Theatre of Hermann Nitsch

A conversation with Hermann Nitsch
Movie Journal
March 28, 1968

Hermann Nitsch, the Austrian artist, gave three performances of his theatre "actions" during his stay in New York, two at the Cine-matheque and one at Judson Memorial Church. The fourth one, scheduled by one of the television stations, was cancelled for fear of causing a riot among the viewers. The three New York perfor-mances were a talking point and created a furor. They also estab-lished Nitsch as one of the most important artists working today in theatre. I interviewed Nitsch just before he left for the University of Cincinnati to participate in their Spring Arts Festival.

### JONAS

You are working with very essential materials, like flesh and blood and brains. How do the different countries react to your work?

### NITSCH

Most of my actions, till now, have been performed in Vienna. And the people of Vienna are very much against me. Only a small group of people in Vienna understand my work and they are very much on my side. Mainly, it's a problem of

the Viennese tradition. Vienna has had a good number
of great names in the past, so now there is this strong hate
of anything that's new in art. It goes back to B r u c k n e r
and M a h l e r, and S c h o e n b e r g. Schoenberg was not
even allowed to conduct his own work, and when he did,
it was a big scandal; he was literally beaten up. Or O s k a r
K o k o s c h k a —he was imprisoned in 1909 and in 1910
for his work, for staging his own play, "Women Hope for
Murder." Kokoschka was one of the first men to work in
expressionistic theatre. People usually know him as a
painter, but for me his early work is much more important.
His early theatre pieces are very, very good. They are
short but they are very good.

### JONAS

What is your main aim, main direction, in what you're doing?
How do you differ from most of what's called "happening
theatre"?

### NITSCH

From the very beginning, I wanted to find a new form of
theatre. Already in 1959, I wrote essays on this subject,
which I consider very important. Already I was concerned
with the problems which I am now putting into practice.
In 1960 I gave the first demonstration of my theatre. The
most important thing about my theatre—which I perform
together with my audience—is that things in it really
happen. In the old, conventional theatre the actor "plays"
the play. It's not reality. But in my theatre all the things
really happen. That is very important. The objects that I use
are real—animals, blood, sugar. They are not symbols
for something else, like in the old theatre. The actor
"plays" being "dead." No! I have here this dead lamb, and
I pour blood into it, and I give it away—it all happens.
I want to make theatre where all the things really happen.
That's why I was very happy when I heard about the
happenings. They came to Europe in 1963. They had
no influence on me, but I was happy to know something
was happening.

### JONAS

Do you think the happenings are too close to the conventional theatre?

### NITSCH

I think that to let things happen is not enough. In my theatre, too, there are elements of the happenings, but I want to go deeper. I like the accidents in the happenings, they are very important—but I want the accident to reach deeper, I want to create situations to provoke accidents which reach deeper into our souls.

### JONAS

In short, you don't care about accidents which are, say, like when you walk at night, you stumble into a chair, the chair falls over—it's an accident, something really happened—but so what!

### NITSCH

I want "aimed" accidents. But do not misunderstand me—I am not putting down happening theatre. Happenings are very important for the new theatre. All I am saying is that there must be more to it. I care very much about drama, classic theatre. I think that the artist in our time must use psychoanalysis, and by using it he can deepen the theatre. The old Greek drama and that tragic depth. Aeschylus and Sophocles had it, and, to some degree, Euripides. Sophocles and Aeschylus are very important to me. They dealt with essential matters, they went deep, they knew how to use effects, how to affect the psyche. They used cruelty, terror, ritual. I like Shakespeare very much, he was a great poet, but he went away from theatre, away from the Greek theatre, which was the best of all theatres.

### JONAS

Shakespeare was "playing" too much ...

### NITSCH

Shakespeare was too much of a literary man. But to me, one of the great things is when King Oedipus stands on the stage, all bloody, and he knows he has slept with his mother, and he has killed his father, and he is blind—that is one of the most important scenes in all theatre. You, I remember, you yourself, you wrote once about Kubelka's films, about *Unsere Afrikareise*, about the dead lion, and you wrote that it was one of the most important scenes

you have ever seen in cinema. And so I say it is the King
Oedipus scene in theatre. I am not a sadist. I don't like
blood. I am against killing and eating animals. But I like
the theatre effect. And I must go back to A r i s t o t l e,
to the catharsis through fear and terror and compassion.

We have to see things with intensity to get the abreaction. The cruelty in theatre can make us free. The theory
of abreaction is very important to the theatre. We have so
many things hidden and suppressed. Our civilization doesn't
allow people to live the way they really want to. So we
suppress all desires and dreams and even ideals. When
there is an accident in the street, everybody comes to look.
When we have no other occasion, we create wars to get
abreactions. Our civilization abounds with such cruel, bad
abreactions. But there is the theatre, and we can provide,
we can create good, cathartic abreactions. I show meat and
blood and brains, the things which cause people to react
with intensity, to see with great intensity. Some people
cannot look at them, they avoid them; but those who look
at them and look with intensity attain the abreaction,
the catharsis, and the beauty through it. This is very
necessary.

This way, the things which are so deeply suppressed
in us that we can't even see them—they come out, they are
pulled out. Why do people like criminal films or westerns?
It's because a lot of people are killed in them. But they
do not provide catharsis. Only art can do it. Only art can
make people more conscious of themselves—not bad art.
N i e t z s c h e said that the Greeks were so strong and so
wholesome and had so much joy that they could laugh about
cruelty. They were not sadists. But I think that people of
our day need this element. We still eat meat. But we never
see the slaughterhouses, we are afraid of them. This doesn't
do our consciousness any good, it breeds guilt. It's wrong.
If we eat meat, we must know that there is an animal
and that the animal is killed to provide us with meat.

### JONAS

In any case, the animal must feel much happier to be used
in a work of art, as you are doing, that is, to serve the
spirit instead of being served in restaurants to people who
stuff themselves to sickness. I was very surprised to discover that many people I know got violently upset when they

found out you are using dead animals in your theatre. But
they aren't squeamish in restaurants. People who will go
to Vietnam and will kill people will be violently upset to see
a dead lamb being used as part of a work of art. Only the
lamb is happy about it ...


NITSCH

To me, however, the reaction in New York was the best.
I discovered that more people here like my work than anywhere else. And what made me happy in particular was that
all the happening artists whose work I admire—like Paik,
Kaprow, Hansen, Schneemann, and many younger
people—they liked my work. Many people whom I don't know
at all came to me to talk, and they understood my work. In
Vienna, this would never happen. In New York, I had at
least two kinds of audience, those who liked and those who
disliked. But in Austria I have only one kind: they all hate
my work. I have been put in prison three times in Vienna.


JONAS

On what grounds? Cruelty?


NITSCH

I am very well known in my own town, mostly by the police.
They accuse me, usually, of provoking public anger. Not
cruelty, not nudity or anything like that. Last time I was
in prison was when they decided that my work is against
religion. In one of my pieces I used toilet symbols and
religious symbols together. But I don't like to laugh about
religion. These are serious matters to me. I am using
symbols (they are always concrete, like, for instance, men-
strual blood) which are two thousand years old, and I bring
them together with the symbols of today—and they don't
understand them, people have forgotten the meaning of
religious symbols, they don't even recognize them when they
see them. So they think I am making fun of God.


JONAS

You mentioned Bruckner, and Schoenberg. Your own show
at the Cinematheque took place after Peter Kubelka's
show. Now, Peter Kubelka is a perfectionist and formalist
as very few artists are today. When I saw your show the
next day I was not surprised at all to discover that you are

as much a formalist and perfectionist as Kubelka (also a Viennese). You are both like Mozarts.

NITSCH

The form for me is very important. Abreaction is only one part of my theory of theatre. In truth, I may be able to live without it. But the main reason why I make my work is because it's beautiful. Kubelka makes films, and I make theatre, but there is not much difference between us. Maybe that's why we like each other's work. We are both for beauty, in the first place. Art must be beautiful. All art, of every age, period, country, is beautiful. Which is to say, it's formal. Without form there is no art. Form is a special aspect of art. In form ALL IS. The real message which art can bring to people is form. Form is that special thing which art is.

JONAS

You keep mentioning ritual, religion.

NITSCH

I have a particular interest in philosophy, particularly in Asian philosophies, in Zen. It may not look that way at first—but Zen is very important in my work. For me, form and art are a kind of religion. I always felt that way. I was very happy when I met Brakhage in Vienna and he told me the same thing in other words. To him film, making a film, is a kind of ritual, a kind of religion. My work, my theatre for me is an aesthetic way of praying, a contemporary way to pray.

I just received a letter from Vienna, from my girl-friend, and she writes that she just saw a birth, and that this new experience helped her to understand my work better— because my work helped her to understand the birth. The birth to her, blood and everything, looked beautiful, very beautiful. There was pain, we shouldn't forget it, but there was also beauty. Many of my theatre actions are like births. And a birth is like a crucifixion and resur-rection together. There is blood and meat and pain, and then comes the newly born child, and he cries, and he begins to live. That's why I work only with scenes of great intensity. To me it's very important. But most people do not know that they live. They live like animals, they live in a dream, they are not there. Through art, through aesthetic experience, I can reach very deep, and it's only on those deep, deep levels that I want to celebrate existence, not on the surface. You know, my big work, if I could really do what I want to do, would last six days, a big feast, with death and resurrection. You have seen only a small fraction of my work. But I may have to wait many years before I can have an occasion to do my big play. People will go in and out of it—it won't be done in a theatre. I need a little village, and the landscape. I want it to be a big ritual celebration of life.

# First conversation with Hermann Nitsch and Peter Kubelka

December 3, 1972

On December 2, 1972, the Austrian artist Hermann Nitsch gave a twelve-hour performance at the Mercer Arts Center, in New York. He was assisted at this performance by Peter Kubelka, who did the cooking. There were over thirty other assistants performing smaller actions and serving as "musicians" in the orchestra, these being mostly either New York artists sympathetic to Nitsch's work or the students of Raimund Abraham, the Austrian architect teaching now at the Cooper Union in New York. The interview that follows was taped the day after the performance, on December 3. Excerpts from the manifestoes were taken from Nitsch's book *Orgies Mysteries Theater*, Maerz edition. Other materials quoted are from my personal archives.

MEKAS

When would you date the beginning of your work which led to the performance on December 2, 1972?

NITSCH

I started in 1958 to write down my thoughts on this type of theatre. In 1962 I began actually giving performances.

MEKAS

Where did you give your first performance?

NITSCH

It was in a cellar that belonged to another artist. It was
really underground, in the center of Vienna. It was part
of a group show of "garbage" works. I did a 9 m long painting
with red color bleed, and I sacrificed a lamb. This was
the first such live performance, and it was on June 4, 1962.

MEKAS

What do you exactly mean when you say you "sacrificed"
a lamb?

NITSCH

I sacrificed the lamb in another place, where the audience
couldn't see it. The audience saw it already sacrificed.
What I mean, they saw a lamb on the cross, and skinned.
The lamb was very very small, because we had no money for
a large lamb. Also, to call it a performance, maybe is not
exactly right. Because I only exhibited the painting.

An excerpt from the O. M. Theatre manifesto of June 1962:

"On the 4th of June 1962, I shall disembowel, tear and pull to pieces
a dead lamb. This is a manifest action (an 'aesthetic' substitute
for a sacrificial act), the sense and necessity of which will become
clear after a study of the theory of the O. M. Theatre project.

Through my artistic production (a form of the mysticism
of being), I take upon myself the apparently negative, unsavory, perverse, obscene, the passion and the hysteria of the act of sacrifice
so that YOU are spared the sullying, shaming descent into the extreme.

I am the expression of all creation. I have merged into
it and identified myself with it. All torment and lust, combined
in a single state of unburdened intoxication, will pervade me and
therefore YOU.

The play-acting will be a means of gaining access
to the most 'profound' and 'holy' symbols through blasphemy and
desecration. The blasphemous challenge is a comprehension of
being. It is a matter of attaining an anthropologically determined
view of existence in which grail and phallus appear as two mutually
necessary extremes.

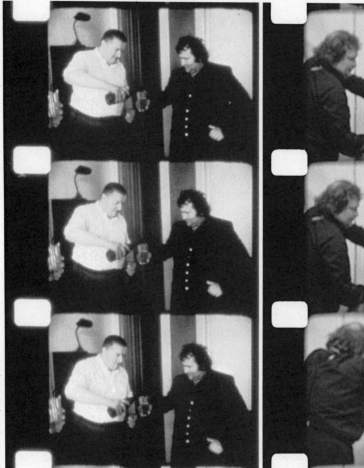

Peter Kubelka and Hermann Nitsch
in Prinzendorf, Austria, 1971

A philosophy of intoxication, ecstasy and delight finally shows that the innermost element of the intensely vital is intoxicated agitation, debauchery which represents a form of existence of the orgiastic in which joy, torment, death and procreation approach and merge with each other.

The consequence of this point of view is that one must recognize the sacrifice as a matter of ecstasy, of the inspiration of life. Sacrifice is another form of passion in reverse which develops differently out of the confusion of the subconscious. Sexual forces change and are translated into the cruelty of the sacrificial act. I affirm the absolute joy of existence, which must develop into pain. Through a complete 'living-out' and experience, the feast of the resurrection is reached.

An existentially understood art form has at its basis, as a result of the acts of experience which it demands, religious sacrifice and abreactive happenings. Except that the 'sacrifice' is spiritualized by art, bloodlessly, symbolically, and in abstract, but is for that no less real. The other 'form of passion in reverse' is changed into art (the 'sacrifice' loses its moral significance, merely a consciously conceived abreaction takes place)."

KUBELKA

I'd like to interject that the first real manifestation of Nitsch's art was a little bit earlier. It was at another art show, and it was there that I discovered him, and I saw that he was a very, very strong artist.

NITSCH

It's true. But I wanted to say here only when I really began working with concrete objects, with reality. Of course, my first really important works were plays, dramas. In them I had various objects included that one could touch and see, objects such as intestines. I wrote them in the late fifties. Then I got in contact with abstract expressionism, De Kooning, Kline, Mitchell, Sam Francis, and I had a feeling that they were doing on canvas what I wanted to do on stage. So I started to paint again, thinking, hoping that I could explain my theatre on canvas, or by means of canvas. I began including the objects in my paintings, and I poured blood and used the floor. I did all this with paints, on very large canvasses. This was one part of my theatre frozen on canvas, or on walls. The process of painting, which was so important in the action painting, was very close to my theatre. My paintings were always connected with my theatre. And when I exhibit my early paintings now, I exhibit them only in connection with my theatre. The first such exhibition, which demonstrated my theatre, was in 1960, and that was the show to which Peter Kubelka was referring, where we met.

MEKAS

Where did that meeting take place?

NITSCH

It was at a very stupid club, very much like the Mercer Arts Center. It was called Loyalty, and it was run by very snobbish

at the Film-Makers' Cinematheque, New York, 1968

people. To them our exhibition was a very big joke. It was very new, and everybody snickered at it and pointed at the blood. It was blood on the canvas. And I had writings on it about slaughtering of the lamb, and I spoke about intestines. Even the titles of canvasses referred to the things I do now in my theatre.

MEKAS

Artists like Otto Mühl, and Brus, where do they come in, in the context of your work?

NITSCH

Otto Mühl came about the same time. Mühl did "garbage" sculptures.

KUBELKA

I should say something here. Nitsch always likes to work, to associate with other artists who do similar things and who are inspired by him. I have always tried to keep him from that because I always found that this was not very good for his own work. Because his own work got mixed with the works of lesser but more sensational artists. But it was Nitsch who gave inspiration to all these others, such as Otto Mühl.

NITSCH

You see, from the very beginning, my friends were joking about the religious concept of the Orgies Mysteries Theatre. I like art, but I never wanted to do only art: my thinking about art has always been closely connected with the religious-philosophical concept. My followers liked my practical ideas and they picked them up, and that was good, that was helpful to the entire development of this direction in art. And there is one man in this group whom I like very much, and I tip my hat to him: Brus. He is a great artist, Günter Brus, he is a really great artist. His work is very close to what's known today as "body art." But he did it like five years ago, a long time ago, when nobody spoke about body art. He is a very important artist. At the beginning, he was influenced by my work, but soon he went on his own strong way. But I don't agree much with Otto Mühl. I think he took a lot of my ideas and then changed them, and I don't like what he came up with. He is always very

Hermann Nitsch, Vienna, 1972

simple, easy to understand, easy to like. Still, after I've said
all this, I also have to say that, in some ways, he is also
strong, and his work has caused him many problems.


MEKAS
Would you attempt to outline the key stages in the development of your work?


NITSCH
In 1963 I did two performances. One took place in March and,
I think, it was really the first action performance in Vienna.
People said it was the first happening done in Vienna. In any
case, for Vienna it was very very new. But this was only a

small performance. It took place in an underground gallery
called Gallerie Dvorak. We did an exhibition of my "paintings" and in the center there was a lamb hanging. There was
very little action, fifteen minutes, or twenty minutes. And
I remember exactly, I had this very, very small lamb. I remember this show like it was yesterday. And it was really great.
Never before did anybody in Vienna do anything like
this in a gallery. On the floor there were intestines, and
I poured blood. And the skins were hanging on canvasses.
I poured blood on the skins, and I poured blood on the
lamb, and I poured blood on the audience, and the audience
moved away. Then I was eating flowers.

MEKAS

You actually ate flowers?

NITSCH

Yes. Tulips.

MEKAS

What a lyrical period …


An excerpt from the O. M. Theatre manifesto of March 1963:

"Everything about me, to the very depths of the psychological, is
rooted in the European, Dionysian, excessive structure of abreaction
for the release of tensions. All the vales of my intensity, the condi-
tioned predisposition in me towards hectically masochistic, sacrificial
satisfaction are released in the action. The 'living-out' experience,
achieved through my actions, their cathartic effect, their immediate
abreactive character satisfies the deeply seated, unconscious need
for "imitation" experiences as opposed to mythical, sadomasochistic
situations, and replaces them indirectly.

In this way, abreactions can be achieved through the
analytically informal way of art without having to be filtered through
mythical experience patterns which demand an unconscious
identification. The intensity which is changed into the seismography
of the outcome of the action, reveals the latent causes of all
mythical excesses.

My painting is the visual (epic) part of the O. M. Theatre,
portrayed on the canvas, derived from the basic excess experience,
and is in direct relationship with the strong sensual excitement

which I feel when I see a smashed egg lying on the street, the mutilated flesh of fruit, cotton wool dipped in urine, white bread soaked in wine, tea roses (wet with saliva) which have been chewed and bitten up by me, a white cloth sprinkled with wine and water, raw flesh and giblets, and when I smell incense and vinegar. The excitement achieved by the tearing up of the lamb is the cause of and not the example for my painting.

The aims of the O. M. Theatre and therefore of my painting:

1. The latter can develop to a painted liturgy, a kind of liturgical means of meditation which demands an affirmation of life.

2. By means of the O. M. Theatre, a central resurrection festival of existence should be created.

3. Every descent into the perverse, the unsavory, takes place in the sense of a healing process of the awakening of consciousness."

NITSCH

And then I took an ax and I threw it into the wall. It was a very short action, but it was very beautiful, and the gallery was full of blood. Then, a week later, the police came to my house. There was a big murder affair in Vienna, a little dance girl was killed, twelve years old, in the opera. So the police came to me. They had heard about my show, so they thought I could be the criminal. I was asleep, and my mother went to the window, and they asked for Hermann Nitsch, they wanted to speak to me. My mother came to me, and she whispered: "Two very clean gentlemen are downstairs..." So I got up very quickly and downstairs, really, there were those two stupid types who looked exactly like from the American movies, with trench coats and all. And they had all my manifestoes. So I suddenly thought: "Well, some rich Americans got interested in my work, and they'll take me to America!" But they spoke German, and they said, "Well, let's go into your flat ..." And I said, "No, it's not possible ... maybe we could go to my studio?" And they liked the idea, and they had this black Volkswagen, and they quickly put me into the car, and my mother was crying. "I'll be back soon!" I shouted. So we went to my studio, and they kept touching the paintings, and kept asking, "Is that blood?" And then they asked me where I was when the girl was killed, and since I had an alibi, they became very friendly and started speaking about art ...

To continue about my work, then, in June 1963— to be exact, on June 28, 1963—I did a performance that

Performance by Hermann Nitsch,
Galerie Junge Generation, Vienna, 1964

represented a very important step in my work. It was an
evening with Mühl and myself. Mühl had a piece, and I had
a piece. The evening started with my piece.

MEKAS

It was at the same place?

NITSCH

No, it was in another place. It was at the cellar gallery
at Perinetgasse 1. The action used the basic elements of my
work: I used the lamb, I used the human body, I used the
intestines. It was a very important show, and not only for me.
It lasted from forty-five minutes to about an hour. And all
went well, until the police noticed it. Then they came in
and stopped the show, and Mühl couldn't perform. And that
was the real beginning for the whole Vienna happening
circle. Many actions followed, and I cannot describe them
all. I'll mention only those that were important for me.

An excerpt from a description of the action of June 28, 1963:

1. Production of a picture. I pour, splash, smear and
spray blood or red dye on the surface of the picture. Then, I stamp
about in the resultant puddles of color, slap the palms of my
hands into the puddles and WALLOW ABOUT IN THEM.
2. A bed, made up with a feather mattress, covered with
a white sheet, and a white cushion (the bed clothes have been
slept in for six nights) is put on the pavement in the street. I get into
bed fully clothed, cover myself up, and stay there for some time.
3. I go into the cellar, where a skinned, dead lamb is hanging from a meat hook, head down on a rope, in the middle of the
room. Beneath it, a white, freshly washed cloth is spread out. I throw
tea rose petals, dipped in vinegar and sugar water, the hair of a
fourteen-year-old girl, which has been dipped in vinegar, wet cotton
wool, greasy sandwich papers, entrails, the fat of entrails and innards on to the cloth. I pour lukewarm water, wine, fatty dishwater
and sour milk on to the cloth. I wrap the hair of an eleven-year-
old girl around the udder and raw meat, cut up these objects with
a pair of scissors and throw them too onto the cloth. During this
action, a tea rose, soaked in sweetened wine, is put into my mouth.
I bite and chew it up until I spit the rose flesh, wet with sweet
spittle. Then, a bunch of wet, fresh, and strongly smelling jasmine

is pressed into my face. (The smell of incense is produced.) I pour blood, fatty lymph, and lukewarm water over the lamb and the white cloth and the objects lying on it, begin to swing the wet, dripping carcass about the entire room, during which action I beat on the head of the animal several times with a clamp.

Finally, I stamp about for some time on the objects lying on the white sheet. The onlookers can view the results of the action. I go out of the cellar into the street (pavement), fold back the cover of the feather mattress, pour urine from a bowl onto the sheet; I put a white paper handkerchief on to the resultant urine stain and put wet hair on it, over which I cut up several revived tea roses, rinsed in lukewarm water, with scissors.

I throw entrails, the fat of entrails, innards, bloody cotton wool smeared with egg yolk and pour sour milk as well as fatty lymph onto the sheet. Then I get into bed fully clothed and cover myself up with the feather mattress. Fellow actors stuff entrails, the fat of entrails, innards, lumps of cotton wool, soaked in dishwater, moist, raw meat, and cooked poppy under the feather mattress from time to time. The actor who is engaged in stuffing objects under the feather mattress always dips them first in hot water; this must take place in full view of the onlookers. Then, they pour hot jasmine tea, vinegar water, lukewarm water in which roses have been rinsed, and the hot lymph and bloody egg yolk mixture on me under the feather mattress. This is continued until the bloody water runs over the edge of the bed and drips onto the pavement. I remove the feather mattress and stand up in the bed. My clothes are completely soiled. They rinse me off with lukewarm water and cotton wool. After this has been done, I wallow about again in the wet bed covered with the objects. I tear the sheet from the bed, carry it and everything on it to the cellar, and slap and throw the more solid objects at the walls and floor. I climb about on the pieces of flesh and innards, bursting the entrails and stamping again on the remains lying on the street (strong smell of incense, slow increase in the intensity of abreaction in the proceedings, occasional breakthrough of destructive sado-masochistic desires).

4. I untie the lamb from its fastenings, take it by the hind legs, and beat it several times heavily against the wall, then I hit the head of the dead animal on the corner of a table covered with a white cloth. Finally, when I have put the skinned carcass down, I kick it, slide it along in front of me and trample about on it and tear the entrails and innards from the breast of the animal. I bite into tea roses dipped in sweetened wine, which are held in front of my face in a bowl.

In 1965 I did an action with two lambs that was very strong.
It was about five hours long. I used in it new things that were important for the further development of my work. The same year, Stan
Brakhage was in Vienna, and I did a special action for him. Kubelka
advanced me some money, like you, but I gave it back. Both of these
actions were important for me. They were followed by other actions,
larger actions, and I ran into trouble with the police and had to
go through the courts and trials. I got half a year sentence. So I ran
to Germany. Those were the last actions I did in Austria.

   In 1966, I was invited to come to London to participate in
the Festival of Destruction Art. This was a very important stop for
me. I did a very successful show. For the first time I used an orchestra, with a screaming chorus, as part of the action. During this
show I met Al Hansen and Yoko Ono and many other artists—
this was a very international gathering of artists. They all saw
my show and liked it. This was the first time, I felt, that my show was
really liked, it was my first real success. And then you and Peter
Kubelka invited me to New York, and I did two actions at the Cinematheque, 80 Wooster Street (March 2 and March 16, 1968) and one
at Judson Church. On April 14 of the same year I did an action at the
University of Cincinnati. These shows were very important for
me. They made it much easier for me to perform in Germany. About
the same time my book, *Orgies Mysteries Theater* (Maerz Verlag,
Darmstadt, bilingual English and German edition) came out, with
your interview, and this was very important.

   In 1969, I did an action in Munich, a two-hour action.
I had a rich backer, and the show was very large. But it also became
a big police scandal.


                      MEKAS
   Where did the action take place?


                      NITSCH
It took place in the Aktionsraum, a theatre where actions
were done. Brus gave a very beautiful performance there.
I had the instruments and screaming chorus and all the
materials I wanted, and I fucked the girl with an artificial
penis, on the cross. The show became a big police scandal
because it was done against their will, they didn't allow
it. The policemen were standing all around—but we tricked
them. We announced the time of the performance, and
the police knew it and waited for it. But secretly, we
told everybody to come earlier, before noon, instead of

1961

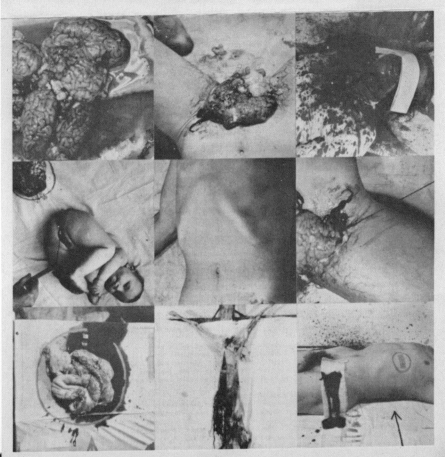

evening, and we did the action and the police didn't even
know about it. This action was one of the greatest performances I ever did. As far as the scandal goes—the press
took my side and attacked the police. The case became
an important victory in the fight against censorship
in the arts.


### MEKAS

So this leads us now to yesterday's (December 2) performance at the Mercer Arts Center. How do you see this
particular action?


### NITSCH

The December 2 performance was the first twelve-hour
performance I ever did with an audience. Before, the
long performances were only when I worked with photographs. So this was a very important performance,
for me.


### MEKAS

All the things that you did at Mercer you had done
before, in individual segments. But you never structured
them all together, in time.


### NITSCH

Yes, this was now. The new thing was to perform it over
a twelve-hour time period. I liked it very much that time
allowed me to work with repetitions. Like a leitmotiv.
Or like in rituals. Primitive people didn't know anything
about the leitmotiv, but they used it instinctively. I like
it very much when things always come back again. Because
the things I like very much I have to see again and again
before I understand them. The same is true with the
audience: it must be much easier for them to understand
my work when there is a repetition aspect to it, easier
than during a short performance. And for me, it is easier
to develop climaxes, accelerations—like in a symphony.
I liked that the people had time to look at it. Like in
a symphony: dramatic pieces, and fast pieces, and slow,
and again strong.

Text of a handout leaflet for the December 1972 performance:

INFORMATION FOR THE VISITOR: The visitors may come and go
as they please, returning at any time they wish. This feast can be considered both an exhibit and a drama. During the quiet parts of the
action, which only SEEM to be pauses, the visitors should walk around
the room and look at the visual results of the actions, which are
a vital part of the whole performance. It is important to comprehend,
sensually and aesthetically, the materials which are on exhibit
and being utilized (meat, blood, intestines).

### MEKAS

I overheard some people who said, "Oh, I think I am not
participating; I think I am not part of it; I'll go home."
And I told them, "I don't think Nitsch means that everybody
should actually participate. You could just look." Am I
right in my supposition?

### NITSCH

You were right. Especially in this play I didn't plan any
special participation of the audience. And I was really glad.
Those things that I wanted them to do, they did. Others
participated by looking and walking around, looking.
There are many ways in which an audience can participate
without actually doing the actions. In a way this performance was between exhibition and drama.

### MEKAS

I brought this subject up because I see a big confusion
around it. Every time they come to an event or action, the
people, particularly in New York, immediately think that
it's planned as "total" participation.

### NITSCH

Of course, I am not against the people participating.
But those are fashions. It is a fashion that people must
participate, that they have to "do" something. It is a fashion.
But on the other hand, I am not against it, it is a very
important part of my plays, particularly in my six-day play.

### MEKAS

Could you say something more about your six-day play, which,
I understand, is the main aim and focus of your theatre.

NITSCH

My big aim and project from the very beginning was the
six-day play. It's stated in my early manifestoes. I want to do
a theatre play which will take six days. It will begin on
Monday, and it will go to Sunday, day and night. The people
will choose when they want to participate, when they
want to come or go—like they did yesterday. They do not
have to stay all six days. Same way as there was no require-
ment that they have to stay all twelve hours. Though
I'dlike very much the people who like my work to stay all
six days.

MEKAS

What will you do in your six-day play that you didn't do in
your twelve-hour play?

NITSCH

The one important thing about this six-day play is that
it will be changed into a feast. The old stage drama, all that
happens in it, is very sad.

MEKAS

You had the feast aspect in yesterday's play, through
Peter Kubelka, who played in it what he called "the cooking
and eating" solo within your larger piece.

NITSCH

True. And this was the first time when people could be part
of the feast. And they had real food and wine. And we had
two large tables.

MEKAS

And then there was a thing when there was a lamb cruci-
fied on the wall, and Peter brought a tray with raw meat,
ready for roasting, and he put it on a small table underneath
the lamb. That made a very, very strong image.

NITSCH

We wanted to show the connection between the things
we eat, the meat we eat, and the animal which is used for
food.

Peter Kubelka's notes on the cooking at the December 2 show:

1. Schweinbraten
    Kümmel, Salz, Zwiebel
2. Lammbraten
    Knoblauch, 1 Guinness
3. Suppe 1
    Fleisch, Leber, Milz
    Karotten, Petersil
    Sellerie, Parmesan
4. Hirn mit Ei
5. Nierndl mit Zwiebel
    Stauben, Wein

6. Lamm Gedünstetes
7. Gr. Paprika, Oregano
    Speck (bacon) Wein
    Br. Butter, Pfeffer
8. Suppe 2
    Knuckles, Knoblauch
    Brot, Rahm, Kümmel
9. Suppe 3
    Mehl, Kümmel
    Rahm

### NITSCH

My hope is that the realization of the six-day play is no longer
an impossible utopia. At Schloss Prinzendorf, in Austria,
the preparations are underway for the production of the six-
day play. The Schloss Prinzendorf theatre will open with
this feast. There I'll use all the elements of my actions.
The inclusion of the surrounding nature will play a big part
in it—the vineyards and real wine cellars and fruits of
the area. The people at the play-feast will drink the wine
of the area and they'll all be heroes of my play. They'll
be able to look into the depths of their souls, they will see
some cruelty, they'll see something about killing, about
meat, about intestines, the whole thing of death and resurrection. They'll see it all, and they'll see their possibilities
and their real reality.

### MEKAS

You keep coming back to the Christian symbology:
cross, resurrection, crucifixion.

### NITSCH

I can't deny that I come from a Catholic tradition. I am not
against the Catholic religion. But I am not *for* the Catholic
religion. But because I come from the Catholic tradition, all
symbols of the Catholic religion are, for me, starting points
to go back to the roots of the development of religions.
For me it is very necessary to make the connection between
the senses and religion, between the sensual centers and
the religious centers.

An excerpt from the "Lamb Manifesto," 1964:

"On the Symbolism of the Lamb: Starting from the sensually felt reality of the bloody, skinned carcass, associations can be drawn with the beginnings of the mythical. The chain of associations so revealed touches directly upon the mastering of the collective surges of human vitality which are continually forcing towards the orgiastic. The lamb appears for the most part in a symbolical relationship with their end-points, sublimations and repressions. The Dionysian frenzy ends in the tearing up of the god Dionysius (of the bull symbolizing him), ends in excess."

The negative image of Dionysian debauchery, passion, ends in the masochistic excess of sacrifice. The Informel, the concrete manifestation of the instinctive in art has an essential similarity with the essence of the Dionysian, as its consequence is utmost excitement, culminating in excess.

The O. M. Theatre utilizes this phenomenon, and in this way achieves a regression within art, a breakthrough of the Dionysian.

The tearing up of the lamb in the O. M. Theatre is the symbolical action for the basic excess experience (ecstatic end point of the abreactive orgiastic.) The sensually real, sadomasochistic situation of the tearing-up is identical with an extreme breakthrough of instincts.

### NITSCH

Of course, my symbolism is very simple. It's very easy to see, for instance, when I am using the lamb's body, pulled open by two men, it's the—I never really say it is this— but it is easy to see that it represents the vagina.

### MEKAS

And then, of course, you have bread and fish ... Both items very Christian ...

### NITSCH

Well, I use those things a lot because they are very sensual media. I use them more for their sensuality than for their symbolism. I use them also for the combination of tension.

### MEKAS

The same you would say about sugar, eggs?

NITSCH

Well, I like the sweet taste. I like the sweet taste because
I like the connection here, working with meat.

MEKAS

Do you like the shape of cubes?

NITSCH

Yes, I like the cube. For me, it's like architecture. I use
it like architecture.

MEKAS

So that you use sugar cubes both for their "essence" and
for their shape.

NITSCH

I like sweetness here.

MEKAS

The lamb, Christ, sweetness ...

NITSCH

I like the connection between "lamb" and "sweet."
Also, between the wound, lamb's wounds, and sweetness.

MEKAS

It makes the wound sweeter.

NITSCH

Yes, yes.

MEKAS

And the color?

NITSCH

There is no paint. It's all red, all blood.

MEKAS

And white materials? White sheets, white sugar?

NITSCH

I like white very much. On the tables, for the blood.
It is very important for me. It's a contrast. White also means

sweetness. The church has always been against my work because I destroy the symbol with reality. I show that reality is stronger than the symbol.

### MEKAS

You place pieces of sugar on the floor. Then you take a crayon and you make a circle around them. You also encircle various organs of animals all laid out on the floor or tables. Is this encircling a formal means?

### NITSCH

Well, I want to make signals. I want to show different things, and I draw circles around things. It's also part of my interest in working with space. It's again, like architecture. To show the space: this space is for liver, this is for the brain, this is for sugar. I make a circle around it so that the audience looks especially at it.

### MEKAS

Like a close-up in cinema.

### NITSCH

Yes. With the lines and circles I want to make very simple connections, which are necessary to see in my work.

### MEKAS

Any connections between different musical instruments that you are using?

### NITSCH

I like brass very much, the wind instruments. Maybe it's the tradition of Bruckner and Mahler. I like the sound of brass instruments very much.

### MEKAS

What was the loop that played all the time, all twelve hours?

### NITSCH

It was an organ loop. I played organ. It connected everything like a background. It connected and held everything together.

Supplement:
Score for the performance on December 2, 1972
Mercer Arts Center

| TIME | ACTIONS | MUSIC |
|------|---------|-------|
| | | richard in charge of tapes |
| 2:00 | exhibition | |
| 2:30 | prelude | |
| 2:45 | silent action | |
| 3:00 | blood pouring and intestines | |
| | " " " objects | orchestra |
| | " " " tables | |
| | audience participates w. test tubes | |
| 3:15 | wine and bread | |
| 3:30 | backstage paul on stretcher | brass instruments backstage |
| | blood and guts on man— blood in mouth | |
| | (n.t. every blood performer has blindfold) and is covered with sheets | brass instr. follow in procession |
| | procession to middle of room beyond the guts | |
| | silent (short) | nitsch whistles |
| | after sheet is removed by g. hendricks from man | orchestra |
| | man remains on the floor | |
| | silent actions— eggs and fishes are opened | flutes |
| 4:00 | paula | |

| | | |
|---|---|---|
| | laying under lamb w. side wound | whistles |
| | nitsch & audience pour blood, disembowelment | orchestra (no cymbals) |
| | opening of lamb j. h. & j. m. & w. | |
| | paul is removed on stretcher | nitsch whistles orchestra |
| 4:30 | food and wine | |
| 5:00 | paula is moved to a different position under lamb | |
| | new white cloth under lamb | |
| | priest robe under lamb | |
| | lamb is pulled wide open, blood is poured into lamb | brass instrs. come & blow at lamb |
| | paula is carried high above heads | nitsch whistles |
| | backstage screaming | orchestra |
| 5:15 | priest robe is placed on lamb | |
| | blindfolded man (blood on head) is brought in from audience entrance, turned around and headed toward | |
| | lamb. when he touches priest robe on lamb, robe is removed. | orchestra |
| 5:30 | silent actions | |
| 6:00 | joanne | |
| | second lamb—sitting under lamb | |
| | side wound—audience partic. as directed | whistles |
| | guts removed | orchestra |
| | lamb is pulled wide open | orchestra, cymbals, screams |

|  | joanne is dragged out screaming | |
|---|---|---|
| 6:30 | silent actions | |
| 6:45 | man on stretcher backstage | |
|  | (paul?) sheet etc. same as 3:30 | |
|  | stephen brought in<br>laid on floor and is undressed | orchestra |
|  | (paul?) nitsch & audience<br>blood pouring | orchestra |
|  | naked man is carried silently out | nitsch whistles |
|  | (stephen) | |
|  | (paul?) stretcher is carried in | nitsch whistles |
|  | procession part-way around room | orchestra procession |
| 7:00 | lamb—side wound | whistles |
|  | guts | orchestra |
|  | opening of lamb | orchestra, cymbals &<br>chorus |
| 7:30 | silent actions | |
| 7:45 | debra | |
|  | is sitting under lamb | |
|  | opening of lamb | orchestra |
|  |  | brass only blowing<br>at lamb |
|  | silent actions | |
|  | debra is dragged away<br>screaming | nitsch whistles |
|  |  | orchestra |
| 8:00 | side wound on middle lamb | |
|  | side wound | whistles and lander<br>recording |
|  | blood w. audience | |
|  | man on a stretcher brought out | |

|       |                                                             |                         |
|-------|-------------------------------------------------------------|-------------------------|
|       | w. sheet covering in procession                             | orchestra in procession |
|       | man on stretcher raised up as blood and guts fall on his stomach | orchestra          |
|       | lamb is opened wide                                         | orchestra w. cymbals    |
| 8:30  | food and wine                                               |                         |
| 9:00  | silent actions                                              |                         |
| 9:30  | lamb                                                        |                         |
|       | side wound                                                  | whistles                |
|       | guts                                                        | orchestra               |
|       | opening—priest robes                                        | orchestra w. cymbals    |
| 10:00 | silent action                                               |                         |
|       | food and wine                                               |                         |
| 10:30 | rope lamb                                                   |                         |
|       | stephen w. ropes tied to penis                              |                         |
|       | undressed by nitsch                                         | orchestra               |
|       | blood on lamb and drops on stephen who is carried out overhead | orchestra nitsch whistles orchestra |
| 11:00 | finale                                                      |                         |
|       | lamb replaced on cross                                      |                         |
|       | silent actions                                              |                         |
|       | blood on guts                                               | orchestra               |
|       | man behind stage (charlotte)                                |                         |
|       | sheet etc.: procession                                      | orchestra in procession |
|       | then uncovered                                              |                         |
|       | lamb side wound                                             | whistles                |
|       | joanne laying under lamb                                    |                         |
|       | guts                                                        | orchestra               |
|       | open lamb                                                   | orchestra chorus cymbals |

| | |
|---|---|
| joanne is dragged away screaming | nitsch whistles |
| charlotte is carried away (silent) | nitsch whistles |
| | full orchestra |
| lamb is opened | brass orchestra blows at lamb |
| lamb is attached to rope in center | lander recording & short sounds from orchestra |
| geoff on cross on floor undressed | last movement of mahler's symphony |
| when naked | mixed w. full orchestra & screaming |
| raising of cross w. geoff | " |
| blood in mouth | " |
| blood on feet by audience | " |
| cross is lowered | " |
| lamb is placed on his body | " |
| people holding lamb open | orchestra cont. |
| geoff's legs are opened by rope | " |
| blood & guts in & out of lamb | " |
| cross is carried to middle of room | " |
| intestines on him—he is carried out normally as in caravaggio's entombment | " |
| | nitsch whistles |
| intestines are placed in middle scrimmage in guts on nitsch's whistle command | full orchestra— to start and stop on command |
| now all guts in middle all comb. to stamp on them incl. orchestra | |
| kubelka arrives with food | back—applause by audience |

# Second Conversation with Hermann Nitsch and Peter Kubelka

Movie Journal
December 14, 1972

This is another conversation with Peter Kubelka and Hermann Nitsch, two Austrian mystics. In this installment they'll talk about the art of cinema, the art of cooking, and the art of theatre.

### JONAS

This year you conducted two film courses, one at the NYU and another at the Harpur College. In both you included lectures and demonstrations on the art of cooking. Could you tell me: Why are you so interested in the art of cooking? I'm using the expression "art of cooking"—should I call it some other name?

### KUBELKA

No, one can say "the art of cooking." I am generally interested in living with all the arts that a person can deal with. That means employing all the senses. And I think that, especially in our time, we should go away from the principle of specialization and live as fully as we can, in various arts. Still, there's an incredible difference between the other arts and the art of cooking. When you cook something, you eat it, and it is a completely different contact with the world from when you just look at something. Cooking is the thing to which you can come closest. Hearing or seeing is only, I'd say, a preliminary contact for humans to scrutinize what they'll be eating. When you eat something, it has very serious consequences for your body. If you see a bad work of art, it may just affect your mood; but if you eat a bad work of cooking—you may die, really die. And if you eat a good work of cooking, you'll be nourished and you'll flourish.

JONAS

We call music an art, we call painting an art, etc. Why do
you speak about cooking as an art?

KUBELKA

Well, you see, I always try to go back to the sources in every
field in which I work. And the conception of art which
most people have is the conception of romanticism, or nine-
teenth-century art where such things as brilliance and
artistry come in, the things that are performed, applauded
by others. But the fields or arts are innumerable. You
can be an artist of walking on the street or pointing things
out or eating things. Art is, I'd say, an articulation of existence, of our existence; it's an articulation of one's view
of the world, or one's understanding of the world. And this
articulation has to be done with the medium.

JONAS

Certain principles run through all the arts.

KUBELKA

Yes. I have already stated that, for example, in the art of
cooking there is a possibility of articulation similar to that
in cinema; namely, to articulate with the sync event, the
simultaneous experiencing of two elements. Say, when you
eat beef with vegetables, you practically participate, you
eat the whole environment where the cow was living. Anyway,
in the context of Hermann Nitsch's work at the Mercer Art
Center, I think that cooking and eating adds another level
to the theatre, which is that you consume, that you really put
it into you, not only touch things or look at things.

JONAS

The art of eating, of course, includes the worlds of plants,
of animals, and of minerals.

KUBELKA

Yes, sure. We eat stones, because of salt. Cooking and
eating involve all the elements. Air. Fire. Water. We consume
practically the whole universe.

JONAS

And you, Hermann Nitsch, in your theatre, are you using
the same elements, or are you restricting them?

NITSCH

The first thing I should say is that I agree very much with
what Kubelka said. For me, it's very important that I show,
with my work, the total experience of the senses. We use
only a small part of our senses, only what one could call
"clean senses." And I think our time is much more true and
we have a more total feeling of our world. Therefore it's
very important that all the experiences available to our
senses are included in my work, or in the work of other
contemporary artists. I want to show something about death,
something about killing, something about cruelty, and I also
want to show the impressions (sensations) which are formally catalogued as repulsive, I want to put them into the
service of aesthetics. From the very beginning, my work
included the use of smells, the use of taste. For me this was
very important. There are arts for the ears, for the eyes,
but no art for smelling, no art for tasting, no art for touching.
And I feel it's very important that we create art for these
senses. So, I use meats in a different way than Kubelka.

JONAS

But Kubelka will cook at your Mercer Arts performance.

KUBELKA

Nitsch's performance, as he says, is very very broad and
encompasses as many sensual experiences as possible. My
function in his play is similar to that of, let's say, a soloist
of a certain instrument in an orchestra piece. So that
what I'll be doing, I'll be playing a cooking and eating solo
within this great piece.

NITSCH

Yes, I agree with that. I have to say again, I agree very much
with what you said at the beginning. It's very near to my
own theory of a total work of art. Many people use this
word, "total," "total theatre," but I think it's really possible
to use it. Because the consequence of my work will be
that people will be able to understand life as a whole better,
they'll get a deeper experience of life as a whole. I often
say my work is a ritual of better use of our senses. And
I think the last sequence of art must be very, very involved
in life. The last consequence is always life.

JONAS
Why do you think this desire exists to experience all
things with all our senses? Why at this point in history?
Because of technology?

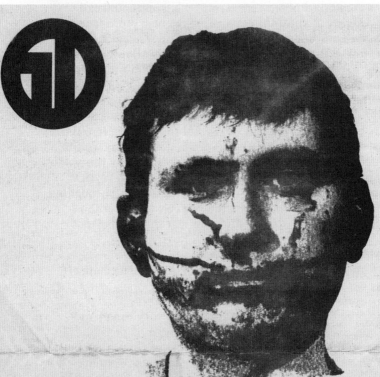

NITSCH

4. Abreaktionsspiel

Welturaufführung        16.Juni 19h
Ausstellung 17.–22.Juni,tägl.16–19h

Galerie Josef Dvorak Wien 3 Lagergasse 2

Performance by Hermann Nitsch, *4. Abreaktionsspiel*, Vienna, 1965

NITSCH

Many different artists, painters, poets, musicians, filmmakers, and, well, theatre people, until the late '50s, worked only in their own disciplines. But in the '50s, it was no longer possible for them to use only their own disciplines. John Cage, I remember, he couldn't work only with sounds produced by musical instruments, he had to use other materials, and he used the sounds of reality, he let something fall down. Many artists began using reality for art. And this is a long, very long development. Just in our time, we all felt that it's very, very important to put parts of reality together in an aesthetic. And maybe you are right, our civilization is so strong, it frustrates us so much that specialist artists have a desire now to get a closer feeling for the world. And I am not against technology. I use technology in my work and in my life. I think it's not because of technology but because of the wrong use of technology that we lose the real taste. Experiments have shown that some people in our society are no longer able to taste the difference between an apple and a potato.

JONAS

What an insult to the potato!

NITSCH

And that's what I like about Kubelka's work and his whole life. Kubelka for me is the only man who is able to find in every country the real food and the food which is concerned with the real way of existence. And maybe we all have to do it, we should all work with all our senses very, very strongly, in order to build the reality which cannot be destroyed by bad or mediocre ways of living. For me it's very important to see the real way of life not only in the past but also in the present. One shouldn't make the mistake of seeing these attempts only as attempts to dig out achievements from the past: good old wines, good old food. I mean, we don't have to go all the way back: we must look into the future. And I think this is a new development, to find and use our senses in the right way. It's part of this development, to want to always have a good wine. I am interested in the whole development of nature, of world, whatever we call it. It is necessary to destroy the mediocrity of civilization, the mediocrity of experience. We must sense and experience better than

average. It's like a religion: everyone, each of us has to live
stronger, more intensively, to use our senses better and
more intensively. I think Kubelka is a very great teacher
of this way of life.


Movie Journal
December 21, 1972


This is the second installment of my conversation with Peter Kubelka
and Hermann Nitsch. We continue our discussion of the art of cooking,
the art of theatre, cinema, and God.

JONAS

Since you travel a lot, what have you found out about the
state of the art of cooking in the world today?

KUBELKA

We have a heritage of cooking, wine-making, eating in various
civilizations. These have been created during processes
of slow development. It was not an enlightened process of,
let's say, an enlightened creation. It was more an unconscious
process of simply growing. And it's fantastic when you
see how Japanese cooking, for example, resembles so much
Japanese architecture, in its cleanliness, in its neatness,
in the purity of how they organize their sensations: and
how Chinese cooking corresponds very much to the Chinese
way, its sense of, let's say, baroque, and its sense of decay
or fermentation, which other countries don't have. So, today,
we can travel from country to country in a very short time,
and we have information about all the countries, and we
even have at our disposal materials from all over the world.
We have at our disposal all the possibilities of all the
traditions of cooking. But in order to do something with
it one has to be aware of the following: one comes to a kind
of common denominator, which is that the arts work with
the senses, and they try to establish something beautiful
or truthful. But the notion of what is beautiful or good comes
from the fact that the senses are geared to survival, and
if you see something, you scrutinize it: Is there any danger
to my life in it? This is important, everything comes down to
that. If you touch something or smell something—all the
senses are made to guarantee the survival of the individual.

JONAS

Darwin's law applied to art.

KUBELKA

Exactly. And from there is derived the notion of what
is beautiful. Because what smells good won't be poisonous,
and the body knows it. My brain is like a computer pro-
grammed through the millions of years of experience
of mankind to decode the messages of the senses in terms
of, let's say good or bad, according to their usefulness
for survival.

If I smell a piece of meat and it smells good, let's say,
fresh, then my computer says, OK, you may eat it. It also
combines with the look of it, and the eyes say: Looks good.
And from there come our notions of beautiful and ugly,
of bad and good. Of course, it also goes for hearing, and for
seeing, etc. And we have now, in our time, we have understood this. So now, we can go to the real thing, not only
representing things like, for example, the painters who tried
to paint a beautiful apple: they tried to paint it so that it
would look from any aspect as good as a good apple would
look. Now, I know how the arts were approached by my ancestors in their desire to be what they called God, the supreme
being, who creates and who lives in his creation. I can
now, let's say, cook and establish a spiritual creation such
as a painter would have done, with my cooking. This is
one aspect of the way we are at the moment, where an
eclecticism in the art of cooking is possible, made possible
by the availability of all the traditions. But this is not the
thing I am interested in. I am interested in going to the
base, as deep as possible. This is why I have such respect
for Nitsch. I think he is the most important man in the
theatre today. And this is because he goes deep. His theatre
is not on the level of brilliance, or of perfection, all these
criteria that we use to describe the things around us.
His theatre is deep, and this is what really counts. It goes
several levels deeper than all the other things that are
done in theatre.

To come back to cooking, let me just describe, let's say,
the roasting of a piece of meat. You have an animal, a
"fellow" animal, which has been, let's say, killed. That means
some vital coordination has been destroyed. The animal
falls down and lies there, and we pronounce it dead. But we

know that modern medicine has proved that the muscle of
a dead man is not dead, because it can be transplanted after
our death. Even the heart is not dead and it can be transplanted and will work again. Which means that when you
slaughter an animal, it is not dead but the various organs
slowly fade out or decay—or whatever you call this process—
or are eaten up by other organisms. And what do we do
now, when we roast it? Imagine our situation in the world,
and the sun, the sun which brings life to creation, and
the warmth, the heat of the sun, when you, let's say, are lying
on the beach and it gets hotter and hotter, and you feel how
this brings all your functions into blossoming; you are growing, the sun gives power to your life. It's slow, but what
an ecstasy. So now we take a piece of the body of the animal
and we expose it to a concentrate of sunlight, which is
fire; and we bring about this process in a fast and ecstatic
way, and we bring it to the point where this living piece
of meat lives its strongest ecstasy. And this is what you call
roast pork. It's like the act of love: you have to be with it
all the time, watch the heat, it must always be … like massag-
ing or stroking it—the heat must be … you must live, when
you roast something—you live with it, and you bring it
to this point, which is a very fertile point also, because it's
a deep insight into the creation, into our situation in the
world. And then—you eat it! You see? This living piece of
meat, in its most ecstatic state—you don't only look at it
and say, "It's beautiful." You not only smell it, you not only
hear it (because you listen to its noises when you roast it),
you get the most intimate contact with it, the most intimate
contact possible in our existence: you swallow it, you
put it in your body. The communion is the symbol of that,
the symbol of taking in God, which means all creation.
So this was an example, let's say, of what, spiritually speaking, is in the normal act of cooking, made possible from
what we know now in our situation.

### JONAS

This is exactly the point where some of the people who have
heard something about Nitsch's theatre and about your
philosophy of the art of cooking and eating, and who, of
course, have never cared to really see it all and experience
it all, usually voice their fears and suspicions: Oh, this
must be some inhuman act being performed, an inhuman

philosophy is being preached. Why should we exalt the
eating of the flesh, they say, etc. So I think that at this point
in our discussion we should clear things up.

KUBELKA

I would like to say something about that. Because this is
one of the very basic and very dangerous errors, that the
greatest humanitarians are declared inhuman. This has
happened again and again throughout history. History
is full of examples of how the people who were most human
and who were really paying respect to creation, to what we
really are—of how they are always declared inhuman. And
this is what happened to Nitsch, and it's grotesque, and
for me it's heart-breaking to see this. Because I've known
him for so many years. He cannot kill a fly! In his apartment
nobody's allowed to touch an ant. He also—he never kills
the animals that he's using in his theatre—he uses animals
which are killed by society anyway. But he confronts our
situation as it is: that humanity is constantly killing everything in nature. This is the situation as it is, and it is very
important to understand this and look the truth in the eye,
not continue living with lies and taboos.

JONAS

And those taboos and lies make our daily actions and
attitudes more abstract and more inhuman.

KUBELKA

Yes. So this is very important to state, this aspect, that Nitsch's
theatre is very humanitarian—even if he himself may not
say so.

NITSCH

Again, I have to say, I very much agree with what you said.
As if I were hearing my own thinking. And it's not only
a problem of my work. The whole world is the same. You
know, I have this theory of abreaction: in our society we are
very frustrated and many of our enemies are suppressed.
I want, with my work—through my theatre—in a humanitarian way, to bring out all the suppressions, to release all the
cruelty. People need sensations, feasts of senses, they have
to let out these energies, they have to come out. And I want
to think about these matters without, or outside, morality.

Of course, when I say, let us forget morality, I want to
forget it only in a phenomenological way of looking at reality.
From the very beginnings of my work, I always wanted to
bring out people's repressions to make it possible to bring
them out in a humanitarian way, with the help of art, with
the help of aesthetics, to bring them to consciousness. Now,
I think I have a much deeper feeling of, let us say, nature.
There is something wrong about saying "nature"; maybe it's
better to say "the whole."

### KUBELKA

I have the same feeling that I never have the right word for
what's called "the world," "nature," "the universe."

### NITSCH

To say "cosmos" is too pathetic, it's not possible for me to
use that word. If I say "nature," it's like saying "God"; it's
a mythic expression. The same with the word "soul," it's very
difficult for me to use it because it's a special expression,
exactly defined. Because now, I think, I have a deeper feeling
of "the whole." And I think there is a very big development
of the whole, and Man is only a part of this development.
And I don't think it's right to stop, to focus everything on
Man. I think there is a development which is going through
us. And I am not too interested in human problems. Well,
of course, I am against death, against war, and all those
things—that's no problem. I don't want to be a stupid, amoral
man. But my standard is this unknown "whole." And so
I hate when I do my work, to give explanations and make
excuses. I am more interested in ecstasy, in creating ecstasy.
I am tired of explaining. I want to show people some
beautiful things with my work.

December 28, 1972

### JONAS

What do you mean when you say "beautiful"?

### NITSCH

Well, I want to create a feast of life in which there will be
meat, dead carcasses, blood, intestines, landscape. In
my six-day play, which I'll start in Prinzendorf next spring,

the landscape will be very important. So I use food, smells,
I use sounds, and what I want to show with it all is really
a glorification of life, of existence. Not only glorification
of the human being: a glorification of every possibility
of being, and of being in a whole, and also the glorification
of forms of beings we don't know.

### KUBELKA

It is a very advanced, a very interesting statement. I think
this brings up a question: What is an artist? And in my view,
if you compare mankind with a single human being, the
artist represents, in a way, the senses, and also the hormones.
In the sense that he makes decisions for the future of mankind. The desires which are in the artists shape mankind
in the future.

When I say "the artists," I mean basic artists, like
in science, you say "basic research"—I am taking an example
from science because science has so much respect today,
everybody concedes that a scientist has the right to be ...
cannot be understood by everybody at the first reading,
everybody would concede that. But in art, we still have this
old concept of art for people in a very wrong way. To really
understand the work of an artist takes a lot of special-
ized proximity and study.

### JONAS

You see, now we always ask art to come to the people, instead
of the people coming to the art. Only at the Anthology have
we restored the proper direction of art. We say, we have
the good thing, and it's up to the people to come to it. I think,
at one point, we wanted to call the Anthology "The Basic
Cinema."

### KUBELKA

Yes, exactly so. Anyway, what I want to say is that the desires
and the creation of artists, of the basic artists, shapes the
essence of mankind in the future. For example, when you see
the old Greek statues, where people have dignity—this is
one of those fantastic examples, that it was the idea of some
people in the early times of humanity, that man should have
dignity. There were these continuous attempts to give humanity dignity. But this was a wish-dream for many, many
thousands of years for many, many sensitive people who were

artists. *They* created it. They had a vision, a wish, and then
they practically created this aspect of mankind through
their work. So that when Hermann Nitsch now comes with
this—there is another wish which will become a trait of
mankind in the distant future, and this is when he says
he wants the understanding, the glorification of "the whole."
Maybe it's what in the old language people called "seeing
God's face."

NITSCH

Yes, yes I always thought so. From the beginning of my
work, till now, I was always very involved with mysticism.
I studied the writings of all the important mystics,
even if I did it in a phenomenological way. And for me,
it was always very important, this identification with
God or with The Whole.

JONAS

That's what I've been wanting to say for some time now:
I always suspected you were goddamn mystics!

KUBELKA

I always said I would like to eat a mystic …

JONAS

I think you are the true mystics. All those who call themselves mystics today, all those swami-lickers, they are
only sissies. They aren't in contact with anything, not talking
about the cosmos! The only thing they can touch is their
own asses, with their heels. You are the true mystics,
no doubt now.

NITSCH

Two mystics at the Heurigen …

KUBELKA

Yes, two mystics at the Heurigen. You know, the wine place,
in Vienna.

NITSCH

People come and look at us and whisper: Look, there they
are sitting there, the two mystics …

KUBELKA

But it's true in a way, because we are. When we drink at
the Heurigen our talks always involve this level of seeing,
of looking at existence. There is no such thing as a banal
thing: you can always look at the truth, at the face of God.

NITSCH

I am not interested in the question of whether there is a
special kind of transcendence. For me, mostly it's transcendence of what we don't know. I have a very deep feeling
for this kind of transcendence. That's not the question.
But I know it all from myself, everything the mystics said,
I have the same feeling when I'm in nature, and when
I'm feeling very well, when I feel that I'm able to use all
my potential. I am not looking at the face of God, but I
have the feeling I'm in the center of the world. And in the
history of mysticism, you always have the point where
the mystic feels he is God. Maybe, let us forget the expression
"mystic." When I am in nature, when I feel very well, and
when the sun is shining, birds are singing—well, then
I am very much in the world, and I think this has something
to do with the development of the world; all forms of
being seem to be surging into this part, into this moment,
and it creates ecstasy. And what I wanted to say at the
beginning is that for me it's possible to feel this, to reach
this state through art. When I hear the symphonies of
B r u c k n e r, well, then I am in the middle, in the center
part of the world. And sometimes when my performance
is going very well, I have this feeling too, of real life, of real,
intensive life. And an intensive life makes us always feel
like we are in the center of the world. And it's not the question at all, whether we are in the center of the world or
not. All I am saying is that this feeling is very, very important.

JONAS

Talking about the center of the world, what are you doing
here, in America?

KUBELKA

I think we are all here for the same reason—Nitsch, and
you, and I. I feel it, and I have said this many times before,
that this is where I want to be heard and where I want my
work to be received. And I am very happy that we now have

an outlet here in America. Because for the artist it is very
important to ... because he is like a hormone in the human
body. It is important that the hormone gets injected in
the right part of the human body; only then can it really
do the work that it is supposed to do. America, at this
time, is the place where the hormones for the future have
the most effective impact for mankind.

JONAS
This includes the art of cooking?

KUBELKA
Especially the art of cooking. Here in America you have
a young person's concern with digesting all the cultural
heritage. You are concerned with the philosophies, and you
are concerned with all the cultures, and I think the situation is that we are at a point where a new art of cooking
is *ante portas*, it will spring up. I know that what I am saying
is completely contrary to the bad reputation that America
has, and everybody says the food is bad here, the cooking
is bad. But it's coming! I am convinced that the age of great
cooking in America is coming. And the art of cooking I am
talking about is completely different from what people think
of as the art of cooking. I mean, it's not gourmet cuisine,
which I detest and which is only an imitation, an unsuccess-
ful imitation of, let's say, French culture. The real new
cooking will be completely different and new, and it will
only learn some things from the past. It will be different.
It will go to the basics. For example, the natural, the organic
food movement is one important step in this development,
a very important step. Because it will provide the basis.
You see, when you have a bad piece of meat, you can cook
it à la *Marengo*, with I don't know what, with bad sherry,
etc.—and it will be just as bad as any of the individual ingre-
dients. Two bad things combined make another bad thing.
So the organic food movement will provide the basis.

# Notes on the Lost Books of Peter Beard

November 10, 1977

"A salvaged windmill known as the easternmost house on Long Island burned to the ground in Montauk on Wednesday night in a spectacular fire that flashed through the frame of the cliffside dwelling.
    The fire in the building, owned by the photographer Peter Beard, consumed thousands of his photographs, a $10,000 processing laboratory, his twenty-year scrapbook diary, a distinguished African library and art collection and an associate's painstakingly assembled photographic history of Montauk." (*The New York Times*, Friday, July 29, 1977)

*Notes from 1970*
He had a bloody accident in Florida, with a bloody wound. But now it's only a brown speck on the page, a memory with no details of the accident. The accident was reduced to this one hieroglyph on the page. Every one of the items in Peter's books is a hieroglyph and nobody will ever decipher the actual—physical or psychological—fact or circumstance. Now, on the page, it's a thing in itself, a reality beyond the original source or impulse.
    I called Peter today. "I lost ten pages of my notes on you," I said. "Oh, good!" shouted Peter in his usual enthusiasm. "That's how it should be, why don't you use losing the notes as part of your notes?"
    Yes, he attempts to retain in his diaries not only the retainable but also the unretainable, the lost. Is this a passion, an inertia, or a sickness, this effort to retain, to preserve the past? Is it a sentimental preoccupation, a child's box of colorful mementos, scraps, miniatures, pebbles? Or is this a laugh into the face of the present, this pompous rooster which, as soon as it's gone, ends up in Peter's book, on one of the pages, and it takes glue to hold it together—that much and nothing more. History, past, all its emotions and its bustle, its dreams, fetishes, all the objects, they are all gone except what's left in Peter's books, displayed there for everybody to see, time metaphors. It's Peter's gallows humor, a joke on reality, history, civilization.

Front cover of *Soho News Weekly*,
Peter Beard's lost books, New York, 1977

The exception is the animals and the trees. That's something else. And, perhaps, K a m a n t e. And B l i x e n. Yes, they are something else. An open window into something else completely. A different feeling comes from them, a different emotion, a different dream. Peter likes to record glimpses of animal strength, their energy, their movement, their pace. Like Peter, going for a swim in an icy winter

river, performing purely physical stunts in *Hallelujah the Hills*.
The desire for the pure physical movement energy.

"To keep a diary, it's like gaining time. Just think of all those
gaps of days which are gone without a memory!"

"The bottle just exploded and went through my wrist.
The blood was dripping, gushing out and I was splashing it over the
book, it was so wonderful. So she picked up and left, she thought
it was a crazy house or something, she just couldn't see how beautiful it all was."

"Look, this book got drowned in the lake. Look what water
did to it, look at the colors, isn't it wonderful?"

"It's not what you see, but what you don't see when you look
at them, that I am really interested in."

Andy Warhol, by means of his cameras, videotapes,
and Polaroids, records life "as is"—as it happens. Peter is obsessed
with recording what's gone, what's not there. He takes his materials from the huge garbage heap of Western Civilization. With his glue
and his scissors he sits among it all, very, very happy.

I don't think he keeps it in order to remember it. I don't
think he's doing it for any reason, purpose, or goal. He just does it, like
some insects or worms do. Collecting the crumbs of civilization into
huge anthills of books and diaries. There was a little tale I read when
I was a child—I have no idea where it comes from nor how it really
goes, but it's about a spider who was collecting all the little crumbs
of bread that fell on the ground, in the grass, wherever humans
happened to pass by, wherever they had their feasts, their civilizations. Humans pick up the big chunks, greedily; the little crumbs they
leave on the ground. And there comes the spider and collects it all,
with great care and love, and puts it all into Peter's books, page after
page, day after day. The spider with the holy cross sign on the back,
punished to do it into eternity.

On every page, it keeps coming back, the dream, the memory
of the uncivilized, the primitive, the original. These diaries, these
books are like his own *Walden*: always animals and birds and green
trees and blood. Even the actresses and fashion models, they are
chosen for their animal grace and animal magnetism, not for their
intelligence or subtlety or culture. No, they are there on those pages
like some African animals, those women. And men—comic-strip,
magazine-page men, from the pages of crime and violence: they are
always there as metaphors of action, of energy, raw energy, beyond
all culture and civilization.

Truly, these books are like a grotesque graveyard of
Western civilization. Details of a civilization collected by chance,

as they fall upon him or as he falls upon them—as he pastes and glues them day after day, day after day. Violence, power, weird deaths, the world of makeup, artificiality, senseless destruction, waste, sadism. And in between of all this: tiny innocent insects, leaves, barks of trees, traces of Peter's own blood—almost every page is painted with blood and ink, every page looks like an open wound of the world, with all its contents pouring out; a ritual, an orgy, the O. M. Theatre of Hermann Nitsch performed over the pages of a diary.

This amazing directness of recording animals in his drawings and his photographs. They resemble the animal drawings of the cavemen. The nonliterary activity of the body, the energy and movement caught in an instant.

"Klee, his whole work is a diary. Same with Picasso."

"I am interested in the possibilities of order and simplicity through the chaos."

1949–50: "First diary, a little book that became four inches fat—all the vacations and food, stones, hair, everything went into it."

1959–61: *Hallelujah the Hills* diaries, all lost, got some pictures; a lot of very straight drawings, very detailed portraits in old master techniques."

"Hallelujah Africa"—"transition book, lost."

Biggest Diary Book, 1963–65, "all in one book. Stopped being diaries, became just a place where I could put extra things which I couldn't put in a day-by-day diary (a smaller fat book kept during the same period) (it fell into Lake Rudolph and was immeasurably improved)."

"In Africa, 1963–64"—"a very small book, has the very smallest writing of any book."

"Hansel & Foetsal" book, "done during 1963 TV day shows after JFK's death (got it at Jerome's)."

Same period, 1963–65, "a photographic diary, seven inches thick, over two thousand photographs." 1967–68: "The diaries turned into yellow pads (pages). I made thirty paintings, they are at Cassis, at Jerome's."

1969—Red & Brown Books: "Started two diaries. Spent five months in hospital. Every single thing was written & every word & memory of the day turned into a drawing. Some pages are homages to friends, people. Both books lost."

Q: "Who are your favorite artists?"

A: "Picasso is the most important, but not favorite. Real favorites are Wols, Chaissac, Ensor, Gauguin, Ryder, Lindner, Klee, Bacon, Rousseau, Bosch."

An address book that "turned into a drawing book."

"In 1970 started the new fat small book."

"See the March blood drawings. The wound bled for a month and a half, so it goes through many pages."

"Roach? Found it in the emergency room, in the Montego Bay hospital."

"Film reel top? It represents $5,000 lost on film that brilliant girl threw into the pool."

"Another book left in Africa, bound in elephant skin. I call it 'Walden,' the place, and the book. I always considered it my Walden."

"When anything really important happens, it's not recorded in the book. Only sometimes some hints, perhaps."

"Andy asked me why my writings are so small. But life is so small. Eighty years means nothing. Smallness makes more room for a lot of trivia."

I have come to the conclusion that it's totally useless to ask Peter why he does it all, or what does it all mean to him. It's more profitable to speak about what they are to me. To me these books look like outgrowths of nature, like all works of art are. Like moss, or fungus.

If you focus all your energy on one page, and work on it day after day with the total absorption that Peter puts into it—it's bound to become something else, another thing in itself. These books are not comparable to anything else in the whole natural or unnatural world. They fall somewhere between the organic and inorganic, between vegetable and mineral. They grow like corals, like the coral islands, very imperceptibly but very organically, bit by bit, by filling the spaces, curves, loops, windings, holes, cavities, even where you don't see any. They grow and they are there and you may choose to live among them or you may choose to ignore them. You may also proceed to nibble away at them, like the Australian coral islands are being nibbled away by the giant starfish. Yes, we can nibble them into nothing with the sharp teeth of our intellect and our psychological etc. etc. analyses, as we have nibbled away entire civilizations. Peter won't give a damn about it. He'll start another diary book.

*Three Notes from 1974*
1. Isn't a cinéma vérité, a diarist filmmaker motivated by the same urges? Peter, L e a c o c k, or myself—we all end up in the same personal, fantasy worlds, expressing not the outside but the inside, the vérité of our minds. How else could it be? Isn't our inside made up of bits and strokes of the outside? And vice versa?

2. Ah, the dead elephants, the dead elephants, the dead elephants!

3. By seeing and reseeing, during the last ten years, Peter's diary books, the uncountable number of "real" details and bits of civilization glued and penciled and splashed upon the pages— every page almost a sutra—signs, signatures, representations I have often wondered if, in truth, any of these details really mean anything in themselves. If there is any meaning in them or to them, it's the design itself, the book itself, the effort, the act of doing it— which is both bigger and more simple than any individual meaning of any individual page or detail. The details and pages dissolve into the whole. All the bits and dregs of our civilization, all disappear into these books, and their meaning can be measured only by the number of hours Peter put into them; the number of pages; the number of pounds, the actual weight of the books, their measurements, their thicknesses in inches...

*Notes from October 1977*
1970—"a complete diary, page by page, day for day."
        Q: "Was it one of those small books?"
        A: "It was about ten inches high, it was a small year."
        Q: "What calendars do you use for the diaries?"
        A: "The bigger ones, the National Diary. 1970 and 1971: those were little Letts Diaries. 1972 and 1973: those were bigger, the National Diaries."
        Q: "The format?"
        A: "Twelve inches high. 1974 was the bigger, super version of the National Diary and that one was a very fat one. But I was doing the mill that year so I didn't really ... it was only an awful lot of photographs and drawings and writing. I was so busy moving the mill, I didn't have time to photograph it. I didn't photograph 1975 either. 1975 was an even bigger National Diary and I had that bound in bushbuck skin in Nairobi. Ah, that was a really good one, very fat. And I have one film of it. Unfortunately, I had no chance to photograph it. And then in 1975—I have it. It was at Meridian Gravure being turned into a series of lithographs for the show, so I got it. That's the Bicentennial Diary. And then I also had a complete book on the making of the mill. It burned. It was a day-by-day diary book on the mill, construction and photographs, doing the cliff and the windmill. Lee gave it to me. It was a specially bound brown-blue diary. And then the Elephant Diary, that was 1971 through 1976. I just filled the whole thing and I still have it, it's right here. "
        Q: "What has really survived? The Elephant Diary and the Bicentennial Diary? Any other?"
        A: "No. But I have pretty good photographs of a lot of them.

I have some very fine lithographs. The 1977 Diary was very raw
and it was lost. I also had a diary on the diaries, remember? With
your introduction, conversations with Bacon and Dalí, Albers,
all the notes—they are gone."

"You should come and film what's left of them. They are
all burned completely, but they still keep the shape. I covered them
up, to photograph them, before they fall to ashes. They look great,
you shouldn't miss the occasion."

A theory of art history ... Our art, our museums,
our art history ...

Time turns everything to dust—paintings, stones, pyramids.
Films fade, frescoes fall off the walls, polluted rains eat up the
architecture. Caligulas, Attilas, Hitlers, Stalins. Churches,
monasteries, museums are turned to ashes. Dresden. San Pietro.
Etc. etc. etc. I am still amazed that we have so much left after all the
wars and clean-ups, dictator after dictator leaving no stone unturned,
the natural disasters finishing what's left. All art is exposed to the
operation of divine chance. What survives, survives only through
a mysterious act of grace, and even so only temporarily. So that everything that manages to survive beyond its own century should be
celebrated as a miracle.

*The End of the Game.* Photographs, diaries, graphics, and film by
Peter Beard. International Center of Photography, 1130 Fifth Avenue,
NYC, November 11 – January 8, 1978.

# The irish photographs of Willard van Dyke

A conversation with Willard Van Dyke
conducted by Jonas Mekas and Hollis Melton
June 11, 1980

I called Amalie Rothschild. For about three years she has been
engaged in making a film about Willard Van Dyke.

"How is the film going?" "Very well. I am mixing this week.
I have a show in St. Paul on October 26 so I have no time to waste."

"What's the title?" "'Conversations with Willard van Dyke.' It's sixty
minutes long." "Anybody else in the film, besides Willard?" "Ah, many
of his friends, such as Ralph Steiner, Ed Weston." "How is
Willard these days?" "Depressed. He was just rejected by the National
Endowment for the Arts grant." "That's incredible." "Do you want
to hear something more incredible? The Guggenheim rejected him
twice in a row." "I can't believe it. Too incredible." "It's true. Willard
wrote thcm a letter that they are discriminating against old age.
And it's true. And it's depressing. They wrote to him to apply next
year. So he wrote to them: 'I may not be alive next year.' So he is
depressed. But he's leaving for St. Paul, for his show, this Tuesday."
 [From a diary entry, October 5, 1980]

Willard Van Dyke, few disagree, is one of the great American photographers. A classic. Practically all his work, though, has been done
in a comparatively short time, between 1929 and 1937. Then he
turned to other work—running the wartime film office in Washington,
making documentary films, running the Museum of Modern Art's
film department, etc. Two years ago, after exactly forty years of
silence, Van Dyke returned to photography, went to Ireland, and
brought back a series of photographs that not only to this writer,
but also to Ricardo Block—the curator of photography at the Saint
Paul's Film in the Cities Gallery, who during the month of October
is presenting Van Dyke's new work—is as significant and monumental
as anything that Van Dyke has done before.

JONAS
Ricardo Block asked me to prepare some notes on you,
on the occasion of your show in St. Paul this fall. This will
be the first major show of your Irish photographs. When
did you do the series?

WILLARD
August 16 to September 24, 1979.

JONAS
What locations?

WILLARD
Many locations in western Ireland.

JONAS
Can you mention any nearby towns?

WILLARD

Clifden in particular.


JONAS

What camera did you use to take these photographs?


WILLARD

I made them with an 8×10 camera that makes 8×10 negatives.
And it happened to be a Deardorff.


JONAS

Is this your '30s camera?


WILLARD

No. I didn't take that camera. Sometimes I wish I had. I still
have my old camera that I worked with in 1929. But I didn't
take it to Ireland because the Deardorff was newer and
had more gadgets to play with. Richard Rodgers gave
it to me.


JONAS

What film emulsion did you use?


WILLARD

I started out with Polaroid but I found that it was far too
difficult to get what I wanted outdoors with Polaroid. But
it's not only that. The emulsion is not good—it was Polaroid
Color II. That had a narrow scope; that is, if I wanted to
get proper colors and proper tones in the whites, all the
blacks would have no definition at all. Or I could go the other
way. But the range was narrow, and so I decided to use
Eastman film.


JONAS

Will you exhibit any of the Polaroid photographs in St. Paul?


WILLARD

Two, maybe. Two may be shown. Perhaps for pedagogical
reasons. They are also not bad photographs. One of them now
is in the Houston Museum of Fine Arts, the other one is
in the Polaroid permanent collection, in Boston, the Kennedy
Gallery, I believe. Both of the photographs that they chose
for their big exhibition have often been chosen by other
people too.

JONAS

Then you switched to Kodak ...

WILLARD

Eastman Vericolor. There are two kinds: one that you can
use with a fiftieth of a second, and the other one a fiftieth
of a second and over. Since I was working outdoors, of course,
I wanted to work with a big camera. I wanted to work with
the long exposure.

JONAS

I don't remember seeing any indoor photographs in the
Irish series. Did you take any?

WILLARD

No. Nothing indoors.

JONAS

On what paper did you print them?

WILLARD

I printed them on Ektacolor, which is an Eastman paper,
type C. I printed them on type C paper. Now, I'd like to make
a point here. Type C—the dyes in the type C are fugitive,
they don't live forever. They will fade with time.

JONAS

How much time do you give them?

WILLARD

Twenty years, if they are properly processed. And the
collectors of photography at this point, and some of the galleries, refuse to show color. Because, they say, the thing is
fugitive. Well, what about C h r i s t o 's fence? Wasn't that only
three days?

JONAS

What about all dance and music performances ...
Nothing more fugitive than dance ... while here they can
cling to it for twenty years at least and get their money's
worth.

WILLARD

So my point about that is that people who invest, they invest
in photographs because they know that these black-and-
white photographs are going to last for a long time, and therefore they'll increase in value. It's a value-oriented thing
rather than a question of whether the artist sees something. The artist sees something, it's exciting to him, and
he makes it, she makes it, and then that exists for a while—
Isn't it as legitimate a work of art as something that happens
to last?

JONAS

Are you going to take the Deardorff to Ireland now, or …?

WILLARD

Oh, I am going to take it … I am using the Deardorff
now. Deardorff has more advantages than the old Eastman
2-D view, which was patented in 1912, and which I first
bought in 1929. They'll both do the same thing on a straight
landscape, but with Deardorff I can do other things.
So that's what I'm going to use.

HOLLIS

Can you talk about why you want to use color as opposed
to black and white?

WILLARD

Well, it happens that Amalie [Rothschild] helped me to get
Polaroid to give me an unlimited supply of color film, and
since I've been so far away from black and white for so long,
I really felt that I needed to divorce myself from it as much
as I could. I wanted to change and do something different.
I wanted to separate the idea, the kind of pictures that I had
been making way back forty years ago, as much as I could
from the pictures that I wanted to make now. And one of the
ways of separating it was color, and that gave me a kind of
goal to find what was good about color, what was there that
I couldn't do in black and white, and I'm still working with
that problem.

HOLLIS

Are there certain things that you feel very passionately
about that you should put in color or …

WILLARD

Well, certainly, I've seen some things that I could've never
photographed in color, and that I liked photographing
in black and white. And on the other hand, there is a kind
of negative thing about the color, which is … Say, I am
just toying with the possibility … if the thing doesn't form
itself in my mind in black and white, ah! What about trying
color? Because the relationships of the colors might make
it. And I am still exploring. But I am afraid that color is
very seductive, as far as I'm concerned. I really ought to be
looking toward black and white rather than color.

HOLLIS

When you go back this summer, are you taking black and
white or color?

WILLARD

Both.

JONAS

Funny though that Ireland is always connected with color.
Green. I don't know any other country so connected with
color. Why did you choose Ireland?

WILLARD

Oh, I chose that for a reason that many years ago I went
over there to do a television show which was largely political,
with Walter Cronkite, and in the process of making
that, I kept going by incredible landscapes that were not
suitable for Cronkite's black and white television examination
of Ireland. This was in 1960. But I kept feeling, my God,
if I ever go back to doing still photography, I am coming back
here!

And there is another thing about this that I've thought
a lot about, and it's the idea of what the material is. And
most of the material has to do with landscape. And when
I first started to work in black and white, I was afraid of
the landscape, and the color released me, set me free to try
landscape and suddenly I …

I read in *Art News* last week, that the classical landscape is something that painters are beginning to tentatively
approach now. And I thought, ah, goddammit, I don't want
to be a painter, I don't want my photography to be painting.

But I am attracted by the landscape. I am ... a lot of my
photographs are landscape, and I hope that the landscape
that I've been doing is not imitative. I feel that it's not.
I think that using the landscape very often, breaking it up
into textural areas, delineated by lines—lines being the
fences ... but I think that the areas are different from the
way in which a classical English landscape painter might
be doing it. But I am the first person to say that I am working
at the opposite end of the spectrum from where L u c a s
S a m a r a s, for instance, is working. It's quite different.
And I am still struggling with it. But the landscape is something that absolutely engrosses me at this point, and I ...
I have to go back now—after several months of looking
at what I did—and find another way of looking at it,
or go to Spain and try looking at it. But I am past the time
when I spent so long trying to utilize the ideas that Weston
had in his pictures, but trying to make them very different so that nobody thought I was imitating Weston. And also
I was fighting the idea of pictorialism, which was the landscape, the presentation of what was there. And at this point
I don't care that people say, "Well, it looks like an English
landscape," or "It looks like a painting," and I wanted
it to be a photograph, and purely a photograph. But I don't
mind that it is classical, or landscape. In a way, it makes
the aesthetic used by many of the people who work in the
same area—say, S t e p h e n  S h o r e—valid.

[Postscript: while looking at prints]

WILLARD
That's a quarry ... marble ... Ireland is known for some
of this marble ... This one for me has more of a feeling of ...

JONAS
A very mysterious tree ... like in a fairy tale ...

WILLARD
It's supposed to be a cypress ... and that's how I feel too,
that it's a fairy-tale tree ... this is just the sun going down
over this little lake ...

HOLLIS
These are all your prints?

WILLARD

Some of them are, some of them aren't. Some of them were
made by a very good laboratory uptown. None of them
are the proofs that I made in Ireland; I had them developed
there, because the negative material has to be kept at
55 degrees or lower and therefore I couldn't sent it back to
the States. They developed the negative, they made prints,
and then I had some prints made here; and some I did.
    ... this was August, and that is the hottest month ...
too flamboyant ... I've always been a fairly good critic of my
own works ... Am I wrong in relating E g g l e s t o n to Shore?

HOLLIS

I don't know ... I think Eggleston is really more emotional
than Shore.

WILLARD

Yes ... Well, I think that would make me closer to Shore
than Eggleston.

HOLLIS

Do you just use a regular lens or ...?

WILLARD

This is a twelve inch, regular ... this was at sunset ... You see
how, when the sunset went down, it made the long shadows
of the haycocks? They are piles of hay with caps like that
on the top so that when the water comes it doesn't go inside
and rot the hay ... This could have been an 18-inch lens;
it probably was, which is a fairly long focal length ...

Willard speaks slowly; his voice is very modulated, comes from
very, very deep, from the entire body; very, very stable; deeply rooted;
with no hurry; as if he had all the time there is; Willard could be
considered tall. As a matter of fact, he walks with a slight bend,
a little bit like a spiteful bull, although there is no spite in Willard,
or if there is, then it's very tamed by culture; Willard is one of the
kindest men I have known in my life, he has given so much of himself,
years, decades of his life to others and with absolutely no regrets;
a few years of creative work, done with a concentration such as
Willard did in the '30s—within a span of a few years he produced
a small, but such an intense, such a perfect body of work that it

provided him with four decades of total abandon—he had no
frustrations about not "creating," not doing photography, not at all—
he did other things.

Long, long ago, I read about Valéry abstaining from
poetry and for ten years not writing; instead, he studied mathematics ... and I thought, young and obsessed as I was with my own
poetry, I thought, ten years! Ah, what willpower!

Willard took forty years out—to help others to make films—
away from photography.

No. It's not willpower. It's only that muses and gods work in
strange ways, they sent Willard back to work—no peace for Willard ...
They pulled the rug from under him and sent him to Ireland.
And again he is on the road & with his camera.

Ah, yes! Once a photographer, always a photographer!—
but let us return to looking at photographs.

WILLARD
... man and wife ... They have a butcher shop and they are
very proud of it ... but I wouldn't have made a picture such
as that twenty years ago, thirty years ago ...

JONAS
What did you look for then?

WILLARD
Well, I looked for much more organized ... if it was to
be a long thing of this kind, then it would have to be very
organized, almost in a design way, whereas here it just
struck me, I don't know why, the relationship of those things
just seemed correct ...

HOLLIS
... even the light here is green ...

WILLARD
... very light green grass on the hill ... but it's true ... I had
to really work to get the green ...

A note made on September 23, 1980:

I met Willard today during the meeting of the Anthology Film
Archives' board, on which he serves. "Welcome back," I said,

"how was your second trip to Ireland?" "Ah," said Willard a little bit sadly. "It rained, it rained every day except maybe two hours every day." So you had to do a lot of waiting," said I, remembering Willard telling me about the first trip, that he had to wait half a day for certain shadows to move to where he wanted them to be. "Yes," he said. "Did you revisit some of the same places?" "Of course! But I didn't bring back much." "Did you take some photographs of exactly the same houses, places? In a different light, angle?" "No, but I was in the same locations. You have to go back to the same places, you know."

# A Dialogue between A, B, and C re the Future of Moving-Image arts and the Regional art centers

The Media Arts in Transition, Walker Art Center
1983

A

Many technological innovations are on the way. So we are told. But when we look through the history of the arts, we find that the most lasting and exciting changes in the directions and qualities of the arts were caused not by the technological changes but by artists of daring ideas and exceptional temperaments. The most innovative and exciting achievements in the American cinema of 1914, 1940–45, and 1957–67 (D. W. Griffith, Orson Welles, Maya Deren, Stan Brakhage, Michael Snow) were made during the times of no (relatively) significant technical innovations. In times of technological innovations, art takes a vacation.

Since the media centers are, or are supposed to be, concerned with the arts—and not with the technologies—

the times of technical innovations should mean trying and
challenging times. Technical innovations usually (in present
times) affect the dissemination (popularization) of arts,
not the creation. If it affects the creation at all, that effect
is totally negative, as is currently illustrated by what
is happening in Hollywood. Video games versus movies.

The main challenge for the art centers, during the next
decade, will be keeping up the standards of the works
shown; how to resist the negative temptations of democracy
in arts. The flood of the second-rate film and video works,
largely encouraged, sponsored, and promoted by state and
federal agencies—via grants that began some years ago—
will continue during the next decade. These are the problems
of democracy—the problems which, nevertheless, are a
hundredfold preferable to the curses of totalitarian regimes.
The art centers will have to learn how to deal with these
problems. Mediocrity will be the main challenge of the '80s.

B

The next ten years will be terrific. Because of new technologies it will be even easier to make moving-image works
than it is today. The numerous state and federal grants will
make it possible for everybody to make films, tapes, and
computer works. The revolution in dissemination will permit amateurs to compete with professionals, and, democracy
triumphing, the amateurs, with their melodramas and sex
and popular politics films, will find it easy to compete with
the "artists." We may even link—via satellites, etc.—with
the amateurs of other countries and continents. We may still
make Youngblood's prophecy come true: we'll make this
world into one village. If you like, you can call it a beehive.
Who wants individualism? Isn't a beehive the most nearly
perfect community system you can read about?

Of course, this will help the "artists" to get rid of their
false ambitions of success and fame. So, after all, if you
want to look at it that way, we are going to perform a "useful" function for artists. They will return to doing their
work just for themselves, as their ancestors of the '20s and
'60s did (Anger, Markopoulos, Brakhage)—which
will restore the standards of their art, standards which,
of course, are only of passing curiosity to the democratic
and socialist masses, no matter how sacred they may be
to the "artists."

C
I find both of you a bit cynical. I myself have a vision of a
great decade for the arts. Technological progress is good for
the arts. Just think of all the great names—I won't mention
them here—that have been added to the pantheon of arts by
the arrival of 3-D and holography. The regional art centers
have a great opportunity to help local artists produce
and show their work and preserve it for posterity. New talent
will emerge. The variety of works presented will educate
both the audiences and the budding artists. The only way
to lift the level of creativity is to lift the level of general
moving-image culture. And that's what the media centers
are doing. It's a little bit pompous to speak only about
art and artists and ignore the public, the people with whose
money, after all, these centers are run.

# On Liberation, Arts & Cultural Imperialism

A conversation between Susan Sontag,
Vytautas Landsbergis, Nam June Paik, and Jonas Mekas
Judson Memorial Church, October 8, 1994

*About the Ungratefulness of America*

NAM JUNE PAIK
I am angry that Americans have forgotten you. You understand? You see, Americans saved trillions of dollars in their
defense budget, because of the collapse of the Soviet Union.

VYTAUTAS LANDSBERGIS
Yes, I think so. [laughs]

PAIK
Also, Americans will make billions in all the oil fields in
Kazakhstan, you know, and from diamonds in Irkutsk.
And you are one of the four guys who did it. Wałęsa, you,

Nam June Paik walking through the Village,
New York, 1975

Gorbachev, and Yeltsin. Four. Only four. And you were
the one who stuck out your neck most. You were the one
who was the most vulnerable, you know? Yesterday, you said
that it was question of dignity. And it was. But death and
torture were waiting for you too, you knew it. Koreans also
know how to die. But we are lucky: we die without being
beaten to death. Gorbachev had his KGB, Yeltsin had his
Party. You were the only one with no real power backing
you. So you were the most courageous guy, you know? And
I was trying to sell your piano concert at Judson Memorial
Church to the American media. And nobody came, nobody
responded, nobody wrote about your coming. I will simply
say that Americans are ungrateful sonofabitches. [laughs]
America gives Lithuania to Germany, then Russia, so they
don't have to worry about it: Lithuanians are troublemakers.

The same they did with Korea when Korea made problems,
they gave half of it to S t a l i n . You see, it's all mega-economy.
They cannot deal with the small guys, so they get rid
of them. But sometimes the small guy can change the world.
You did it. They wanted to give you the Nobel Peace Prize,
they ended up by giving it to Gorbachev ... V y t   B a k a i t i s ,
the poet, said yesterday: the media would like you better
if your name would be shorter, if they wouldn't need two
columns ... Vyt instead of Vytautas. Like V y t   G e r u l a i t i s ...
       When I was a small child growing up in Korea, look-
ing at the world globe, I was always looking at Guinea,
at one end of the world—it was the smallest in that part
of the world; and Lithuania, the Baltic countries which were
on the other side of the globe, the same size as Korea ...
Guinea and Lithuania ... the two smallest entities, you know?
Korea is one third of Japan, and 3 percent of China ...
By Asian standards Korea is small.

LANDSBERGIS
I have tried to explain to the politicians what you just said,
about the great savings for them in their military budget,
and that they could help us immediately. But they didn't do
anything.

PAIK
Yes, because Americans make money in defense. So that's
a double-edged sword, you know? They need some little
enemies ... to keep the industry going. Still, it's a tremendous
saving. Which year—1988, 1989—did it become clear that
you would overcome the Soviets?

LANDSBERGIS
It was with the establishing of the liberation movement
S ą j ū d i s as a mass movement—it was the summer of 1988.
One year before the fall of the Wall.

PAIK
When did you become leader of the liberation movement?

LANDSBERGIS
It was in November of 1988. The Sąjūdis movement was
established in June. Initially, there was no chairman, only
the council. But we soon became an official opposition to

the official ruling communist party. And being accused, and having confrontations on the streets, and having to make a lot of quick decisions, the council decided that we needed one responsible spokesman, because some things had to be decided immediately. And they elected me to be that person.

PAIK

You weren't scared? Because you could have been assassinated by the KGB.

LANDSBERGIS

No. A campaign of hatred was immediately initiated against me and the movement, and KGB agents were planted amongst us, but I was quite calm about it. Because, if they had decided to kill me, nothing would have prevented them from doing that. The bodyguards were needed only as a protection from common crazies.

PAIK

So the things started building up. Your name began appearing here in 1988, if I remember right, and it climaxed during Desert Storm, when Gorbachev thought he could crush you unnoticed. The only way to remind America of what you did for them would be to print a picture of you speaking from a tank. At that time, there were already many correspondents stationed in Vilnius—*The New York Times, Washington Post, The Financial Times*—there was a lot of press.

LANDSBERGIS

But we thought that the collapse would take longer. I thought it would take several years. But it all collapsed in one year. We thought that it would be better for us if the collapse took several years. We wanted only Lithuania to be recognized as an independent country, and we wanted the rest of the republics to stay in the Union several years longer. It would have been much better for us not to be in the same group. Now we are lumped together with other Soviet republics, as "former Soviet republics." But in truth we have been occupied countries! The way we saw it, the Soviet Union did not consist of fifteen republics: it consisted of twelve republics and three occupied countries. I was always trying to explain this to the West, but it was too difficult

for them to understand that. Even today, they talk about us
as "former Soviet republics."

PAIK
I hear Lithuania is doing very well ...

LANDSBERGIS
Not very well ... Sometimes it looks like we have been
forgotten.

PAIK
Yes, I have felt that myself. I have been trying to persuade
the press to write about your concert. A former President, and
one who saved America trillions of dollars, and plays piano—
that would be news, OK? That was my speculation. It didn't
work out. [laughs] That's what you were saying: you have
been forgotten.

JONAS MEKAS
In some way, it may prove to be good, to be temporarily
forgotten. It helps to invent your own ways of doing things.
Still, eventually Lithuania will have to connect itself with
the rest of the world.

*Media, Seoul Olympics, and the Collapse of the Soviet Union*

PAIK
So, by 1988 you were sure you'd win.

LANDSBERGIS
Yes. It was only a question of time.

PAIK
But even then *The New York Times* was against you. They
wanted a slow transition, remember? And Bush didn't
receive you for a long time.

MEKAS
How much do you think was contributed to the collapse of
the Soviet Union by the media? By the radio, TV satellites,
the information that was coming into the Soviet Union
from the air, something that was difficult to stop.

Vytautas Landsbergis.

Marx, Engels, Lenin,

George H. W. Bush,
President of the United States

Tanks from the Soviet Union

That's why I said yesterday, that when I heard Bob Dylan songs coming through the windows, in Vilnius, I knew the end was coming.

PAIK

We should add the Olympic Games to the media. Many people have told me about the importance of the role that the Seoul Olympic transmissions played in the breaking up of the Soviet Union. They were always told that South Korea was very poor and military. But through the sports coverage they saw that Korea was not so poor. And that played on people's minds. That produced a very concrete effect.

LANDSBERGIS

Yes. We all saw it. It showed that a small country could defend its independence and achieve so much, compared

with North Korea. It was a very clearly seen difference
between the two systems. What happened in Seoul,
also, it was the victory of the Lithuanian basketball
team. But Lithuania was never mentioned by the Soviets ...
It was the Russian team! That didn't contribute to the
dignity of the Lithuanians who got the medal ...


PAIK

The same happened in 1936, in Berlin, where the
Koreans could only run under the Japanese flag. So when
a Korean won a medal, and a Korean newspaper sent
a picture of the winner, with a Japanese flag, the paper
erased the flag from the picture and printed it. The paper
was closed the next day ...


*Intellectuals and Karl Marx*


PAIK

Do you think we can save any part of Karl Marx theory?
I don't think we should try to save it.


LANDSBERGIS

It is a strange situation when Western leaders, heads of
state, and politicians are talking 90 percent about the
economy, as if that were the most important issue. Why?


PAIK

But Marx as an economist failed. I remember A d o r n o
said that after Auschwitz nobody can talk about poetry. Then,
after the Hungarian revolution, there was all this enthusiasm for Karl Marx. That was really an irony. I think it
was the American hegemony. You see, we can decide! We'll
decide! They should have listened to what happened in
Hungary, in Poland, at that time. After that the intellectuals
should have never talked about Karl Marx, after 1956.
Nothing can be saved. Of course, American intellectuals
today cannot say they are pro-communist. But they can
say that they are anti-anti-communist ...


MEKAS

I know people, right here in New York, and in Paris, very
bright people, who say, yes, it all failed in the Soviet Union,

but it proves nothing! They say, there is nothing wrong
with Marxism or socialism or even communism: only
that it happened in the wrong country at the wrong time,
and fell into the hands of the wrong politicians, and it
was all done in the wrong way ...

PAIK

But it also failed in Sweden and England.

MEKAS

That doesn't enter their heads.

PAIK

Sweden and England are among the most educated people.
And if it failed there, where could it succeed? It can't succeed
in Uganda or Congo or Madagascar or Korea. One hundred
years of experiments should prove it was enough ...

MEKAS

No, they don't take that as proof.

PAIK

That's amazing. We knew it—Jonas and I were two anti-
communists in the avant-garde.

LANDSBERGIS

But they did it effectively in Romania: they shot Ceaușescu
and retained the system. It was an effective solution.
Gorbachev was absolutely proud when he informed
the Congress of People's Deputies in Moscow about it.
I was there when he reported the events in Romania, about
the execution of Ceaușescu. He was his guy. Goodbye,
Ceaușescu ...

PAIK

And President Bush?

LANDSBERGIS

Yes. I asked President Bush four or five times to make some
political moves to protect Lithuania from a Soviet attack,
which was already prepared. He didn't believe it. He thought
that it would be disastrous for Soviet policy to do that.
They won't do it, he said. But Gorbachev did it in three weeks,

in one month. I met President Bush again in May of 1991,
after the hearings by the Commission of Human Rights,
in the Congress, and again, in September, when I went
to New York to participate in the United Nations General
Assembly, when we were accepted as members.

PAIK

How do you feel, working in politics, as a piano player?

LANDSBERGIS

Sometimes I use my ability to play on various informal occasions. For example, during a pleasant evening—and there
was some Icelandic music—someone asked me, and I played
piano, old folk songs. I also remember, when President
Mitterrand visited Lithuania, he and his wife in my office
in Vilnius, I played for them, it was my gift. I also played
for the Danish and Swedish royal families ... They asked
me to play, because they saw a piano in my office.

*Fluxus and Liberation*

PAIK

Paderewski and Landsbergis ... You were a close childhood
friend of George Maciunas, the Fluxus guy. He had
an extraordinary sense of humor. But I also remember that
your tactics against Soviet tanks also had a great sense
of humor. You shared the sense of defiance and the laugh.
George used to say that when he dies, he would like to
come back as a frog. In the Asian tradition, a frog always
has humor and it always has defiance.

LANDSBERGIS

I remember the situation, when I was pressed to give an
answer to Gorbachev's ultimatum, in April of 1990. It was
his second ultimatum. It was three days after the proclamation of Independence. He asked us to denounce the
proclamation, and he sent a long list of accusations treating
us as breakers of the Soviet laws, demanding that we
implement all their demands in three days. And it was
Friday, Easter Friday, and we had a press conference,
and the journalists were asking me what my answer will
be, and I said, it's a weekend, and it's Easter weekend,

and it's Easter Friday, so we are going to celebrate Easter,
and we'll decide it all later ... let them wait three days.

PAIK

Humor gives you some distance. Sometimes it's the only way
to survive. I am used to doing little things, I cannot imagine
how one feels when one is in charge of the whole country,
or the world, you know.

LANDSBERGIS

Lithuanian business was always very small ... And the
question was always: Should our policy be based on justice
or on pragmatism? We chose justice. But that was uncom-
fortable for America. We have been troublemakers, creating
troubles for the good Mr. Gorbachev. Washington always
called us asking not to create problems because Gorbachev
was doing a nice job ...

PAIK

That sums up *The New York Times*, you know. When is the
next election in Lithuania?

LANDSBERGIS

In two years. The Russians are pressing us very strongly
now, that is, our government. Our government has already
promised to sign a treaty for military transit through
Lithuania, which would mean inclusion of Lithuania into
the Russian military sphere. It's not signed yet, but the
president has said that the treaty was prepared for signing.
In addition, there is some minor bad news. Our Foreign
Ministry signed an agreement with the Russian Foreign
Ministry about regular consultations on foreign policy,
to consult about the issues voted on in the United Nations,
which way to vote, etc. So we are in danger of again
becoming a satellite.

PAIK

It's very dangerous.

LANDSBERGIS

The more so because we cannot see any necessity for
that. It's curious, though, that when President Brazauskas
recently visited the United Nations and spoke there, his

speech was OK. But after visiting the State Department,
in Washington, he began speaking differently. For instance,
now he says that we shouldn't rush to join NATO—we
should not "provoke" Russians—that we should enter NATO
one by one, and not all at once. These are exactly the
Russian arguments. The same words, the same argumentation.

PAIK

Is it because Russia is giving you oil?

LANDSBERGIS

Russia has been successful in blocking the building
of our own terminals, which would enable us to get oil from
the West. This has been done through the KGB and some
corrupt Lithuanian officials.

PAIK

But actually, it's the Americans who control the oil flow.
They could have helped. But American policy is to divide the
world and live in peace ...

LANDSBERGIS

Now Kissinger is speaking reasonably, he is criticizing
Clinton's policy. As for Bush, in general, Bush was not so
bad. He played his own game, an official game. But he really
helped us to preserve our fragile independence. Of course,
when we were endangered every day, we were angry with
him. It seemed to us that it was so easy and such a small step
for him to say just a little more ...

*On Čiurlionis and George Maciunas*

PAIK

I live near Bonn. So I often go to the Kunsthalle, which is
run by Pontus Hultén. That's where I saw the paintings
of Čiurlionis for the first time.

MEKAS

Hultén was the director of the Moderna Museet, in Stockholm, when I met him first in New York in 1959. I think
it was at Alfred Leslie's place. Hultén liked Leslie's work
very much. It's at that time that I gave to Pontus a book

with reproductions of Čiurlionis's work. He was impressed
enough by what he saw to go to Kaunas, Lithuania, to
see his work in originals, and later he included it in all
the major shows of twentieth-century art.

PAIK

They had a whole room of his work at Kunsthalle. And it
was very interesting because there was one musical score in
which he made fun of musical score writing, like John Cage
would do, you know, only that he did it fifty years earlier.

You know, I was a music critic for two years and I
majored in Schönberg, I spent three years on Schönberg.
So I know something about music professionally, and
the two last pieces of Čiurlionis that you played at Judson
Memorial Church, I can say, that I can trade Schönberg
for Čiurlionis any time. Schönberg was a very arrogant man,
I don't think he would have recognized Čiurlionis, he didn't
even recognize Stravinsky or Bartók. [laughs]

LANDSBERGIS

Same with Nina Kandinsky, who kept denying any
influence of Čiurlionis on Kandinsky, even when it was
very evident and witnessed by Kandinsky's friends, and
Kandinsky's letters to Čiurlionis from Munich.

PAIK

I know that the Lithuanian language is still the closest
language to Sanskrit. Which means Lithuanians are very
stubborn people who resist foreign influences. I know that
George Maciunas was sending you some materials and
letters—you even wrote Fluxus music pieces, in your letters
to George. You also contributed pieces to Mieko Shiomi.

LANDSBERGIS

Yes, I sent him a few pieces. It was interesting for me to find
out about the happenings and performances, so I suggested
to him some events of my own. Later, I saw my name appear
in Fluxus publications. I was a little bit surprised, and
embarrassed, not knowing how the communist powers will
react to it all. But they ignored it.

PAIK

You saw George for the last time during the war, in the fourth
grade, just before he left for Germany?

LANDSBERGIS
Yes. And I never met him again.

PAIK
And your father?

LANDSBERGIS
My father lived in Australia. He went to Germany in 1944,
looking for my brother, who was fifteen and was arrested
by the Germans with a group of underground fighters and
taken to Germany. My father went to Germany in search
of him and they were both liberated by the American Army
and went to Australia—same way as Jonas came here.

MEKAS
I almost went to Australia, too. As a displaced person.
I signed up to work on a ship that was cruising between
Sidney and Le Havre. While me and my brother were
waiting to be called on the ship, an invitation came from
Chicago, to go there. So we said, why not, what's the difference, let's go to Chicago. But we never went to Chicago: the
boat landed in New York, we looked at the skyline of New
York and said, "Ah, New York! Why go to Chicago?" And they
were angry there in Chicago. They had an apartment there
for us, and jobs. Here, in New York, we had nothing. But this
was New York! You are in the center of your dream and
you're going to go to Chicago?

PAIK
But you didn't want to be a businessman.

MEKAS
But some people are telling me that I made a big mistake.
They say, with my persistence, I should have gone to Wall
Street ...

PAIK
But if *you* are too stubborn on Wall Street, you lose money.
You have to be very flexible there ... [laughs. To Landsbergis]
Did George live far from you?

LANDSBERGIS
I met him in second grade. It was in 1939. He lived very near
to my parents' house. We played boy's games there.

We were just two little boys. We were interested in electrical trains. Later, we only corresponded, but we were spiritually connected. We lived in two different worlds, and separately, for many years. But then we connected, somehow, once more. And all this time, separately, each in our own way, we were working on actualizing the idea of personal independence—personal independence, as practiced by George, and national independence, which was my work. I see George and Fluxus as representing a very basic idea of independence, independence from the establishment—to be a little bit in, but not completely in, to preserve the best. But in 1939 we were just two kids playing with little electrical trains.

### PAIK
His father was a railroad engineer ...

### LANDSBERGIS
And my father was an architect.

### MEKAS
George's father was a railroad engineer. A very good one. That's why the American Army immediately hired him, after the war. All those wrecked railroads ... He worked in Wiesbaden. That's why George went to Wiesbaden. That's why the first big Fluxus event took place in Wiesbaden. I spent a year there too, after the war, in a displaced persons camp.

### PAIK
George's father was a professor.

### MEKAS
Yes. He taught at the City College and published papers on railroad engineering in scientific journals. His mother worked as a secretary to Kerensky.

### PAIK
Besides you, Fluxus also had an artist by the name of Milan Knížák, he lived in Prague, he was a very close friend of George. He was arrested by the communists three hundred times. He is now a very high-ranking official in Czechoslovakia.

MEKAS

I was told he is one of the presidential candidates there.

PAIK

George reconnected with you around 1965?

LANDSBERGIS

Yes. I wrote to him asking him to send me some archival
materials on Čiurlionis. But he sent me materials on Fluxus
instead ...

PAIK

But I think, from listening to Čiurlionis's music yesterday,
that he will become part of the classical musical repertory.
Because pianists need new pieces, and these are wonderful piano pieces.

LANDSBERGIS

But sometimes I think that Čiurlionis's music is not for
those who want to show themselves off, not for the brilliant
technicians. And it's also contrapuntal, which probably
is the reason that his works are not yet played by world-
renowned pianists.

PAIK

And then, Americans do not play much piano ... 25 percent
of Juilliard students are Koreans. The Japanese, Chinese,
Israelis, and Canadians make up the rest. [laughs] America
is going all pop ... Susan Sontag did not mention it yesterday, but most pop music, American pop music is actually
Afro-American music. So that Americans do not need
to have a bad conscience pushing their culture to the Third
World because that's where it came from. They are only
packing it here ...

MEKAS

Here is one anecdote about Susan. A few years ago I was
in Japan, in the Kyushu area. And it was time to eat.
So my Japanese friends said we should go to Susan Sontag's
restaurant and have some noodles. I said, what? Susan
Sontag's restaurant? Yes, they said, a couple of years ago
Susan Sontag came here and ate noodles and she thought
she had never known what it means to eat noodles until

she came and ate here. So they decided to rename the place "Where Susan Sontag Ate," so of course I said I wanted to go there. We went and the noodles were absolutely great. And right by the sea. Right at the spot where Korean culture jumped into Japan.

*About Art & Liberation, Cultural Imperialism, and Bob Dylan*

### LANDSBERGIS

The arts have very deep and strong roots. But at the same time, there is constant change in the arts. And it should be noted that the arts are the most free of all human actions. And among all the arts, music is the freest.

In the seventeenth century, a musical textbook was published by the University of Vilnius. It was in Latin: *Ars et praxis musica*. And the author wrote, in his introduction, as his first sentence: *"Musica ars inter liberalis nobilissima"* —music is the noblest of all the liberal arts. In various periods of our history the songs that were sung by the people have been our spiritual sustainers. And even under the Soviet occupation, when the armed resistance in Lithuania continued for ten years, many songs were created about this struggle. These songs are the expressions of the desire to be free, expressions of the free soul. Sometimes I think: Why do people want to die for liberty, what makes them like that? Is liberty something more than abstraction? How can it be described? The experiences of various people who have been imprisoned by totalitarian regimes, relate that one sometimes feels more free in prison than outside of it. There was a cartoon which sums up what I am trying to say. It shows a man in prison. And a prison window. And a voice comes out from the prison, through that window: "I am free! I am free!" He felt more free in prison than the others outside—and this is the point for me. The freedom fighters who died in the forests during that decade, they knew that they were going to die. They left their homes to die. For a few weeks, some for a few months, they were free men. And they died free. And they died with dignity. Personal dignity and national dignity. So that when I think about what the arts means for liberation, I think about this dignity of spirit.

MEKAS

I remember, when I was in Lithuania, in 1977 ... actually
it was in 1971 ... I was walking through Vilnius, and through
the open window I could hear Bob Dylan. So I knew that
the ice was breaking, that a new generation was coming, that
the liberal arts were reaching them and you couldn't stop
it. When I heard those songs coming through the window,
I knew, I had a feeling that something must be happening.
And, of course, it was happening. And, of course, it
happened, but we also knew that many artists sang the
greatness of Stalin.

SUSAN SONTAG

Well, since I'm here with two Lithuanians, perhaps I should
mention my own connection with Lithuania. My grandfather
was born in the mid-1870s in a village ten miles outside
of Vilnius. But when he was two years old, the family left
for America, so I am a third-generation citizen of the United
States—a big country that is very different from Lithuania.
I have a somewhat different idea than the one I've just heard
expressed about the relationship of art and tribes, or art
as the affirmation of a national struggle for liberation and
dignity. Not that my views are based only on an American
experience. I have spent about a third of the last eighteen
months in a small country called Bosnia; I have been made
an honorary citizen of Sarajevo; I am going back again next
month. So I know from personal participation in various
arts activities in Sarajevo something about the role that
the arts can play in giving victimized people some sense
of dignity. But, of course, you don't have to spend time in
a small, martyred country to know that art is connected with
human dignity.

But for all that—and with due respect for the Lithuanian context and the presence of a man who is both a
distinguished pianist and played an important part in the
national struggle of his country—I have to say that I am
extremely unsympathetic to the connection of the arts with
tribalism. Let me, in the context of this discussion, give
you the other point of view. Though it may be that the most
ancient function of the arts is to express the spirit or soul
of a tribe or community, I am struck by the fact that nowhere
is the spirit and the soul of the tribe and the people more
alive today than among the Serbians. We all know that

art can be used in the service of the most loathsome regimes. But I'm not speaking of art which praises dictators—films celebrating Hitler, odes to Stalin. I'm thinking of folk music, the genuine art of the people and the tribe. It can become the vehicle of the most terrible, racist, fascist sentiments. Folk arts are often mobilized precisely to affirm the claims of an invading tribe. You don't find this in Bosnia, seventy percent of whose territory was seized by Serbia when the present aggression began in April 1992. But you do find it in Serbia and among the Serbs fighting in Bosnia. And I don't think I'd be very happy to see more art celebrating the United States of America, and the soul of our many-faceted tribe.

I also beg to differ with Jonas Mekas—not about his joy, but about the meaning of hearing Bob Dylan coming out a window when he was visiting oppressed Lithuania twenty years ago. I'm sure you can hear Bob Dylan, or Kurt Cobain, or whatever is the latest emanation of American mass culture, in China today, or in Iran—though perhaps behind doors, and not out a window. Let's not forget that this music we've loved is part of the American business machine: weapons and entertainment. The United States is the biggest exporter of mass entertainment. But the fact that this mass culture, of which Bob Dylan may be the high end, can be found in the living rooms and bedrooms and cellars of oppressed people all over the world, doesn't make them free. They can have their American mass culture—the fun, the games, the clothes, the songs, the movies, the videos— and still live under a dictatorship.

If we leave aside expressions of the soul and spirit of the truly oppressed tribe, or the tribe that pretends to be aggrieved or victimized, like the Serbs, there are some really important and valid connections between art and liberation that are not necessarily tribally indexed. First, art can play an oppositional role to many kinds of tyranny. President Landsbergis has invoked the notion of "inner freedom"— you can be free in prison, he said. Though I find that idea a little harder to assent to after spending time in Sarajevo, the biggest prison camp in the world ... Let's agree there is such a thing as inner freedom. Then I would say that art has a role of building or enlarging various senses of inner freedom, in opposition to various senses of tyranny. For if there are other senses of freedom than the usual political sense, there

are other senses of tyranny or oppression or totalitarianism
than the kind exemplified by secret police and gulags and
*lagers,* and the imperial takeovers of small countries. There
is also the tyranny of inanity. There is also the tyranny
of shallowness. There is also the tyranny of mindlessness.
There is also the tyranny of a culture that makes people
ashamed of being serious—that severs the links between
their consciousness and their lives, which makes seriousness
possible. This suggests another oppositional role for culture, another way that the arts can defend human dignity.

   Now I return to America and the culture this country
sponsors and has made such a huge success—the most
successful system of arts in the history of the world. I think
that system of culture and arts can also be the enemy. The
art that I care about is an alternative activity, alternative
to the main system of production, and is dedicated to main-
taining the credibility and the experience of the serious.
For me this is the most valid connection between art and
liberation.

### MEKAS

Art and liberation is a complex subject. I think there are
different layers, different dimensions in art activity. I think
there is one art that is very deep, it's like the blood of a
country, of a group of people, that comes from very deep
memories and sustains that little country or that group
of people. And then there are arts that are more artificial
and open to manipulation and are manipulated by politicians
and are more temporary. I think when we speak about the
arts, we should be aware of these different levels. And on
some level, art always remains art and you can not do
anything to it or misuse it and it deals with whatever is best
in us. And the other parts or layers can be manipulated.
And that, of course, happens. And back to Dylan: liberation,
again, is a very complicated thing. I mean, the breaking
up of the Soviet Union did not happen just because of people
desiring only the good things—the desires for some "bad
things" were included in it too. For example, their wanting,
maybe, to have everything that the Americans have. The
liberation process is a complicated process. There are
good things and there are some very bad things connected
with it. And the liberation that we see taking place all
across Eastern Europe, and going to the Ural mountains and

further, is not complete yet. OK, the system has collapsed,
the Soviet Union collapsed. But the liberation is continuing
on other levels. It's not yet finished.

### LANDSBERGIS

I would like to go back to the idea of dignity in life and art,
as an opposition to humiliation. We can see this humiliation in the arts too. Susan mentioned the commercial arts.
Commercial arts are a humiliation of the human soul.
The uprisings in art are uprisings for the liberation of the
soul's dignity. You have to defend your soul—so you rise
up, to save the arts against artificial arts, because in art in
general, there are always genuine things, essential things,
and surfaces, fake things, fake arts. In a moral sense,
art is an expression of love. I can't imagine … it would
be very hard to see art as an expression of hate. It would
be a protest, a very painful protest—but not one of hate,
of somebody or something. Art always appeals to humanity.

### SONTAG

I don't think there's anybody in this audience who doesn't
realize that there are many senses of the term "art." But
we can't use the term only for the art we like. As Duchamp
taught us, put the bottle rack or the pebble on the beach
in the right context, in a museum, and it too is art. So art
can be what we consider art—an enterprise embodying
a certain kind of consciousness—though what interests me
is art that offers other models than the reigning models.
That's the enterprise that Jonas Mekas has been conducting
for decades: giving people in this city a larger idea of what
filmmaking can be, to give them another canon, another repertory, so they won't be discussing whether *Forrest Gump*
is a good movie or not. They won't give a damn about *Forrest
Gump*. Instead, they'll go to the Anthology to see a movie
by Béla Tarr because his most recent movie, *Sátántangó*,
is showing at the New York Film Festival, and I first discovered Béla Tarr at the Anthology, which showed one of
his earlier films, *Damnation*.

But I don't believe, as President Landsbergis seems
to think, that art is fundamentally connected with love, and
cannot invite us to hate. Though I think the greatest thing
human beings do as a species *is* to make art, I know that art
is not necessarily a vehicle of positive or humanistic state-

ments. Still, art is the best vehicle of transcendence we have, the one that has the greatest continuity, the longest and most complex history with which we can connect.

[Question from the audience]

### SONTAG

The question was why I said that American culture was the most successful in the history of the world. I meant success in the most literal sense. It's the culture which has reached the largest number of people ever. It's like acid rain. Wherever it goes, to any tribe, any outpost in the world, people respond by giving up their local, ancient traditions and turning on their television sets and putting tapes in their cassette decks. Go to Africa, to Asia, anywhere, places that are really remote. Ask them, "What do you like about these things, the TV, the movies, the music, and so on … They'll answer in one form or another: "It's fun." America is where fun comes from. They'll say: "It's liberating!" (Remember, that's our high-minded topic today—Art and Liberation.) But what they mean is: it's liberating them from their own cultures. There is an international culture. And I'm not speaking of the global village, don't buy that nonsense. There is an international mass culture, since the 1960s at least, which has unprecedented appeal to people everywhere. Never before has a culture been so exportable.

### LANDSBERGIS

For me, the most impressive product of American culture is New York City. It's impossible to export it or import it, and for me it's an essential consideration in this little discussion.

Jonas Mekas at the Frick Collection,
New York, 2015

# A Story about a man who went to the frick Gallery to look at a Vermeer

Movie Journal
April 18, 1960

Once there was a man. He lived, he worked, he ate, and he slept like
everybody else. One day, I do not know how or why, he went to
the Frick Gallery and stood in front of a painting by Vermeer.
As he stood there, watching the subtle play of light and color, he
began to feel pleasant currents go through his whole being. Later,
at home, and at work, he could still feel Vermeer's presence. He
felt a kind of electricity in the subtle and tiny ends of his senses,
a current which went further, into his thoughts and through his heart.
He knew that something that had been atrophying and dying in him
was suddenly given new life by Vermeer. And he felt richer for it.
He wasn't a shrinking man: he was expanding. All his life he was told
that art and beauty were ephemeral and unreal. Now he knew that
in actuality both art and its workings were concrete and real. Vermeer
had locked into his painting the energy, the subtle vibrations of light
and line which can wake up and come into action as soon as there
is a sign of any approaching frequency of vibration in the onlooker—
and it lifts that lower vibration of the onlooker into its own field.

Knowing this, the man now frequently visited the gallery
to spend time with Vermeer. It was like going to school and learning
and growing—only the facts learned were not the facts of profession
and craft but rather the facts of aesthetic sensibility. If in school, he
felt, his thinking powers were strengthened and the know-how facts
were instilled into his memory, so here an entire area of his being
that he didn't even know existed was strengthened and developed and
now seemed to give meaning to the rest. He also understood now
that the expression which he had heard so often in school and among
his friends, that art is a reflection of life—now this expression had
little meaning for him. Art was not a reflection of life: Art *was* life.
Art was energy. Art was more life than he was, very often ... More
soul was locked into this painting than into some of his friends. The
separation was not between life and a reflection of life but between
the different phenomena. A man is one thing, a tree is another thing,

a stone still another, and a painting by Vermeer still another. And each of the four was a field of energy and they acted upon each other and all four were life.

As the years went by, while his visits to the Frick Gallery continued, he used to stop occasionally in the street in front of some artist selling his paintings. And he was always disappointed not to receive from them any of the feelings he got from Vermeer. A confusion of muddled tones seemed to come out of these amateur paintings— a vibration of a much heavier quality and frequency which almost by force was pulling down his own frequency, dulling his senses, jarring with them, making him almost physically sick, and he had to rush away. He knew by now that the artifacts of man can act both ways— they can lift one up or they can drag one down, all depending on where the onlooker was in his own development and where the creator of the artifact—"the artist"—was when he was creating the artifact, where he was in his own development, how pure, how clear an instrument he was himself, what kind of note could sound through him.

# *Notes for Allen Ginsberg*

April 2, 1997

10 p.m.
Allen just called. His voice was very, very weak … He said the doctors told him he had only about three months to live. Liver cancer, and other horrible things. But he was in a good mood. He said he had accepted death and is not worrying or panicking, it's all very normal. I asked him if he had enough care, if he needed anything. He said, no, he has a nurse, and even a very special hospital bed that is very easy to control … no, he needs nothing. He said he's writing a lot of poetry, for a book which could be entitled—if I remember it right—"Poems from the Bed Thinking about Death." I may be misquoting. Said, come and visit me. I felt he has some special need for it, for me to visit him. I promised to visit him mid-next week. His new apartment is all cluttered, he said, but very comfortable, a lot of paper stuff. Bob Dylan called, and Hiro called and cried, he said … We talked for some twenty minutes, and it wasn't a sad conversation, I just couldn't feel sad, hearing his voice so relaxed. Actually, we both laughed a lot, talking about it, about him knowing that

he only has three months to live, and all that unfinished business—
which we both agreed was total nonsense anyway—as we go from here
to there. I said we laughed; actually, he only chuckled, a sort of
familiar, classic Allen chuckle. Anyway, it was not a sad conversation,
strange as it may sound to some. But that's Allen's special gift,
I guess.


April 5, 1997

     Noon
Bill Morgan called. Said, sit down. I said, just say it. Allen died last
night 2:40 a.m. Funeral service, Monday 9 a.m.–1 p.m., Shambala
Center, 118 West 22nd Street. Wednesday he came back from hospital.
Was in good working spirit. Worked all day. Thursday he felt sick
again. Friday night had a stroke, went into a coma. Never woke up.
Fell asleep ...

     5 p.m.
Sent messages to Paris, Tokyo.
     Hiro called. Said, come to Allen's house.
     There were some fifteen or ten of Allen's friends when
I came. And four or five Tibetan (?) monks, sitting around a low
tea table, chanting.
     Allen's body was still in the bed, where he died, at the north
wall of the room, by the windows draped in blue—a wind was now
moving the drapes, gently—his head west—head turned sideways, sort
of toward us, but not exactly, he was somewhere else. Rosebud was
there, and she turned on the lights for a minute because the part
of the room, the long room where Allen was lying was in semi-dark-
ness—so I could videotape him and see him. He was sleeping, thought-
fully sleeping, that's the impression I got—with a touch of romantic
sadness in his face. But relaxed. Reminded me of Raphaelites,
I don't know why.
     The monks chanted all evening. Occasionally they held
little conferences among themselves, trying, I guess, to determine
if Allen's spirit had really left the body—because nobody should
touch his body until the spirit leaves it—but since the results were
negative, the monks kept chanting and ringing bells and burning
things, etc., as we all sat around the room, silent, or talking quietly—
Rosebud, Rani, Hiro, Patti Smith, Anne Waldman, Peter
Orlovsky, and a few others. Allen did not want, neither did the
monks, to have any strangers or press or TV around: they wanted

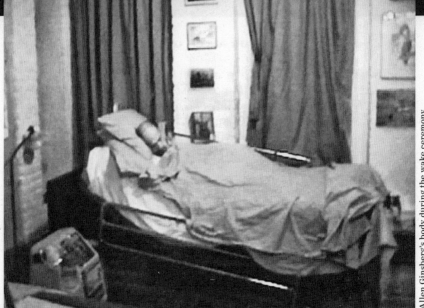

Allen Ginsberg's body during the wake ceremony, New York, 1997

Poet Peter Orlovsky praying in front of 405 East 10th Street, New York, 1997

Allen's spirit to leave the body in quiet peace. Peter—he said
he was only sixty-eight—he was so broken by it all, so beaten down.
But he was happy at the same time. He was bent down in body
but totally upright in spirit, I thought. He seemed to be completely
somewhere else, only half aware of what was really happening,
he was in some kind of blissful dream.

It was about quarter to twelve when the monks decided
that Allen's spirit had really left the body and it was OK to remove it
from the premises. Funeral home people came, all neatly dressed,
and in a very matter-of-fact way, very professionally wrapped up
Allen's body in the funeral shroud, put it on the stretcher, and wheeled
him out. It was about five or ten after midnight.

I walked into the street. I caught a glimpse of the black limo,
on my video, with Allen's body in it. Then I saw Peter, so sweet, so
sweet, with his hands put together for prayer. Then the limo started
moving away, and Peter waved bye-bye in the sweetest possible
way, I have never seen anything so sweet—bye-bye, Allen—and the
limo disappeared among the street lights, and Peter went to the
405 East 13th Street door and searched for a key in his pocket—
and this action, somehow, searching for a key in his pocket, after all
of this—this seemed to me so incongruous, so out of place and so
totally somewhere else: returning back to reality. This searching for
a key in the pocket, and opening the door, was a reality that had not
yet hit him, really. I turned my video toward First Avenue. It was
full of lights, taxis, and Lower East Side life. I turned toward it, my
camera still running.

Allen Ginsberg and Peter Orlovsky,
Central Park, New York

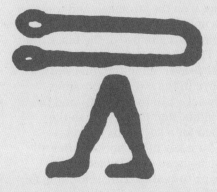

the looks of words

creations, objects, photos 1960 - 2000

**Schuldt**

with a preface by

Jonas Mekas

jan van der donk - rare books, inc.

2001

601 w. 26th st. 12th. fl. - new york, ny 10001

## In Praise of Crazy Wordsmith Schuldt

When you talk to Schuldt you have to be prepared to be inte rupted in every sentence as he jumps on one of your word the sound of it, and begins to twist it this way and that wa and then he permits you to continue, until he pounces agai He does it with an immense pleasure and joy, with a glee his eye. You can almost see in it some kind of animal ple sure. I have never known anyone as crazy about words Schuldt, and that includes not only the spoken words, but di tionaries, wall writings, advertisements of all kinds, cann food labels, absolutely everything where you can see or he a word.

**Bauer** *Akupunktur* **Bezzel** *F* 
**Czernin** *quirlen* **Feyrer** *obu* 
**Fritsch** *Apparat* **Gappmayr** 
**Garnier-i** *wir* **Garnier-pi** 
**Geerken** *Rad* **Heißenbüttel**

From the very first of his posters, all the way from 1960 yc can smell that obsession. I first met Schuldt in 1969 when was running the 80 Wooster Street Cinematheque. He did happening there, a performance. He threw into the audienc lumps of crumpled paper, bunches of words, and had an exh bition of his ingenuous posters, word puzzle objects, letter mirrors, and other word things.

Schuldt's craziness about a word always has something els attached to it - usually another word. He clashes them, ma gles them, collages them, he dismembers and reassemble them in different reincarnations. And he laughs and chuckle as he splatters them over his posters, his word-manglin objects and machines, his puzzles and performances. Whi he does it all, he seems to descend to some Urstate of som Urchild who is just beginning to babble, terrifically excited pronounce the very first word ever spoken, just barely emer ing from the Urschlamm or Urschleim of language.

Schuldt works from some kind of ever-boiling state of solalia. And the amazing thing is that the result of all this craziness is poetry. Yes, Schuldt is one of the very few makers of poetry today. A playful inspired obsessed pulator and inventor, being irresponsible with words as ets have always been, for the sake of poetry.

ah, always that chuckle. Playfulness. That's in the work ll the wordsmiths and pranksters, be it Khlebnikov, itters, Frank Kuenstler, Mallarmé or Schuldt. Or the folk s, those word twisters and spinners that you find among illage, country people. They are masters of their art but never lose that twinkle in their eyes and voices even the work is deadly serious, as serious as only some- that is totally pure, can be. Schuldt's work has that total, lete purity.

## Words into Shapes

### A Thing Out There

I was quite a greenhorn and a whippersnapper to boot when I got involved with writing and language trans-formation at the end of the fifties, but soon I began to think of my work not only as "what I do", but as "what is in front of strangers". To think of writing as that thing out there that confronts the gaze of an uninitiated person who hasn't a clue as to my innermost hankerings or weirdest theories or deepest scholarship. It dawned on me that the work has to make it on its own, standing on its own feet. I won't be there to babysit it, and besides, who'd want to talk to the babysitter? So I began to see my creations much like a furniture maker looks at his chair. Ultimately, what it boils down to is what other people hold in their hands or have before their eyes or in their ears. And those physical ways are how the writing gets to their minds, their sensibilities, their memories.

### Craft

Of course there are concepts, ideas, thoughts, words, invention, imagination, not to mention obsession and a few other things. Poetry is not just craft. But neither should it stop short of craft - or else it may well be anemic, wasting, craftless, a limp and faceless orphan. Come to think of it, craft should mostly be on the outside, on the boundary (in recent parlance: the interface, the mug that gets in between). Deep inside, work, or art, is driven by invention and discovery. The practical, down-to-earth sense, the skills and taste that come with craft, may hamper invention. On balance, crude invention is more likely to be invention.

Poster (detail) for "Steinigung", 1960. K..P.Dienst and Schuldt

### The Body's Typography

Maybe this is all a fairy tale but it does explain how I came to take charge of as much of the outside of my work as I can handle. I started out as a pale adolescent mumbling gibberish poems to small audiences. Soon I shifted gear. If the poems were incomprehensible, wasn't it all the more necessary that the words be clearly enunciated? Otherwise the point would be lost, no? I became a performer. I taught myself to project the words clearly. I thought of them as frisbees, sail-

Pamphlet by Schuldt, published by jan van der donk - rare books, New York, 2001

ing up to the ceiling at the far end of the room. I never sit, I read standing up. It's better for the typography you make with your body. Then I realized I didn't want the furniture, the desk in front of me, the mike stand, all those paraphernalia. Nothing should come between the poet and the audience, nothing except perhaps sheer incomprehension.

## Punishment

Graphic design and tape editing and all these chores of competence may just be the punishment for not sticking to our calling in its primitive, original form. That's what we get for no longer relying solely on the voice, on breath, mouth and the physical presence of the shaman, the medicine man, the griot, or at most the multi-media approach of the snake charmer on Djemaa el-Fna. It's the price we pay for all this new-fangled technology, for man-made materials like paper and liquid crystal and ink and magnetic particles of rust on plastic ribbons and bouncy electrons all over the place. The binary displaced the canary and puts us to work.

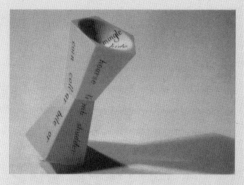

Ivory Textbody, London. 1963. English version.

## Transformation

A work - whether it's music or painting or poetry - is driven by invention but made by transformation. One can't ever create anything wholly new. The beach is there, the sky, the stars, the letters. The pigments are there, the wavelengths, the sounds, the words. You cannot actually make a new wavelength. But you can put things in a new order, you can transform materials into a new entity. I cannot insist enough on this point. Transformation is central to my ability to make work (more so than the "word" that Jonas Mekas has singled out), and this fact (long before I thought of "trans-formation") must have attracted me from the start to the tasks of determining the shape of my work in various media or materials. Every time you make a manuscript into a printed sheet or an audio piece or do it on stage or make it into a sculpture or a mural, there are new transformations in addition to those that were brought about in the manuscript, and hard choices to call. The new transformations will restrain and intensify the work and

perhaps bring out strands in it that I hadn't counted on. I le more about the manuscript, and I have to figure out how make it work in a different medium, a different material i envi-ron-ment. I have to find out what the damn thing really The public may have a different perspective on this, but the artist, the work is not what he knows. It is the unknow is where he hasn't been before. It is unfortunate that he invariably compelled by the world to talk about it as though (she), of all people, were the expert on it.

## Not Poetry

A rider. In the last thirty or forty years I haven't used the w poetry as many times in an afternoon as I have here. T may be rather misleading. I am, I admit, often referred to a poet. It is not of my doing, though. The work I do is motiva by curiosity (more than by greed). I want to see the outco of certain combi-nations, separations, and transformati that I think up and execute. I want to figure out the answ to certain questions. And no doubt I enjoy playing; Jo Mekas is very right about that and some Chinese friends me lao wan tong, a venerable old man who has left the ca of the world behind him and plays like a child. In all of t deciding whether it is poetry or not is not an issue, and wh I think about it at all it is peripheral to my interests and h more to do with which particular section of a bookstore works are found in.

## Hypertext before its time

Many branches grow from one trunk. Soon after I began w ing I noticed how things could head off in different directic all originating in the same first line. Different word compo tions, each giving rise to another tune, to other sensatic other flavors. It seemed rather a shame that all of these one had to be sacrificed in the writing. You had to settle one thing, and would never find out where the others wo have taken you.

Cube Puzzle (single element, London, 1966/New York 19

I toyed with ways of keeping at least some of this potenti some of the alternatives, in the finished writing. Or you mi say: to keep the writing less finished and with more of

ential showing. The reader would then be able to switch
ween different routes, different states of the piece.
wadays this is called hypertext, but this was 1961 and
ody had ever thought of such a thing. I drafted 48 phras-
r half-sentences or clauses, short statements of a theo-
cal nature (an essay on language, meaning, writing) that
ld readily combine into longer structures. They were to be
ted on some-thing the size of a business card; all 48 cards
e packaged in a carton cube big enough that they would
te freely; all six faces of the cube perfectly the same so
ody could have an idea of what was top or bottom, and
reader, upon breaking open the box, would have to
ume that the cards were in random order, no longer the
the printer had packaged them. The order of cards would
carry the authority of the writer. Any order was explicitly
orized. I was happily imagining two people seated at a

Pullout (detail) from "Unquel the Dawn Now", with Friedrich
Holderlin and Robert Kelly. Kingston, NY 1998.

Jan van der Donk gratefully acknowledges
support for this exhibition from the Consulate General of the
Federal Republic of Germany

Published by Jan van der Donk - Rare Books, Inc.
Designed by Jonas Mekas, Schuldt, Jan van der Donk
copyright 2001 by the authors
Printed in the USA by Official Press, NYC

Glass Textbody, London 1965. German version.

e, each shuffling their own set, and arguing that I had said
thing while disputing that from the same set of state-
ts helped to another meaning by a different sequence. I
ted to give a three-day-and-night reading from this (mod-
on the 6-day bike races) and a computer to keep track of
h potential sequences I had already used up. The poor
hine would have had to deal with 48! (48 factorial).
puter experts advised me that this was beyond the
acity of any computer then existing.

## t Bodies

ndon 1965-66 I returned to these questions and created
text bodies and the original small-scale Cube Puzzle.
se are true hypertext sculptures. There is thorough unity
ject and words: the shape of the sculpture is the gram-
of the text. The shape is not an illustration or a pun, as it
Apollinaire's Pear or Rain and in so many works of visu-
etry.

need to show different strands of writing in parallel arose
in and was resolved in elaborate five-color pull-outs in
uell the Dawn Now / Am Quell der Donau, a work based
poem by Hölderlin and written with Robert Kelly in the
published by McPherson & Co. in 1998.

Jonas Mekas in "Infinity Waistnippers, Washington Square Park,
April, 10 1999.

# In Praise of Crazy Wordsmith Schuldt

1995

When you talk to Schuldt you have to be prepared to be interrupted in every sentence as he jumps on one of your words, the sound of it, and begins to twist it this way and that way, and then he permits you to continue, until another word comes his way that he gets all excited about and there he pounces again. And he does it with an immense pleasure and joy, with glee in his eyes and a chuckle. You can almost see in it some kind of animal pleasure. I have never known anyone as crazy about words as Schuldt, and that includes not only the spoken words but dictionaries, wall writings, advertisements of all kinds, canned food labels, absolutely everything where you can see or hear a word.

Craziness or playfulness it is, I don't know. Actually it's both. It's also, obviously, an obsession. From the very first of his posters, all the way from 1960 you can smell that obsession. I first met Schuldt in 1970 when I was running the 80 Wooster Street Cinematheque. By then he was already very deeply obsessed. Or pos-

sessed, more correctly, perhaps. He did a performance, a performance where he threw into the audience lumps of crumpled newspapers, bunches of words, and had an exhibition of his ingenious posters, word-puzzle objects, and other word-related things. It has to be always word-related, everything that Schuldt ever does is always word-related.

Now, suddenly I am becoming aware that the word "word" doesn't fully explain what Schuldt does. Because his craziness about a word always has something else attached to it, and that is, most of the time, there is another word—what else?—attached to it. He clashes them, he mangles them, he collages them, he dismembers them and reassembles them again in different reincarnations. And he laughs and chuckles seeing what new meanings and sounds emerge from that mangle as he splatters them over his posters, his word-mangling objects and machines, puzzles and performances. While he does it all, he seems to descend to some URstate of URchild who is just beginning to babble and is terrifically excited to pronounce the very first word ever spoken, just barely emerging from the Urschlamm or Urschleim of language.

Yes, Schuldt works from some kind of ever boiling state of glossolalia. And the amazing thing is that the result of all this joyful craziness that you hear and see is poetry. A poetry that emerges from the chance juxtapositions, breakings-up of words, words ripped out of the contexts of cultural and daily semantic contexts and histories, and displayed nakedly and by themselves in completely fresh chance situations and constructions.

Yes, Schuldt is one of the very few true makers of poetry today. A playful inspired obsessed manipulator, inventor of word arrangements, groupings, makings of words, being irresponsible with words as all poets have always been, for the sake of poetry. A lover of words. Meanings, structures, shapes, rhythms and everything else follow. But at the beginning is always the word. Written or spoken. But a word: logos.

And, ah, always that chuckle. Playfulness. That's one thing one can always notice in the work of all the wordsmiths and pranksters, be it Chlebnikov, Frank Kuenstler, Mallarmé, or Schuldt. Or the folk poets and jokers, folk poets, word twisters, and spinners and smiths that you find among old village, country people—they always have a touch of humor, a chuckle. They are master smiths of their art but they never really lose that twinkle in their eyes and voices, even when the result of their work is deadly serious, as serious as only something that is totally pure can be. Schuldt's word/meaning poetry has that total, complete purity.

# Andy Warhol's Street Diary

August 2010

*Andy the Diarist*
A couple of decades ago, when I asked Kenneth Anger to send me brief descriptions of his films, he sent me information such as: the movie was shot such-and-such year, the camera used was Bolex, the film stock was such-and-such, and the print was struck from the original negative, year such-and-such, on film stock such-and-such. All very, very factual.

Store window, New York, 1986

I have never forgotten that lesson. He was giving me the essential facts that determined the physicality of his movies. Nothing that determined the content of his films.

I remember now G o e t h e's dictum, that we should discuss works of art only in their presence. Be it films, paintings, or photographs, we have to confront them directly, each of us, and they mean different things to each of us.

I will try to follow Kenneth's model in my short introduction to the A n d y   W a r h o l photographs in this exhibition.

*Camera*

I was informed, by those who worked closely with Andy, or researched
his life and work for the books they did on Andy, that he was given
a Brownie camera when he was eight or ten years old. Together with
his brothers, he managed to convert the family's basement into
a darkroom. I am also informed that later in his life he took some
photography lessons from his close friend and former roommate,
Ed Wallowitch (who, at Andy's direction, made the still-life
photographs in 1962 from which Andy produced paintings and drawings of the Campbell's soup cans). And his brother John, together
with their cousin, also John, ran a photo-booth business called
"Johnny's Photo Shop." They even handcolored some of the photographs. In short, photography was part of Andy's life from childhood.
Which also means he was looking at things since childhood.

This brings me to the question of what camera or cameras
Andy used to take the pictures in this exhibition. When I posed the
question to Deborah Bell, she did her own legwork and informed
me that she had learned from sources at the Andy Warhol Foundation and the Andy Warhol Museum that, beginning in 1976, Andy
used many small, point-and-shoot 35 mm cameras to make the kinds
of pictures that you will see in this exhibition, and that Andy had
a collection of such cameras. As it has been documented, Andy had
been introduced to the new Minox 35 EI model on a trip to Zurich
in 1976 by Thomas Ammann, who was then working for Andy's dealer,
Bruno Bischofberger. This Minox, which was especially small
for 35 mm cameras at the time, remained one of Andy's favorite models.
Andy didn't use larger, "professional" 35 mm cameras such as
Leica, Nikon, Olympus, or Canon because he preferred the miniature
ones that were relatively new on the market. From that moment
in 1976 when he discovered the point-and-shoot camera, it replaced
for him, almost completely, the Polaroid SX-70 camera, which he then
reserved primarily for his studio work. Besides being small and
light, the point-and-shoot cameras were self-focusing and had built-
in light meters, so Andy did not have to worry about setting f-stops
and shutter speeds. It was all about portability and convenience
for Andy, and he wanted to be as inconspicuous as possible when
taking these street photos. I am told that Andy frequented the camera
stores in the Herald Square area, such as Willoughby's. He'd look
in the windows and then go in and buy these small cameras, of which
he owned a lot. He would misplace or break them and then he'd go
buy a new one or send an assistant out to buy another.

I remember now my visit to Stan Brakhage, in Colorado,
in 1966. He had all these different film cameras, 16 mm and 8 mm,

all around the place. Every one was in use, but for separate films—
different films were slowly growing in each of the cameras.

### The Prints

The information I have tells me that Andy did not make the prints
himself. There is nothing very unique about that. Some of the
greatest photographers have used other printers. I remember visiting
Robert Frank around 1960. There was a developing tank in the
room. I assumed that he was making his own prints there. No, he said,
I hate making prints. I like taking pictures, but I have a good friend
who prints for me.

Some of Andy's prints were made by Christopher Makos,
in his own darkroom. Later the printing was passed on to some of
his assistants. For film processing, Andy used a lab, which also made
the contact sheets. Andy edited the contact sheets and Christopher
or his assistants made the prints almost immediately, often within days
of Andy taking the pictures. The prints in the exhibition measure
8×10 in. or the reverse. As a rule, there were no duplicates made unless Andy was going to use the images for his stitched, or sewn, photographic composites, in which case he would order 11×14 in. prints
of the selected photographs.

Andy primarily used Agfa Portriga-Rapid paper, though
there were some other brands once in a while, such as Kodak.
He liked Christopher Makos's choice of materials—same papers
and printing methods.

The prints with white borders, showing the black lines around
the image, were made before the prints that are bled to the edge of
the paper. Andy started doing the full-bleed prints in 1982. The prints
in this exhibition were made between 1981 and 1986, during the last
decade of his work.

### Selection of Prints in the Exhibition

The photographs on view here exclude the well-known subjects of
Andy's other photographs, such as the fashion world and the Beautiful
People. As the exhibition title conveys, it concentrates on the lesser-
known part of Andy's work. I am told that there are over a thousand
of these "street" photographs.

I always thought Andy was a diarist. A diarist in art is one
who is totally open to all possibilities all the time. One who doesn't
throw out anything; everything eventually is used. Andy was recording everything. With a still camera, with a video camera, Polaroid
camera, Sony tape recorder, pencil. A diarist's work never ends.
He snaps everything all the time. He is an open eye; he is the garbage

can into which everything can fall, can be thrown. Celebrities, yes, there were many of them; they needed him, they flocked to him. Andy didn't need them. He photographed them the same way he photographed shop windows and garbage cans during his street walks. With no judgment passed. The umbrella is just an umbrella. The neckties are just neckties. And so are the Body Girls; they are just Body Girls. Sometimes one can perceive a tiny, tiny smile in some of them, but it's the unusual, typical Andy-smile that one can see in many of the photographs of Andy. Sometimes that smile shows up in the subjects he chooses to photograph, sometimes in the writing in the photographs, sometimes in the simple boredom of the subjects themselves—in their simple "dailiness"—such as spoons, or a window full of shoes (Andy's first love ...).

So he walks the streets of New York and snaps, snaps, snaps. I have always argued with the people who have talked about Andy as a voyeur. No, Andy was not a voyeur; Andy was a gazer. He gazed at things, at people, at reality. A very special gaze. There was no pathological obsession in it. It was a very natural state of gazing. Andy was an open eye. He was a looker. You see it in all aspects of his work, in his art. Maybe he was also the most democratic artist at the same time. The diaristic form in art is both the most personal and the most democratic.

Now that I have told you the basic facts about the physicality of the photographs in this exhibition, please look at the pictures themselves if you haven't yet seen them. And I hope that someday a major museum will give us the chance to see reunited all of the street photographs by Andy from which these twenty-five were extracted.

*From an unpublished interview with Gregory Corso on an unmade film on Rimbaud*

In 1969 I lived at the Chelsea Hotel. Gregory Corso lived—
most of the time—there too. We had many drinks together at the hotel
bar, Quixote. One day, Gregory proposed we do an interview for *The
Village Voice*, where I was writing at the time. I taped it, but over
our next drink at Quixote Gregory expressed some reservations about
the interview. He thought we should do another one. But as time
went on, we somehow got involved in other things and forgot about it.
        The other day I was looking through my old papers and I
found a transcript of the interview. It was supposed to appear in
*The Voice* as one of my "Movie Journal" columns. Here is an excerpt.

Pasolini is making movies. Susan Sontag is making movies.
And so are Marguerite Duras and Robbe-Grillet. Who is the
next literary person to make movies? It's Gregory Corso, of course.
His Chelsea Hotel room is cluttered with film, all over the floor. And
he holds his Bolex like a wife: he talks to it, he praises it, he takes
better care of it than his typewriter.

### JONAS MEKAS
What's this stack of movies here? What are you after?
Why are you budging into enemy territory?

### GREGORY CORSO
I just want to make a few particular movies. Always wanted
to see the life of Rimbaud, Shelley. But you need a
beautiful movie man to do it and the few there are, are in big
money films ... man, but I got the right spirit, and so there's
only me I can go to, and I went and bought me a real nice
camera, a Bolex Reflex with a Vario-Switar lens—which you
so graciously recommended—thank you—and it cost me
all my poems ...

You see, I've been writing like always, but I don't always
publish what I write—in fact, I've not submitted a book to
be published in eight years.

JONAS MEKAS
Why not? Why don't you accept the fact that you are a poet?

GREGORY CORSO
My reasons are, firstly, I found myself writing topical stuff,
things that demanded immediate publication ... Well,
I decided that the best way to call them apples was to forego
publication altogether. I mean, it's no good, this being in
demand. It was 1960 or so, I think, when my publisher, New
Directions (who's always been straight with me), told me
I was one of the ten best-selling poets in the country, like,
I bet, those people on the best-dressed list who spend a
good deal of their time dressing FOR the list. So, anyway,
like all things, I've changed. Years ago, I had something
to say ... I gave readings and got into print. Today, like most
souls of truth, I have something to do, and I'm yet muse-
blessed to say it vondrously [sic]. Poems to thrill the heart
and brighten the head—the task of alerting, enlighten-
ing, protesting, heralding, was an electricity of joy for the
young poet.

So I have no regrets about taking myself out of the
daily image self-lineup. Where it works for Allen, it wouldn't
for me. Allen gets high on activity, I get wild on the unpredictable. To give a reading was always a heavy business.
I'd painfully read poems that were never meant for public
utterance, more than once. Now the only thing film has
to do with all this is I bought my $1,400 camera with a good
deal of the poems I've written these past years—sold them
to a college library where they'll always be cared for and read
by those who care. What with my traveling about and no
one stationed place to call home, only getting them published would ensure their safety, or giving them to a college
archive. Because I've lost a lot of poems, suitcases full,
and by the looks of the poetry I see coming out, I know
I shouldn't lose mine ...

My Rimbaud movie will not be exactly about Rimbaud.
Rather it will be about a young hippie genius—before
these mere hippies—called Arthur Rainbow, and he'll come
from a small town, like Rimbaud, and go to New York City—

Gregory Corso, New York, 1975

as Rimbaud had Paris—and make his way there. Meets
Verlaine, whom Ginsberg could play—ha—and so forth,
all in exactitude with the beautiful Frenchman's young life.
Goes to Tangier (instead of Aden), deals in grass (instead
of guns and slaves), gets cheated in his bizarre quest to get
rich (like King Menelech screwed [Rimbaud] with gun
roster), discovers perhaps some rare anthropological artifact
(like Rimbaud did territory in his explorations) and
ultimately returns to the states, loses leg, sees the influence
of his poesy on youth (like symbolism on French youth)
in the birth of the hippie breed, and dies …

This, of course, is a simple outline. Things like crossing
the Alps in the dead of winter, his drug cures, love woes,
getting shot by Verlaine (such as Ginsberg would never do).
But after all, Rainbow ain't Rimbaud, nor [Verlaine]
Ginsberg—just a famous elder poet suffices.

# Notes after reseeing the Movies of Andy Warhol

1970

On reseeing the movies of Andy Warhol, in bulk, old and new—
a task which involves a good number of working days—the first thing
that strikes one is the uniqueness of the world presented in them,
and the monumental thoroughness with which it is presented;
a uniqueness in the sense that there is no other artist in cinema
similar either in subject, form, or technical procedures. Warhol went
into his work with such an intensity, concentration, and obsession
that one whole area of experience—the people, the visual ideas,
the ways of doing it—was so totally covered that there is practically
nothing left for anybody else to do in that area.

We have other similar instances in contemporary
cinema: Stan Brakhage, Gregory Markopoulos, and Jean-
Luc Godard went about their work the same thorough way:
there is nothing much left for any other film artist to do in the areas
they passed through. Huge areas of form and content have been
covered in all these four cases, with all the formal questions, technical procedures, and solutions explored. In Brakhage we have
one area of content, form, and technical procedure explored;
in Markopoulos, another; in Godard, still another; in Warhol, again
another. Neither the content nor the form nor the style nor the
technology is the same in any of the four cases. Each artist came
and revealed a different vision of the world.

Sometime in 1965, Stan Brakhage came to New York.
On his mountain in Colorado, nine thousand feet up, he had heard
about Warhol and *Sleep*. He sat down at the Film-Makers' Cooperative
and he said: "Enough is enough. I want to see the Warhols and
find out what the noise is all about." So he sat and looked through
reel after reel of *Sleep*. I think he even said he looked through
all of it. I was working by the table, and Stan stood there suddenly,
in the middle of the room, and he started raging in his booming
mountain voice. He told us that we were taken in, that we were fools
for sure. Plus, he said, he was leaving New York. Something to
that effect. Sitney was there too, I think, and perhaps Kelman.
I walked ten times across the room, listening to Stan's rage.
Something shot through my mind: "How did you project the film,
16 frames per second or 24 frames per second?" I asked. "Twenty-
four," said Stan. "Please, Stan," I said, "do us a favor. I know it's
hard for you, but please sit down again and look at *Eat* and *Sleep*
at 16 frames per second, because that's how they were intended
to be." Which Stan bravely did, honoring us, and for which I
honor him. We went across the street, to Belmore, for some coffee
and for some wound-licking, and we left Stan alone to watch the
films. When we came back, much later, we found Stan walking back
and forth, all shook up, and he hardly had any words. Suddenly,
he said, when viewed at 16 frames per second, suddenly an entirely
new vision of the world stood clear before his eyes. Here was an
artist, he said, who was taking a completely opposite aesthetic
direction to his and was achieving as great and as clear a trans-
formation of reality, as drastic and total a new way of seeing reality
as he, Stan, did in his own work. Stan left the room, without any
more words, and had a long walk. I have never seen him before,
or since, as shaken up by another aesthetic world as he was that day
after watching the movies of Andy Warhol.

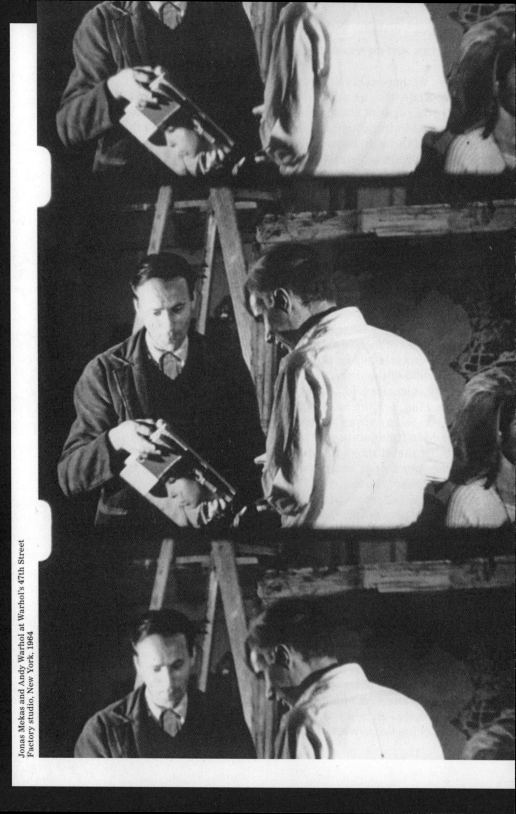

A very simple, a very simple displacement indeed. From 24 frames to 16 frames per second. But that's the story of all of Warhol's art: it's always so unbelievably simple a thing that makes it work. One little thing rightly chosen shifts the whole to a totally new angle, becomes the key to the essence of the work. To see that one simple but unique angle, that one unique formal idea (or concept), has been Warhol's talent, a talent that runs out over the boundaries of his art and spills into life in general. It's commonplace knowledge by now, from *Vogue* to *The New York Times*: it is the unique eye of Warhol to discover, to single out the right faces. A face that Andy Warhol singles out will eventually reach the covers of *Look*, of *Life* or *Vogue*. The same goes for shapes, objects, and ideas. If one could call the cinema of Brakhage a cinema of retinal impacts—or simply a cinema of impacts—then one could call a great part of Warhol's cinema a cinema of presences. One of the special gifts and hallmarks of Warhol's cinema has been this ability to distinguish, to find, to see the cinematically and conceptually photogenic.

"But it's so easy to make movies, you can just shoot and every picture comes out right."—Andy Warhol[1]

Only the next decade will begin to gain some perspective on the cinema of Andy Warhol. As I sat, now, reseeing all his movies again, I was again getting involved in them from the beginning and in a new way. One of the problems of preparing a Warhol filmography, for instance, is that the original presentations of his films have been so much like the films themselves. For example, at the original show, the different reels of the film entitled **** were projected in double superimpositions (one reel on top of the other). Today, on the shelf, what's left of it is a pile of individual thirty-minute reels with no information of any kind as to how to look at them. One can look at them any way one wants. I viewed them as separate thirty-minute films; one reel—one film. During the premiere screening, *More Milk, Evette* was projected as a double-screen movie—there was another movie, I don't remember which (and no use asking Andy, his mind is blank on such matters), projected beside *Evette* on the same screen. A number of other Warhol movies were shown sometimes in single projections, sometimes in double projections, sometimes in superimpositions; sometimes two thirty-minute reels were projected one after the other, running for sixty minutes; at other times the same two reels were projected side by side at the same time, running for thirty minutes. At the end of 1964 and throughout the year 1965, immediately after the Expanded Cinema Festival (at the Cinematheque), Warhol went through a period of projection experiments, experiments which culminated in the Velvet Under-

ground series at the Dom and *Chelsea Girls*. During such experimental projections the projectionist could do practically anything
he wanted—with Andy standing behind him, of course. The projections at the Factory were always very casual, that is, with people
milling around, walking in front of the screen, the music going
on at the back. The chance aspects of *Chelsea Girls*, the overlappings
of reels in sound and image, drove some reviewers to desperation:
they never knew if they were seeing the same film as their colleagues.
In short, the aesthetics that went into the making of the films spilled
out into the presentations of the films, into the theatre. This un-
compromisingness and thoroughness of the cinema of Andy Warhol
is carried thus to its ultimate purity (or call it extreme) in every
area, whichever area of his cinema we happen to touch.

  This thoroughness sometimes provokes curious paradoxes.
For instance: as huge and monumental as the achievement and
body of the cinema of Andy Warhol is, one could also entertain an
argument—and it's quite a popular argument in certain circles—
that Andy Warhol doesn't exist at all in practicality. Andy Warhol
is a concept, an idea, a myth, a Madison Avenue concoction, a product
of the advertising agents.

  "The problem is that he had almost nothing to say, and
therefore substituted camp and, at best, put-on. He was and is,
however, a cunning self-publicist, and there are always some unwary
critics around ready to find significance in amateurish improvisation."—Hollis Alpert[2]

  Warhol is like America: America is only an idea, after
all, they say. They say, even New York is not America. The early
Warhol is all La Monte Young or Jackson MacLow or Paik.
The later Warhol (I'm speaking about Warhol's cinema) is either
Ronald Tavel or Chuck Wein; still later it's maybe Viva, or
maybe Paul Morrissey, who knows. And the mystery of it all
remains how it all holds together! Again, it's like the United States:
the idea, the concept, they say. That is, the essentials ("the Revolution") come from Warhol, and the particulars, the materials, the
people come from everywhere and they are molded and held together
by the central spirit, Andy Warhol—Andy Warhol who has become
almost the symbol of the noncommittal, of *laissez-faire*, of coolness,
of passivity, of *tabula rasa*, almost the Nothingness Himself.

  "In many ways inaction is preferable to unintelligent action,
for it has at least the merit of not creating further sanskaras and
complications. The movement from unintelligent action to intelligent
action (i.e. from binding karma to unbinding karma) is often through
inaction. This is characteristic of the stage where unintelligent

Still from the film *Award Presentation to Andy Warhol* at Warhol's 47th Street Factory studio, New York, 1964

action has stopped because of critical doubt, but intelligent action has not yet begun because no adequate momentum has arisen. This special type of inaction which plays its part in progress on the Path should in no way be confused with ordinary inaction which springs from inertia or fear of life."—Meher Baba, *Discourses*[3]

I have watched Andy Warhol at work, and I have seen certain ideas grow and change and never reach realization because something somewhere didn't click: the approach, the angle, the shape, the setup didn't exactly work out. So I know well that nothing or little that Warhol does during those "passive," "careless," and "casual" shooting or painting sessions is really that careless or that passive. His aesthetic senses are behind it all, always awake, letting it all happen. But when everything is "just happening" and when everybody thinks that "things are happening by themselves"— there he stands, like he isn't even there, and with an unnoticeable, single, simple switch from 24 to 16 mental or formal "frames"— with one single conceptual switch he transposes the "uncontrolled" realism into an aesthetic reality that is Warhol's and nobody else's. Those "16 from 24" switches are very unnoticeable—it may be a shrug, it may be a word, it may be a deadpan, it may be a touch or a swing of the camera—they may be very slight but they are always there, and nobody sees them—neither their meaning nor even their very existence—but the Artist himself and that's exactly where the origin of the myth of the Permissive Andy comes from, from the fact that he is the Total Artist and sees what no one else really sees.

"Why is *Chelsea Girls* art? Well, first of all, it was made by an artist, and, second, it would come out as art."—Andy Warhol[4]

"Marcel Duchamp reduced the creative act to choice and we may consider this its irreducible personal require-ment. Choice sets the limits of the system, regardless of how much or how little manual evidence is carried by the painting." —Lawrence Alloway[5]

This controlled, and I stress, totally controlled cinema—I insist that instead of total permissiveness he has been exerting a total control—because of this inversion, the yin and yang of permissive-ness control, the film division of the Factory attracted to itself all the sad, disappointed, frustrated, unfulfilled, perverted, outcast, unreleased, eccentric, egocentric, etc. etc., talents and personalities. A whole generation of the Underground Stars produced by Jack Smith, Ron Rice, and Ken Jacobs were there, on the brink of Waiting to Be Used. And there he was, Saint Andy, letting them all into his orbit, into his quarters. Effortlessly and painlessly he moved

them and coordinated them and used the energies and forces that
were pouring in, balancing them, clashing them—a most subtle
maneuvering of the most extreme temperaments and personalities
in town, a maneuvering that culminated, on the one hand, in *Chelsea
Girls,* and on the other, in the Velvet Underground light projections.
The Dom series of the Velvet Underground, with projections, were
the most energy-charged performances I have ever seen anywhere.
The filmmaker here became a conductor, having at his fingertips
not only all the different creative components—like sound controls,
a rock band, slide projectors, movie projectors, lighting—but also
all the extreme personalities of each of the operators of each piece
of equipment. He was structuring with temperaments, egos, and
personalities! Warhol maneuvered it all into sound, image, and light
symphonies of tremendous emotional and mental pitch (Exploding
Inevitables was the other name) which reached to the very heart
of the New Generation. And he, the conductor, always stood there,
in the balcony, at the left corner, next to the projector, somewhere
in the shadows, totally unnoticeable, but following every second and
every detail of it, structure-wise, that is.

　　"The Plastic Inevitables (Velvet Underground; Warhol
and Company) performances at the Dom during the month of April
provided the most violent, loudest, most dynamic exploration
platform for the intermedia art. The strength of Plastic Inevitables,
and where they differ from all the other intermedia shows and
groups, is that they are dominated by the Ego. Warhol, this equivocal,
passive magnet, has attracted to himself the most egocentric personalities and artists. The auditorium, every aspect of it—singers,
light throwers, strobe operators, dancers—at all times are screaming
with an almost screeching, piercing personality pain. I say pain;
it could also be called desperation. In any case, it is the last stand
of the Ego, before it either breaks down or goes to the other side.
Plastic Inevitables: there remains the most dramatic expression of
the contemporary generation—the place where its needs and desperations are most dramatically split open. At the Plastic Inevitables
it is all Here and Now and the Future."[6]

　　　The exhausted and tired academic art squeezes all and any
content into worked-out, accepted, likeable forms. They are no longer
aesthetic forms: they are molds. They give the illusion of strength,
security, and harmony. There is this aspect of new art: a feeling of
things placed on the verge of out-of-balance. It's like Taylor Mead.
I saw him the other day at the Factory. He was complaining about
a film he was doing with somebody, how he was cut and edited to
pieces. "Wynn said he'll keep in *only the essential parts* of my scenes,

SCRAPBOOK OF THE SIXTIES

where *the thing happens.* Nothing will be left," he said, "only the controlled." Because what his scene was really about—and Andy understands this and permits it—can be revealed only by means of *duration.* Yes, the duration, that's the word. There are certain ideas, feelings, certain contents which are structured in time. The literal meanings you can spell out through climaxes, through the scenes "where the thing happens." That's why Godard's films are so literal. But the real meaning, the one that is beyond the literal meaning, can be caught only through structuring in time. That applies equally to feelings and thoughts. One of the essential misunderstandings about art and thought has been the belief that thought is opposed to aesthetic activity, to art. And particularly that thought has no place in cinema, which is images, man, images! But the modern scientists tell us that the thoughts are governed by the same structural processes as art, that is, by pace, rhythm, duration; the durations and repetitions of thoughts and feelings and actions. Much of philosophical and mystical writing attracts us not because of the ideas but because of the rhythms and pacings, the structures of thoughts, the meditative and contemplative structures of those writings. The literal meanings are of secondary importance. Most of the criticism of Andy Warhol films (apart from their "poor technique") rests on the fact that his movies seem to be lacking any literal meanings, any ideas, any scenes in which "things happen."

"With us, people can be whatever they are, and we record it on film. If a scene is just a scene, with a lot of ideas that have nothing to do with the people, you don't need to make a movie, you could just type it."—Paul Morrissey[7]

When you go beyond the literal ideas, beyond the sensory shocks, when you begin to deal with more essential movements of thought and spirit, when you try to register more subtle human qualities—and the cinema of Andy Warhol has always been concerned with man—you begin to structure in time.

"These other Yankees don't know that I'm from the South, so they don't bother me, but the South has a feeling toward the human person that the North doesn't have."—Andy Warhol[8]

"I still care about people but it would be so much easier not to care. It's too hard to care ... I don't want to get too involved in other people's lives ... I don't want to get too close ... I don't like to touch things ... that's why my work is so distant from myself ..." —Andy Warhol[9]

"With film you just turn on the camera and photograph something. I leave the camera running until it runs out of film because that way I can catch people being themselves. It's better to act natu-

rally than to set up a scene and act like someone else. You get a
better picture of people being themselves instead of trying to act like
they're themselves."—Andy Warhol[10]

We have one more of those curious paradoxes with which
Warhol's work abounds. There is this popular notion that Warhol
is *the* commercial artist of the Underground. That notion is promoted
by both the wider public and by the aestheticians of the avant-garde.
The paradox is that the cinema of Andy Warhol, more than any
other cinema, is undermining the accepted notions of the American
entertainment and commercial film. The cinema of Brakhage or
the cinema of Markopoulos or the cinema of Michael Snow has
nothing to do with the entertainment film. They are clearly working
in another, non-narrative, non-entertainment area, as in a classical
way and sense we say all poetry is in a different area. But the cinema
of Warhol, *Chelsea Girls, The Nude Restaurant, The Imitation
of Christ*, is part of the narrative cinema, is within the field of cinema
that is called "movies," it deals with "people," is part of it. Is part
of it but is of a totally different ilk. That's why the movies of Andy
Warhol cannot be ignored by the commercial exhibitors. At the same
time, once they are in, and they are in, they undermine, or rather
transform, or still more precisely, transport the entertainment,
the narrative film into an entirely different plane of experience.
From the plane of purely sensational, emotional, and kinesthetic
entertainment, the film is transported to a plane that is outside the
suspense, outside the plot, outside the climaxes—to a plane where
we find *Tom Jones* and *Moby Dick* and Joyce and also Dreyer,
Dovzhenko, and Bresson. That is, it becomes an entertainment
of a more subtle, more eternal kind, where we are not hypnotized into
something but where we sort of study, watch, contemplate, listen—
not so much for the "big actions" but for the small words, intonations,
colors of voices, colors of words, projections of the voices; the
content that is in the quality and movements of the voices and expressions (in the Hitchcock or Nichols movies the voices are
purposeful, theatrical monotones)—a content of a much more complex,
finer and rarer kind is revealed through them. And these faces and
these words and these movements are not *bridges* for something else,
for some other actions: no, they are themselves the *actions*. So that
when you watch *The Imitation of Christ*, when you watch this protagonist who does practically nothing, who says very little—when you
watch him from this new, transported plane of the New Art (all
minimal art exists on this transported plane)—you discover gradually
that the occupation of watching him and listening to him is more
intellectually fruitful, more engaging, and more entertaining than

watching most of the contemporary "action" and "entertainment" or serious "art" movies. A protagonist emerges with a unique richness of character. All the mystical and romantic seekers of Truth and God have left their marks in this character. Patrick is the hero of the end of the twentieth century. Every little word, sound, hesitation, silence, movement reflects it totally and completely. Not that Warhol *made* him act that way, be that way: he chose him perfectly and flawlessly and allowed him to be himself within the context, and chose him for those qualities and in that place.

"I'm so mad at Andy," she said. "He just *puts* you out there and makes you do everything."—Ingrid Superstar[11]

"I have Andy now to think ahead and make the decisions. I just do what he tells me to do."—Viva[12]

And this is one of the achievements of Warhol's work, as one discovers when one reviews it again today: this total exploration of these unseen, imperceptible aspects of changing reality, of using his art and the technology of cinema to register them; the structure with those subtle human qualities and changing, emerging, new realities which escape even the wizards of cinéma vérité.

"What Warhol does not permit is that his machine and technique become the stars of the film. In most so-called 'documentary camera style' features being screened these days, the supremely slick results and absolutely astonishing feats of technical wizardry defeat whatever hope of evoking reality the film's creator's may have had in mind. Their standards, in which all things are perfect, may be said to establish a visual fantasy. Warhol's technique establishes visual reality, in which nothing is perfect. but it is real, and his films are all the better for it."—Dennis J. Cipnic[13]

And do not think for a moment, dear reader, that the actions, the choices of the artist, *why* he chooses this or that procedure at that particular moment in history, are meaningless or do not express man fully! Do not ask him to explain it all to you, why he did it that way, and please do not say, when you find that he can't answer, that his silence means that he *didn't* know what he was doing. No, every moment of his life, his whole past grew and grew and mounted and led to this moment of unconscious choice. What I'm saying is that the protagonist and the feeling and the content of *The Imitation of Christ* is pure Warhol.

"Warhol himself, I suspect after talking with him, doesn't know where he's really at, what he's really stumbled into." —Richard Whitehall[14]

What amazes one, when one resees Warhol movies, the entire bulk of his film work, is the amount, the vastness of the gallery

of people, of different dreams, faces, and temperaments that his films are filled with. Andy Warhol is the Victor Hugo of cinema. Or maybe Dostoyevsky, a little bit sicker, that is. And then, again and again this preoccupation, or should I say obsession, with the phenomenal reality, with the concrete reality around him, as he's trying to grasp it and record it again and again, and each time it escapes him. As if the deeper you dig into the human aspects, the more you swing into the material aspects—one deepens the other.

"All my films are artificial, but then everything is sort of artificial. I don't know where the artificial stops and real begins."
—Andy Warhol[15]

"I've been thinking about it," conceded Warhol. "I'm trying to decide whether I should pretend to be real or fake it. I had always thought everyone was kidding. But now I know they're not." He looked worried. "I'm not sure if I should pretend that things are real or that they're fake. You see," said Warhol, craning his head absently, "to pretend something real, I'd have to fake it. Then people would think I'm doing it real."[16]

"Well, I guess people thought we were silly and we weren't. Now maybe we'll have to fake a little and be serious. But then," Warhol said, going on like a litany, "that would be faking seriousness which is sort of faking. But we were serious before so now we might have to fake a little just to make ourselves look serious."[17]

The reality seems to be constantly slipping away from under the feet, so he turns to another way of doing it, coming to it from another angle—again and again—with such untiring persistence and obsession that it borders on both the titanic and the insane. Yes, only in a factory—it could be done only by a factory, and not by a human effort. No, the face, held for no matter how long on the screen, no, it doesn't reveal it *all*; nor do the endless conversations reveal or register it *all*, they do not reveal the existence totally. So he zooms in and out and swings the camera and runs it wild, at the Dom, and in the studio, trying to catch it through the medium itself, through the materials and chances of his medium, indirectly, sneakily, from the sides—putting blind snares to catch the truth, the reality, the existence—and that doesn't do it either. So he goes to two screens, to three screens, to superimpositions and strobes and music—or he just leaves the camera by itself—maybe it will do it when nobody sees it, looking at IT by itself, as the eye of a newborn baby—maybe it's there, IT, but we don't know how to see it again—yes, how to see it or look at the world as if you have never seen it? So he places the camera there and it watches life—it stares at life, like a baby, and it's difficult to stand it, that naked look, so you become conscious of it, you begin to reveal yourself to the child, you show to the child what you'd never reveal to even the closest of your friends, those certain secret emotions, certain secret, subtle, fragile, curious motions of the soul.

"Experiencing things and objects as things and objects is the outcome of holding certain attitudes, and to hold and apply these requires a constant effort."—Sinclair [18]

The other day, I was looking through some old English texts. Then I dug out *La Chanson de Roland*, and *Vogelweide*. Oh, the beauty of the Old French, and the High German, and the Old English! Why is it so that languages seem to become slicker with time? They seem to lose those raw edges, that earth quality. Or is it only an illusion, all those mysterious spaces, those unknowns and those in-betweens? Anyway, I thought, whatever the case, the language of the Warhol sound movies (I am talking about the language of cinema) and the language of much of the Underground in general, beginning with 1960 or thereabouts, when compared with the Hollywood film or the European art film, has all the qualities of Old English, of Old French, of High German. It has those raw edges, those mysterious areas where the imagination can roam, where we can erect our own under-textures and under-structures—those mysterious blanks, spaces, muddled noises which can be interpreted two, three, four, ten different ways—that crackling sound—that unpolishedness which at some point becomes pregnant with personal meanings. Like La Monte Young's music into which, while listening, you can project one million of your own melodies. That's about the most significant difference between the language of the New Cinema (the Underground) and the film language of the Old Cinema. The only thing is that usually *Old* refers to the origins, to the sources—but in cinema, until now, *Old* meant everything that had become so polished, had reached such a degree of functionality, specialization, and prac-ticality that it had lost all its mystery and origins. The only paral-lel between Old English and a similar notion of cinema would be to speak about Lumière. And that's where the early cinema of Andy Warhol went: to the cinema of Lumière. He did it very instinctively, but with that act he rehabilitated the meaning of *Old* in cinema, he pushed it all the way back to its true origins. At the same time, he became the first modern film artist who went back to the origins for a readjustment of his art, for the refocusing of the medium.

"Andy Warhol is taking cinema back to its origins, to the days of Lumière, for a rejuvenation and a cleansing. In his work, he has abandoned all the 'cinematic' form and subject adornments that cine-ma had gathered around itself until now. He has focused his lens on the plainest images possible in the plainest manner possible. With his artist's intuition as his only guide, he records, almost obsessively, man's daily activities, the things he sees around him.

"A strange thing occurs. The world becomes transposed, intensified, electrified. We see it sharper than before. Not in dramatic, rearranged contexts and meanings, not in the service of something else (even Cinéma Vérité did not escape this subjugation of the objective reality to ideas) but as pure as it is in itself: eating as eating, sleeping as sleeping, haircut as haircut.

"We watch a Warhol movie with no hurry. The first thing he does is he stops us from running. His camera rarely moves. It stays fixed on the subject like there was nothing more beautiful and nothing more important than the subject. It stays there longer than we are used to. Long enough for us to begin to free ourselves from all that we thought about haircutting or eating or the Empire State Building; or, for that matter, about cinema. We begin to realize that we have never, really, seen haircutting, or eating. We have cut our hair, we have eaten but we have never really seen those actions. The whole reality around us becomes differently interesting, and we feel like we have to begin filming everything anew. A new way of looking at things and the screen is given through the personal vision of Andy Warhol; a new angle, a new insight—a shift necessitated, no doubt, by the inner changes that are taking place in man."[19]

"In effect, then, Warhol insists on *our* personal commitment, to ourselves, rather than his (the observer can no longer be as passive toward art as he has been for the last four hundred years or so), by giving so little and demanding so much. (How do you fill the time in which you are supposed to be looking at the picture?) Like it or not, it appears that we are being expected to alter our accustomed patterns of perceptual rate, our attention span, and our notions of fitness."—A l a n   S o l o m o n[20]

The viewer is, thus, confronted with his own blank mind. Here is cinema that doesn't manipulate him, doesn't use *force* on him: he himself, the viewer, has to search, to ask questions, sometimes unconsciously, other times consciously, and still other times by throwing objects at the screen. The *serious* art and the *good* entertainments are supposed to shake *you* up. Here, however, is an art which asks that *it* be shaken up; by *you*, filled up with ideas, by you! An art that is a *tabula rasa*. A cinema that leaves the viewer standing alone, in front of it, like looking into the mirror. Didn't we always say that art mirrors reality? So here it really is! Before, it was always true that man mirrored art. Now we straighten things out. We liberate man from art's slavery ... Isn't the mirror empty and

silvery too, like Warhol's face, like the silver of his hair, like the silver
of Warhol's Silver Flotations, the silver of the Factory walls, the
silver of his paintings?

"To do this once is forgivable. It is a kind of dadaesque joke
mocking art—and hell, I'm all for it. People and artists do tend to
take themselves too seriously at times. If one has enough money from
selling Brillo boxes at $200 apiece to waste six hours of raw stock and
developing (such as in the movie *Sleep*) to create a mammoth joke—
well man, go ahead. But to do it again and again and then ask people
to sit through it is pushing things a bit too far. A joke's a joke, but I
for one would be embarrassed to play the same boring joke on people
more than once."—P e t e r   G o l d m a n[21]

During the early years of the decade, the early period of
Warhol's film work, whenever I went to a university, lecturing, I used
to take one of Andy's films, usually *Eat*. And always the same thing
used to happen. The film starts rolling, the audience sits quietly,
for a minute or two. The catcalls and crack remarks begin. In the
fourth or fifth minute, however, they begin to realize that I have
no intention of stopping the film, and the reports from the back lines
reach the front lines, that the reel is *big* (forty-five minutes). The
most unsettling thing, however, is the fact that no amount of noise or
cracks seems to do any harm to the film! Its nonchalant, obstinate,
and don't-give-a-damn imperturbability on the screen seems to
reject or absorb anything you can throw at it. It almost grows stronger
with every whistle. So the students begin to leave the auditorium.
After ten minutes or so the impatient ones leave or give up, others
resign, and the rest of the show proceeds quietly. Later, from the
discussions, it becomes clear that there is always a period—to some
five minutes, to others fifteen, to some still longer—a period of
*jumping the reality gap*, or what we could also call the period of
aesthetic weightlessness; a period of adjusting to the aesthetic
weightlessness, to the different gravitational pull. From there on
you are floating through your mind, from there on the movie—*Sleep,
Eat, Haircut*, and exactly the same applies to the later sound movies,
say *The Imitation of Christ*—from there on everything becomes
very rich. You are watching now from a new angle, every detail reveals a new meaning, the proportions and perspectives change—
you begin to notice not only the hundred-mile movements but also
one-inch movements; not only is a crashing blow on the head an
action, a touch of a butterfly wing is also an action. A whole new world
opens because of this shifted angle of vision, of seeing, a world in
which there is as much action, suspense, tension, adventure, and
entertainment as in the former place—and more!

"When we speak of fashions in thought, we are treating philosophy lightly. There is a disparagement in the phrases, 'a fashionable problem,' 'a fashionable term.' Yet it is the most natural and appropriate thing in the world for a new problem or a new terminology to have a vogue that crowds out everything else for a little while. A word that everyone snaps up, or a question that has everyone excited, probably carries a generative idea—the germ of a complete reorientation in metaphysics, or at least the 'Open Sesame' of some new positive science. The sudden vogue of such a key-idea is due to the fact that all sensitive and active minds turn at once to exploiting it; we try it in every connection, for every purpose, experiment with possible stretches of its strict meaning, with generalizations and derivations. When we become familiar with the new idea our expectations do not outrun its actual uses quite so far, and then its unbalanced popularity is over. We settle down to the problems that it has really generated, and these become the characteristic issues of our time."—Susanne Langer [22]

One could say that the cinema of Jean-Luc Godard is the cinema of applied propaganda. His is an ingenious and total usage of all the means of cinema, the vocabulary, the syntax, for the purpose of putting across certain literal ideas. As a result, the medium is misused, and the ideas themselves distorted, as all propaganda is.

The cinema of Brakhage is the cinema of the truth of the eye, of seeing. The preoccupation with the processes of seeing in its own turn revolutionized the means of registering the seeing; it expanded the medium though which man expresses or retains his visual memories and ideas.

The cinema of Andy Warhol is also about the truth and life as is, or, rather, men as they are. It is a cinema or a passion to record people and their feelings as they are—but without any stress on it, without any illusions, without any sales talk about truth and life as is—in other words, doing it but remaining silent, letting the thing itself speak for itself. Everybody, all the cinéma vérité filmmakers are trying to catch the truth in order to show it to *others*; Warhol is doing it as a private passion. The truth caught in Warhol movies remains in the shadows, under the palm trees, no light is being thrown into its face, and it's visible only to those who themselves put in an effort to see it, who light their own lamps, so to speak. The very humble and transitory look of his films seems to pay respect to the truth's privacy.

Again, it was Stan Brakhage who, on his last visit to New York—as he has done on every other of his previous visits—was lamenting the transitory aspects of his art. He slumped into the chair with his long legs on the floor, helpless, almost defeated, talking about the cathedrals and frescoes, and wondering which of his films, if any, will remain in the year 2200, when some of the originals are already fading and crumbling today. There was Jerry Joffen, we remembered, six years ago, who worked, had influence, including influence on Warhol at some early stage—and where is his work today? It all went with the wind, only the memories left. The ephemerality of Warhol's screenings, all the chance elements of them, and the changing states and shapes and lengths and even the titles of his films—Warhol seems to have incorporated all the transitoriness of things into his very aesthetics, looking at his own work nonchalantly, and cool, very cool, no dramatics, no lifted voice about it. And that's why it seems to me that his cinema is really about the transitoriness of the medium and the transitory state of all things. About the transitoriness of all existence and all art.

I bumped into Andy the other day. We spoke about this and that, and about my own film diaries. He spoke about how much he wanted to do the same: to record everything that he saw, everything that happened around him. "But it's impossible," he said, "it's impossible! I tried, but it's impossible. It's impossible to carry with you a movie camera, a tape recorder, and a still camera at the same time. I wish I could do it."

So he is still at it! Still trying to catch it all—by all possible means. It's an obsession unto death!

"We're going to start making serious movies," said Andy.

1   Andy Warhol, quoted by Gretchen Berg in an interview, *Los Angeles Free Press*, March 17, 1967.
2   Hollis Alpert in *Saturday Review*, quoted in the advertisements of the film, *Coming Apart*.
3   Meher Baba, *Discourses*, p. 113.
4   Andy Warhol in an interview with Gerard Malanga, *Arts Magazine*, vol. 41, no. 4, 1967.
5   Lawrence Alloway, *Systemic Painting*, The Solomon R. Guggenheim Museum catalogue, 1966.
6   Jonas Mekas, *The Village Voice*, May 26, 1966.
7   Paul Morrissey, quoted in an article by Neal Weaver, *After Dark*, January 1969.
8   Andy Warhol in an interview with Gerard Malanga, *Arts Magazine*, vol. 41, no. 4, 1967.
9   Andy Warhol, quoted by Gretchen Berg in an interview, *Los Angeles Free Press*, March 17, 1967.
10  Andy Warhol, quoted by Gene Youngblood, *Los Angeles Free Press*, February 16, 1968.
11  Ingrid Superstar, quoted in *The Realist*, August 1966.
12  Viva, quoted by Barbara L. Goldsmith, *New York* magazine.
13  Dennis J. Cipnic, *Infinity*, September 1969.
14  Richart Whitehall, *Los Angeles Free Press*, April 28, 1967.
15  Andy Warhol, quoted by Gene Youngblood, *Los Angeles Free Press*, February 16, 1968.
16  Andy Warhol, quoted by Leticia Kent, *The Village Voice*, September 12, 1968.

17  Ibid.
18  Sinclair, *Conditions of Knowing*,
    quoted in the Stable Gallery program
    note (Warhol show).
19  Jonas Mekas, excerpt from text
    of sixth independent Film Award,
    in *Film Culture*, no. 33, 1964.

20  Alan Solomon, Boston Institute of
    Contemporary Art catalogue
    (Warhol show, 1967).
21  Peter Goldman, *Village Voice*,
    August 27, 1964.
22  Susanne Langer, *Philosophy in a
    New Key*.

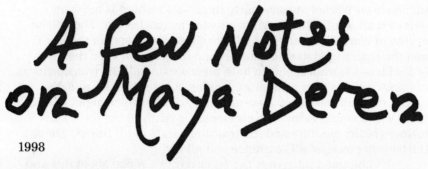

# A Few Notes on Maya Deren

1998

I am thinking about Maya Deren. More specifically, I am thinking
about images of Maya Deren herself, as she presented herself in
her films and photographs. And I am thinking about myself, how do
I present myself in my diary films? All my films are basically about
myself. The way I see it, whenever I film my friends, the world around
me, I try to be as casual in my filming as possible. But as I am reseeing my films, my film diaries, I notice that whenever I film or allow
others to film me, I begin to act. I assume one or another persona.
I am this, and I am that, and I am again someone else. I am clowning,
I am posing, I am hamming. But in every one of those cases I am
projecting myself into a persona, a role I never really was but many
times I wanted to be.

　　　　Maya was much more serious than I am. Or, rather, when
necessary she could look at things with more detachment. One of
the strongest disagreements between Maya and myself had to do with
this detachment. Maya was totally against improvisational, spontaneous, diaristic cinema. A film, every detail of it, had to be planned
with utmost seriousness. When I now think about Maya's images of
herself, I know that they were all carefully planned. Still, I think
that on that careful, calculated mental level, she was doing much the
same thing as I, or Cindy Sherman, or Claude Cahun. She
was projecting herself into imaginary selves. I say imaginary, but in
reality those were, or are, the many real selves of Maya Deren. The
only difference, a tiny one, is that while Claude and Cindy go through
different and drastic surface changes in their self-representations,
bridging generations, ages, and centuries, Maya stuck very closely to

who she was in real life. Instead of changing her makeup, she changed the context, the background, the story. Her makeup alterations were slight, but essential. As a matter of fact, Maya would improvise in real life, during her famous New Year parties, assuming more extreme impersonations than any that we see in her films and photographs. She had a collection of exotic dresses to help her. But all of these slightly different personae or impersonations together made up

Maya Deren, c. 1943

one Maya: an intellectual, inquisitive soul of Maya in search of something, and that something could have been anything, including the Holy Grail.

Actually, in all three cases—Maya, Cindy, and Claude—the artists create a complex network of impersonations, and we drift with them. No one persona is the real Maya or the real Cindy or the real Claude: they are, in effect, all real. They are all different petals of the same lotus flower.

It was in 1953 that I first met Maya. I was searching for a copy of *An Anagram of Ideas on Art, Form and Film*, a little book, or what Maya called a chapbook, which she had published in 1946. I couldn't find it anywhere, not even at Gotham Book Mart, the publisher of the book. Because I had been told that it was the most intelligent attack on the documentary film form, and a key to the understanding of Deren's films, I became obsessed with finding it.

Most of the people I spoke with about the *Anagram* shook their heads: the book was far above their heads. I have to add that, even today, Maya's book, which undoubtedly ranks with the three or five most important pieces of writing on cinema ever published, is still approached by most film anthologists with the same kind of fear and trembling.

Finally, a friend who knew Maya suggested that I call her and borrow a copy of the book from her directly. I was just a young nobody from Lithuania: a displaced person, a so-called immigrant. After four years of "living" in the postwar displaced person camps, I was brought to the United States by the United Nations Refugee Organization. I was living at that time on 95 Orchard Street, an escapee from two years in Williamsburg, Brooklyn. I had such great respect for Maya that I felt it was almost sacrilegious to bother her with such a request. But I had no other choice. I was obsessed with the need to read the *Anagram*. So I called her and asked if I could borrow a copy of the book. She sounded surprised but said, "Of course, I'll lend it to you."

I went to Maya's Morton Street apartment, in Greenwich Village. As I was climbing up to the third floor, or was it the fourth, I looked up and there at the top of the stairs, like in her film *Meshes of the Afternoon*, stood (fortunately, with no knife) a bushy-haired woman, peering at me with her big eyes. She stared at me so intently that against my better judgment (for fear of being impolite) I had to ask her, "Is anything wrong?" "No," she said, "no, only that you looked so much like Sasha that I was sort of in shock."

That's how Maya and I met. As in some of her films, I was transformed by Maya into somebody else. I dissolved into S a s h a—

Alexander Hammid—her second husband from whom she
had separated a few years earlier. Thanks to my resemblance to him,
however, Maya and I became friends instantaneously. Despite my
ritualistic transformation on the stairs, our relationship remained
always intellectual, or down to earth, two souls who met and
recognized each other and remained together to help each other.
We argued, we disagreed, but we always remained friends.
Sexually we were completely somewhere else. During that period
sex didn't exist for me: I was totally immersed in poetry. In addition
to that, I had a feeling that Maya was beyond sex. She was, to me,
sort of androgynous. Despite her bohemian reputation, Maya was
located somewhere beyond sex. Actually, I thought it was her bohemi-
anism that betrayed her real ultra-sexuality. She was a woman,
but she was also something else because she was an artist. She was
embraced by the gods. Not unlike Claude and Cindy.

Of course, I never had a chance to meet Claude Cahun.
My first introduction to her work came during a torrential downpour
in Naples, in 1994. I was sitting in the studio of Giuseppe Zevola
and drinking my morning espresso when I heard water dripping.
I discovered that Zevola's roof was leaking, and the rain was falling
on a book on a nearby table. I picked up the book, and luckily it was
only slightly wet. It was a copy of *Aveux non avenus* inscribed,
on the front page, by Claude to André Breton. Zevola had picked it
up by chance, a few months earlier, from a street book vendor. He
had promised to send it to the Musée d'Art Moderne for Claude's first
big Paris show. By saving that book from destruction, I felt somehow that I was given a connection to Claude. When later I saw Claude's
show in Paris, I thought I understood her and loved her, the same as
I think I understand Cindy and I love Cindy—me, the obsessed diarist
who I think doesn't really know anything about the ways of real
humans. And because I thought there was also a connection between
Claude and Cindy, I sent a copy of Claude Cahun's Paris show
catalogue to Cindy. That was in 1995.

But let us return to Maya.

She was strong, but she was also fragile and even helpless at
times. Since my brother Adolfas and I admired her, we became
very close friends. We helped her at her yearly screenings, organizing
the technical part of her lecture series at the Living Theatre,
and at one time even running her Creative Foundation office on
Morton Street (down the street from where she lived). Adolfas practically became her chauffeur, driving her around the city in a Jeep,
which, coincidentally, we had purchased from Sasha Hammid, without knowing that he was once married to Maya.

On her part, Maya acted like my mother. She even tried
to be a matchmaker, searching for a suitable wife for me—and
she almost found one, although not quite. But that is another story.
During her last year of life, Maya, Teiji (her young third husband),
Adolfas, and I saw each other at least once a week. It seems strange,
but I do not remember any "memorable," "intellectual" discussions
together. It was all talk about what had to be done for the next event,
or else about what we had seen, or our friends, or memories of
Europe—and Adolfas and I used to go home all excited and not be
able to sleep half the night. And then we would wake up and forget it
all and another day would begin.

We also used to play drums together. Maya and Teiji
had some drums in their apartment, and Maya would put on exotic
dresses and dance. I think Adolfas also danced but I was too shy.
Maya used to practically transform herself into some kind of gypsy,

dancing for hours on end with a wildness and excitement and also a total seriousness.

That's the kind of relationship we had. Adolfas was always there, and his relationship with Maya was slightly different from mine. During that period he was very involved in reading cards. He was telling the past and future, but especially the present. He believed that the best test of card reading was to describe the present. That's what got Maya. Maya had an incredible, almost fatalistic faith in Adolfas's card-reading ability. And it was not based on what he was telling her about the past or the future: it had to do with what he told her about her present state, her relationship with Teiji, and her work.

Now, looking back in my memory, remembering it all in glimpses, in single frames, I see Maya's face, always very intense, never making small talk. There was always a very special subtle laugh behind that intensity, which would come out in brief spurts. Those who didn't see this lighter side usually were a little bit frightened by Maya. The intensity is reflected in all of Maya's faces, in her films. The exception perhaps is one of her most frequently reproduced images: Maya as a face from B o t t i c e l l i. Curiously, though, that image was filmed and "directed" by Sasha Hammid, and I think it represents his dream of Maya: he threw her back to the Renaissance. All the other faces of Maya are rich with the reverberations of twentieth-century modern art.

As for Adolfas and me, I have to admit that we did not exactly identify ourselves with Maya as an artist. Our friendship had little to do with her art. We liked her intensity and her activism as the spokeswoman for avant-garde films. As for ourselves, we felt that we were from a different, postwar generation. Although I was thirty when I met Maya, and Adolfas twenty-seven, we both felt psychologically like teenagers. The war, the forced labor, and the displaced person camps had taken away a full decade from our lives. One would think that because of all that we had gone through it should have been just the opposite; it should have aged us by a decade. But not in our case. For us, the day we left our home we got suspended in the middle of an unfinished dream. We froze as if someone had placed us in a time capsule to awaken a decade later in New York City, in 1949. Thus Maya, who in reality was only five years older than me, was seen by us as old, old, old. She was already part of film history, whereas we had just entered its ring of fire.

Still, we were very close to each other. There were all kinds of intellectual and exile reverberations between Maya and the two of us. After all, she was born only a stone's throw away from our village. The distance between Kiev, birthplace of Maya Deren, and Semeniškiai, where Adolfas and I were born, is about the same as the distance between New York and Poughkeepsie. Maya needed friends and conversation. She liked us, I don't know why.

As far as her films went, to us they were part of classical cinema. We admired them in the same way that we admired the films of Man Ray or Hans Richter, Jean Cocteau or Marcel Duchamp. But we were waiting for something that would come from our generation. For me, that something happened with Stan Brakhage's first New York show in 1956 at the 100th Street Living Theatre space. Suddenly I felt here was the cinema that touched the deepest nerves of my sensibility: it was electrifying. It was no longer just a continuation of '20s or '30s cinema. It had nothing to do with symbolism, surrealism, or classic, eternal aesthetic values. It was all about the filmmaker himself, standing almost naked in front of us.

It was always a very sensitive subject with Maya: the surrealists, the '20s. Any reference, in the press, or in real life discussions, to her work as containing elements of surrealism made Maya mad. And I think she had a right to be mad. I think that surrealism was imposed upon Maya by Sasha who was the co-maker of her first film, *Meshes of the Afternoon*. When Maya began making her own films, they turned toward ritual and away from surrealism. Although she was educated in Europe, in the classical tradition, in her films after *Meshes* she was searching desperately for an alternative, trying to get away from that crowd that was still surrounding her. All the surrealists and dadaists had converged on New York, and she was looking for an escape into something else. You can see that in her face, in *At Land* especially. She never got to that something else. But she made a huge leap for it in *Choreography for Camera,* a leap across space and time. She landed on the shores of an ocean and froze there, intensely gazing into the future just before the cultural explosion of the '50s and '60s.

# Bum-ba Bum-ba: Conversations with John & Yoko

It was December 1970. I had one of those sudden irresistible urges to see my friends' films. An orgy of films. Since I don't like watching films just by myself, I rented the Elgin theatre for seven days, just before Christmas, and announced a 7¾ New York Film Festival.

One of the people I called for films was Yoko Ono. I wanted to see some of the films she had made with John in London. After hearing what I wanted to do, Yoko said, "Yes, yes, but don't you think I should make something new for the festival instead of showing old films?"

"Yes," I said, "it's a terrific idea. But we have only two weeks to Christmas. You have only two weeks to make your film."

We left the idea right there. A few hours later Yoko calls and tells me: "John and I decided to make *two* new movies for your festival. That's it."

John and Yoko's film team, supervised by Steve Gebhardt and Bob Fries, moved at full speed. Yoko and John didn't sleep. Things moved hectically and with great excitement. The whole artistic community of New York was immediately involved. Two films were under way. They became known as *Legs* and *Fly*. Both were completed in time for the December 18 screening at the Elgin.

The conversations that follow began the evening after the screening, late at night. We were all totally exhausted. It was a trying week for all of us. We couldn't do anything else but talk.

1. December 18, 1970. Regency Hotel, New York City.

JONAS
So what do you want to do with these movies now?

JOHN
I don't know …

YOKO

I think that the sound was very good, you know?


JONAS

I liked the camera sound in the background.


YOKO

Fantastic ...


[*Legs*—365 members of the New York artistic community were invited
to appear at the studio where Steve Gebhardt was waiting with the
camera, to film their legs. Legs were filmed to just about a few inches
above the knees. Some 333 of those called showed up and were
actually filmed.]


JONAS

Many failed to recognize their own legs, when they saw the
movie. It's amazing.


JOHN

They didn't recognize their own legs ...


JONAS

No, they didn't. But what amazed me most is ... I thought
these would be all very beautiful legs. But they were
not ... All that collection of pairs of legs, but no leg in any
of the pairs looked alike—that's the amazing thing.


YOKO

But they were like sculptures.


JONAS

No Roman or Greek would really like these legs.


YOKO

But Jonas, it's a very deformed age, you know?


JONAS

I didn't expect to see that, that's all. I expected anything
but that. Some small ... some crooked ... fat ...


YOKO

It's not a Greek or Roman age.

JONAS
Yeah, I know.

JOHN
But the Greeks and the Romans, all we have is pictures ...
It's like just showing Hollywood, you know, or Playboy.
People don't look like that.

JONAS
But still, one has certain ideal images, projections ...

YOKO
But those legs match this New York landscape better.
They seem so crushed and pushed and lonely ...

JONAS
Now, it would be interesting to shoot another three hundred
legs in some other place ...

YOKO
They might look different, you see. It might be on some
island, a nice island where there's less pressure. The legs
might grow better, you know. But I enjoyed it and I also
enjoyed the idea that everybody was a star, you know?
Like, not one *prima donna* performing in it. Everybody who
went up on the platform became a star immediately. You
said something about preferring *Legs* over *Fly*. Why is that?

[*Fly*—Twenty-minute film showing a fly crawling or sitting on a nude
female body. Towards the end more flies join in.]

JONAS
Well, I prefer just straight things. Now, here, in *Fly*, there
is an idea ...

YOKO
Did it project any specific idea?

JONAS
There was an attempt at dramatization, I thought. Maybe
I am wrong. But at this stage, you know, of where I am now,
what touches me most is something that is very direct,
not dramatized. That's why I very much liked *Apotheosis*.

YOKO
Yes, I understand.

JONAS
Where was it shot, *Apotheosis?*

[*Apotheosis*—The film begins with a close-up of John and Yoko, but then it immediately opens on an aerial view of a snow village, a small medieval-looking old village. The camera (in a balloon) slowly floats up, gradually disappearing as we go higher, as the balloon softly floats along, and then it goes into a cloud ... stretching into infinity.]

JOHN
In an English village, down South.

YOKO
That is my favorite, too.

JONAS
When did you make it?

JOHN
Last year sometime. About a year and a half ago.

JONAS
That village looked very medieval.

JOHN
Well, it's a classic English village, you know. It's preserved still. It's one of those beauty spots ...

JONAS
What was the name of the village?

JOHN
I don't remember but when we got there, we didn't know what village it was—the cameraman picked it, I think. You know, he just said, "That's a good place to shoot." We said, "Just get us a village square somewhere."

YOKO
And it started to snow at night.

George Maciunas's notes for John Lennon and Yoko Ono's

Historical Boxes

Yoko 1933   Vit B2 { Kuhn, szent Gyórggi & von Jauregg.   Fluorescent light.

reflecting pond stock

Roosevelt - New Deal - campaign button.

Bank crisis.    Sholokov:

Fed. Bank. Deposit Insur,   seeds of Tomorrow.   ( FM radio. E. H. Armstrong fragment

USSR - dipl. rel. with US - Flag

Tennis shorts   start purges,   bullet

    & comic book   16 mm sound projector

Hitler to power - arm band.

Repeal of prohibition - bottle   Actatine Plutonium Promethium Neptunium

Japan + Germ. withdraws fr. League,   disc McMillan & Abelson

Stavisky case.   Cage: Sonata for clarinet & 6 short inventions.   Riboflavin ACTH it disc

John 1940   pure penicillin 24 Aug.   Gödel - math. Jeep.   &. Radar turbo jet.

Butter, sugar, bacon rationed in UK

Evacuation of 400,000 children fr. London.

Finno- Soviet peace treaty.   penicillin   Sholokov Don Flows Home to Sea.

Germany attacks Norway, Denmark.

Trotsky killed *   Belgium. Holland, Lux + France *

Churchil. Blood + toil speech.   Nylon stocking

Dunkirk evacuation. — sand fr. Dunkirk

France - armistice - 400,000 french soldiers surrender Vichy

Germans → channel Islands. "Sea Lion"   Th. Mann transposed heads.

* Battle of Britain — RAF 1st raid on Berlin — Massive attacks on London

50 US destroyers to UK.   Cage - Living rm. music.

Hi Sea Lion postponed.   Italians attack Greece.

"Barbarosa" plan   Lend Lease.   Africa war

George Maciunas' notes for John Lennon and
Yoko Ono's "historical boxes." In the
finished boxes, each note item is represented by a "symbolic" object.

JOHN

Yeah, it started to snow the night before, and they were
all saying, "Oh, why did you choose us? 'Cause we're a famous
village?" You know. We said, "No, we never heard of it."

JONAS

And the snow did it. Without snow it would be something else.

JOHN

Well, we made it twice, once without snow. We had to shoot
it a few times. It was beautiful without snow, yeah. But it
wasn't as good as with snow.

JONAS

It's very peaceful, it's very ... Did you, was it ... the noise, the
cackling and the barking, that was recorded in the village?

YOKO

In the same village.

JOHN

From the balloon.

YOKO

[says something in the background]

JOHN

It was recorded on the ground and in the balloon.

JONAS

That sound really came up there?

JOHN

Yes, yes, you could hear it for miles around. We didn't have
enough of it, so I had to repeat it sometimes. Because they
kept getting it wrong. We kept sending them up again to get
me a decent sound. And, uh, we couldn't get a better one ...

JONAS

Did you get up in the balloon yourself?

JOHN

No, no. We went up in the air for about ten feet ...

YOKO
It's very scary up in the air in a balloon ...

JONAS
And then the balloon went into the cloud and for a minute
or two there was absolutely nothing to see, you know. The
screen went blank, white. So they [the audience] began making sort of funny remarks, and whistles. They were whistling.

JOHN
They had a long night ...

JONAS
There were people there who didn't even come to see
the movies: they came to see you.

JOHN
Yes.

JONAS
So, at that point I went up front and I asked them why they
had come here, why, this generation of peace and love ...
I said: You come here and you think you are a generation
of love and peace, but you behave like you are a generation
of anger and war ...

YOKO
[laughs]

JONAS
I mean, you cannot just look and watch, just watch the clouds,
you know, you always want to be entertained ... Don't come
back, I said ... And at that moment the balloon came out
of the clouds, and into the blue sky, and suddenly everybody
realized it wasn't just an empty "artistic" gimmick: the camera was passing through a cloud: There was a gasp. They saw
their bad faith ...

YOKO
It's a very pure film.

JONAS
It is. It's a very classical film, it has a classical structure.
And it produces catharsis.

JOHN

Ah ...

JONAS

I think it does. Really.

YOKO

Yes.

JONAS

*Give Peace a Chance* is very different. Maybe we should
have run it on a different evening ... The compilation films,
interview films concerning the NOW generation, they are
always made by some Hollywood man, or by some old square,
and they use all that footage, and they twist it, you know.
But in this case, in *Give Peace a Chance*, it comes from the
inside. So it's a document, in that sense, not a concoction.
There is no wrong note in it, neither in how it was made
nor in what it says. I think it's a very important document for
future students of the period.

JOHN

Yeah, we'd like it to go out to colleges.

YOKO

How did you like *Two Virgins*? That was right before
*Give Peace A Chance.*

JONAS

[reluctantly] I didn't like it that much. Do you like it yourself?

YOKO

I thought, it's ... because it's so ... you know ...

JONAS

Maybe one has to be in the proper mood for it.

JOHN

It's a home movie, you know.

JONAS

Yeah. [pause]

JOHN

We didn't show *Smile*.

JONAS

... and the self-portrait.

YOKO

Yes.

JOHN

*Smile*, it's very amazing, when you look at it.

[*Smile*, also known as *Film No.5*—John smiling in a garden filmed twenty thousand frames per minute—three minutes telescoped into fifty-two minutes.]

YOKO

And also the music is ...

JONAS

Oh, there is music to it?

YOKO

... I mean, bring your own instrument, you see, and everybody comes with their own instrument and plays it to this sort of ...

JONAS

Oh, I see ...

YOKO

It's an event, you see.

2.


JONAS

[addressing Yoko] R i c h a r d  F o r e m a n was listening to your record the other day, and he said, "That's what rock music will be ..."

YOKO

He said that's what rock music will be?

JOHN

Great.

JONAS

… or "should be."

YOKO

I don't know …

JONAS

Who knows what rock music really …

JOHN

I think that's the way it will go, you know.

YOKO

I just feel that people will become more desperate and,
uh, they would like to, sort of, really just express themselves
in sound rather than in words, you know …

JONAS

What about your music … You studied music?

YOKO

The music is always around me, somehow, because …
My father wanted me to be a pianist. He was a very good pianist, but he didn't make it as a pianist, he became a banker,
you know. And he always regretted that because his father
was a banker. When his father died, he left word that
he would like very much for my father to become a banker.
So he felt that the first child he has, has to be a pianist,
you know, so when I was a little girl, he was always trying
to sort of find out if my hand was big enough for piano.

JONAS

Whether your fingers were long enough …

YOKO

Yes … but I was a very nervous child and they hammered
me too much into practicing piano and also into composing
music, Western-style music, you know. And that was what
developed an inferiority complex in me. I didn't like music
and I didn't want to take piano. But then, you see, I was

always interested in songs. That's different from the piano
and all that ... So I think I was always ... at Sarah Lawrence
I was always sort of composing songs. And after that, when
I came back to New York City ... I've done a lot of ... like
the one that you were performing in too, at the Carnegie
Recital Hall. I did all these, you know, sighs and moaning
and things, and people didn't understand me in those days.
Jill Johnston wrote something about a little girl who
was sighing and moaning ... There was Richards, something
like that, in *The New York Times*, too. He was saying, well,
you know, maybe she might become, in the future, she might
become a composer, but that now it seems like she knows
only how to compose titles, the titles were sort of nice, like
*Grapefruit*. So I think they took it as that, you know, so-so ...
And the audience was laughing, you know? It was in the dark,
complete darkness, all this moaning and groaning. They
were saying, "Why, I'd like to see her having orgasms," you
know, sort of kidding me. Things like that. And in London,
too, the things I was doing ... Probably people didn't appreciate it so much because it just sounded like screaming.
[laughs]

JONAS

Have you heard what Meredith Monk is doing?

YOKO

No, I don't know what Meredith Monk is doing.

JONAS

She has been going in that direction for some time. But
completely different sounds. I have never heard anybody
else singing like you, your kind of sounds. Is there anything, something that maybe comes from your Japanese
background?

YOKO

I don't think so. I think the Japanese will think, probably, that ...

JOHN

It's Western.

YOKO

It's Western, you know. I mean, it's something like ...

JONAS

Is there in your singing, is there any singing in Japan, that is,
I mean, that is Western?

YOKO

Well, I was trained, actually I was trained in Western music,
German, you know, songs and all that, and Italian songs,
in Japan.

JOHN

Just trying to sing, in Japan …

YOKO

… to sing, you know, in Japan. And, they said, I had a good
operatic voice and I could eventually sing in La Scala,
you know … And I was dreaming about that. So my voice
training has been very Western. But then, at some point,
in New York, I started to feel sort of too desperate just
singing operas.

JONAS

But still, one knows that one can not escape where one comes
from, from the race and cultural memories. There must
be something you are bringing from back there, and you are
merging it with … something … not easy to define …

JOHN

I think it's got more kinship with just childhood than any part
of the world because when I first heard her stuff, I've never
heard anything like it, the voice stuff. But a lot of the stuff
she did and does was like when you'd lie in bed on your own,
you know, at night, and you'd do "uh-arrh-aahh," and just
entertain yourself for an hour or two if you couldn't sleep …
And doing noises like that—I don't mean that stuff when
she takes off singing—but a lot of just trying to find all the
different noises you can make with your throat, immediately reminded me of doing it as a child, you know.

JONAS

When did you begin singing this style, going into this
direction?

YOKO

About 1959 or something ... Around the time when I was
starting to, you know, in that loft, the Chambers Street loft,
do you remember?

JONAS

Yes.

YOKO

But the singing and groaning are things that people
do anyway, you know. It's universal, singing and moaning
and groaning ...

JONAS

Nobody thinks of it, or does it, though, as music ...
consciously so.

JOHN

It's like Andy painting the Heinz soup things ... It took him
to do that, to make everybody aware of that. It's the same
thing, isn't it? She's just making us aware of our own voice,
you know.

JONAS

... of certain vocal, sound qualities that could not be
expressed in any other kind of singing ... very emotional,
direct and rough qualities that would disappear when
polished. Very personal and very, very abstract at the same
time. But very, very real.

YOKO

Well, you see, I think people don't like it mainly because it's
too real. For instance, you see, composers are used, especially Western composers, I don't know, Oriental composers
as well, I am sure, but, uh, what they do is, they have, say,
some sad emotion and they try to refine it into an accepted
music style, you know. So instead of saying, "Oh, I am sad,"
or something, you say, [singing in lilting voice] "Oh-h, I'm
sa-ah-ad, oo-hh, oo-h, oo-hoo-hoo-hh, I-I-m sa-a-ad, I-I-mm
sad." You know like if you put it in operatic context or
something, then people are willing to listen. But I think
that, especially when I'm very sad or very tired, I start to

stutter. And then people are saying, "Well, you don't stutter."
And then I realize that I don't really stutter. But in my
mind I'm stuttering, you know, and I'm very carefully trying
to hide it. Like when I want to say something so desperately to you, you know, and I'm shy, I don't know what to say,
or I think I'll be hurt or something. Then I'm stuttering or
I might say, "Juh, Juh, Juh, Juh, Juh, Juh, Jonas, ah, ah, ah,
ah, ah, could ..." something like that. And then I control
myself, like anybody in the social context does, and I say,
after I control myself very well, I say, "Oh, Jonas, by the way,
would you mind putting my film in your theatre?" or something like that. But actually people, in their minds, they are
always stuttering.

JONAS

But isn't that, in your case, also a formal device of breaking,
structuring the raw reality, because, if you don't break
it up, formally, those emotional, whatever, outbursts,
then they'd look like pancakes. That stutter is a formal
device.

YOKO

Yes, yes. Maybe, because I was brought up in a very musical
environment I have to formalize it, maybe, and maybe that
is actually the sort of ...

JONAS

It's very organic because, at the same time, you go to the
very roots ...

YOKO

Yes, yes ... yes, I even think that my screaming and shouting,
and those things, are too formalized. But people think that
it's just screaming and shouting. They don't even see any
rhythmic, you know, communication or anything in that. But,
the point is, I don't believe that in real life, in the soul and
in the mind, people are so smooth as to say, "Oh, how
are you, Jonas?" But music is brought up into, grown into
a very refined form. They are talking just as smoothly as
people talk, you know, and it is wrong, it's not real. And in
our minds, actually, instead of saying, "How are you," "Yes,
I'm fine," we are just screaming and crying and shouting
and always covering that.

So, what I do in my music is, instead ... I want to
do something that's not phony for me. So, like, I can't say,
you know, like "Oo-h, oh Jonas, oh Jonas," something
like that. I can't say that. I have to say, "Juh, juh, juh, jo-on."
That's the way I feel, you know.

JONAS

Uh-hm.

YOKO

And so my music is stuttering all the time. It's that that I
feel the most. [sighs] And especially, for instance, you know
the one that was accompanying the *Fly* film?

JONAS

Yes.

YOKO

That one, actually, I think I was doing a passage from
an opera, something like, I forgot the tune, but ...

JONAS

Maybe that's why I said I thought *Fly* was an opera film.

YOKO

[humming a melody] Da-da-da-da, dah-da, dah-da, or
something ... but distorted. You see, like, when you're very
young and fresh and you don't know anything about life,
you can sing with a clear voice. But then you start to have
all sorts of pain, distortion, and anguish in life. Then you
say, "da-da-da-da," you know. You say, "a-a-h, a-a-h, ah,
oo-h, oo, oo-h." I was changing into that, and "u-u-h-h-, ah,
uh, u-hh, uh," you know. I just took a theme out of an opera
and repeated it many times. But it's almost distorted to
the point that it's not recognizable that it's a theme from
an opera.

JONAS

It's like Ken Jacobs taking an old Hollywood movie and
reshooting it, in his own way, repeating frames, by projecting
it, slowing down, running it backwards, resuming at some
other spot, on the screen, filming it—it becomes like his own
stutter on the theme of the original film.

YOKO
You see, like I'm too much in pain, as a person, to, you know,
organize anything, so I just have to go there, you know,
like the immediate stutter ...

JONAS
So this is like action painting with voice.

JOHN
Yeah, that's what I said, because people's reactions to her
music are just like I imagine people's reaction to abstract
and action painting was. It's just that people have an
intellectual—even non-intellectuals—have such an intellectual barricade against anything real or anything spontaneous that they need for it to go around, Route 66, before
they can accept it, and her stuff breaks that down ...

JONAS
The conditioning is very very set, in singing—same in theatre
voices, all the uses of voice, they are so set that it's hard
to escape that conditioning.

JOHN
When you hear real old blues singers and real folk singers,
say, in Britain, you know, the old ones that they recorded
before they died, they would sing, whatever, like, "I'm going
down the mine, um-uher-erm," and they'd do it, a big voice
thing after each word, you know, it'd be acceptable. I think
it's like ... Just the fact that they use their throat, you know,
they weren't trained singers and they wouldn't just sing
a story but add their own personality to it. They'd sing, "Down
the mine, um-hu-um-m," and that would be their sort of
trademark. But, they'd be showing off their voices ...

YOKO
But you see, for instance, I met John and I found something
else again. And this is great progress for my work. You know,
in electronic music—when I was in New York, most of my
friends were doing electronic music and all that—and I
was ... very deeply depressed, you know, because the direction they were going was too impersonal, for me, you know?

JONAS
Yeah, and ...

YOKO

... and too intellectual, for me. And I was doing this, "Uh-h, uh-h, uh-h, uh," and I felt like that, you know. And when I did that at the Carnegie Recital Hall, all my friends who were very cruel New York artists, they thought I was too personal and uncool. And that was a comment that meant that you are sort of animalistic, not cool enough. The New York art direction was coolness, you know, cool art ...

JONAS

Jack Smith was doing something in your direction ...

YOKO

Yes, I understand, yes. Yes. So, what happened was I suffered from that and I went to London, and it was a great thing that I went to London.

JOHN

I thought so ...

YOKO

... and I met John and, you see, they were playing this music
that I wasn't able ... I had no chance to get into until then,
you know. I didn't know about pop or anything. And in electronic music they have this very complex rhythm. And they
were doing just "dumm-da-da-da-da-da-dat," one-two-three-
four beat. So I said, "Why do you do a one-two-three-four
beat?" And I didn't understand it. They said, Well, there's
many complicated rhythms, like a [gives an imitation] ...
and all that, you know." And then I suddenly realized, you
see, the heart beat is "one-two, one-two" ...

JONAS

Isn't it "one-two-three"?

YOKO

Your heart goes one-two-three?

JONAS

Oh, I see ... One doesn't always know one's heart ...
Maybe there is something wrong with my heart! It has a
waltz rhythm.

JOHN

Right.

YOKO

Not like a first six-five and then eight-five. It's not like that.
Wavelength music is highly complex rhythmically but almost
going to an intellectual realm with it, you know? And the
thing is, I realize that, sort of, electronic music was somehow
out of touch with people. There was some miscommu-
nication, you know. And the reason was not only because
it didn't have the personal, animalistic aspect that I was
concerned with, but it also sort of went further and further
away from the real heartbeat rhythm. Because heartbeat
is the most basic, intimate rhythm that we have, you know.
"One-two, one-two, one-two." [voice imitative of actual sound]
Because that's how we are living. That's why we are alive
because we have a heartbeat. And so classical music in the

beginning was one-two, one-two. Then it went into one-two-three, one-two-three, one-two-three, sort of waltzy rhythm. It went into all sorts of complex rhythms, went further and further away from our body. And, of course, our mind is so refined that we have very complex mind rhythms. So the minute I met John, I saw why rock and roll is popular, no wonder. Because people are actually very honest, you know. People are ... You can't deceive people. You can't deceive people with intellectual, sophisticated, electronic music in a phony way. You can't do that. You see, people like rock and roll because there's that heartbeat, "bum-ba, bum-ba," you know.

JOHN

You see, I've converted her.

YOKO

So, these days, now, there was one review saying, "Miss Ono's music is pretty simple." You know, like ...

JONAS

[to John] I hear that you are becoming more complex ...

YOKO

[laughs]

JOHN

But the music isn't complex ... I, myself, yes.

YOKO

No, but ... "Miss Ono's music is actually pretty simple, isn't it? It doesn't have the complexity of Stockhausen or ..." But I, I prefer this. I want to have a beat underneath all my music. And maybe, my voice can do complex things, maybe the mind rhythms, you know. Show the mind rhythm in my voice and keep the body rhythm with the accompaniment. And so ...

JOHN

Who said that? I'm sorry ...

YOKO

There is something about that in the review ...

JOHN

No, no. I mean, about my music getting more complex.
It isn't at all.

JONAS

No, no. I said it only to see how you'd react to it. Nobody
said it ... I didn't mean to ...

JOHN

Yeah, I didn't get into complex music. No, I might have
headed towards it for a bit, but ...

YOKO

I think he's always being too real to go into something,
you know, that sort of sophistication.

JONAS

Yeah, I think that the richness of means doesn't mean that
the music is more complex or, as you progress ...

YOKO

No, no, it doesn't. So his album this time too, shows himself,
uh, just saying what he wants, and just having a very
simple guitar accompaniment, or whatever ... And I think
that we're both going in that direction ... But I know that,
instead of saying, "Why, why, why, why!" if I said, "Wh-hy, oh
wh-hy, oh why-y" (slower, operatically slower), you know,
then people would think it's easier to listen to, and I know
that. But I can't do it.

JONAS

But in your music, there is some electronic sound.

YOKO

Oh yes, yes. You see, that's another thing. I'm not against
using any electronic device as long as it works, you know.
And I know that many sophisticated composers would say ...

JONAS

Again, we are talking about the richness of means ...

YOKO

Yes, yes. But they would say, you know, listen to my things
and say, "Oh, all she did was put an echo in," you know,

or something like that. And it's not a very complex electronic
means that I'm using. I'm just using it because it worked.
And I remember those days when the, you know, very "in,"
snob crowd was saying, sneering about some music that just
used echoes, "That's just an echo effect," or "playing the
tape backwards," you know.

3.

JONAS

I was a little bit bothered by the audience's reactions to the
*Fly* film. Actually, they reacted to the soundtrack. They
thought, I think, that you were trying to imitate the sounds
of the fly—of some Essential Fly, or something—and they
began making similar sounds.

YOKO

[surprised] Really?

JONAS

Yeah. I have it on the tape. I taped the first part of it, when
you sing. But they gave up, eventually, and just watched.
I thought maybe the sound ran too parallel to the image,
maybe.

JOHN

It's just like two straight lines, you know …

YOKO

I think that the music in the *Fly* becomes very independent.
I almost felt that …

JONAS

… after one got used to it, one felt it was …

YOKO

… when I saw it with the music I thought, "Well, maybe
the film is the accompaniment for the music. [light laugh]
You didn't know which one was an accompaniment for
which, you know. The film can be the accompaniment for
the music. [laughs lightly again] In the beginning, when
I was making the film, I'd say, "Maybe we should collect flies
and have noise and all that. Fly noise." It just didn't sound

right. But that thing that John did with the guitar, you know,
made sounds almost like flies.

JONAS

That was very good, that added another dimension, I liked
that. That came about ten minutes into the film.

JOHN

Fifteen minutes.

YOKO

You see, like ... I'm sure that many people who now understand my music would never have understood it unless
I hadn't ... I introduced the element that I was influenced
by John, you know, on the guitar, and things like that.
You know, the beat rhythm part. And so it's great now, in
that sense. I think, with that thing underneath, it becomes
a little bit more acceptable ...

4.

JONAS

[addressing John] And how is all this influencing you?

YOKO

John? [light laugh]

JOHN

Uh, Yoko influences me just about in everything that I do.
I don't know how to express it, really.

JONAS

I think that one needs more time to gain such a perspective.

YOKO

Yes ... You can't be objective about it.

JOHN

Actually, she's influencing me in the way I sing, you know.
I mean, I was becoming a formalized rock-and-roll singer.

JONAS

I noticed new sounds in your new record.

JOHN

I was becoming a formalized rock-and-roll singer. You know,
the same as an opera singer, in a way. And after being
with Yoko and hearing her voice things, I realized that ...
how limited, what limits I put on my voice. So, she ...
I opened my throat again, you know.

YOKO

And also I think that ...

JOHN

It brought some realism into it.

YOKO

And also, what he did, I don't know, maybe it was always
true, you know, in the guitar section of *Why* he goes really
mad with the guitar, you know? I think, because we both
influence each other in sort of like a dialogue. I enjoy that
the most when we are improvising and then I get into his
thing and he gets into my thing and it goes like that ...
Another thing I think is ... You see, he was making 8 mm
films and all that—home movies—and they were just pretty
good. Like, they were sort of B r a k h a g e style.

JONAS

Where are they now? You still have them?

JOHN

Yes. They are all home.

YOKO

Before I met him, he was doing that. And then I met
him and [in whisper] uh ... what was that one? He made
a self-portrait film, and then he made *Apotheosis*.

JOHN

No, she did ... that. I mean, all that was due to her.

JONAS

Is *Apotheosis* ... whose film is that?

JOHN

That was mine.

JONAS

Oh, I see.

JOHN

That's why we put titles on it, Jonas. Like, eh …

JONAS

Yes, I forgot … I forgot what the titles said.

JOHN

I had the idea after she told me her idea for *Up Your Legs Forever.*

JONAS

How old is that idea?

JOHN

Oh, very old. So was *Fly.*

YOKO

You know, I told him about my idea for *Up Your Legs Forever* and he liked it very much and then he thought of the *Apotheosis* idea.

JOHN

Which is *Up Your Legs Forever* [light laugh] … for real.

YOKO

… going up … But, you know, I feel that *Up Your Legs Forever* was very physical. *Apotheosis* was very spiritual. And then, about half a year later, it suddenly occurred to me, I thought, but my God, it's a great film! You know? And I was very proud of him. But at the same time I was very jealous and very upset and everything. It's a fantastic film. It's almost like … I thought I was doing this film work and suddenly he came and he stole the scene … It was so good, you know. I thought, "My God, it can't be so good!" And so I thought, "Well, if they're going to show it in New York …" [laughs]

JONAS

It's one film of which I wish I'd have my own print.

JOHN
Good. I'll give you a print.

YOKO
Yes, yes. It's the kind of film that I wish I had made
that film.

JONAS
It's a metaphor.

YOKO
Everything, everything, everything …

JOHN
As soon as Yoko showed me, uh, a kind of … not a dialogue
… I don't know, she sort of made me aware of …

YOKO
… instructions.

JOHN
Well, the instructions, yes … of how to express something
in film. Whereas before, films had always been something
I'd seen, you know. Like from Hollywood or whatever it
was. And I had seen a few underground films but it was all
like, you know, nothing special. But then she showed me
how to express it in films, through her instructions and being
with her. I'd always thought, before I went into films, I'd have
to, you know, know about this and know about that. But she
opened my mind up and I realized I could just say it in a
film the same as in a song or in a poem. A poem, you know.
It's a poem that has no words. And I think almost, I approach
films the way she approached rock and roll, you know. What
she did in rock and roll with her voice and the sound and
the ways she edits and fixes tapes. I realized how tight I
was, you know, that I was beginning to get old about it and,
uh, tighten up in my expression. And she blasted me open.
And I blasted her open too, because she was an intellectual.
We burst each other's pretensions.

YOKO
As a debut film, *Apotheosis*, you can't go higher than that.

JOHN

I don't think there is anything special about it. But now
you're all starting to talk about it and I'm now beginning to
worry about it ... I didn't think about it, you know, it was just
a poem that was inspired by her work and I did it. It gave
me experience just to see it ...

JONAS

Well, you can still look at it that way. But once it goes into
the world ...

JOHN

Yeah, it's begun to take on a life of its own since you showed
it here.

YOKO

And I suffered a little because I thought, well, *Up Your
Legs Forever*, you know, the idea of going up was my idea.
But then it's all right, because, you see, it's like ... It's very,
very different. It was very different and also I suddenly
realized that it's almost like ... You know, John sometimes
strums a guitar harmony for me, you know. And maybe he
used that harmony in another song or something. But when
I do it, it becomes completely different. Anyway, I was on
the defensive almost. I said, "Oh, if you're going to do a film
festival, *Apotheosis* is going to be the only film that's good,
so I have to make something. [laughs] And I made these two
films, you know, for you. But, in a way, I have mixed feelings.
I'm very proud of having a husband like that too. [laughs]

JOHN

I have the same thing about her voice things.

YOKO

Yes, yes ...

JOHN

... thinking, "I should have done it."

YOKO

John likes my voice. [laughter] So we're very happy, in
that sense, you know. We're lucky that we like each other's
work and all that.

JONAS

[addressing John] *Self-Portrait*, that's your film?

JOHN

Yes.

YOKO

Yes, that's John's film.

JONAS

I still have to see it.

JOHN

Well, all it is, is a close-up of my prick for twenty minutes or something, you know. It's a little bit of a drag to look at. The idea's more fun than the film. It wasn't filmed well either, it's just this sort of ... I like the idea better than the film.

YOKO

No, I think *Self-Portrait* is a ... You see, some people, probably, in the avant-garde, they did show their anatomy before, you see. So they say, "Oh, it's been done." But ...

JONAS

That's George's style.

YOKO

Yes.

JONAS

George is ... He is always referring to whoever was the first to do what ...

YOKO

Yes. But if you see John's *Self-Portrait*, you see that's done very straight, you know. Nobody did it that way. They will always have a string around the penis or something, doing this. I saw that done in Denmark. But this is a very pure, straight film, you see.

JOHN

That one was also inspired by *Smile*, 'cause *Smile* is three minutes of face blown up to fifty-two minutes. And it's just fantastic. It's like seeing into somebody's soul. It's like a moving portrait on the wall, like a Renoir, but it smiles at you. And then I thought that ...

[tape runs out]

5. [continued] December 21, 1970

JOHN

So where were we?

JONAS

Eh-h, your 8 mm films.

JOHN

Oh, those, yeah. Well, uh ...

JONAS

You'll have to pull them out some day.

JOHN

Yes, I suppose so.

JONAS

They may look different, you know. When did you see them last?

JOHN

Probably maybe a year and a half ago, or more. I made them about four years ago, you know, when I first started hearing about the so-called underground films. People like Bruce Conner were sending us films over. Some used our Beatle music in the background, things like that. And, well, we've been messing around with 8 mm films a long time, making silly films, like comedies, trying to make funny films on eight mil, like home movies. I just started filming everything in slow motion and just superimposing things on it all the time. So it's all self-edited. Each four-minute film is a film itself. Some of them are stuck together—one time I edited a few together but it's such a bore and ...

JONAS
It's becoming more and more editing in the camera.

JOHN
Yeah, right, right. So after I'd shot a few and edited them
while I was shooting them, you know, I thought, "Well, let's
have a go at editing. Let's try and edit them and see if
I can do something." But it was always better just to shoot
it and make that the editing, you know.

JONAS
Of course, you can edit it all later, too. But then you have to
go through a completely different process.

JOHN
Oh, yeah, there's always things like filming water, you know,
like the swimming-pool water and then winding it back and
filming something else on top of it so that it had all these ...

JONAS
... superimpositions.

JOHN
Yeah, superimpositions, all the time. But once they went
into Super 8 ... it took me about a year to learn how to
handle an 8 mm Canon camera. And then the cameras were
changed and I could never learn again to do another one,
so I stopped doing it.

JONAS
And the footage ... a film like *Give Peace a Chance*—who put
that one together?

JOHN
It's mainly Yoko's work. I mean ...

YOKO
*Give Peace a Chance*?

JOHN
The editing and all that were mainly her stuff. I've had
no experience of any kind of editing. I've learned a lot from
her, you know.

YOKO
Well, for that type of film you have to have a different
mentality.


JONAS
It's an information film in a way.

YOKO
I have to … It's still in the editing process. I am not
very satisfied with it. I think I have to cut ten minutes,
maybe more.


JONAS
I noticed you kept the whole thing on Capp.


YOKO
That was good.


JONAS
He is such a … And the footage speaks for itself.


JOHN
I think the idea here is that I have no real idea. So when I am
confronted with something, it frightens me. So when I first
go into a studio, it frightened me having to transfer all these
different tracks onto one track. But seeing her work, just so,
tam-tam-tam-tam, you know, like that—it made me feel a
little bit confident in handling it. She hadn't done a lot of anything, but seemed to me like she'd been doing it all her life.


YOKO
No, no, it's not that. It's just that, I think, you know, I probably,
I don't know, I am probably just sort of not afraid of doing
it. There are many things that I am afraid of doing, but this
thing is something, one of the very few things I am not
afraid of. I think everything is just a matter of whether you
are afraid or not.


6.


JONAS
My feeling is that your strength, in film, is in the concept,
in the idea for the art. *Legs*, *Smile*. Which is not exactly
collecting materials and information.

YOKO

There was a point in my life when I was just giving concerts,
where there was no sound at all except, I would say, the music
of the mind, and everybody who comes starts to get into
their own mind music, I guess, getting involved in an event
situation without any sound at all. So, instead of listening
to the physical, material sound, they were listening to their
own minds, you see. And I went into that, and I gave many,
many silent concerts in London and other places—it started
in New York. And meanwhile I stopped screaming and
shouting, which I was doing here around 1960. I don't know—
I was dying to shout and scream, you know. By the time
I met John, I was really ready to scream again. It's like that,
you see. For instance, the film, too. At the time when I came
back from Japan, 1964 or something, I remember, I gave you
that script, you know, *The Six Scripts to Jonas Mekas*, and
then you were telling me, "Why don't you make those films?
If you make them, I'll give you one night at the New Yorker
Theatre," you know. And for me, it meant a lot, you know.
So I said, "My God, I have to make these films." But the point
is, physically for me, it is impossible to make a film. First
of all, I didn't even have money to buy a camera or film stock,
and I didn't know how to operate the camera. I mean, it was
almost like if you say, why don't you fly to the moon. Like
that. So, it was at that point that, thanks to you, I decided
to make films of instructions. All the film instructions that
I gave you in those days actually are my best instructions,
I think. They were sort of half imaginary instructions, you
know, or some that you can't even do. So when you said,
"Why don't you make the films?" I was almost trying to tell
you, Jonas, my films are instructions, somebody has to
make them—but I said it stuttering, I always just say it
in my mind, and I can't say it to you, you know. I can say,
maybe, "But, Jonas, t … t … t …" but I can't say the rest
of it. And I didn't know how to communicate the idea that
I was an instruction filmmaker.


JONAS

And my problem is that I am always trying to hook everybody
on making films, instructions or no instructions …


YOKO

So the *Bottoms* film, and all that … they are basically instruction films which anybody can make.

JONAS

Peter Kubelka is very proud of the fact that in five hundred years anyone could, from his notes, reproduce *Arnulf Rainer* [film]. All films may disappear, either because of the fragility of the materials or the stupidities of men, but his film will be there, he says. But now I see he won't be alone: your films will be reproduced from your instructions, very, very easily ...

YOKO

And the notes are very short, you know.

JONAS

It's one whole genre of cinema, the Fluxus genre.

YOKO

And also, the *Fly* film, it was depending on the movement of the fly. You just have to edit according to the movements the fly made ... those are your notes ...

JONAS

It will be more difficult to reproduce the *Fly* film than *Legs*, though ...

7.

YOKO

The *Legs* film was more like an event, or happening. But the *Fly* film, it took so much energy out of me and I feel like a fool, because *Apotheosis*, we didn't use so much energy.

JONAS

The *Fly* film took more energy than the *Legs* film?

YOKO

Yes. But *Apotheosis* turned out to be a better film, I think. So the thing, that is, the kind of thing I was always telling people, laughing about people like Stanley Kubrick using millions and millions of dollars and many, many years to make a film, and it doesn't convey as much as things that we make with a very small budget and in a short time. And John taught me ... he just did it, while I was thinking of it. And the thing is, even now I think it is a crime to use a

1. Harvey Kramer
2. Ann Nagy
3. Shelly Petnov
4. Kathy Cox
5. Jonathan Cott
6. Dan Richter
7. Donna Gray
8. Jim Moore
9. Lorraine Knox
10. Michael Cuscuna
11. Taylor Mead
12. Lindsay Maragotta
13. Jim Moran
14. Peter Delacort
15. Susan Pinsker
17. Noel Behn
18. Bruce Litmin
19. Michael Turner
20. Larry Rivers
21. Brendan Atkinson
22. Tom Lightburn
23. Garth Summerville
24. Kristin Steer
25. Beth (c/o Norm Seaman)
26. Lisa Negrin
27. Gay Seaman
28. Evelyn Seaman (c/o Norm Seaman)
29. Vali
30. Jim Rieh
32. Nervel
33. Michael Ridley
34. Richard Ryan
35. Dean Duck yes
36. Sam Jones
37. Yvonne Ruskin
38. Ira Cohen
39. Andy Smith
40. Patti-Lee Chenis
41. Piere Heliczer
42. Peter Hansen
43. D.A Pennybaker
44. Cynthia Pennybaker
45. Pete Bennett
46. Jeff Hewitt
47. Utah Phillips
48. Mike Kramer
49. Harriett Black
50. Beryl Stone
51. Randy Brown
52. Bici Hendricks
53. Geoff Hendricks
54. Danny Cohn
55. John Skoszyk, 1200 Broadway, New York, N.Y. 100

56. Ralph Shultz
57. Tomi Riley
58. Suzannah Sedgewick
59. Al Steckler
60. Renie Bergen
61. Lillian Ocasio
62. Ellen McDonald
63. Basil Cox
64. Asha Coorlawala
65. John Wenner
66. Derek Carter IV
67. Donora Johnson
68. Denise Johnson
69. Richard Jones
70. Diane Newman
71. Alan Newman
72. Malcolm Bailey
73. Dave Kroll
74. Ken Reiderman
75. David Bergen
76. Dick Bellamy
77. Joe LaGuidice
78. Walter Keilery
79. Anna Pomaska
80. Secondhand Rose
81. Joe Butler
82. Letty Eisenhauer
83. Sandy Noyes
84. David Kurzman
85. Rhett Brown
86. Bob Brown
87. Velvert Turner
88. Gustav Sjoberg
89. Andrea Zlatkin
90. Howard Zlatkin
91. Ronnie Rosenblatt
92. Peter McGuilam
93. Bieka
94. Loren Standlee
95. Austin Chinn
96. Jack Smith
97. David Poisal
98. Don Plumleigh
99. John Miele
100. Henry Geldzahler
101. Gordon Minard
102. Susan Buck
103. Jerry Cole
104. Jane Rose
105. David Simon
106. Jillian Hewitt
107. Michael Findlay
108. George Catha
109. Peter Ferrara Broadway, New York
110. Michael Page

List of leg actors for the film *Up Your Legs Forever* by John Lennon and Yoko Ono, page 1, New York, 1970

lot of money to make a film, when there are so many starving
children. Some filmmakers use enough money to build a
city, you know.

JONAS

Yes, but then we come to the question of the different
genres of film, the narrative film, historical film, musical film,
etc. And as soon as one begins to want to tell a story, to go
into all the fiction that one's imagination can produce—
one has to go into expensive stagings, and masses of people,
and actors, and etc. etc.—and one can not do that without money.

JOHN

After all, how many blank canvasses can you show? How
many sorts of movies of the Empire State Building can you
make? So once you made *that* statement, I understand it.

YOKO

That is all right. I have done a lot of things like that.
Like Danny was saying: What about those intellectual artists
of New York who are just doing these things that do not
communicate at all. You know.

JONAS

Everything communicates ... Even nothingness
communicates.

YOKO

Yes. But being highly sophisticated and being in their own
shell, just communicating to their in-crowd, you know ...
and whatever, all right ... But I criticized a lot of that side
of me. For instance, in London, by the time I did the show
at the Indica gallery, and my gallery show had many instruction pieces—some people started to understand my things
and, you know, these young students, they came to my things
like to something very special, like to a shrine, you know.
So when I made the *Bottoms* film, in London, it wasn't the art
critics and the painters, the artists who liked it ... But there
was a taxi driver who said, "Oh, I like your film," and he
shook hands. I thought it was very good, you see. Of course,
there are many levels ... But also, it's a nice feeling when
you are just communicating with somebody you never meet.

| | |
|---|---|
| 111. Livy Merchant | 167. Jerry Parker |
| 112. Patrick Tirpo | 168. Fumio Yoshimura |
| 113. Susanna De Maria | 169. Robert Mollot |
| 114. Leslie Talbot | 170. Jan Van Raay |
| 115. Fred Raskind | 171. Poppy Johnson |
| 116. Michael Gaseman | 172. Silviana |
| 117. Judy Kramer | 173. Laurie Deutsch |
| 118. Pat Farrell | 174. Nancy Seizman |
| 119. Mary Pat Haberle | 175. Bruce Gedman |
| 120. Paul Krassner | 176. Evelyn Oliver |
| 121. Gerald Weiner | 177. Jim Buckley |
| 122. Mary Jane Hayes | 178. Fonjo de Vre |
| 123. Joe Dragon | 179. Beverly Tangen |
| 124. Elena Hernandez | 180. Stewart Krane |
| 125. Mark Sloane | 181. William Brownrigg |
| 126. Fred Billingsley | 182. Linda Patten |
| 127. Jann Hodenfield | 183. Charles Bergengren |
| 128. Michael Thomas | 184. Ron Rosenbaum |
| 129. Deborah Gwyneth | 185. Countess Svietlana vonStr |
| 130. Lillian Roxon | 186. David Lee-Bergen |
| 131. Karen Back   George Back | 187. Eileen Smith |
| 132. Karen Back | 188. Kevin McCarthy |
| 133. Mark Rutzky | 189. Roy Robinson |
| 134. Don Schaffer | 190. Jan von der Marck |
| 135. Kathy Streem | 191. George Segal |
| 136. Lee Jaffee | 192. Peter Max |
| 137. Carol Friedlander | 193. William Holderith |
| 138. Willoughby Sharp | 194. Peter Beard |
| 139. Tom Lea | 195. Jeff Rose |
| 140. Liza Bear | 196. Tim Lippman |
| 141. Robert Polidori | 197. Diane Ostendorff |
| 142. Donny Burks | 198. Valery Herouvis |
| 143. Andy Harlow | 199. Arthur Tarres |
| 144. Pamela Francis | 200. Silvain Mizorahi |
| 145. Steven Drangel | 201. Bill Murcia |
| 146. Barbara Clark | 202. Jeffry Lewis-Green |
| 147. Peter Yokum | 203. Al Goldstein |
| 148. Andy Siehel | 204. Mallory Geitheim |
| 149. Mark Monstermaker | 205. Bob Linderman |
| 150. Jonas Mekas | 206. Pete Gaylor |
| 151. Richard Robinson | 207. Debby Ross |
| 152. Lisa Robinson | 208. Robert Acciani |
| 153. Julia Leonard | 209. Michael Acciani |
| 154. Susan McLaughlin | 210. Richard Dostal |
| 155. James Pietsch | 211. Shirley Clark |
| 156. Dave Walley | 212. Temple Boon |
| 157. Jon Hendricks | 213. Stanley Amos |
| 158. Elliot Ingber | 214. Gary Williams |
| 159. Dick Beahrs | 215. Bob Fall |
| 160. Carl Mirasola | 216. Bill Collins |
| 161. Harvey Stromberg | 217. Daphne Erwin |
| 162. Linda Jackson | 218. Patrick Hulsey |
| 163. Glenn Doddo | 219. Berta Orsita |
| 164. Eugene Seaman | 220. Jim Everett  Broadway, New York, N |
| 165. Glenn Johnson  Broadway, New York, N. | 221. Bruce Bettinger |
| 166. Des Eisenstein | |

List of leg actors for the film *Up Your Legs Forever* by John Lennon and Yoko Ono, page 2, New York, 1970

And, of course, some artists—when I started to make the
*Bottoms* film, it got a lot of newspaper coverage. Not really
for what it was, but the sex aspect, you know. So many
artists thought I sold out, and all that. But I enjoy that aspect
of being able to communicate.

8.

JONAS
Regarding *Legs*. How many legs, pairs of legs did you have
in the film?

YOKO
363.

JOHN
365.

YOKO
It was 365, you see …

JOHN
… days of the year.

JONAS
But now I think it's only 333 or something like that. Why?

YOKO
Yes, I think, I am afraid so …

JOHN
Like the *Bottoms* film, it's called 365 bottoms, but there
weren't 365 bottoms.

YOKO
It's a conceptual number. It was only 280 bottoms.

JOHN
Same thing. 333. But it will always say 365.

YOKO
Because that's the concept. A conceptual number.

222. David Robinowitz
223. Emil Schou
224. Jerry Marcel
225. Mark Gerge
226. Peter Moore
227. Hala Pietkiewicz
228. Victor Herbert
230. Wm Rockmacher
229. Jerry Ordover
231. Julie Hymen
232. Sue Shenn
233. Ralph Severini
234. Nancy O'Connor
235. John Lobsitz
236. Ann Silverstein
237. Grace Charleton
238. Shirley Basler
239. Virginia Lust
240. Susan Anderson
241. Jud Yalkut & Jeni Engel
242. Allen Kline
243. Howard Smith
244. Patti Oldenburg
245. Bunny Dexter
246. C.H. Ford
247. Paul Mozian
248. Al Aronowitz
249. Larissa Jarzombek
250. Bob Rosen
251. Jan Spiegelman
252. Bob Adleman
253. Walter Gutman
254. Cyrinda Hatzikian
255. Pedro Meroney
256. Dave Stein
257. Gabriel Stenziano
258. Joe Shepherd
259. Marc Stanton
260. Steven Hirsch
261. Chas. Rose
262. Katherine Dunfee
263. Christopher Makos
264. Kevin Donnelly
265. Gregory Chepard
266. Rick Salmon
267. Jack Hopkins
268. Emily Shin
269. John Cain
270. Paul Shepherd
271. Jerry Singley
272. Diane Meltzer
273. Louis Newman
274. Isabel Questell
275. Leo Waldbauer
276. Steve Black

277. Ron Anderson
278. Dolly Latzenic
279. John Amon
280. Bob Hankins
281. Seth Feigenbaum
282. Maureen Simone
283. Lennie Gruen
284. Richard Rheem
285. Jan Teitelbaum
286. Joel Homer
287. Diane Friedman
288. Jon Gaynin
289. Gail Gaynin
290. Roy Manvell
291. Leonard Wienstien
292. Dusty Moss
293. Francesca Moss
294. Allen Taylor
295. Michael Chender
296. John Buscemi
297. Sid Bernstein
298. Joel Weinstein
301. Shelly Landers
299. Tony Biel
300. Diana Biel
302. Phylis Banek
303. Tamil Termos
304. Isabel Figuredo
305. Rudi Echeverri
306. Jeff Dubren
307. Rachel Dubren
308. Milton Schneider
309. Peter Morris
310. David Smith
311. Barb Sellwin
312. Pat Depew
313. The Ort.
314. Bob Fries
315. Joshua Deutsch
316. Chris Fries
317. Marilyn Landers
318. Annie Leibovitz
319. Barbara Neidleman
320. Miguel Wica
321. David Johansen
322. Diane Podlowski
323. Merlo
324. Trisha Podlowski
325. Phyllis Vampolsky
326. Bert Shavitz
327. Bill Sontag
328. John Southard
329. Janet Hodgieo
330. Steve Gebhardt

Apple Records Inc., 1700 Broadway, New York.

List of leg actors for the film *Up Your Legs Forever*
by John Lennon and Yoko Ono, page 3, New York, 1970

JONAS

Like the centipede ... a centipede seldom has more than
80 legs. But it will always be called a centipede ...

YOKO

It's nice that we are starting to enjoy film, isn't it?

JONAS

There will be more demand, I think, for this kind of film
when the cassettes arrive. For private use. Be it for fun,
to entertain one's friends, or whatever ...

JOHN

Right now, we could be selling 8mm versions of all our
films, for anybody that wants them. But the thing is, it costs
so much to make them, with sound.

YOKO

I think it will be difficult. Like, my *Grapefruit* was
very difficult to sell. Because I am so impressed with it,
I can't stop talking about it, but, like, *Apotheosis* ...
The *Bottoms* film is like Andy Warhol's things, you know
—it was talked about a lot and it is the kind of film that
people talk about. *Apotheosis* is the kind of film that gives
you such a spiritual affect you don't want to talk about it.

JONAS

Yes, but there are always people who buy books of poetry,
books that aren't talked about. The same "minority" art that
we have in other arts we have now in film too. These are the
laws of life and you can't change them fast. There are always
bestsellers in prose, and they buy them in millions. Let
it be. You can't go by numbers. Still, film is more accessible
than, say, books. Although you could consider Brakhage
and Pound on the same level of difficulty, Brakhage will
be viewed by many more thousands than Pound will be read.

YOKO

You say, Brakhage is working commercially?

JONAS

No. I am only comparing him with the most difficult [of] other
forms of arts. Cummings or Pound. Stan is not making

commercial films. But he is easier to accept, or sit through,
the eye seems to be able to tolerate more than the mind.
I am speaking comparatively.

> YOKO

Andy is the most commercially accepted.

> JONAS

I think it's more in the press than in actuality. He gets a lot
of publicity, is much discussed, but his films are not as widely
shown or seen as those of Brakhage. I know it because
there are figures and records at the Film-Makers' Cooperative. But Brakhage is never mentioned by the mainstream
press.

> YOKO

Really?

> JONAS

Yes, I know it for sure.

> YOKO

What kind of market is it, college circuit?

> JONAS

Colleges, universities. Then, museums, galleries. It's all
widening up. Anyway, Warhol is not the filmmaker that rents
most. There are others, like A n g e r and Brakhage, that
reach many more people. Of course, I am not talking about
films like *Trash*, which is not Warhol, it's M o r r i s s e y,
which is something else. That is a commercial independent
cinema. I am talking about the Warhol of *Sleep*, *Eat*,
or *Empire*.

> YOKO

Kenneth Anger distributes through the Film-Makers'
Cooperative?

> JONAS

Yes.

> YOKO

How about Peter Kubelka?

JONAS

He distributes exclusively through the Cooperative.
You have to keep in mind that these films are distributed
through a number of cooperatives, not only the New York
Coop. Different filmmakers' cooperatives cover differ-
ent geographical areas. There are co-ops in San Francisco,
Chicago, London. At this moment your best chance
I think is also through the cooperatives.

9.

YOKO

Did you see *Rape*? What did you think of *Rape*?

JONAS

I should see it once more. I had to run out of the theatre
for ten minutes, to get something for the theatre, so I missed
about ten minutes at the beginning.

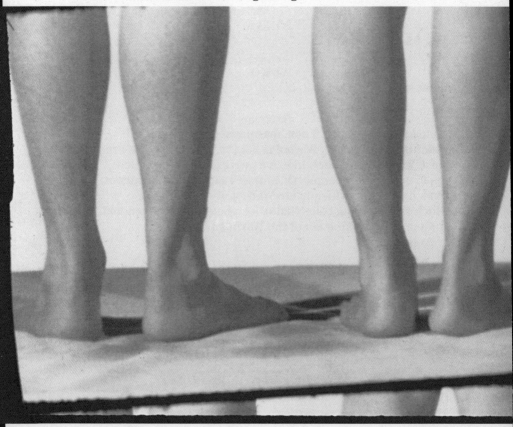

JOHN

It was made for Austrian TV.

JONAS

The audience, they wanted to see the real rape. They wanted
to be entertained by rape, I think. That's what they wanted
to see, and they couldn't accept that there was no usual rape.
Maybe there was a different kind of rape, but not what
they expected.

JOHN

It was a rape, it was the rape we all go through. We don't
always get physically raped, by somebody. But we all get that
kind of rape, from society. But it was beautiful. It was on
Austrian TV, you know, it caused a riot. They commissioned
us to do it, this man came over ...

JONAS

Where was it shot?

JOHN

It was shot in London, but it was shown in Austria, on TV.
It is a very square place, Austria.

YOKO

They suddenly decided to come to London, and said,
well, John and Yoko, if you make a film, we'll commission
you, we can put it on TV.

JONAS

Did they actually televise it?

JOHN

Yes, it was shown, and it got the biggest reaction in phone
calls of any film ever shown.

JONAS

On TV, it was probably more effective than in a theatre.
The rape became more private.

JOHN

It comes over on TV—we watched it—what was the place?
We saw it in Austria, no?

YOKO
Yes, but ... We did, actually, in Switzerland.

JOHN
The Austrian TV people put it in the Montreux TV Festival.
It didn't win anything, but it sort of split people.

JONAS
But *Rape* is, in a way, an entertainment film ... only on
a different level. Nothing is exploited for sensation, but ...

JOHN
The girl didn't know she was filmed.

JONAS
What do you mean she didn't know?

JOHN
I mean, she didn't know what it was all about. Nobody
told her. She was picked arbitrarily; she was not told
anything.

JONAS
So, actually, you met her for the first time through the lens
of the camera, on the street? I mean, the cameraman.

JOHN
We made a few test films on different people. Just arbitrary
people we met in the park, and then, finally, because
you could never go long enough, they always got into a bus,
or a car, and went home, we had to find somebody who
had a friend or sister, so this sister of a girl I knew, we got
the key to her flat from her sister, and the girl actually didn't
know, so she wasn't acting, she was really going through
that thing. Later on, when the press saw her, she said
she was an actress, so everybody presumed that she acted
in it. But she didn't. She really didn't know what they
were doing.

JONAS
But probably she knew from the faces. She knew that
it wasn't that bad a situation yet ... She could have called
somebody for help.

JOHN

Her sister kept the line blocked, she couldn't make calls.

JONAS

Ah ... I see ... I couldn't understand why she couldn't make calls. The film doesn't show that.

JOHN

She was really panicking in that room. She didn't know who they [the crew] were, and the only person she got through to was her sister, and she was saying, in German, or Austrian, "Help me, help me, these people won't go away, you know, the ones I told you about yesterday, they are still following me."

JONAS

So the sister had the telephone locked, I see.

YOKO

She was on our side.

JOHN

She called her sister, and said, "Get the police," in German. Like everybody, when confronted with a real situation, we don't actually call—we don't know what to do. It was a long time before she decided to call, you know.

JONAS

She looked real. All her reactions were very real. Then, in the room, I thought, maybe there she already knew that it was just for the movie.

YOKO

It was the second day, she was really upset.

JOHN

She was waiting to go out, she had a date, and she didn't know what to do. She picked up the telephone once and she couldn't get through, and the second time it rang, something happened, and her sister was at the other end. She was telling her sister, "Look, I have to go out, I want to go to the embassy, I want to call the police." And she just didn't know what to do. But nobody believes it. It's really real, that film.

JONAS

To film reality so that it looks real is a real art ...

YOKO

But you see, the thing is, she just came to London, as a tourist, for about a week, just visiting her sister who lives in London, and she couldn't speak English properly, she didn't know the streets ...

JOHN

What do you say when you are actually attacked? You say, "Help!" And all she said in German, was "Why don't you leave me alone?" "What is this?" "Why aren't you leaving me alone?" "What is this?" "Why are you doing this?" It was good that it was in a foreign language, for most people.

YOKO

It's a very real film, you know. I could have made it more dramatic by setting up an obvious situation, but I didn't want to do it.

JOHN

If you get some of it translated, you can see that she didn't know, you can hear what she's saying. "I don't know what it is," she says. At first, she tried to woo the cameraman, and the soundman, and she's sort of flirting with the cameraman. "Oh, come on now, what is this, this has been going for a long time." By the time they got to her flat, she was just so stunned that they got in with the key. She knew she couldn't fight three men, and they wouldn't speak to her.

YOKO

And you see, the thing is, we were in the hospital. I was having a miscarriage, and John was staying with me, in the hospital, and we were there for five days. And all that time they were filming, we never went to the actual filming of it. And everyone that the cameraman followed started out by saying, "Oh, this is for TV?" Some got furious. There were many interesting people that they followed. But they didn't follow ... I said, you must follow until they faint ... and they said, we can't ... So every take was very short. And then, finally, they said, OK, we'll follow. Because,

the cameraman, he was a very shy cameraman, and he'd
say, "I can't do this to people ... terrible ..."

JOHN
We held a press conference, at the Montreux television
festival, and some of the press people got very upset.
"Why did you do this, why did you do this?" They have a
TV festival there. So they got very upset, saying, "Well, isn't
this interference with people's private life?" The press
people are not to be believed.

YOKO
"Why did you do that to the girl?" And all that, you know.

JONAS
And they themselves, they interfere with people's lives
through their papers every day in every home.

JOHN
Right, right. That is why it was such a joke.

10. [Later that evening ...]

YOKO
Most of my things were instructions, like the *Grapefruit*.
Only instructions. Because, for practical reasons, it was
very difficult to physically realize them; most of my films
were conceptual, or, because I am a person who sort of cannot
physically realize them, like that, sort of ... I don't know ...
Before I have a chance to actually physically realize a film
I just put it in notes, you know, instructions. And then I went
to London, and after I met John, it suddenly started to ...
I don't know ... because John really understands my things,
my instructions ... So, he sort of gave me the incentive to go
ahead and actually physically realize it. Like for the *Fly* film,
you know. At one point I was thinking: My God, I am using
all these people, and these people are tired, and I started
to feel very guilty. And I was saying to John: "Look, I feel
guilty about ..." In the middle of it. And John said, "No, no,
if they don't like it, they don't have to stay around, they
can leave you. So don't worry." That kind of encouragement
and practical advice.

JONAS

There are little, tiny films which one can make by oneself.
One doesn't have to bother anybody. One just does it, just
the camera and me. And then, there are films that involve
many people. On the level of the Underground film, *Fly*
is a Hollywood production ... It needed cooperation from
many different people ...

YOKO

Yes, yes. I just really felt that it was like a Hollywood
production. Lights and editors and, you know ...

JONAS

And whenever you work with more people than one,
you always have this feeling, OK, maybe I am misusing them,
you always have to go through that kind of questioning.

JOHN

Maybe I will stick with one-shot films ...

JONAS

That is needed also.

YOKO

You know, I am very aggressive ... So, it's working out,
actually. I am beginning to get courage. Instead of saying,
"Oh, I can't do anything," I let people just film my things,
with my instructions.

JONAS

And you did it in an amazingly short time. I had doubts,
myself, whether we should really go for this date. But then,
I said, I think she's going to make it.

JOHN

I wasn't sure whether she'd finish it either.

JONAS

I was really quite certain about it. Once I saw you shooting
it, I no longer had any doubts. And I knew that Steve
can make the technical side happen, because he's used
to deadlines, his TV things, etc. So I knew he would manage
his part.

YOKO
Everybody was marvelous. And it was very beautiful.

11.

JONAS
How long is the *Bottoms* film?

YOKO
I think it is about an hour.

JONAS
Is it like the early version you did with George?

[1966 version of *Fluxfilm No. 4*: Close-up shots of buttocks of some
12 different performers; 5 minutes.]

YOKO
The early version didn't have any sound.

JONAS
Is the London version black and white?

YOKO
Black and white. It has a lot of very interesting sound.

JOHN
London's swinging intellectuals, giving these amazing
reasons, intellectual reasons, why they are taking their
trousers off, you know. All that kind of …

YOKO
They would pull S a r t r e, G u r d j i e f f, and P r o u s t,
and those things out. You see, intellectuals cannot take their
pants off without making some big philosophical remark
about it. All these people that came, very highly intelligent
people, but before they take off their pants, they have to go
through this big discussion. And it was very interesting, and
that is all in the soundtrack. Some girl saying, she wouldn't
take her pants off without being paid a lot, because she's
a model, you know. Things like that.

JONAS
And there she goes …

YOKO
There was a good reason to make a very long version.

JONAS
Are there any other films that you made in London that
you didn't bring with you?

YOKO
Well, we brought *Bottoms*, *Smile*, and *Self-Portrait*. We didn't
bring *You Are Here*.

JOHN
After I first met Yoko, I sort of blasted open in my head. I had
a gallery show, out of the blue—I had never done anything
like that before. I had a show called *You Are Here*, and
I dedicated it to Yoko. And it was just a canvas with *You Are
Here* on it. And things of that kind. I made a film with ...
we filmed everybody from behind the door.

YOKO
You see, it was a gallery.

JOHN
The film is not worth showing.

YOKO
You insist on it, but I think it should be shown. You see,
you walk into the gallery, and there is nothing there.
And you go downstairs, in the gallery, and there you see
a white canvas, and you have to go close to it. And you
go closer, and it just says, YOU ARE HERE.

JOHN
We had a candid camera and we filmed the people, reacting
to your art. You see, they come to John Lennon's first
gallery show and all that, and they think there's going to be
some action ... But we had some of the challenge boxes,
they had to go through all these challenge boxes to get there.
Once they got there, we gave them a badge, and the badge
would say YOU ARE HERE. We just filmed that.

JONAS
How long is that one?

JOHN

Twenty minutes.

YOKO

But you see, the point is …

JOHN

I never liked it, it's just a good memory. I never really
released all the balloons with YOU ARE HERE on them,
and the instructions to bring them right back to where
they got them …

YOKO

But, you see, it was like, a kind of gallery show, that was in
the Fluxus tradition, very pure, you know, but because he
was John Lennon, the whole world, the reporters, they made
it into a completely different thing.

JOHN

That's why we filmed it.

YOKO

And it's a very interesting document of those people
making different things. I liked it. I believe in the Fluxus
tradition. [Picks up and reads from a text she wrote on
October 22, 1968.] "This year, I started thinking of making
films that were meant to be shown in a hundred years'
time. Like taking different city views, hoping that most of
the buildings will be demolished by the time the film is
released. Filming an ordinary woman in her full gear knowing that in a hundred years' time she'd look extraordinary
anyway. It's a lot like applying the process of making vintage
wine to filmmaking. This, in fact, would mean that as a
filmmaker, you don't really have to make a film anymore but
just put your name on any film and store it. Storing would
then become the main endeavor of a filmmaker." But then,
the idea started to get too conceptual. You see, the thing
is, in that sense, this is a fantastic film. It's like vintage wine,
in ten years it will become fantastic.

JONAS

This summer I think I'm going to my own old town, in Lithuania. I don't know how many people are left there, but I

want to film a hundred faces, one minute of each, everybody
in the old village, like an anthropologist. A hundred Lithuanians. Then you'll be able to see how Lithuanians look.
Because they keep asking me: Are you a typical Lithuanian?
Is George a typical Lithuanian? So I am going to show
them how a hundred Lithuanians look, and they can decide
where I fit. But if somebody had taken pictures of a hundred Lithuanians a hundred years ago, I think that would
be really fantastic to see, all the faces, and how they are
dressed, etc. It's the same with the legs. The value of your
*Legs* film will increase with time. There will be meanings and values imposed upon it, art or no art. It will be
a valuable and curious document of the legs of artists
and intellectuals—they were not exactly from the street—
New York anno 1970.

#### YOKO
It has to be intelligent legs, I thought. First of all, I asked
them to collect intelligent legs. And now, when people
come and see the legs, they suddenly see that they are just
ordinary legs.

#### JONAS
But they don't care about their legs, they don't take good
care of their legs.

#### YOKO
They don't.

#### JOHN
It was very interesting. A lot of people, they were saying,
"Oh, can't I leave my underpants on?" A sign of individuality.
Or some wanted to leave their boots on. A lot of people
think that with clothes on, the clothes become their individuality, they really suspect that they would all look alike
without them. It's strange.

#### YOKO
And the thing is that it's just very nice to take legs. One
person said: "I wonder if N i x o n has very ugly, violent legs."
But there is no such thing as ugly legs. Even Nixon, if you
see his legs, they would look the same. And I just wanted
to show that we are all all right. We are all very peaceful.

John Lennon and Yoko Ono during the filming of *Up Your Legs Forever*,
New York, 1970

Even the meanest person, when he's asleep, he'll look beautiful, like a baby, or naïve. Because our body is very naïve,
you know. And when I saw the film, I thought, very, very sad,
very sad, because of the deformity, you know.

JONAS

It is a very sad film.

YOKO

The deformity. And everybody is so insecure. They don't
want to look that ugly, and everybody's out there. And it's sad.
Because in this world they are desperately trying to hide
that ugliness and they are trying to look beautiful.

JOHN

They struggle to be beautiful.

YOKO

And it's not their fault that their legs are ugly, that they
are ugly. People have to suffer for being ugly. Even if it's not
their fault. They feel ashamed. And it was a very sad film.
People showing their ugly bodies. But also, at the same
time, when it was under that light, I thought they were all
beautiful.

JONAS

When I was watching them, during the filming, when I saw
them in their totality, with their faces and all, and in that
context, they looked all right. But when only the legs are
framed, in front of you, right there on that screen, they
become more exposed to scrutiny.

YOKO

There was one producer who has millions and millions,
and he came and he showed his legs—he was too shy to …
But he showed his legs, and I saw that with all his money he
couldn't change his legs, and also legs showed that he was
too fat and was getting into old age. And he couldn't do
anything about it, with his money and power. So, actually,
everybody is, like, very vulnerable. Like, we showed our
bottoms, too, they didn't look anything special.

JONAS

They were ... you noticed, you got a big round of applause ...
[laughs]

YOKO

But also, there was a big silence, when we were on ...

JOHN

All day, there were a lot of jokes, and talking about us
being in the film. But then we went on, and there was this
silence, very, very silent ... "Hm, what kind of legs do they
have ... Maybe they'll look like insect legs or something ..."

YOKO

We have very modest looking bodies, you know ... And despite
all that, we love each other's bodies. So I felt very sad at
the same time. I know that every one of those legs is something very, very special, to that person who loves. I mean,
John's body is very, very special for me, I love him very much.
And to me, it's a very special body. Of course, it doesn't
have a silver lining, or something ...

JOHN

I think it's a rather special body ...

YOKO

Yes, it is very special. So, people are very fat beings. But they
create poetry about each other's legs, you know.
    I think of the *Legs* film as an event too. It has a lot
of the elements of an event, in the sense that everybody came
there and became a star and they were all happy that they
were stars, they were all happy on that stage. Another thing
is, one of the critics called me up. Well, she went to see
the *Legs* film but didn't stay until the end: it's a film mainly
for the people who are in it, you know ... So they still have
that kind of concept.

JONAS

Like with *Apotheosis*. The camera went into the cloud, they
couldn't see anything for a minute or two, so they immediately
started shouting.

JOHN

The screen was white. But it was moving all the time. It was real clouds.

JONAS

Though one couldn't see them on the Elgin screen. For two or three minutes or so. So the audience went into attack.

YOKO

Somebody who saw it said: Why was it completely white? He felt like he was suffocating. Provocation. And then, when it came out into the blue sky, out of the cloud, he just felt like, aah, the suffocation is over.

JONAS

Somebody sitting next to me turned to me and said something nasty about the film. So I said, "Don't you like a nice white screen?" And he said, "Oh, but cinema is mo-ve-ment, the camera is mo-ve-ment!" So I had to step aside, he was hopeless. Today, I just came from Jack Smith's *No President*. He had shown that film before, on a number of occasions, and he always changes it, makes changes. It's never the same. So, now, everybody, two hundred or so people, are sitting there, and Jack comes, and he's very late, and he's in the projection booth, still making splices—and finally the film comes on, but those two hundred, everybody wants to see it exactly the way they saw it the last time, you know! But Jack had not only reedited it; he continued working on it even while it was being projected. He covered the image here and there, and fooled with the music—he continued editing the film right there on the projector, and the film we had all seen before now became something slightly different, like I never saw that film before. So somebody stood up, angrily, and started shouting: "It was great before, when I saw it. What is he doing, why is he destroying it?" "Sir," I shouted at him, "is it every day you get a great artist like Jack Smith to come here and edit, make a film right for you, right here, aren't you lucky?" And the man kept squeaking: "I have seen this film, it was great," and "What is he doing now?" They are so used to ... They always want to see the same over again. Even if they see it only once, they are so easily ... We talk about Pavlov's dogs. But this is worse! No dog will ever ask for the same after only one impulse. But these

people refuse to see, they remain blind to whatever is
happening right there before their eyes. Smith or no Smith.
And Jack was working there, upstairs, in the projection
booth, going through his trances, just to make it greater for
them, and it was very great to see it.

12.

### YOKO

When I was just writing instructions, I was at the point
of disappearing. Because, I couldn't physically materialize
myself. And I was disappearing, sort of. I was becoming
a concept. But now I am just starting again to materialize
myself, you know. But you see, the *Fly* film has many
levels and many things in it. Like the fact that the girl had
a very alive body. And the fly was on her. And the fly usually
comes on a dead body … And it's a feeling of, sometimes,
maybe the body is dead or maybe it's alive. Like we all
go through that, every day, for twenty-four hours. Sometimes
we are dead, and sometimes alive, and sometimes we are
both, you know.

### JONAS

There was an Austrian journalist, news journalist, from
Vienna. She came and kept asking me questions, "Who
photographed this film? Every image in it is like a painting,
the composition, and …"

### YOKO

Yes, yes. For the first time I was trying to do very strict compositions. Everything was, in that sense, very strict. And as
the film goes along, the body was supposed to look more and
more dead. And then, finally, even the fly leaves the body,
you know. At first, I was trying to make a film of, say, just
when you film the toes, it's very young. Gradually, when the
camera gets to the buttocks, it becomes older and older,
using different women, you know. And then, finally, when
it comes to the face, then a very old face. But instead of
a fictitious scene like that—I just tried to show that from
the toes to the head is like our lifetime …

### JONAS

But the very last shot … There is this hand, and there
is like a movement that happens, a slight shake, maybe

accidental—and the fly flies away, and out the window.
That worked perfectly.

YOKO
I tried not to show that. You see, that is because the fly
flies off.

JONAS
Yes, but the hand actually moves? So that the impression
is, OK, maybe she was sleeping, not dead at all, and now
she's waking up and makes this movement—the first visible
movement in the film—there may be others but to me this
was the first visible movement. At the same time, this was
the end of the film. The fly flies away. So that it was sort of
mysterious and metaphorical, I thought, and I liked that.

YOKO
Yes, maybe it was meant that way.

JONAS
Whatever that metaphor is, it's OK.

JOHN
You see, and we tried to cut out that movement. She cut
at least a couple of frames off, because it would look like she
shook the fly off.

JONAS
Maybe that's good. Otherwise it may have been too
big a movement. Now it's just a suggestion of movement.
Just a touch of movement.

JOHN
Dawn.

JONAS
Maybe it's the soul leaving the body ...

YOKO
Yes, yes ...

JONAS
A mystery ...

YOKO

Another thing, I tried to be very honest with it. And the
thing is, like, the fact that the camera is always sort of on her
body, and pretending that camera is not there seemed very
dishonest. So I thought maybe I should make it in such a
way that from the beginning it looks like a dead body, somebody shooting it, and showing camera flashes all the time,
psch, psch, psch, you know—I thought it might give the film
another feeling, sort of smash through the lyricism ... You
see, I think in a way we live in an age where we are sort
of ashamed of lyricism. I thought that was sort of like almost
the maximum bearable line of lyricism.

JONAS

Or maybe it became sort of like an expanded slow-motion
haiku.

YOKO

Yes, yes. That is another thing that I learned from John.
"Working Class Hero," his song, you know. That melody sends
the rhythm ... But I learned that it's all right to sing. So
that that film is singing, you know. We came to an age where,
sort of, singing melodies, one is shy to sing melodies. And
if you sing, "She shouldn't be like that," they will think ...
To sing is almost like a sentimental gesture or something
that people shy away from. But I learned that it is all right.
Yes, we are human, we are sort of naïve people, not too
sophisticated. We are singing. So what's wrong with it?
So in *Fly* I sing a ballad. It's like a ballad. I mean, I sang ...

JONAS

You sang in both image and sound.

YOKO

Yes. I didn't mean in the soundtrack. But it's like a ballad.
It's all right to do that. The thing is, that there is a trend,
definitely, among the artists that, you know, they shouldn't
express things too subjectively, too personally. I was in that
too. So, whenever I had to do something, instead of saying,
"I am sad," or "I am crying," I try to maneuver in some
way, instead, so that it's like a third person. Instead of saying,
"I feel this way, and please see how I feel," or something,
I say, "Oh, there was a girl once in Long Island, and she used

to cry." Just to hide the fact that it's me, and thinking that the more you deviate like that the more artistic it is ... And I think that most of my dry stuff, like the books and the films, have that side, of shying away from my real emotions. And it's lying. But that's what I did.

But I am that girl who is dying, I am the girl who is dying with flies, you know, and I am the one who is moaning and crying underneath. You have to allow some personal, emotional stuff like that, instead of just flickering the lights or something—I just cry out. You see what I mean? So I know that this is a very awkward ballad of somebody really ... awkwardly trying to show her emotions.

TEXT CREDITS

On Alban Berg & Anna Sokolow
December 18, 1954
(not published)

In Defense of Perversity
November 21, 1958
Diary entry (not published)

Absolument Moderne
After reading the first issue
of *Big Table*
1959 (published in *Naked
Lunch@50: Anniversary
Essays*, University of Southern
Illinois, 2009)

To the Editor
May 9, 1959 (not published)

"Here and Now with Watchers,"
or Dance as a Modern Art
A conversation between
Erick Hawkins, Lucia
Dlugoszewski, and Jonas Mekas
1961 (not published)

"Totentanz"
Bread & Puppet Theater
of Peter Schumann
May 15, 1962 (not published)

A Note on Jean Genet's
Film, "Un chant d'amour,"
and Harold Pinter
1964
(published in *The Brooklyn
Rail*, February 11, 2006)

On John Cage
January 2, 1965 (not published)

A Salute to Carolee Schneemann:
In Praise of Surface
March 1965
(published in *The Brooklyn
Rail*, April 2, 2010)

Jim Dine's "Natural History
(The Dreams)"
May 1, 1965 (not published)

Notes on Shooting "The Brig"
(published in *The Village
Voice*, "Movie Journal,"
June 24, 1965)

The Living Theatre:
From the Conversations
with Judith Malina
and Julian Beck
Cassis, August 1966
(published in *Living Theatre*,
Edizioni Morra 2003, Napoli)

Interview with Gerd Stern
and Michael Callahan: USCO
June 1966 (published
in *Film Culture*, no. 43, 1966)

On Expanded Cinema
Selections from *The Village
Voice*, "Movie Journal"
(published in *The Village
Voice*, February 6, 1964 –
June 23, 1966)

Texts on Ken Jacobs
June 25, 1985;
September 3, 1995;
April 11, 2001; May 2004
(not published)

39 Notes on Dance
(published in *Dance Perspectives*, no. 30, Summer 1967)

A Conversation between
Pier Paolo Pasolini, Jonas Mekas,
and Gideon Bachmann
Rome, July 1967 (published
in *Film*, October 1967)

Theatre of Richard Foreman
A conversation between
Richard Foreman, Amy Taubin,
Michael Snow, P. Adams Sitney,
Ernie Gehr, Jonas Mekas,
Joyce Wieland, Ken Kelman,
and Margaret Ladd
March 15, 1969
(not published)

A Conversation with
Susan Sontag
(published in *The Village
Voice*, "Movie Journal,"
October 30, 1969)

A Conversation with
Emile De Antonio
(published in *The Village
Voice*, "Movie Journal,"
November 13, 1969)

Jack Smith,
or The End of Civilization
(published in *The Village
Voice*, "Movie Journal,"
July 23, 1970)

The Invisible Cathedrals
of Joseph Cornell
(published in *The Village
Voice*, "Movie Journal,"
December 31, 1970)

O. M. Theatre of Hermann Nitsch
A conversation with
Hermann Nitsch
(published in *The Village
Voice*, "Movie Journal,"
March 28, 1968)

First Conversation
with Hermann Nitsch and
Peter Kubelka
(published in *The Village
Voice*, "Movie Journal,"
December 3, 1972)

Second Conversation
with Hermann Nitsch and
Peter Kubelka
(published in *The Village
Voice*, "Movie Journal,"
December 14, 21, and 28, 1972)

Notes on the Lost Books
of Peter Beard
(published in *Soho Weekly*,
November 10, 1977)

The Irish Photographs of
Willard Van Dyke
A conversation with Willard
Van Dyke conducted by
Jonas Mekas and Hollis Melton
June 11, 1980
(not published)

A Dialogue between
A, B, and C re the Future
of Moving-Image Arts
and the Regional Art Centers
(published in *The Media
Arts in Transition*,
Walker Art Center, 1983)

On Liberation, Arts &
Cultural Imperialism
A conversation between Susan

Sontag, Vytautas Landsbergis,
Nam June Paik, and Jonas Mekas
Judson Memorial Church,
October 8, 1994
(not published)

A Story about a Man
Who Went to the Frick Gallery
to Look at a Vermeer
(published in *The Village
Voice*, "Movie Journal,"
April 18, 1960)

Notes for Allen Ginsberg
April 2 and 5, 1997
(not published)

In Praise of
Crazy Wordsmith Schuldt
1995 (not published)

Andy Warhol's Street Diary
August 2010
(published in Deborah Bell
Photographs catalogue
for *Andy Warhol's Street Diary
Photographs 1981–1986*,
September 2010)

From an Unpublished Interview
with Gregory Corso on
an Unmade Film on Rimbaud
1969 (published in
*Poetry Project*, Summer 2001)

Notes after Reseeing
the Movies of Andy Warhol
1970 (published in
John Coplans, *Andy Warhol*,
New York Graphic Society,
1971)

A Few Notes on Maya Deren
(published in *Inverted
Odysseys*, edited by Shelley
Rice, The MIT Press,
Cambridge, Massachusetts,
1998)

Bum-Ba Bum-Ba:
Conversations with John & Yoko
December 18 and 21, 1970
(published in *Jonas Mekas
présente Fluxfriends:
George Maciunas, Yoko Ono,
John Lennon*, Centre Georges
Pompidou, Paris, 2002)

IMAGE CREDITS

pp. 11, 12, 16
Credit: Author's archives,
1954

p. 23
Credit: Author's archives,
New York, 1961

pp. 23, 32
Credit: Author's archives,
extract from the program
*Here and Now with
Watchers*, New York, 1961

pp. 41, 42
Credit: Bread & Puppet
Theater

p. 44
Credit: Anthology Film
Archives, New York

p. 47
Photo: Robert Haller,
New York, 1975

p. 48
Credit: Carolee Schneemann's
Archives, 1964

p. 51
Credit: Author's archives,
New York, 1965

pp. 55, 57
Photos: Stills from
the film by Jonas Mekas
and Adolfas Mekas,
New York, 1964

p. 59
Photos: Storm De Hirsch,
New York, 1964

pp. 66, 70, 71
Photos: Lloyd Jasper,
Cassis, 1966

p. 78
Photo: Ken McLaren,
Cassis, 1966

p. 78
Photo: Ken McLaren,
1968

p. 81
Photo: Ken McLaren,
Cassis, 1966

p. 82
Photo: Ira Cohen,
New York, early 1960s

p. 82
Photo: Lloyd Jasper,
Cassis, 1966

pp. 89, 90, 91, 97, 101, 116, 121
Credit: Author's archives

p. 121
Photo: Geo Saito,
1964–1967

pp. 128, 131
Credit: Author's archives

p. 142
Photo: Still from
unedited film footage by
Jonas Mekas

pp. 144, 147, 148
Credit: Author's archives

p. 151
Credit: Anthology Film
Archives

p. 156
Credit: from the film
*Travels* by Jonas Mekas,
1967

p. 183
Photo: Friedl Bondy,
New York, 1976

p. 186
Credit: Richard Foreman,
New York, 1970

pp. 195, 196, 205
Credit: Author's archives

p. 225
Photo: Diana Foote, 1975;
Credit: Anthology Film
Archives

pp. 230, 233
Credit: Author's archives

p. 237
Photo: Jonas Mekas,
New York, 1962

p. 245
Credit: Anthology Film
Archives

p. 256
Credit: from the film
*Reminiscences of
a Journey to Lithuania*
by Jonas Mekas, 1971

p. 256
Credit: from the film
*Scenes from the Life of
Hermann Nitsch*
by Jonas Mekas, 2013

p. 259
Credit: from the film
*Reminiscences of
a Journey to Lithuania*
by Jonas Mekas, 1971

p. 259
Credit: from the film
*Scenes from the Life of
Hermann Nitsch*
by Jonas Mekas, 2013

pp. 262–263, 267, 270, 284,
296, 300–301
Credit: Author's archives

p. 315
Credit: from the film
*He Stands in a Desert
Counting the Seconds of his
Life* by Jonas Mekas, 1975

p. 319
Credit: Stills from
the film *Lithuania and the
Collapse of the USSR*
by Jonas Mekas, 2008

p. 334
Photo: Sebastian Mekas,
New York, 2015

p. 338
Credit: from the film
*Scenes from Allen's Last Three
Days on Earth as a Spirit*
by Jonas Mekas, 1997

p. 339
Credit: from the film *As I Was
Moving Ahead Occasionally
I Saw Brief Glimpses of Beauty*
by Jonas Mekas, 2000

pp. 340–341, 342–343
Credit: Author's archives

p. 346
Credit: Deborah Bell
Photographs, catalogue for
*Andy Warhol's Street Diary:
Photographs 1981–86*, 2010

p. 348
Credit: from the film Scenes
from the *Life of Andy Warhol*
by Jonas Mekas, 1990

p. 353
Credit: from the film
*He Stands in a Desert
Counting the Seconds of his
Life* by Jonas Mekas, 1975

pp. 356, 359
Credit: from the film *Award
Presentation to Andy Warhol*
by Jonas Mekas, 1964

p. 365
Credit: from the film *Scenes
from the Life of Andy Warhol*
by Jonas Mekas, 1990

p. 373
Credit: Author's archives

p. 375
Photo: Alexander Hammid,
1943; Credit: Author's archives

p. 383
Credit: Author's archives

p. 395
Credit: from the film *Walden*
by Jonas Mekas, 1969

pp. 411, 413, 415
Credit: Author's archives

pp. 418, 429
Credit: from the film *Happy
Birthday to John* by Jonas
Mekas, 1996

Back cover
Jonas Mekas in front of the
Chelsea Hotel, New York,
1968. Photo: Gideon
Bachmann, New York, 1968

Jonas Mekas
Scrapbook of the Sixties
Writings 1954–2010

Book concept:
Jonas Mekas, with
Fabian Bremer and Pascal Storz

Editor:
Anne König

Editorial assistants:
Ames Gerould, Wilma Träger

Graphic design:
Fabian Bremer, Pascal Storz

Typesetting:
Fabian Bremer, Tim Wetter,
Adriaan Van Leuven

Lithography:
Günter Hansmann, Berlin

Copyediting:
Charity Coleman, Simon Cowper

Proofreading:
Simon Cowper

Printing and binding:
Kösel GmbH & Co. KG,
Altusried-Krugzell

Acknowledgements

Charity Coleman, Ryosuke Fujii,
Gloria González Fuster, Natascha
Gikas (German Filmmuseum,
Frankfurt am Main), Maurice
Göldner, Sebastian Guggolz,
Christian Hiller, Jakob Hoffmann
und Raum 121 e.V., Inga
Jarmoškaitė, Schorsch Kamerun
and the Golden Pudel Club,
Giedra Kregzdys, Ramune
Krikstanaityte, Rebecca E.
Marshall, Sebastian Mekas,
Philipp Neumann / mzin, Marcos
Ortega, Adomas Paltanavičius,
Modestas Rimkus, Georg
Rutishauser, Bernd Scherer,
Peter Sempel, Edith Spettig,
Peter Starzec, Thomas Tjiong

All the photographers
who contributed to the book:
Anna Blau, Friedl Bondy,
Ira Cohen, Diana Foote,
Robert Haller, Lloyd Jasper,
Geo Saito, Stephen Shore,
Daniel Vittet

Photos and documents:
personal archives of Richard
Foreman, Peter Schumann,
Hermann Nitsch, and the author.

Second edition
Printed in Germany
ISBN 978-3-95905-033-3

Published by

Spector Books
Harkortstraße 10
D–04107 Leipzig
www.spectorbooks.com

Distribution

Germany, Austria:
GVA, Gemeinsame Verlags-
auslieferung Göttingen GmbH &
Co. KG, www.gva-verlage.de

Switzerland:
AVA Verlagsauslieferung AG,
www.ava.ch

France, Belgium:
Interart Paris, www.interart.fr

UK:
Central Books Ltd,
www.centralbooks.com

USA, Canada, Central and
South America, Africa, Asia:
ARTBOOK I D.A.P.,
www.artbook.com

South Korea:
The Book Society,
www.thebooksociety.org

Australia, New Zealand:
Perimeter Distribution,
www.perimeterdistribution.com